A GENE
OF MANNERS

A GENEALOGY OF MANNERS

TRANSFORMATIONS OF SOCIAL RELATIONS IN FRANCE AND ENGLAND FROM THE FOURTEENTH TO THE EIGHTEENTH CENTURY

Jorge Arditi

THE UNIVERSITY OF CHICAGO PRESS
CHICAGO & LONDON

Jorge Arditi is assistant professor of sociology
at the State University of New York, Buffalo.

The University of Chicago Press, Chicago 60637
The University of Chicago Press, Ltd., London
© 1998 by The University of Chicago
All rights reserved. Published 1998

07 06 05 04 03 02 01 00   99 98   1 2 3 4 5
ISBN: 0-226-02583-7 (cloth)
ISBN: 0-226-02584-5 (paper)

Library of Congress Cataloging-in-Publication Data

Arditi, Jorge.
    A genealogy of manners : transformation of social relations in
France and England from the fourteenth to the eighteenth
century / Jorge Arditi.
        p.   cm.
    Based on the author's thesis (doctoral)—State University of
New York at Stony Brook.
    Includes bibliographic references and index.
    ISBN 0-226-02583-7 (hardcover : alk. paper). — ISBN 0-226-
02584-5 (pbk. : alk. paper)
        1. Etiquette—France—History.   2. Etiquette—England—
History.   3. Diplomatic etiquette—Europe—History.
4. France—Foreign relations—England—Diplomatic history.
I. Title.
BJ1881.A73   1998
395′.0942—dc21   98-23581
                                                            CIP

To Olivia and Chloe

CONTENTS

ACKNOWLEDGMENTS

I began working on what eventually became this book when I was a doctoral candidate at the State University of New York at Stony Brook. My first and greatest debt is to my dissertation advisor, John Gagnon. Although this text is vastly different from the fruit of that first effort, many of the central ideas of this book developed through long conversations in John's office. With time, he has become a teacher and friend; I am fortunate to have been his student. The other members of my dissertation committee, Diane Barthel, Lewis Coser, and Richard Howard, were a constant source of support and inspiration.

Among the many people at Stony Brook who read my work, discussed my ideas, or otherwise helped in innumerable ways, I would like to thank Eviatar Zerubavel, Michael Kimmel, Rose Laub Coser, Mark Granovetter, Stephen Cole, John Sumser, Chris Nippert-Eng, and especially Liora Gvion-Rosenberg. Liora was the most helpful and wonderful of friends. Neil Smelser and Ann Swidler were extraordinary in their support and friendship after I moved to the University of California at Berkeley. Neil read and commented on the changing versions of this manuscript and provided invaluable support. Ann was not just my next-door neighbor; our ongoing conversations and friendship have proved priceless. Among my former colleagues at Berkeley I would also like to thank Kim Voss, Michael Burawoy, Loïc Wacquant, Peter Evans, Claude Fischer, Trond Petersen, and Arlie Hochschild. Fernando García Selgas, Luis García Abusaid, Shana Cohen, Jakie Orr, Natasha Kraus, and John Martin were always stimulating. Raka Ray occupies a special place both as friend and colleague.

Special thanks go to Mark Gottdiener, whose friendship and support, intellectually and otherwise, have been critical during my years at the State University of New York at Buffalo. Most of my indebtedness at Buffalo, however, is to my students. Minjoo Oh and Paul Fuller have been exceptional in every possible way. The participants in the informal discussion groups on Foucault and Bourdieu have provided the intellectual stimulation essential for my work. I also would like to express my appreciation to Paul DiMaggio, Stephen Mennel, and Richard Brown, who read and commented on parts or all of the manuscript. Doug Mitchell at the University of Chicago Press has been an ideal editor. Sue Thur and Judith Johnson helped in ways neither of them may suspect. Finally, the manuscript would have taken much longer to complete without the help of Amy Hequembourg, my research assistant at Buffalo, who contributed more than I can acknowledge. I dedicate the book to Olivia and Chloe Arditi; it is as much theirs as it is mine.

Manners, Social Relations, and Power

The cause of the origin of a thing and its eventual utility, its actual em-
ployment and place in a system of purposes, lie worlds apart; whatever
exists, having somehow come into being, is again and again reinterpreted
to new ends, taken over, transformed, and redirected by some power
superior to it; all events in the organic world are a subduing, a *becoming
master,* and all subduing and becoming master involves a fresh interpretation, an adaptation through which any previous "meaning" and "purpose"
are necessarily obscured or even obliterated.

Friedrich Nietzsche, On the Genealogy of Morals

Some Reflections on the Advent of the Term *Etiquette*

THIS BOOK ANALYZES transformations in infrastructures of social
relations in Europe, England, and France in particular, from the fourteenth to the mid-eighteenth century. It explores how certain forms of relating to one another give expression to the collective self of a dominant
group in a society, and how these forms—to echo Nietzsche—are eventually taken over, transformed, redirected, and placed in an entirely different
universe of practices by new groups in the process of "becoming master."

The exploration begins with a deceptively minor detail of the history
of the English language: the introduction, towards the middle of the eighteenth century, of the word *etiquette* to denote good behavior or propriety.
The Oxford English Dictionary records the first appearance of the word in
a letter Lord Chesterfield wrote to his son on March 19, 1750. "Without
hesitation," Chesterfield admonished the young Philip Stanhope, "kiss his
[the Pope's] slipper or whatever else the *etiquette* of that court requires."[1]
The experience might not have been pleasant, but it was useful, and certainly the young man followed it the best he could. Etiquette, in this example, is associated with ceremony, and more precisely with "the prescribed
ceremonial of a court and the formalities required by usage in diplomatic
intercourse." The scope of the word rapidly expanded, and by 1768 it came
to be applied not only to formal acts but to any "conventional [rule] of
personal behavior observed in the intercourse of polite society." In this

context *The Oxford English Dictionary* quotes Laurence Sterne's *Sentimental Journey*—although, as we shall see, credit for this new meaning should go again to Chesterfield.

The word is supposed to have come from the French for "ticket," or "label," and how it came to designate something related to politeness is not clear. Oscar Bloch and Walter von Wartburg, in their *Dictionnaire étymologique de la langue française,* propose a plausible though not very satisfying explanation.[2] Its origins, they argue, may be traced to the court of Philippe le Bon, Duke of Burgundy, who, to compensate for the lack of the kingship that he had sought in vain, imposed on his court a previously unknown solemnity—which included the registration of all daily events and activities on official forms. Then, apparently, both the custom and the word reached Vienna, and later Madrid, when Marie de Bourgogne married Maximilian of Austria in 1477. Why the court of Bourgogne used *etiquette* to designate Philippe's arrangement and what happened to the word after it reached Madrid remain mysteries. The major French dictionaries record the earliest written use of *étiquette* in a letter that Madame de Maintenon, the overly religious companion of Louis XIV, wrote to Madame de Brinon in 1719.[3] Madame de Maintenon used the word with the same sense as in Chesterfield's letter; not until 1778 did the word acquire its broader meaning in French. This last fact is significant, for it shows that the term was first associated with polite behavior in England, not France; thus, any attempt to understand its emergence should be grounded on a study of British, not French society.

As we know from the work of Norbert Elias,[4] for the preceding two hundred years, since the early sixteenth century, the word used to speak of breeding and politeness was *civility,* a word that had itself come to replace another, *courtesy.*[5] *Civility,* quite an ancient term alluding to ideas of civil polity and government, was first associated with the notion of proper deportment, as Elias has pointed out, by Erasmus of Rotterdam in his small book, published in 1530, *De civilitate morum puerilium.* In part a continuation of early courtesy manuals, in part a true revolution in the conception of politeness, *De civilitate* spread the idea that propriety of behavior meant something important for the conduct of civil life—of life, that is, within the spheres of the body politic. In spite of Erasmus, however, *civility* was not commonly associated with good behavior until the end of the sixteenth century. The *Dictionnaire de la langue française du seizième siècle,* for example, lists three senses under *civilité:* (1) "enfranchisement, citizenship"; (2) "science of the civil [i.e., legal] thing"; and (3) "political activity."[6] There is no mention of "politeness of manners." The impression is reinforced by *The Oxford English Dictionary:* only one of a large number of sixteenth-century quotations reported under *civility* refers to "behavior proper to the intercourse of civilized people."[7] In one form or another, all remaining quotations refer to the same three main entries of the French dictionary. The association of civility and the body politic, of civility and the practices connected with behavior within a specific plane of power, seems to have been taken for granted. I suggest that its replacement by the word *etiquette* towards the middle of the eighteenth century points to a complete transformation of that plane of power and to a reconfiguration of the infrastructure of social relations that it helps constitute that was provoked by a new group in the process of "becoming master."

I will argue that the practices associated with *etiquette* developed as part of the shift from a highly centralized system of power-practices that supported the absolutist tendencies of the English monarchy to a system that affirmed the aristocracy as a group. These practices and the new term associated with them served as one of the mechanisms by which the aristocracy constructed and affirmed its power. The word itself marked the emergence of a new concept of behavior that put an end to the practice of defining behavioral propriety according to a set of coherent moral principles. It marked the breakdown of what had been taken as a necessary connection between manners and ethics and, just as important, their reconnection to a different ground: the group in itself. This shift implied the unfolding of a new way to relate to things and to people, of new ways of acting and thinking that substantially changed the terms according to which English men and women in the higher classes of English society related to one another and construed their understandings of the social, of others, and of the self. And it was precisely the elaboration of a system of practices affirmative of the group in itself that, I suggest, helped the English aristocracy to establish and affirm its power.

My general argument does not differ much from Elias's. Elias sees in the change from *courtesy* to *civility* a sign of far-reaching transformations in the constitution of social reality. To him, concepts of propriety are not simple words alluding to a somewhat similar thing at different periods of time, nor are they mere offshoots of fashion, gaining or losing favor because of the whims and fancies of an epoch. They are terms that have not only plain, denotative meanings but involve some precise conceptions regarding their referents. If at some point in history people adopt a new word at the expense of an established concept, they do so because the word gives expres-

3

sion to an entirely new way of being in the world: to new patterns of behavior, new relations of power, new institutional arrangements, new emotional and psychological boundaries between people, a new texture of social relationships. Each concept reflects a specific mentality, a particular way of engaging in social intercourse, of perceiving people. Each conveys a different constellation of social and cultural constructs. According to Elias, the sanction of the word *civility* at the beginning of the sixteenth century marks the coming of a new order of social relations, and of a transformed person. It marks an unfolding of material and psychological boundaries between persons, a growing separation of bodies and psyches out of which emerged, two hundred years later, the modern, "civilized" individual. And it marks the formation of a new matrix of social practices that both enable and shape the rise of the modern state.

The study of the advent of the term *etiquette* during the eighteenth century expands the scope of Elias's work in critical ways, however. First, the suggestion that "etiquette" involves a disconnection of propriety from ethics calls our attention to a characteristic of manners before the 1700s that finds no expression in Elias: their full embeddedness in ethics. The incorporation of this element adds a new dimension to our understanding of propriety at the time, and forces us to rethink its history. Books that are virtually invisible in Elias, among them some of the most influential of their time—Baldesar Castiglione's *Book of the Courtier,* first published 1527, or Nicolas Faret's *L'honneste-Homme ou l'Art de plaire à la Court,* published in 1630—become suddenly central. Others, like Erasmus's *De civilitate morum puerilium,* the book at the heart of Elias's study of the civilizing process, acquire a vastly different significance. The medieval concept of courtesy takes a very different meaning from the one Elias gave it. At its core we find the elaboration of a code of behavior based on strictly defined religious ideals. Indeed, courtly love, benevolence, kindness, cheerfulness, and the ideal that encompassed them all, *courtoisie,* developed as the result of a widespread permeation of everyday medieval practices by Christian ethics. In this sense, *courtoisie* involved an affirmation of Christianity and, as I discuss in detail in chapter 2, emerged as a function of the power of the church and the clergy, as part of the infrastructure of social relations through which the religious powers fashioned their collective self. The advent of *civility* involved the constitution of a new infrastructure of social relations and a displacement of power from a plane of practice affirmative of the church to one affirmative of the monarchy—of civil, as opposed to ecclesiastical, power in general. The shift from *courtoisie* to *civility* is the topic of chapters 3 and 4. Chapter 5 examines the consolidation of the infrastructure of social relations associated with *civility.* Chapters 6 and 7 describe the initial formation and the consolidation of the infrastructure that gave rise to *etiquette.*

Second, the suggestion of a disjunction of manners and ethics points to the beginning of a new chapter in the history of social detachment in the West, a chapter in which the processes of physical and mental separation, whose beginnings Elias traced to the early sixteenth century, appear to have attained a new dimension: the conceptual. Elias, indeed, helps us to realize how detachment, gradually, became a central element of people's experience. We can almost sense how the boundaries that started to form between people provoked a changed experiencing of other and, by extension, of self. With the fading of behaviors rooted in practices of touching, of corporeal familiarity, of spontaneous intimacy, it is not difficult to understand how people started to experience themselves as separate beings, each with his or her own body and personal space. Yet, although the experience of detachment was becoming common, its interpretation was still highly problematic. Ample evidence suggests that for most people the feeling of detachment was, at best, an incongruity. For the men and women of the sixteenth and seventeenth centuries, detachment was defined in mostly negative terms: as an abnormality, as a moral aberration, or even, as in *Hamlet,* as a prelude to madness.[8] It did not find expression within the conceptual frames at the core of their culture. Within the frames of etiquette, on the other hand, detachment not only came to be defined as normal but, because it had become part of the very processes of thinking, came to be experienced as natural. The distinction is not spurious, for the change that we witness with the coming of etiquette is not uniquely in the literal interpretation of detachment—whether detachment was something good or bad, normal or abnormal. It is, we shall see in chapter 7, a transformation in the nature of the experience of detachment—all of people's experiences, including now the experience of the very process of thinking, indicated the positiveness of detachment.

The picture that we get, then, is not limited, as in Elias, to the straightforward increase of social detachment, to a continued separation of bodies and psyches prompting an increasingly keener experience of individuation. It is one of expansion, of detachment reaching new frameworks of experience—each movement prompting a different way of sensing and interpreting the self, a different attitude towards one's own self and other persons, a different method of defining oneself in relation to these others and to the social structures shaping one's practices.

Indeed, the suggestion of a disjunction between manners and ethics takes Elias one step closer to a concept of discontinuity—although it does not totally forfeit the idea of continuity. The very suggestion of an incrementally expanding scope of detachment clearly points at a continuity, at the idea of one moment being made possible by the preceding one, of the present forming an uninterrupted sequence with the past. The history of Western societies during the last five hundred years may be seen, in this light, as entailing a continuous movement towards the further constitution of detachment, its fundamental characteristics expanding into different levels of social reality. As we shall see, a new infrastructure of social relations is always a function of the conditions of possibility created by an existing infrastructure; that is, the power of a new group always develops from conditions set by the hegemonic mechanisms of an existing group.

The Concept of Infrastructures of Social Relations

Conceptually, this book draws as much from Elias as from Michel Foucault's ideas concerning the constitution and eventual demise of historically specific modalities of order, as elaborated in his early works.[9] One way to look at Foucault's early work, indeed, is to see it as engaging the idea of order, problematizing it, and transforming all order into something contingent, partial, and inevitably embedded in power.[10] The concept of infrastructures of social relations that I introduce here uses Foucault's particular insights on historically specific modalities of *thought* to convey a notion of historically specific modalities of *being*.[11]

The Specificity of Classificatory Systems

The problematic nature of order finds explicit expression in the introduction to *The Order of Things*—a book that, to some extent, expands and transforms the tradition of the sociology of knowledge initiated by Emile Durkheim. Behind that book, as background premises, lie Durkheim's ideas on categories of thought and systems of classification as developed in *The Elementary Forms of the Religious Life*.[12] The very first paragraph of *The Order of Things* brings Durkheim's ideas to mind, which Foucault, by his quotation of the well-known passage from Borges, problematizes and expands significantly.[13] Foucault points out how the bestiary invented by Borges makes us aware of the impossibility of thinking in certain ways, and he makes it his task to identify the specific characteristics of classificatory systems that render certain thoughts thinkable, others unthinkable.

The question raised by Foucault goes well beyond Durkheim's remarks regarding the need for "harmony" among collective representations. In the conclusion to *The Elementary Forms of the Religious Life,* Durkheim refers to the "fact" that even "true" concepts—concepts that are in accord with "the nature of things"—might not come to be thinkable. "If they are not in harmony with the other beliefs and opinions, or, in a word, with the mass of the other collective representations," he writes, "they will be denied; minds will be closed to them; consequently it will be as though they did not exist."[14] The idea reminds us somewhat of Kuhn's concept of a scientific paradigm, which is closed to thoughts and observations that cannot be given expression from within its theoretical and empirical frameworks.[15] Concepts that cannot be expressed in the terms of the paradigm remain unthought; observations that are not recognized by its concepts remain unrecognized. Foucault's point is of a completely different order, however; to him, the limits of the thinkable are not a result of the contents of what is thought, of their "harmony" or "structural closure," but—as Borges's imaginary encyclopedia revealed to him—of the logic by which systems of classification are constructed in the first place.

Foucault in effect transforms what Durkheim calls a "framework for the intelligence" into a shifting, historically contingent ground—what he calls the "episteme"—on which the very principle used to associate one thing to another changes with time. In this sense, he does not question the existence of order but raises the question of what constitutes an order to begin with. For him, the thinkable and the unthinkable, what becomes an "order of knowledge," is not simply a function of the divisions according to which we place things together and, by extension, differentiate among them; it is a function of the logic that we use in attributing similarity to things, of the specific method that we apply to associate and differentiate, to order things. Each method involves a different experience of thinking, a different modality of thought, and each yields an "order of things" that is of a completely different order from the others.[16] What I intend here is to elaborate and expand this idea of different modalities of thought into an idea of different, shifting, historically contingent "modalities of being."[17]

The Specificity of Infrastructures of Social Relations

One of the beauties of a concept of modalities of thought lies in its ability to convey an idea of epistemological difference and thus to provide a discourse

7

capable of conveying the kind of transformation involved in a discontinuity. According to Foucault, in effect, cultural discontinuities cannot be gauged by the simple emergence of new material artifacts, new styles in art, or new statements—even contradictory statements. For him, a discontinuity involves a complete epistemological reorientation—a mutation or, more correctly, a metamorphosis of the very grounds (read the practices of association and differentiation) from which thought arises.

The concept of infrastructures of social relations helps us to theorize an idea of ontological, as opposed to epistemological, difference. A proper understanding of the transformation of orders of social relations requires a concept of ontological restructuration as sensitive to metamorphoses in the material configurations of social reality as the concept of modalities of thought is to metamorphoses in its mental frames. The concept of infrastructures of social relations, in other words, should allow us to speak of a transformation as disjunctive in its effect on the grounds of social action, as Foucault's concept of the episteme allows us to do with regard to the grounds of mental activity.

As used in this study, the phrase *infrastructures of social relations* refers to the patterns of association and differentiation in a society and to the practices through which these patterns are produced and reproduced. Each infrastructure involves a different pattern, a different logic by which people establish relations of similarity and difference with one another and thus develop an understanding of themselves in relation to others. I place equal emphasis on both the construction of similarity and dissimilarity, and the logic of relationality, or what I call the pragmatics, that develops with each infrastructure. Each of the three infrastructures that I examine involves a different way of establishing similarity and difference among people, and each involves practices of relating to one another, a pragmatics, that is, of an entirely different order. Moreover, each helps to bring into being and consolidate the power of a different social group—the high clergy, the monarch and his court, the aristocracy.

In the infrastructure of social relations that embodies the power of the church (analyzed in chapter 2) people establish similarity and difference in terms of a series of concentric circles along which every person is located. People are considered in relation to their distance from the common center, God, and otherness is a function of the space separating a person from that center. This takes actual expression in what I call a pragmatics of revelation, which is grounded on a reality founded on the circulation of belief. The parameters of the experiential are established in practices that sustain and are sustained by theism. Truth, rightness, and truthfulness, the perception and experience of the world, society, and self respectively—the "ordering of things" in general—are functions of an engagement in practices of divination, that is, in discovering hidden meanings and essences assumed to originate in some supernatural power, divine or otherwise. Rationality itself is defined in terms of divination, and knowledge arising from some other basis, like modern principles of science, defies comprehensibility.[18] And both the concentric order of things and the pragmatics through which it receives concrete expression are marked by the coalescence of bodies and psyches discussed by Elias.

In the infrastructure of social relations that embodies the power of the monarchy (see chapters 4 and 5), the patterns of similarity and difference are still concentric, but they are marked by the development of individuation, and now the body of the monarch replaces God at the center of the circles. The modes and practices of relating to one another become, as a consequence, of a different order and now follow what I call a pragmatics of grace. The pragmatics of grace is founded on the circulation of honor, a currency that derives from the monarch and circulates along the lines of relationality centered in the figure of the monarch. Truth, rightness, and truthfulness follow from an engagement in practices that affirm royal centrality and from the preservation of the mechanisms by which honor circulates. As faith is the essence of symbolic capital in the pragmatics of revelation, honor is the symbolic currency, so to speak, that gives the pragmatics of grace its essence—the essence by which the collective self of a court society develops. Monarchical hegemony operates by having everybody revolve, physically and symbolically, around the figure of the king.

In the infrastructure of social relations that embodies the power of the aristocracy (see chapters 6 and 7), the patterns of similarity and difference are no longer concentric. The infrastructure becomes multicentered, composed of multiple axes of relationality that radiate from the body of each aristocrat. As such, the infrastructure prompts a repositioning of the person within the realm of a new, multiaxial plane of practice. Action and self-understanding no longer follow from one's relation to a single center or the social networks organized around and leading to that center, but from a multiplicity of relations to a multiplicity of focal points. And it is precisely by making those points the focus of practice that, I suggest, the hegemony of the English aristocracy during the eighteenth century operates. Practice follows what I will call a pragmatics of systemic relationality that embodies the multicenteredness of the infrastructure and whose major currency is the very allegiance to the multiplicity of points that constitute its essence: the aristocracy itself as a group.

Elaborations

Three elements of Foucault's concept of modalities of thought are relevant for a study of the infrastructures of social relations.

Heterogeneity First, to Foucault, the difference between one form of knowledge and another is not primarily one of content. Their contents are different, of course (and important in their own way, as we will see), but they differ primarily because they are functions of different logics of association, because they are grounded on different and incommensurable epistemological fields.[19] One of the most remarkable yet least understood characteristics of these epistemological fields concerns their capacity to yield a multiplicity of statements, concepts, ideas, discourses, beliefs, and even paradigms that contradict each other when evaluated from within the mode of thought they produce. Indeed, according to Foucault, every epistemological field yields statements that are diametrically opposed to one another—each statement being doubled, so to speak, by its own mirror image. Cultures are therefore not homogeneous, harmonious systems of meaning; on the contrary, they are heterogeneous and contradictory, in a sense tautological constructs constituted out of a single logic of association. Thus, for example, the mode of knowledge of medieval societies was equally geared to the elaboration of the most pious religious discourse and to (from the perspective of that discourse) the most heretical forms of magic. Religion and magic are functions of the same epistemological field, yet they imply perfectly contradictory beliefs and practices. The same is true of the simultaneous affirmation and derogation of courtship during the sixteenth century and of the discourses of identity and decenteredness that emerged in England a century later. If the new and contradictory are structured on the same epistemological grounds, then we have addition, increment, a richer constellation of ideas, perhaps, but not a discontinuity. Then the language of "progress" makes perfect sense.

I suggest that we can identify this same characteristic in the infrastructures of social relations. That is, we should not expect the range of experiences that emerge from an infrastructure to be homogeneous or harmonious. The range of experiences is inevitably circumscribed by the infrastructure itself. Just as some thoughts are thinkable and others are not, depending on the logic by which a culture constitutes the boundaries between things, some experiences are existentially possible and others are not, depending on the infrastructure that serves as the ground of experience. Any infrastructure of social relations limits the number of experiences that we can have, making certain experiences (all those that we cannot have because the ontological conditions for experiencing them are not present) impossible.[20] We have only to consider, for example, our own inability to experience the fluidity of corporal and psychic boundaries that, according to Elias, characterized reality during the Middle Ages, to realize the limits of our own range of experiences.

Still, like an epistemological field, each infrastructure of social relations makes possible an almost endless number of experiences that, however similar they look to an outsider, to an insider seem totally opposed: extreme piety and witchcraft, identification with the ways of the courtier and conscious resistance to them, an experience of normalcy or alienation regarding the multicenteredness at the core of etiquette. Each pair of opposites is grounded in the same infrastructure and develops as a function of a same logic of association and the same pragmatics. This property of the infrastructures of social relations is what makes a heterogeneous, dissonant, and—from the perspective of the insider—irreconcilable complex of practices into a culture, into a complex that in spite of all its diversity shares a ground from which the differences develop.[21]

Reality as Deployment   Second, like most theorists of knowledge during the last thirty years, Foucault develops a concept of practices of thinking that, interestingly, is implicit in Durkheim's analysis of rites and ritual activity.[22] To Foucault, in effect, epistemes are not deep structures in the sense used by structuralists like Claude Lévi-Strauss or Noam Chomsky. Although contents are a function of the logic of association in which they take shape, this logic of association in turn exists only through what is thought and said, in the actual practice of thinking through it.[23] Epistemological fields, that is, exist only in their actual deployment through discourse—through a plurality of sometimes contradictory discourses.

Similarly, I suggest (and in this, although my formulation differs from that of others, I am obviously not alone) that infrastructures of social relations exist only in their actual deployment in behavioral practices. To echo my own formulation: while practices are a function of the infrastructure of social relations in which they develop, infrastructures of social relations, in turn, exist only in the multiplicity of apparently incongruous practices that they make possible. Individuation itself exists only as people engage in individuating practices—in a system of courtly manners, for example, as Elias showed, or in the religious practices of Protestantism and ascetism, as Max Weber suggested.[24]

Change as Gradual   Third and last, as my earlier use of the term *metamorphosis* rather than *mutation* suggests, to Foucault the idea of discontinuity implies neither abruptness nor the immediate end of what existed before. Either claim would be sufficient to dismiss Foucault without a second thought. Foucault shows, however, repeatedly and at length, how discontinuities take time to form, how a beginning can take more than a century to permeate thought and practice.[25] What *is* more or less abrupt is the moment at which we can begin to see that thought in general is following a new modality, which has now become dominant. Neither does the coming into dominance of the new imply the immediate end of the old. Foucault affirms that the practices of thought generated by a former epistemological ground continue to be present after a new practice has become dominant—even if they are eventually bound to subside.[26]

Nevertheless, we must not allow our awareness of the continued existence of the old to blind us to the emergence of the new. For the significant point is not that everything that preceded the new ceases to exist, even though much of it eventually does, but that the new itself comes into being. The advent of a new modality of thought or of a new infrastructure of social relations signifies the emergence of something different, something that did not exist before, and this point of difference, not the lines of continuity, is what we want to explore. I intend to address the emergence and deployment of new infrastructures that are instructed by logics that cannot be derived from the earlier practices of power. The continuation of older modes of thinking and being does not diminish, let alone refute, the importance of the new.

The concept of power that follows from the present approach is, on the other hand, different from Foucault's. While Foucault sees power as nonlocatable and nonpossessed, the present study, in some ways more in the spirit of Nietzsche, sees power as fully located, as a function of the affirmation of a person or a group.[27] To define power as located has two significant consequences. First, it means that infrastructures of social relations develop from some center and are deployed outward, yet they do not reach everywhere or affect everything with the same force. Different groups of people experience the same infrastructure differently and generate different strategies of action in relation to it.[28] We may therefore introduce a concept of hegemony. Second, it means that we can envision the existence of more than one infrastructure of social relations at a time and conceive therefore of a multiplicity of synchronous "planes of power."[29] The dominance of an infrastructure is always limited, challenged by the presence of other powers—past and future—attempting to affirm their own presence, to set the foundations of order, to become, in turn, dominant. The resulting concept of power is thus more flexible and less totalizing than Foucault's, and allows us to speak of infrastructures of social relations in terms of *partiality*—a terminology that, as I shall argue in conclusion, makes possible the formulation of a nonessentialist concept of social foundations.

Finally, I should note that any attempt to give a substantive as opposed to a formal definition of the concept of infrastructures of social relations would defeat its own purpose. As should be apparent, it is impossible to identify a quality or substance that could be deemed constant in the constitution of infrastructures of social relations. No single, fixed property of social relations exists on which to construct a continuous understanding of order. Each infrastructure is composed of a different "substance," a different texture of social relations in whose materiality action takes place: "coalescence" during the Middle Ages, increasing degrees of detachment later; centered structures of practice before "etiquette," multicentered structures of practices during and after etiquette; and so on. In the transition from courtesy to civility, properties of centeredness or multicenteredness are spurious; in the emergence of etiquette, in contrast, the constitution of multicenteredness becomes fundamental. Any attempt to produce a substantive understanding of infrastructures of social relations is in fact bound to generate a text as perplexing as Borges's Chinese encyclopedia—a text in which the different properties of order are as incongruous, as devoid of a common ground, as the categories in Borges's story. A discursive continuity—from coalescence to detachment, or from centeredness to decenteredness, for example—can be formulated, as Elias did, only with regard to the transition from one infrastructure to another; it cannot be done when attempting to understand more than one transition. The quality that undergoes metamorphosis, in effect, changes from transformation to transformation.[30]

Methodology: Etiquette Books and Infrastructures of Social Relations

As should be apparent by now, manners and changing concepts of propriety are indeed ideal vehicles for analyzing the emergence and transformations of infrastructures of social relations. Manners represent one form through which such infrastructures come into being. They convey a sense of the practices attending the construction of similarity and dissimilarity within a dominant group, and of the logic of relationality—that is, the pragmatics—at their core. The manners that Lord Chesterfield advocates, for example, imply multicenteredness, as we shall see, and following those manners implies producing and reproducing a multicentered reality. The manners promoted by Castiglione or Faret, in contrast, imply centeredness, and following those manners produces a centered reality that constantly affirms and reaffirms the power of the monarch. Chesterfield's etiquette gives full expression to the pragmatics of systemic relationality through which the English aristocracy constructs itself as a group in itself. Castiglione and Faret give expression to a pragmatics founded on the circulation of grace, a property that derives from the monarch and orients behavior to its procurement.

Many sociologists may find my focus on the manners of dominant groups, of "elites," vastly confining and oddly outdated. Not only might they see the focus on the higher classes as "unrepresentative" and therefore as telling little about society, but in the view of many scholars today, the practices, structures, and logic of the social life of a dominant group develop only in relation to an "other," as a function of practices of subjection of and distinction from this "other." In not recognizing the "other," my approach runs the risk of being essentializing and totalizing.

Given the theoretical orientation of this book, the first point is not a difficulty. An infrastructure of social relations is not supposed to be representative of an entire population. Quite the opposite, it represents, so to speak, the positivities of the dominant classes alone.[31] An infrastructure is a function of the power of the dominant groups, and only in connection to these groups should we expect to see a coincidence between that infrastructure and practice.

The second point raises a more serious difficulty. But my position is grounded on the suggestion, to be explored throughout the book, that an infrastructure is primarily a function of how the members of the dominant group construct *similarity* among themselves, a process that I argue cannot be understood in reference to practices of difference alone.[32] I would argue, for example, that the specific type of multicenteredness found at the core of etiquette cannot be understood except as an expression of the need felt by the aristocracy to construct itself as a unique group. Multicenteredness is in this case a function of, and an instrument for, the need to give equal expression to the body of each aristocrat, not an effort of the aristocrats to separate themselves from others. And it is precisely through the deployment of practices that affirm the similar as defined by the powerful group—through practices of essentialization and totalization—that the group exercises its power among others. Certainly, a recognition of the essentializing tendencies of power does not imply the formulation of an essentializing theory. In order to avoid essentialization, a theory must elude the trappings of power: it must shy away from the temptation to define others in its own image, to see others as an extension of itself. The question of how my approach fares on this score is a topic that I discuss in the conclusion.

The very usefulness of etiquette books, I suggest, lies in their capacity to convey to their readers the pragmatics in terms of which the collective self of a powerful group takes shape. Etiquette books are not written for the dominant classes, for whom knowledge of the infrastructure comes naturally—naturally in the double sense that they learn it from birth and that it indeed coincides with their daily experiences.[33] Etiquette books are for the most part written by and for members of the social groups immediately below the dominant classes, by and for people who aspire to belong to and succeed among the dominant classes. What is most important to them is not simply to learn the manners of the elite but to master the logic instructing their manners—not just to know a set of rules, but to capture and come to possess the logic instructing those rules. As Baldesar Castiglione put it more than four hundred years ago, the important thing is not just to learn "how to behave" but to absorb that knowledge so thoroughly that the behavior appears to be the natural disposition of the person, who is thus "like a singer who utters a single word ending in a group of four notes with a sweet cadence, and with such facility that he appears to do it quite by chance," or like a painter with the skill to paint "a single line which is not labored, a single brush stroke made with ease and in such a manner that the hand seems of itself to complete the line desired by the painter, without being directed by care or skill of any kind."[34]

My decision to study only the most successful etiquette books of each period therefore makes methodological and analytical sense, for in these books the grammar of social behavior, which must be mastered as one masters music or painting, is best expressed. I complement the knowledge that we gain from etiquette books with readings of literary works, both high and low, of personal diaries, of memoirs, and information from the extensive secondary literature on each of the topics that I touch upon. My focus on books of etiquette creates a manageable scope for my task and provides a sense of continuity; I use these books to build the backbone of my argument. For the sake of a manageable scope, I also sacrifice breadth for depth: instead of superficially reviewing a large body of literature, I analyze only a small number of books and diaries whose value I justify from case to case.

Only by taking a very long view of history can I make my point. Here, again, I run against current practices; however, the short view of history dominant in academia today makes the processes that I am about to explore invisible. The concept of an infrastructure of social relations can only be properly clarified by taking the long view, and only from a broad historical perspective can the processes of ontological continuity and discontinuity that I focus on be analyzed.

I must carefully qualify the scope of the present study. I am definitely not suggesting that a study of manners or of concepts of propriety exhausts the dimensions involved in the constitution of infrastructures of social relations. Admittedly, propriety represents but a small portion of the realities of European societies during the period from the fourteenth to the eighteenth century. Even less do I intend to suggest that transformations in manners explain the political shifts that I analyze below. Issues related to the formation of nation-states, or to industrialization, or rationalization, to mention only a few, are certainly central to the evolution of Western societies during the period that I cover in this book, yet I leave those issues aside.

What I suggest is that a study of propriety is necessary for understanding the evolution of European societies during the sixteenth and seventeenth centuries, and that what little has been written on the topic must be revised. Moreover, I suggest that a study of the deployment of practice through manners is indispensable to understanding the formation of infrastructures of social relations and, as I will argue in detail towards the end of the book, that the insights we gain by studying propriety cannot be attained through any of the dimensions that are current in our explanations of the rise of modern societies. The transformations that I analyze in this book are significant and should be interwoven with a general understanding of European history. That, however, remains beyond the scope of the present book.

In the next chapter I attempt to develop an understanding of the infrastructure of social relations embodied in the practices of *courtoisie*.[35] These practices follow a logic of ordering things, of relating to one another, of existing in a social space, that are foreign to our perceptions and understandings of reality. The language of these practices, to use Nietzsche's formulation, has been again and again reinterpreted, taken over, transformed, redirected—it is a language that has disappeared, that has become "silent." I do not follow Foucault's archaeological method to reconstruct the lost language of courtoisie from its textual vestiges, however. Instead, I begin by presenting two texts that help define one of the central dimensions within which the multiplicity and heterogeneity of perception inherent in the world of courtoisie unfolds. Then, gradually, I incorporate other dimensions, weaving an increasingly larger, albeit never complete, tapestry of the infrastructure of social relations of medieval societies. The danger of projecting the sensibilities of our own geography and time are always present and, to a point, unavoidable.[36] In the attempt to recapture the language and experience of courtoisie, therefore, we should proceed as carefully as possible, as self-consciously as possible, to avoid filling the silence with an echo of ourselves.

CHAPTER TWO

Centeredness, Social Coalescence, and the Hegemony of Ecclesias

I have not tried to write the history of that language, but rather the archaeology of that silence.

Michel Foucault, *Madness and Civilization*

The Order of Ecclesias
Bors de Ganis and Pridam le Noir

THE FIRST TEXT that I examine, taken from *The Quest of the Holy Grail*,[1] an anonymous Arthurian romance written in Old French prose most probably between 1213 and 1223,[2] relates the following incident. Sir Bors de Ganis, Knight of the Round Table, son of King Bors and cousin of Lancelot, arrives, after a day of wandering, at a fortress and asks for hospitality. Eagerly, the guards let him in. What follows provides a singular view of the sensibilities of the time. I quote at length.

> And when he was unarmed they led him into an high tower where was a lady, young, lusty, and fair. And she received him with great joy, and made him to sit down by her, and so was he set to sup with flesh and many dainties. And when Sir Bors saw that, he bethought him on his penance, and bad a squire to bring him water. And so he brought him, and he made sops therein and ate them. Ah, said the lady, I trow ye like not my meat. Yes, truly, said Sir Bors, God thank you, madam, but I may eat none other meat this day. Then she spake no more as at that time, for she was loth to displease him. Then after supper they spake of one thing and other. With that came a squire and said: Madam, ye must purvey you tomorn for a champion, for else your sister will have this castle and also your lands, except ye can find a knight that will fight tomorn in your quarrel against Pridam le Noire. Then she made sorrow and said: Ah, Lord God, wherefore granted ye to hold my land, whereof I should now be disherited without reason and right? And when Sir Bors had heard her say thus, he said: I shall comfort you. Sir, she said, I shall tell you there was

here a king that hight Aniause, which held all this land in his keeping. So it mishapped he loved a gentlewoman a great deal elder than I. So took he her all this land to her keeping, and all his men to govern; and she brought up many evil customs whereby she put to death a great part of his kinsmen. And when he saw that, he let chase her out of this land, and betook it me, and all this land in my demesnes. But anon as that worthy king was dead, this other lady began to war upon me, and hath destroyed many of my men, and turned them against me, that I have wellnigh no man left me; and I have nought else but this high tower that she left me. And yet she hath promised me to have this tower, without I can find a knight to fight with her champion. Now tell me, said Sir Bors, what is that Pridam le Noire? Sir, said she, he is the most doubted man of this land. Now may ye send her word that ye have found a knight that shall fight with that Pridam le Noire in God's quarrel and yours. Then that lady was not a little glad, and sent word that she was purveyed, and that night Bors had good cheer; but in no bed he would come, but laid him on the floor, nor never would do otherwise till he had met with the quest of the Sangreal.[3]

The next morning Bors raises early, says his prayers, and proceeds to meet the older sister's champion.

Now departed the one knight here, and the other there. Then they came together with such a raundon that they pierced their shields and their hauberks, and the spears flew in pieces, and they wounded either other sore. Then hurtled they together, so that they fell both to the earth, and their horses betwixt their legs; and anon they arose, and set hands to their swords, and smote each one other upon the heads, and they made great wounds and deep, that the blood went out of their bodies. For there found Sir Bors greater defence in that knight more than he weened. For that Pridam was a passing good knight, and he wounded Sir Bors full evil, and he him again; but ever this Pridam held the stour in like hard. That perceived Sir Bors, and suffered him till he was nigh attaint. And then he ran upon him more and more, and the other went back for dread of death. So in his withdrawing he fell upright, and Sir Bors drew his helm so strongly that he rent it from his head, and gave him great strokes with the flat of his sword upon the visage, and bad him yield him or he should slay him. Then he cried him mercy and said: Fair knight, for God's love slay me not, and I shall ensure thee never to war against thy lady, but alway toward her. Then Bors let him be; then the old lady fled with all her knights.

So then came Bors to all those that held lands of his lady, and said he should destroy them but if they did such service unto her as longed to their lands. So they did their homage, and they that would not were chased out of their lands. Then befel that young lady to come to her estate again, by the mighty prowess of Sir Bors de Ganis. So when all the country was well set in peace, then Sir Bors took his leave and departed; and she thanked him greatly, and would have given him great riches, but [he] refused it.[4]

Obviously, the story cannot be taken as a description of reality. Even acknowledging the difficulty of perceiving the medieval world from our present perspective, much of the story evidently belongs to the domain of pure fiction. The hero, Bors, a quasi-mythical figure, is indeed too good, too honest, too eager and willing to serve. In this text we follow what for him are quite routine activities: arriving, by chance, at an isolated fortress; receiving and accepting hospitality; socializing with the lady; praying to God; fighting Pridam le Noire; showing courage and power; saving his opponent's life; saving, too, the fortune and honor of the young sister. Other texts from the same narrative depict a character of extreme piety, extreme beauty, extreme strength and valor. As an act of penitence, he lives on bread and water and sleeps on the ground, his head resting on a hard object—a stone, a chest, or a tree-branch. He is instantly recognized as one of the chosen by those who possess the power of knowledge, usually hermits. According to the present version of the legend, he is, with Galahad and Perceval, one of the witnesses of the miracle of the Holy Grail. Not only is Bors too good to be real, but the wicked are too wicked, the humble too humble, and the courageous too courageous. Pridam has a prodigious reserve of blood in his body and is able to deliver a speech while in the utmost agony.

The version that I am quoting from was written by a fifteenth-century English gentleman and scholar, Sir Thomas Malory, and would seem to convey as much of a thirteenth-century text as of Malory's own perception of reality. Malory could not avoid projecting his personality, or the general perception of things particular to his world and his station, and therefore could not avoid transforming the French text into an image of his own times.[5] The differences between Malory's text and one dating from the thirteenth century are most revealing and, as I argue below, most helpful in our own effort to identify and understand the specificities of the infrastructure of social relations of medieval societies—or rather, of one dimension of that infrastructure.

The thirteenth-century French version, for example, places great emphasis on the negative side of the relationship between the two sisters, and in its text the younger lady is not just "young, lusty, and fair" but penniless and, in truth, quite pitiful. Bors is indeed gladly lodged—for good reason: the young lady knows that her end is approaching. Contrary to what we read in Malory, however, he displays no politeness whatsoever. He shows respect for his hostess—she is a noblewoman, and as we will see, Bors is obliged to honor her—but he refuses the food that she offers him without comment (there are no pleases and thank-yous in the French text), leaves without ceremony immediately after the fight, and, worse, shows stupendous contempt for his inferiors. He is also surprisingly indifferent to the value of human life. In the earlier text Bors does not threaten "to destroy" the vassals who refuse to pay the young lady homage, a phrase that may mean a number of different things, but threatens to *kill* them, which he does. He does not "chase" the people "out their land," as Malory writes, but, assisted by the young woman's knights, he slays all who fail to show her respect—as he does with all those who pay *him* homage. These differences do not change the substance of the story, but they change our perception of Bors, the perfect *courtois,* modify our understanding of courtoisie, the embodiment of virtue, and as a consequence, sharpen our first picture of the infrastructure of social relations of medieval men and women.

Indeed, the fictional character of the story does not affect our ability to see the infrastructure at the core of medieval reality. However grotesque the details of the narrative may appear to us, they nevertheless begin to delineate the space of the imaginary of their time and place. They convey a sense of the conceivable, of what may be thought and done, of the cultural ordering within which representation happens, and of the ontological ordering within which acts become possible. Without taking anything literally, we nevertheless form a vision of the roughness and violence, the honor and courage, the piousness and devotion, the sensibilities and the assumptions of the society that produced them—medieval society and, in particular, French society during the twelfth and thirteenth centuries. We see the ferocity of the combat, the emotional intensity of the people, the religiosity of the characters, the formality of social intercourse, the strength of social bonds—and in all these images what strikes us most is not their alleged happening but the very fact of their representation in the romance.

Malory's text, with its transformations and inventions, helps to highlight the foreignness of this representation. Malory's attempt to make Bors into a more "human" character—more compassionate, more ethical, more polite—points, precisely, at the transformation of the concept of humanity in the period between the two versions of the romance. As I mentioned, to the men and women of the Middle Ages, Bors *is* the ideal courtois.[6] He is rude, violent, and contemptuous, yet he respects the young sister in spite of her misery, offers her his services, and keeps his word even in the most difficult circumstances. He fights for justice and, in a sense, for the defense of the law of God. And surprisingly, he spares his opponent's life, for in spite of his apparent disregard for human life, killing Pridam would have been an act of the utmost barbarity, an act that would have erased Bors's image as a celestial knight of perfect courtoisie.

To gain a fuller understanding of courtoisie, however, we turn our attention at this point to a second narrative—one that introduces us to its mirror-image: villainy.

The Terms of Villainy

The terms *courtoisie* and *villainy,* indeed, evolved together, as opposite sides of the same historical movement, and it is in their conjunction and the traces left by their paired evolution that we shall begin capturing the medieval world in its diversity, its heterogeneity, its tensions and contradictions—and its inevitable power dimension.[7]

Like the first, the second narrative, *Le chevalier au barisel* ("The Knight and the Keg"), a "pious tale" dating from the early thirteenth century, was written by an anonymous French author.[8] It tells the story of a knight, as unreal as the first, albeit obviously very different. I again quote at length:

> Between Normandy and Brittany, in a faraway country, once lived a powerful man of great repute. At the limits of the land, near the sea, he built a castle, fortified with so many towers and battlements, so strong and well armed, that he feared no king, no count, no duke, no prince, no viscount. And that powerful lord I am telling you about, was, as I was told, fair of body and face, rich of goods and birth. By his appearance, it could be thought that there was no person in the world more generous or nobler than him. But he was crooked and disloyal, so conceited and deceitful, so proud and arrogant, and so cruel, that he feared neither man nor God.

To put it in one word, he had ravaged and ruined the entire land around his estate. He could not have a vassal he did not hurt and dishonor. His lust for evil was immense. He watched the roads closely and killed all the pilgrims and robbed all the merchants. He spared no priest, no monk, no recluse, no hermit—as for the nuns and *freres convers,* the more they were attached to God, the more he made them live in shame, and the same was true with ladies and damsels, widows and maids.[9]

The text continues in the same vein for a while. We learn that the un-named knight refuses to marry, seeing wedlock as a humiliation. We learn that he never respects the days of fast, never goes to church, never prays—that he rejects all things religious. "Think of all the misdeeds that a person is capable of, in words, actions, or thought: he had carried them out all,"[10] the narrator concludes.

One Easter day, at the instigation of his vassals, he agrees to accompany them to the church's door—mockingly, contemptuously, swearing at ev-erybody and everything. Full of scorn and sarcasm, he consents, too, to go into the chapel, and for no precise reason other than allowing the story to unfold, he agrees to confess his sins to the priest. He tells his sins reluctantly, angrily, cursing and smiting at the vicar. At the end, he refuses to repent. The priest implores,

"What! Won't you do any good? Yes, you'll do one good deed, if it pleases God and you are able to, before leaving us. I only ask you, in the name of God Almighty, to take my little keg to the river. You'll dip it into the water—that would not be difficult for you—and if you bring it to me full, you'll be absolved of all sin and free from penance; you'll have nothing to fear, for I'll take your sins on myself."

As he heard him, the knight began laughing disdainfully and answered: "It won't cause me much harm to go to the fountain and then do my penance. I accept, whatever I might think of it."[11]

Of course, not a single drop of water falls into the keg, and the more he tries, the angrier he becomes, and the less he succeeds. He is too proud to admit defeat, however, and the next section of the story tells of the knight's journey through many lands, determined to release himself of his charge. He grows hoary, weary, dirty.

He has no clothes and no castle, and cannot find shelter. Quite the contrary, he runs into hesitant, impervious people, hard and

23

cruel, who, seeing him so deprived, so big, so strong, so well-built and so ugly, so dirty and suntanned, tattered and bloodstained, fear to lodge him. As a consequence, he often sleeps in the fields. He had lost all joy and was tormented with anger and resentment. But I can warrant to you that he never made an effort to show modesty and to soften the harshness in his heart; he contented himself with complaining about his lot to God, but like an arrogant, not a penitent.[12]

He wanders for the most part of a year until, beaten, he decides to return to the priest. He arrives at the church on Easter day, exactly one year after he left. At first the priest does not recognize him, but seeing the keg, noting that it is still empty, and realizing that the knight has not changed, he begins to cry. He offers to God his soul for the knight's, and then the miracle happens: deeply affected by the immensity of the cleric's love and kindness, the knight repents.

"Verily, I see something magnificent that fills my heart with wonder, since this man, who does not belong to me, and does not depend on me the least, this man who belongs only to God, Sovereign King, incurs damnation for me! For my sins, he cries and grieves. . . . Ah! Very sweet Lord, if that is Your wish, accord me so much remorse, by your virtue and mercy, that this prud'homme be consoled, he who is in great pain. God, do not allow that pain to be fruitless. I received this keg because of my sins, and because of my sins I took it: very sweet Lord, if I acted wrongly, I plead guilty. True God, I ask for Your mercy. Now, do Your will: I am ready . . ."

And God, who saw his [repentance] and that he wanted to work honestly on his salvation, and that with no hypocrisy, did a noble and beautiful feat, and highly *courtois*. It is not to highlight the act that I mention it for He never committed a villainy; but listen to what God did to soothe his new friend: He makes the water in [the knight's] heart rise to his eyes, and a big tear, that the Lord drew from a real spring, darted, straight as an arrow, into the empty keg. And the legend tells that the keg overflowed, and that the water gushed everywhere.[13]

The knight, finally redeemed, dies shortly afterwards, his soul escorted to heaven by an army of angels, while the Devil, in fury, watches helplessly. Clearly, this is not an Arthurian tale of epic dimensions. It is a fable or, more precisely, a *conte pieux,* a "pious tale," and by its very nature it is moralizing and intensely Catholic.[14] It relates, as we have seen, the tale of a powerful knight who carries a personal war against God. He is redeemed after he sheds a tear of true repentance. It is as unrealistic as the first and, like the story of Bors, should not be taken, in any of its aspects, as a literal description of reality. Yet, like the first, or rather in conjunction with the first, it speaks of something real, something that, in some ways, resonates with the lived experience of its public. As a popular tale, it was probably told many times by minstrels and storytellers in public squares, and it may well have reached a wide audience.[15] It is conceivable, too, that it reached all social classes, projecting a certain way to perceive the world, helping, however lightly, to constitute that perception.

The complementarity of courtoisie and villainy emerges fully in the opposition of the two main characters—the arrogant, cruel knight being indeed the reverse image of Bors. The long introduction of the fiendish knight at the beginning of the tale could not have been more eloquent. He is presented as a proud and vicious tyrant, as a source of misery to men and women, old and young, weak and strong, stranger or friend alike. He has no experience of love, and can muster only contempt for everybody and everything. He is the worst sinner in the entire world. The symmetry is incontestable. While Bors the courtois receives hospitality instantaneously, the knight never has a door opened, and never opened his to anyone. Whereas Bors is faithful and generous, the villain shows only treachery and greed. The first is full of piety and lives to serve God; the second lives in blasphemy. The *conte pieux* makes the opposition of the two concepts explicit, for not only is the knight the epitome of villainy, but the priest—the God-loving, generous character of the tale—is, textually, a "prud'-homme," a gentleman. And none other than God is characterized as courtois. I quote the thirteenth-century version of the text:

> *Et Diex qui vit son desirier,*
> *Et li voloit à droit aidier,*
> *Là li fist une cortoisie,*
> *Et pour chou ne le di-jou mie,*
> *Vilounie ne fist-il onques.*[16]

Together, indeed, courtoisie and villainy drew the lines of a moral order, albeit not the only order, in reference to which medieval men and women related—interpreted, judged, negotiated, subjected, opposed—their daily experiences. This order should not be confused with the infrastructure of social relations of medieval societies. It was a constituent of that infrastructure, embodying the specific logic in whose terms people positioned themselves in relation to others, developed systems of classification, and attributed similarity and difference among themselves. It was one among many, sometimes contradictory, orders in the shape of which that logic attained expression, and whose exercise helped bring the infrastructure into being. As the two tales suggest, it was also an order deeply permeated by Christian ideals, giving body to those ideals, promoting their incorporation into practice, helping transform the partial reality of *ecclesias* into a hegemonic foundation for medieval societies in general.

The Permeation of Christianity

The Christian dimension of the tales is unequivocal. Although, as we will see, the discourse on the Grail incorporates many pagan and magical elements, Bors is nevertheless engaged in an essentially religious quest, and its success is a function of the character's purity, of Bors's virtual sinlessness. He prays, keeps penance, and waits for the guiding hand of God, and these activities form the core of his daily existence. God rewards him by gracing him with adventures; sinful knights, indeed, are bound to wander for days, months or years—depending on the severity of their offenses—experiencing nothing at all.[17] Bors's very triumph, as we will also see, is a logical consequence of his closeness to God—and I use the word *logical* advisedly. The knight of the *conte pieux*, on the other hand, is engaged in a struggle against faith, against the church. His behavior is not merely antireligious, it involves the literal rejection of *ecclesias* (from *ecclesia*, "church")—a term that conveys both the ideological and the structural dimensions of medieval Catholicism.[18] And it is by means of a purely religious act—the act of genuine penitence—that he is, in an instant, transformed from villain to *courtois*.

As far as the *Quest* is concerned, the Christian dimension is even more marked. The romance involves a literal translation of biblical texts into chivalric symbols—knightly figures replace evangelical characters, and many details of the narrative parallel the scriptural writings.[19] This characteristic of the medieval text explains the mostly negative attitude of many church people at the time to Arthurian romance in general, to whom the literal transposition of the Scriptures would seem vastly heretical. This characteristic, too, already points at one of the ironies that mark the processes of infrastructural transformation at the core of the emergence of the concept of civility during the sixteenth century. For such transposition can be used as much to assert the domination of ecclesias over the feudal institutions of society as to justify the priority of the secular over the ecclesiastical once the secular powers have taken them over and have "become masters." In this sense, the romances become potential, and eventually actual, instruments of resistance and renewal.[20] Neither the heretical character of the romance nor its possible use as an instrument of resistance, I should note, negate its permeation by religious concepts and ideals. On the contrary, these two characteristics, as I discuss in the subsequent section on the discursive deployment of ecclesiastical hegemony, appear to reinforce rather than deny the argument at hand.

The historiography of everyday life during the Middle Ages is on this point instructive. Until the 1970s most historians saw religion as arguably the most important component of medieval daily life. Johan Huizinga used the term *saturation* to describe the pervasiveness of religion in the medieval mentality.[21] "Never was faith more completely worthy of its name," wrote Marc Bloch.[22] And Robert Delort, one of the leading authorities on medieval everyday life before the 1980s, maintained that "the Western World was inhabited exclusively by Christians, and every facet of man's daily life— morals and his attitude to sin, family life, and his relations with his fellows—was directly interpreted, influenced, and even provoked by religion."[23] Prompted in part by the excessive role assigned to religion in the constitution of everyday life by people like Delort, scholars in the 1980s turned that perception upside-down, viewing religion as an existing yet minor component of everyday reality.[24] In some cases, as in Maurice Keen's *Chivalry,* for example, religion disappeared almost completely.[25] But this position is as problematic as the first, and ample evidence shows that religion was far more important than the new scholarship suggests. Certainly many practices and thoughts, to use Matilda Tomaryn Bruckner's formulation, "conflicted or competed with, or simply coexisted alongside of, the views and teachings of the Church."[26] Moreover, medieval societies were composed of innumerable local cultures, specific and unique.[27] But it is equally certain that many practices, including those that conflicted or competed with the practices of ecclesias, and many of the local cultures, even though always maintaining some of their specificities, were nonetheless *permeated by* religion. They were not totally constituted by religion, as Delort suggests, but permeated by it, a verb that denotes the properties of diffusion and infiltration that help make sense of a concept of hegemony.

This permeation was visible in many fields of practice and experience. Ecclesiological referents were of substantial consequence in the ordering of time and space, for example.[28] Daily activities were punctuated by liturgical offices and the sounds of bells coming from the church; prayers and masses helped to mark and divide the days and the weeks; religious festivities helped organize the year, the Christian calendar accompanying and punctuating the rhythm of the seasons. The routine described by Delort might not have been strictly followed, but it gives a feeling of the significance of the festivities. I quote a brief passage:

> The winter solstice was marked by the great festivities of the Nativity (25 December), the Circumcision (1 January), the Epiphany (6 January), the Adoration of the Magi, and the Baptism of Christ. During the previous period, Advent, there were three fast-days a week: Monday, Wednesday, and Friday. The weeks that preceded Lent were marked by other festivities that varied with the social stratum but were particularly typical in the rural environment . . . : Candlemas on 2 February, celebrated with pancakes and the blessing of the candles; Shrovetide just before Ash Wednesday, when the faithful crossed their foreheads with hallowed ashes to symbolize the fate reserved for the body. Then began forty days of abstinence from meat, except on Sundays and at Mid-Lent, in preparation for Holy Week.[29]

Whether or not one was pious was not very important, for regardless of a person's religiosity, the festivities served as markers and as occasions for breaking everyday routines. Moreover, they were fully imbued with Christian meanings, and by extension they imbued with Christian meanings all the activities associated with them. Indeed, to the extent that we accept the structuralist postulate that "things" attain meaning only by virtue of their relations with other "things," the whole forming a relational system of meanings (however unstable and tension-ridden that system might be), the significance of the constant presence of religious signs in medieval everyday life cannot be easily denied.

Religious signs marked also the structures and uses of space.[30] The church and its position in the geography of towns, the spatial organization of rites, the presence of religious objects and relics in people's households, or the centrality of holy sites in the imagined cartography of the time, for example, helped deploy religious codes everywhere, which imbued medieval cultures, however localized, with Christian meanings.

The permeation of the imagination by religion is difficult to convey in a few sentences. People's imagination was not just populated with saints of all sorts, miracles, demons, the fear of eternal punishment, ideals of redemption, superstitions, and so on, but was fed, as many scholars have argued, by an "immense appetite for the divine."[31] The divine, in all its forms, was lived with intensity and practiced in innumerable rituals—not just perceived but experienced as real. To medieval men and women, a figure like the Devil was not a mere invention of the imaginary but a real, dangerous creature, always at work, appearing everywhere, constantly seeking—in the guise of a handsome youth, an attractive woman, a defenseless elder—to induce someone to sin.[32]

Moreover, the lines separating religion from many spheres of practice whose boundaries today we take for granted did not exist, and therefore the fusion between the religious and those other spheres was complete. Bryan Turner's discussion of sickness makes the point neatly:

> Categories of sin and sickness have evolved into separate and specialized components as the outcome of a process of secularization, although it is also recognized that medical discourse still contains a moral viewpoint on individual and social organization. In medieval European culture, these distinctions did not exist, and Christian sacramentalism retained the notion that the cure of souls and bodies could be brought about through the rituals of penance. It was traditional in Christian cultures to recognize a parallel between the work of the priest and that of the physician. . . . The connection between the sinner/confessor and patient/physician was clearly recognized by theologians like Grosseteste, who identified a connection between moral vices and physical sins.[33]

The practices of knowledge, Foucault's modalities of thought, were also imbued with a religious, Christian consciousness; "knowing" during the Middle Ages involved the identification and association of what were believed to be primordial signs created by God at the beginning of times into what I would call a semiotics of revelation.[34] This practice did not generate a singular or homogeneous type of knowledge, as we might easily presume, but took many forms, yielding a plurality of sometimes disconcertingly different discourses. The practices of resemblance that Foucault saw as the primary episteme of the Middle Ages were but one of the forms taken by this semiotics of revelation, and the discourses of resemblance are consequently only one among the many discursive forms made possible by this semiotics.[35] The practices of "figural interpretation" discussed by Erich Auerbach produced, for example, a very different discursive form.[36] Rather than identifying resemblances between signs, figural interpretation involved reading events—past and present—as expressions of the Scriptures, as figurations of events described in them. The Scriptures contained the truth, and the happenings in the material world reproduced, literally, the happenings inscribed in the holy texts. This practice generated a figural discourse, a discourse of scriptural semiotics, as opposed to a discourse composed of listings as described by Foucault—two discursive forms that, on the surface, could hardly be more different from one another. And we must relate the *Quest* to the practices of figural discourse; the potentially heretical or subversive character of that text points only at the plurality of expression made possible by a single discursive form.

In these and many other examples, hegemony works *through* permeation. It works through the spread and penetration of religious signs, meanings, and forms of knowing into almost every field of experience—by virtue of the absence rather than the presence of boundaries between the religious and other lifeworld practices. It works through the fusion of religion with these other practices, in the "undifferentiated experience" of religion and everyday routines.[37] And precisely what permeates is very clear. It is not simply "religion" in some general, abstract sense. All the religious practices that we have briefly covered—prayers, feasts, confessions, penances, diets, cares of the body, superstitions, discourses of resemblance and figuration, courtoisie and villainy, and so on—are functions of the power of ecclesias, providing contexts within which that power comes into being and deploys itself. In this sense, hegemony works by tending to make everything similar, according to the terms of similarity determined by a power, in this case ecclesias, as an expression of its own "essence." It works, indeed, by essentializing, by attempting to make everything over in the image of the power.

Heterogeneity and the Silencing of the Other

But power is not only the result of mechanisms of permeation or essentialization; it is also a product of practices of differentiation, of the establishment—often violent—of lines of separation and difference within the heterogeneity of practices that constitute a reality. Here I do not refer to the most obvious practices, like paganism in the context of ecclesias, that are foreign to the hegemonic power and as a consequence become evident candidates for exclusion—although even in these cases the power often attempts to permeate or co-opt before excluding. I refer, rather, to practices, like magic, that emerge from within the infrastructure of social relations generated by the hegemonic power and as a consequence give body to the same logic, the same modality of action, the same pragmatics as the one defining the terms of the similar.

Richard Kieckhefer, one of the major authorities on magic during the Middle Ages, beautifully showed how magic and religion indeed shared the same pragmatics or, to use his term, the same "rationality."[38] Discursively, magic seemed to follow the same semiotics of revelation as religion or what at the time was ordinary science. Like religion and ordinary science, magic worked through the reading and organization of signs and the alleged effects of certain properties of these signs on the natural world. Nicole Oresme, for example, explained the workings of magic "as the result of properties or 'configurations' inherent in sublunary objects and verbal formulas."[39] Writers explained the effectiveness of specific astral configurations by definitions of the characters of planets, sympathies and antipathies, the recourse to hidden powers, and so on—arguments that follow the same practices of thinking that, according to Foucault, gave the natural sciences of the time their shape. Moreover, the identity of magic and religion also involved an experiential dimension, the two producing and reproducing not only a semiotics but, quite literally, a pragmatics of revelation—a specifically medieval pragmatics, that is. Indeed, medieval religion and magic shared the same "immense appetite for the divine," evoking the same attitude to everyday things, fostering practices that, although often representing opposite sides of the same coin, were, by the same token, congruent.[40] The line separating medieval magic and religion was, at best, blurred. "The terms 'magic' and 'religion' were both current in medieval discourse," noted Kieckhefer, "but they would not usually have been viewed as opposites or even as essentially distinct categories. The distinction between 'magic' and 'miracle' would have seemed more familiar to medieval Europeans. Both were extraordinary phenomena, inexplicable solely by the known laws of nature, and in each case the defining feature was the operation of exceptional forces: demonic intervention, occult virtues within nature, or divine intervention."[41] Here, Kieckhefer points at the characteristic that separated the different forms of knowledge, namely, the alleged type of force in operation. Both the theistic origins of these sources and the method by which knowledge was generated, however, remained constant. To use Kieckhefer's terms, medieval magic, unlike paganism, was by no means irrational or nonrational; it partook of the same rationality as religion. Magic was perhaps "irreligious," but most definitely not "nonreligious."[42]

In this example, we observe not only a heterogeneity of discourses but, as I have suggested, a heterogeneity of practices—the same pragmatics yielding, for instance, religious pietism, practices of natural magic, or sorcery.[43] The pragmatics of revelation indeed generated more than two general practices, religion and magic; it triggered multiple forms of religion and multiple forms of magic, or rather, a blurred field of multiple religious and magical practices.[44] The lines that emerged, then, were not those between religion and magic but those between the religious forms consolidated in "religion" and only some among the original forms of magic: the forms, that is, that represented the greatest threat to the collective self of ecclesias.

These were in fact dispersed forms that cannot be easily categorized in terms of specific domains such as "love magic" or "medical magic," for there was no relation between the domain to which magic was applied and its acceptance or rejection by the ecclesiastical authorities. There were forms of love magic that were forbidden, others that were encouraged; forms of medical magic that were banned, others that were bolstered; forms of astrology that were legitimized, others that were condemned; and so on.[45] Their inclusion on one or the other side of the divide had nothing to do with the substance of the magical activity itself. Both legitimate and illegitimate magic made use of potions and spells, or relied on incantations.[46] What determined their designation was solely the extent to which they were perceived as disrupting the order of ecclesias, the extent to which they were indeed seen as violating its collective self—a self given ideal expression in the ethos of courtoisie.[47] Spells and potions alleged to be harmful to marital relationships as defined by the church—for example, by promoting infidelity or, conversely, impotence—were severely condemned and violently opposed; spells and potions alleged to help marital relationships—by restoring potency, for example—were in turn encouraged.[48] The condoned practices were defined as curative, as divinely healing, as fomenting a restoration of the essence of Christianity, and were assimilated within the spaces of religion. The threatening ones were redefined as sorcery and witchcraft and consigned to the other side of the line, to a space of "difference." Their practitioners were marked as "not belonging to the collective self," as "others" whose practices had to be effaced and whose voices had to be silenced.

The suggestion that most acts of magic designated as negative were associated with activities of women raises important questions concerning the gendered nature of the divide—questions that I cannot pursue in this study.[49] The significant point for our purposes concerns the very establishment of the line and the perception that in this case hegemony works through the effacement and silencing of practices made possible by the very reality that the hegemonic power generates. Although magic is certainly not unique to medieval Europe, the forms that it takes in Europe during the Middle Ages, the pragmatics and the rationality in terms of which it is exercised, the semiotics that gives it meaning and shapes its activities, are specific to medieval Europe. And precisely what the dominant power must efface and silence are some of the practices of this specifically medieval magic. Certainly, too, these practices of differentiation, the practices of naming certain others as "not belonging to the collective self" help to fashion that collective self. By definition, naming "others" helps set the boundaries of "self." By definition, too, as I argued in chapter 1, a power comes into being and exists through the multiplicity of its practices, including its practices of difference. Yet to suggest that the practices of difference determine the collective self, to assume that that self comes into being only through practices of difference, is to ignore the importance of practices of similarity in the constitution of infrastructures of social relations in general. Indeed, neither the semiotics nor the pragmatics of revelation that I have discussed can be explained through practices of difference. The collective self of the dominant power develops from a combination of practices of similarity and difference, of mechanisms of permeation and differentiation, the first providing the foundations on which the more specific lines of differentiation develop.

The Logic and Practice of Centeredness

Courtoisie and villainy involve the generalized, and idealized, perceptions of self and other that follow from the many lines of differentiation that we see unfolding in medieval Europe as a consequence, and instrument, of the power of ecclesias. Courtoisie represents an idealized self; villainy, a paradigmatic other. They also illustrate how these lines involve the division of a single foundation, the two concepts emerging from the same infrastructure of social relations, each representing the mirror image of the other. But to fully understand these concepts, we must introduce a second dimension to our understanding of the infrastructure of social relations at the core of the order of ecclesias, namely, its centeredness. Indeed, the identification of a semiotics and a pragmatics of revelation provide an understanding of the foundational modalities of that infrastructure, of the "plane," so to speak, on which the social relations of ecclesias unfold. We still need to develop an understanding of the actual interactional orders that develop on that plane—of what makes an infrastructure of social relations into precisely that: an infrastructure of *social relations.*

The term *centeredness* here refers to the specific configuration of social relations in terms of which the order of ecclesias takes shape. It refers to a system of gradations in which social positions are perceived and organized in the form of concentric circles, the value of each stratum depending on its distance from the central point. Like all attributes of ecclesias, it is deeply imbued with religion.

Ernst Cassirer showed how medieval thought combined elements of Christianity and Neo-Platonism to generate what he called "the concept and general picture of a *graduated cosmos.*"[50] Inspired by Platonic thought, medieval cosmology saw the world as composed of two essences: a "sensible essence" composed the sensible world, a world of phenomena and appearances, and an "intelligible essence" formed the antithetical, intelligible world, a world of ideas and noumena. According to Plato, each was the precise reverse of the other, and each precluded the other. There was a qualitative difference between these two worlds, and their essences could not be reconciled. Everything that the one was, the other was not. The world of appearances implied movement, multiplicity, and indetermination. The world of ideas involved permanence, pure identity, and determination. They constituted two irrevocably separate entities. There was no going from the one to the other, no way of understanding the one in terms of the other.

Cassirer showed how medieval men and women adapted this vision of the cosmos to their beliefs and sensibilities. To them, God's descent to Earth and His incarnation in Christ implied a reconciliation of the two worlds. God, the eternal, the immutable, had assumed through the body of Christ the form and essence of the temporal and multiple. He thus united phenomenon and idea in a spiritual, divine bond. Cassirer describes the consequences of this reflection beautifully.

> [Across the] abyss of negation, a spiritual bond extends between the two worlds. From one pole to the other, from the super-being and super-one, the domain of absolute form, reaching down to matter as the absolute-formless, there is an unbroken path of mediation. The infinite passes over to the finite on this path, and the finite returns on it back to the infinite. The whole process of *redemption* is included in it: it is the Incarnation of God, just as it is the deification of man. In this conception, there is always a "between" to be bridged; there is always a separating medium that cannot be jumped over but must be traversed step by step in strictly ordered succession. . . . Thus, all being emanates from God in

determined degrees of radiation, only to gather up again in Him and to re-concentrate in him. . . . Just as these radii come closer together the closer they get to the centre, so the union of essences prevails over their separation the less distant they are from the common centre, the source of being and of life. And with that we also have the justification, the actual theodicy of ecclesiastical order, which is essentially nothing but the complete reproduction of the spiritual-cosmic order.[51]

In a sense, the opposition between the sensible and the intelligible remains in this transformed Platonism. God is unmodified, absolute Being; the material world we inhabit, and of which we are part, is "phenomena"— bits of modified, finite, incomplete being. The two essences are still intrinsically different. But now a new element emerges: while still of a different order, the absolute radiates over the universe, creating, by virtue of its concentric effects, a hierarchical arrangement of things.[52] That which is closer to God is, axiomatically, of a higher order.[53]

As Cassirer saw it, the adulterated Platonism became as a consequence an adulterated Aristotelianism. In contrast to Plato, Aristotle held the notion of a continuity of being evolving in a single, uniform process. To Aristotle, the movement of the intelligible towards the sensible, of the divine towards the terrestrial, was a *logical* movement, a movement that denied the dualism of Platonic thought. To him, reality was one, and appearance and idea were not incommensurable states of being. The one developed into the other, and together they formed an existential unity. As Cassirer noted, however, for Aristotle the process connecting the two states of being was one of development and not, as in medieval cosmology, of emanation. The difference is most significant, for freed from any Platonic conception, Aristotle's metaphysics became a logical theory in which one language was able to interpret all reality. Medieval thought, in contrast, had to resort to its Christian sources in order to resolve its inherent contradiction. For if no transformation of the intelligible into the sensible was possible, the divine could penetrate the terrestrial only on account of its very power, by virtue of a miracle whose origin—God—made it incomprehensible to terrestrial beings. People did not have to understand; it simply was, and their certainty depended on faith, not comprehension.

It would not be difficult to see in this theodicy, to use Cassirer's term, a simple instrument of ideology, a construct that helped to justify and sustain a well-established, oppressive order by concealing the relations of power at its root. Religion would seem to play the role that Marx attributed to it, that of the opium of the people: "the sigh of the oppressed creature, the sentiment of an heartless world, and the soul of a soulless condition."[54] Yet, however seductive such a reading might be, any interpretation along those lines would fail to take into consideration the specificity of ecclesias. It would fail to recognize the extent to which religion was for the order of ecclesias what capital is for the order of capitalism. In the order of ecclesias, religion did not conceal; it was the resource with which power was exercised and the means by which hegemony was achieved. Religion may have become an opium where it has ceased to be the essence of the dominant power, where indeed it conceals rather than comprises the mechanisms of hegemony of the new power. To paraphrase Marx, in the order of ecclesias, religion was the essence of the oppressing creature, the sentiment of the ecclesiastical heart, and the soul of its essentializing self.

To European men and women of the Middle Ages religion was indeed concrete and material, not only maintained but constantly reproduced through the complex of practices that it permeated—the prayers, feasts, confessions, penances, diets, health practices, superstitions, discourses of resemblance and figuration that we covered above, and now also the centered practices of hierarchical organization that we begin seeing. People did not have to understand this, or the theodicy described by Cassirer, to experience and practice it.

To recognize the significance of religion during the Middle Ages of course does not mean that we should reduce everything to religion. Nor does it mean, for that matter, that ecclesias was the only power in medieval Europe. As I indicated above, local cultures and local practices abounded at the time. Moreover, the power of feudal lords and feudal institutions, discussed in the next chapter, should not be ignored. Yet from the perspective of our present purposes, neither the existence of local cultures nor the power of feudal institutions lessens the importance of ecclesias. For ecclesias nevertheless permeated large domains of medieval experience, including the feudal, making the infrastructure of social relations through which it developed into a hegemonic foundation, though not the only one. The argument that I am advancing is about permeation, boundary-making, and hegemony, not total constitution. For the purpose of understanding the transformation of infrastructures of social relations as expressed in concepts of propriety, the exclusive focus on the order of ecclesias is justified, for courtoisie, the dominant medieval concept of propriety, took its place within the order of ecclesias and helped give body to the power of ecclesias—not the power of the alternative feudal institutions.

The actual configuration of social relations in the world of ecclesias was indeed fully congruent with the perception of centeredness described by Cassirer—a perception, as we saw, grounded on a complete acceptance of religious principles. For most medieval people, the divine origin of the authority of bishops and kings was inarguable.[55] Here, the signs that God had placed everywhere were already revealed, and their truth was indeed incontestable. As He had wished for all things in the world, He had wished, too, for a just and proper organization of the universe. He had placed in His proximity the monarch and the high priest, whose functions were to rule the world according to His intentions. Then, as part of the divine plan, He ordered society in a complex yet precise system of precedence, each stratum down the ladder receiving less of His glow. And indeed, the basic distribution of medieval society was congruent with this idea, yielding, at its most general level, a tripartite ordering of social relations. At the top was the clergy, followed by the nobility (with the major exception of the king), followed by the masses of peasants, merchants, and townsmen. But each order was itself divided into several groups, and we find within each basic state a further hierarchy. A prince was "more" than his vassal, and the vassal "more" than his own servant, though all could be of noble origin.[56] A bishop was more divine than a simple priest, and a yeoman farmer was of higher status than a serf.

All this received practical expression, for instance, in the position the different groups occupied in a church, or in the marching order of processions. Bishops always led processions, preceded only by an image of Christ, their one and only lord, and thus expressed their preeminent position in the concentric organization of the cosmos.[57] Then came the priests, then the deacons, the subdeacons, the sacristans, the readers, and the exorcists. Then came the noblemen, according to their rank, the great landlord in front, the vassals following, the richer and more powerful first, the lesser vassals behind. Then marched the commoners, guilded craftsmen, and free peasants leading the way for a mass of serfs, poor laborers, and vagabonds. Finally came the women, forming, to use Shulamit Shahar's expression, a "fourth state."[58] And, as Georges Duby has noted, "since the issue was one of value, of relative proportion of good and evil, an order of this kind was of course inviolable. To have broken ranks would have been sacrilegious."[59]

Every person's position was then first determined by birth. Either one was born a noble, in which case one was enlightened by definition, or one wasn't, in which case the person had to live in the shadow of his or her superiors. Nobody was born into the clergy, but the place that someone came to occupy in the ecclesiastical hierarchy was again largely fixed by ancestral distinction. Birth was instrumental in foretelling a person's occupation and, to a significant extent, in establishing the limits of his or her ambitions. A serf's son was practically doomed to become a serf; his daughter, destined to marry into serfdom. A merchant's son most likely became a merchant, and a knight's son, willingly or unwillingly, a knight. God forgive the youngster who was not dubbed a knight at the proper time: he was violently rejected by his peers, scorned by his lessers, and, worse, was bound to become a villain.[60]

But not everything depended on the vicissitudes of lineage, for as we learned from our two stories, distance from God was also a question of behavior. People who behaved according to the principles of courtoisie were rewarded with a special beam of divine light. Virgins and chaste widows were accorded special privileges at church and during processions.[61] Faithful knights became not only soldiers of a terrestrial lord but, like Bors, fighters in the celestial armies, combating the enemies of the church.[62] Saints, the makers of miracles and conquerors of temptation, became instant celebrities and were rapidly ordained members of the nobility.[63] Conversely, the unfaithful—Moslems, Jews, and heretics of all sorts, including witches—were seen as the worst enemies of society, of humanity itself.[64] They did not occupy even the lowest place in the hierarchical order—that place was occupied by women. They were completely outside of it, in total obscurity, out of reach of the divine glow. Laborers and craftsmen who worked with materials considered taboo were defined as outcasts: butchers, executioners, and surgeons who came in contact with blood; dyers, fullers, and cooks who worked with dirt and impurities; traders who used money.[65] Sinful priests were scorned, sinful commoners scorned, tortured, or put to death, sinful noblemen obscurely castigated by God.[66]

The practices of centeredness make manifest the place of courtoisie and villainy among the hegemonic mechanisms of ecclesias. Centeredness itself involves a configuration of social relations that gives full body to the power of ecclesias, combining into a single frame, as the very conjunction courtoisie/villainy attests, mechanisms of similarity and difference: mechanisms of similarity, first, since its practices are fully permeated by the collective self of ecclesias and contribute to transforming that self into something tangible, evident, and "essential"; but also, quite clearly, mechanisms of difference, since the practices of centeredness simultaneously establish and ground a complex of lines differentiating people into degrees of selfness and otherness—lines, indeed, marked on the foundation produced by the similar. The suggestion that the practices of centeredness order people in *degrees* of selfness and otherness is important. On the one hand, it allows for a more nuanced perception of self and other than a strictly dichotomous one. On the other hand, it allows us to look at centeredness in terms of a continuum within which the effort to engage in practices able to bring someone closer to God—the effort to conform, to become part of the similar, to become a courtois, that is—is constantly fostered. In this light, courtoisie becomes an instrument of normalization. It is a vehicle by which people are prompted to become "normal," to engage in practices of similarity, to identify with and fashion themselves as subjects in terms of the similar as defined by ecclesias. It is a referent in relation to which, as I mentioned earlier, medieval men and women interpret, judge, negotiate, subject, and even sometimes oppose their daily experiences—in which case, depending on the extent to which such opposition erodes the authority of the church, ecclesias turns to its more violent forms of subjection. Courtoisie is also an idealized referent. As it prompts people to identify with the collective self of ecclesias, it simultaneously makes everyone who develops such an identification feel incomplete, inadequate, guilty, and thus driven to engage in even more practices of normalization.

Now we are able to understand the inevitability of Bors's victory over Pridam le Noire: any other outcome would have challenged the logic of ecclesias. Bors represents the perfect courtois, God's chosen, loyally realizing His will, voluntarily embracing the hardest trials of faith. His triumph is a foregone conclusion. And we understand the meaning of the parable of the knight and the keg. It is a tale about resistance to ecclesias, about the refusal to be normalized, and about the extraordinary transformation that a person undergoes who willingly becomes one with the church.

The Ontological Condition of Coalescence

As we will see in the next two chapters, the ethos of courtoisie will gradually wither away as domination in medieval societies shifts from the ecclesiastical to the secular centers of power. A new ethos, giving body to the power of a monarchical infrastructure of social relations will then emerge—using, misusing, taking over, and transforming many of the properties of courtoisie. One important dimension is still missing from our understanding of the infrastructure of social relations at the core of the world of ecclesias, however. This is the dimension that the work of Elias calls our attention to, namely, the coalescence (my term) that characterizes social relations during the Middle Ages in general.

Coalescence refers to the particular texture of social relations that results from the softness and permeability of interpersonal boundaries and from the roughness of everyday life identifiable in medieval Europe. As the texture of a cloth refers to the way a fabric or substance feels to the touch, the texture of social relations refers to the way in which self and other, as well as "things" in general, are experienced. It refers to the quality of social relations that sets the terms of the thinkable and of what can be experienced—terms that in the case of coalescence, of the merging of bodies and psyches, and of the roughness of material life that Elias describes, we are unable to reproduce today. Indeed, we should not confuse coalescence with what today we variously call attachment, involvement, or commitment. Coalescence speaks of a fundamental condition of fusion, of a blending and amalgamation of properties into one single body. It speaks of a condition that makes the experience of individuation impossible. Attachment, involvement, and commitment, in contrast, belong to the same universe of possibilities as individuation and represent conditions that are the opposite, the mirror image, of individuation. Like individuation, they are modern phenomena, emerging out of the same historical and sociological processes. Attachment, involvement, and commitment are functions of a previous act of separation; they describe the action of two necessarily separate monads.[67]

The infrastructures of social relations of ecclesias, including the principles and practices of courtoisie, developed within the conditions of experience made possible by coalescence. Consider the ideal of behavior portrayed in the *Quest*. Many of Bors's behaviors, however rude they might appear today, are understandable given what we have already learned about courtoisie. His refusal to accept food from his hostess, for instance, is not a sign of discourtesy, it is an act that brings him close to God. His disdain for the lady's vassals is similarly unexceptional, for given their distance from God, they are simply not worthy of respect. Yet we still cannot understand Bors's cruelty, or the violence and apparent absence of humanity that mark the *Quest*. These inclinations are integral to the behaviors defined as positive, if not virtuous, within the confines of ecclesias and which make sense only in the context of coalescence.

Literary and visual representations of medieval reality suggest that the behaviors described in the *Quest* were perceived as quite ordinary at the time. In fact, compared to other narratives, the story of Bors is rather bland. Here, for example, is how *The High Book of the Grail* describes what Perceval, a better-known and more perfect courtois—perfectly chaste, impeccably well-behaved, divinely protected—did upon his return to Kamaalot to eleven of his mother's enemies whom he had defeated in combat and led to captivity:

> He bade that a great vat be made ready and brought into the mid-
> dle of the court; then he called for the eleven knights to be led
> forward, and had them beheaded in the vat and left to bleed as
> much blood as they could. Then he had their heads and bodies
> thrown out so that only the pure blood remained in the vat. Then
> he called for the Lord of the Fens to be disarmed and led before
> the vat with its great fill of blood. He had him bound tightly, hand
> and foot, and then, mocking, cried:
> "Lord of the Fens! Lord of the Fens! You could never have
> enough of the blood of my lady my mother's knights, but I will
> give you enough of the blood of your own."
> He bade him be hung in the vat by his feet so that his head
> was plunged in the blood up to the shoulders; and he had him
> held there until he drowned to death. Then he ordered that his
> body and the bodies of the other knights be taken to an ancient
> burial-pit beside an old chapel in the forest, and the vat with all
> the blood was thrown in the river, so that the water ran red.[68]

Countless *fabliaux,* short stories, scenes from longer narratives, or draw-ings from the epoch convey a similar landscape of ferocity and aggressive-ness.[69] Again, the relevant issue does not concern whether or not people actually behaved that way but the ordinariness and unproblematic character of the representations. What is notable is the evidence that this behavior could be imagined and expressed in such an extensive range of cultural objects. All of these representations suggest a different configuration of ex-periential boundaries—a different attitude to behaviors that today we would unequivocally define as violent. Like the behaviors at table or the practices of caring for the body (or, from our perspective, not caring for the body) that Elias describes, what we note is that these representations did not offend, did not transgress the boundaries marking people's sensibilities.

The attitude to torture, documented not only by Foucault but, much earlier, by Huizinga, for instance, suggests the connection between the rep-resentations and the actual sensibilities of medieval men and women. Hui-zinga tells of the citizen of Mons, who "bought a brigand, at far too high a price, for the pleasure of seeing him quartered, 'at which the people re-joiced more than if a new holy body had risen from the dead.' "[70] And he tells of the people of Bruges, who, in 1488, "during the captivity of Maximilian, king of the Romans, cannot get their fill of seeing the tortures inflicted, on a high platform in the middle of the market-place, on the magistrates suspected of treason. The unfortunates are refused the deathblow which they implore, that the people may feast again upon their torments."[71]

Indeed, as Elias maintains, what we are seeing is a different constellation of sensibilities, in which feeling appears to have been shaped by experiential boundaries of an order altogether different from the ones we experience today. From our perspective, feeling during the Middle Ages would seem rougher, emotional expression freer of inhibitions and constraints—as if, as Elias suggests, the boundaries between body and body, and body and nature that characterize much of today's behavior did not exist. This is suggested not only by the violent tenor of life, the manners at table, or the attitude towards the natural functions that Elias discusses, but by the architecture of homes, small and large alike, the precariousness of everyday life, and the attitude of medieval men and women towards death.

Houses were small and, except for those of the very rich or of city people, usually had only two rooms.[72] The main room was the kitchen, where people not only cooked and ate but also spent much of their scant free time. There, families gathered and their members did whatever they had to or wanted to do. Dogs, chickens, and pigs strolled about at will. Children played among themselves or with the animals. Men drank, played dice, or told stories. Meanwhile, women worked and took care of everything. The other room was the bedroom, and there all the family slept together, sometimes in the same bed. Privacy, intimacy, or personal life were by today's standards scant and, if they existed at all, seem to have had very different meanings.[73] Rich noblemen who could afford to have private rooms used to invite their guests to share their beds—the guest sleeping on one side, the host's wife at the other, and the nobleman himself between them. The very existence of chapters on behavior in bed in advice manuals even from much later periods suggests the ordinariness of such behaviors.

Or consider the expanse of the countryside, the insecurity of the roads, the incertitude of nature, the hopelessness of disease, all characteristics of life that concurred to make the medieval world dangerous and precarious.[74] Between feudal castles was a vast, empty space, a literal jungle where the strongest and the harshest made the law.[75] Roads were narrow, tortuous, and infested with robbers, hungry beasts, and knights of more than doubtful reputation. Wolves invaded towns and country in search of food, attacking cattle, poultry, and humans alike. The darkness of night was absolute. Death seems to have been a daily presence, a constant contingency, ever possible in famines, diseases, wars, the cold of the winter, plunder, burglary.

The entire attitude of medieval men and women towards death seems to have been mediated by a set of taboos and fears different from our own.[76] Death in the Middle Ages held no terror and was not, as it often is today, a discreet, lonely, frightening occurrence. It was a common event, and people confronted it in an open manner, as a normal element of the order of things. Death, to make use of Philippe Aries's term, was "tamed." It was seen coming, and the dying prepared themselves to meet it. To evade its warnings, to reject it, to hold onto life meant to expose oneself to ridicule. Nobody fought death, and nobody, even though living alone, ever died alone. When in 1219 William Marshall, Regent of the Kingdom of England, felt his end coming, he gathered his many vassals, and together they made the journey from London to Caversham, his manor.[77] For two months he waited for death. For two months his court waited with him. He had ample time to dictate his will, in front of everybody, and he took leave of all, one by one. He died sumptuously, to the sound of bells, his sons and vassals close to him, weeping copiously. The night of his funeral a big banquet was organized in his honor, a banquet over which he was supposed to preside, seated at the place of the master of the house.

To paraphrase Elias, it would indeed seem as if the wall of feelings which appears now to mediate not only contact between one human body and another but experience in general had not yet developed, or rather, was of a different order.[78] People seemed to stand in a different relationship to one another, as they did to the world of objects and of nature, than we do[79]—as if their sensibilities, marked by a softness and fluidity of boundaries, had indeed a different structure and character that generated a reality of interwoven selves and bodies and of a more immediate relation between self and nature than we experience—a reality, that is, of selves and bodies embedded in one another and in nature. As I mentioned above, coalescence involves a condition very different from attachment, which effectively implies the union of autonomous, unembedded individuals. And its opposite is not detachment but individuation: the emergence of a condition in which selves and bodies are no longer interwoven. It is a disengagement that involves the literal removal of self and body from the collective of interwoven selves and finds expression not only in the negative practices of punishment but, as importantly, in positive practices like the search for spiritual growth in solitude—as in hermitage.[80]

The reality that I am describing is highly reminiscent of Durkheim's "mechanical solidarity," yet very different.[81] Like the type of order that emerges under a condition of coalescence, mechanical solidarity conveys the idea of a collective as a single social body in which punishment consists mainly in a severance of the offender from the one body. But while undifferentiation between people is for Durkheim a function of the similarity of activity that follows from a little-developed division of labor, in terms of coalescence it is a function of a quality of interpersonal and perceptual boundaries. For Durkheim, what forms the collective and determines the absence of individuation is a likeness of experience, but in the concept of coalescence, as Elias beautifully shows, it is the interwoven constitution of selves. The difference is critical, for to Durkheim and to many other nineteenth-century theorists of premodern societies,[82] similarity and solidarity are given. They are the very essence of the social body that develops from a limited division of labor—a point that, incidentally, by now has become vastly discredited.[83] A theoretical perception in terms of coalescence, in contrast, makes no assumption about similarity, let alone solidarity. The suggestion that selves are interwoven does not imply that all selves are similar, or that people experience the same activity similarly, or that they develop "solidarity" with one another. As courtoisie itself makes evident, coalescence can coexist with practices of gradation and difference, as well as practices of antagonism and conflict. Coalescence is only one dimension of an infrastructure of social relations, and both the practices and substance of the similar, like the practices and substance of the different, are seen as functions of the entirety of the infrastructure—or rather, of the power that realizes itself in and through that infrastructure.

To return to the metaphor that I used above, we can say that coalescence provides the fabric in which the order of ecclesias is embedded. The interwoven makeup of interpersonal structures involves an interactional foundation within which the power of ecclesias operates. It simultaneously conditions its mechanisms and, as we shall see in the next chapter, is transformed as power itself changes. The development of courtoisie attests to this embeddedness of ecclesias in what I have characterized as the ontological condition of coalescence—as it does, for that matter, to the embeddedness of power in an interactional foundation in general. For it is only in light of this further characteristic of the infrastructure of social relations of ecclesias that we are able to understand courtoisie and its apparent insensibilities or exaggerations.

Thus, for instance, chastity, a central element of the ethics of courtoisie and one that participates, as we shall see below, in the practices of centeredness and normalization of ecclesias, takes a most surprising form. For given the absence of corporeal boundaries in medieval societies—a condition that, among others, appears today to foster a perplexing intimacy— few could resist the lure of the flesh. Bors, an imagined figure of perfection, showed his virtue by having "never" committed the act of flesh "but in one time that he begat Elian le Blank."[84] William Marshall, lying in his death bed, worried for the future of his only unmarried daughter, the young Jeanne, for he knew that "maids with no support, no dowry, have difficulties in finding a taker," and that "if their weddings are delayed for too long they may well turn . . . 'into shame.' "[85] In medieval society it was the inhibited, the inordinately prudish, the excessively mannered who were sanctioned as evil and immoral.[86]

The courtois, in like manner, was not supposed to have been "gentle," or to have behaved in a "humanitarian" manner. Rather, he was supposed to fight the unfaithful and the villain who dared oppose the power of the church and of the king, the order of God.[87] It was also natural for him to weep at the death of the virtuous and disdain the death of the villain; to mourn at the grave of the lord and the friend and rejoice before the corpse of the enemy.[88] Thus, as we see Bors and Perceval killing mercilessly, we see them shedding tears unsparingly after Galahad's death, "as ever did two men."[89] And now we can appreciate Bors's immense compassion in saving Pridam's life.

The Discursive Deployment of Ecclesiastical Hegemony

Most contemporary medievalists tend to see the secular texts that I discuss above as forms involving irony or parody, implying an act of resistance to or subversion of the established, hegemonic order. This is true not only regarding the interpretation of Arthurian romances, but also studies of popular medieval literature like the *fabliaux* or the advice manuals and non-Arthurian romances that I analyze below.[90] The extent of sexual license portrayed in these texts, for example, is seen as an act of resistance to the practices of chastity advocated at the time by ecclesiastical and feudal institutions alike. Thus, instead of reproducing or deploying the order of ecclesias as I suggest they do, they subvert it and contribute to its eventual transformation. Yet, as Douglas Kelly observes, most romances treat sexual license, at least in its extramarital form, as immoral and sinful, and rather than protesting chastity, they exalt marriage and fidelity in conjugal relations.[91] Rather than subverting the established order, they try to control what from the perspective of that order is a "disorder," namely, the sexual practices that emerge from coalescence. They inhibit, rather than promote the forms of behavior that follow from coalescence and induce people to different experiences and practices of their bodies and minds—experiences and practices, I should add, that ultimately transform the very condition of coalescence.

Here we perceive the role that the codification of courtoisie into a system of behavioral rules—the elaboration and promotion of a code of manners, that is—plays among the instruments of power of ecclesias. Given the eminently moral dimension of courtoisie, we should not be surprised to learn that most books, or parts thereof, that would qualify as manuals of courtoisie during the twelfth and early thirteenth centuries were actually morality books. Courtesy books, books devoted primarily to the elaboration of a code of behavior, to *manners,* were virtually nonexistent at the time.[92] With one or two exceptions, all the earlier texts emphasized morals over behavior, values over the codification of a precise set of norms. Manners, most suggestively, were (when at all discussed) presented as extensions of the moral discourse. They were presented as practical expressions of the ideals embodied by courtoisie and thus effectively served as vehicles by which ecclesias, quite unintentionally, attempted to induce the kinds of experiences and practices that I briefly alluded to above. And clearly, to the extent that people abided by the rules, ecclesias succeeded in permeating and fashioning their bodies and minds.

In this sense, manners involved an aesthetic translation of the ethical code at the heart of courtoisie. They involved a translation of the morality of ecclesias into form, of ethics into behavior, and conversely they were one of the forms through which the moral acquired concrete expression. They were one of the forms through which the moral, and the power at its root, came, literally, into existence.

Medieval authors established a perfect congruence between corporal and spiritual beauty, between urbanity and hierarchy, between individual or social harmony and divine order, between the ceremonial of what we call today etiquette and the "perfection required for the vision of God."[93] Elizabeth Keiser describes how this congruence takes shape, for instance, in St. Thomas of Aquinas's exegesis of "temperance" in part 2 of his *Summa Theologica.* "The fusion of aesthetic, ethical, and religious impulses," Keiser writes, "had strong appeal in medieval society; it comes to expression in a wide range of works, but perhaps nowhere so strikingly as in St. Thomas of Aquinas in his exposition of temperance as one of the moral virtues":

An affection for nobleness, what Aquinas calls *honestas,* enables one to shape conversation and actions, general comportment and even outward apparel into a well-formed life suffused with spiritual beauty. Although pretentiousness is a vice, we are nonetheless urged by St. Thomas to take care about manners and appearances for our soul's sake. Considering the virtue of modesty as that part of temperance which governs outward apparel, he observes that deficiency in style is a vice that presents itself in two ways: "First from negligence, as when a person fails to attend to and take due pains about dressing as he should. Second, by seeking glory from your very lack of care about dress." As he drily continues, "in bodily things not only dazzle and pomp but also dirt and drabness can be ostentatious."[94]

We find a similar reasoning in Andreas Capellanus's *On Love,* a work written about 1185.[95] *On Love* is a lengthy, definitely humorous book on a most profane subject, carnal love, and is often used as an example in arguing for the ironic, subversive nature of secular medieval texts in general.[96] Following Ovid's *Ars Amatoria,* Andreas, a cleric at the court of Champagne, sets out to discuss in detail issues concerning how to win, buy, and preserve love. He discusses the different stages of such a process, their effects, and the relations that should develop depending on the lovers' social conditions. And he addresses not only the question of how to recognize the approaching end of a relationship but, quite unabashedly, how to dump one's lover. The details that he addresses obviously have little relation to the actual amorous practices of the time, and the humorous, zestful character of the book is everywhere apparent. Andreas discusses at length, for instance, the different rules that clerics, nuns, or harlots should observe as they engage in games of seduction (and more), depending on the social status of their lovers—a discussion that is obviously unrelated to any reality and is intended in jest. But although much of it is fantasy and intended as play, it is nevertheless play "with a recognised point in a society whose conventions make such fantasies meaningful."[97] And it is as play, or jest, and not as irony, that *On Love* seems to have been understood by its intended audience, an audience composed primarily of other clerics.

Indeed, in spite of its playfulness, the treatise is ultimately uncompromising in its rejection of the behaviors that it discusses. The humor becomes a rhetorical device by which an otherwise scandalous theme could be discussed without excessive sanctimoniousness. As P. G. Walsh explains, "An-

dreas knew that his clerical readers would be pleasurably scandalised by the
studied contrast between his own analysis of love and its more theological
counterparts, and it was a daring and flamboyant gesture to handle at length
such topics as 'The love of clerics,' 'The love of nuns,' and 'The love of
harlots.' . . . But the sober treatment of these subjects, wholly acceptable
from the Christian viewpoint, belies the presence of any ironical intention."[98] When his contemporaries scolded him, it was mostly for having
gone too far in the jest, not for representing a danger to the order of ecclesias.[99]

And the same technique of congruence or translation about which Aquinas was so explicit instructed Andreas's treatise, effectively "transposing
many of the positive aspects of *amor Christianus* (the power of love, the
importance of chastity, the asceticism which eschews sexual relations) into
the secular ideal."[100] Moreover, Andreas not only transposes the religious
ideals of love to the secular, but uses the very structures of centeredness
discussed above to help frame the text through dialogues in which the social
status of the participants varies. The "manners" that Andreas advocates
become an integral element of the infrastructure of social relations of ecclesias, simultaneously a product of it and a vehicle for its production and
reproduction. The twelve "chief precepts of love" that he sets forth during
a dialogue between a man and a woman of nobility, for example, involve
a perfect translation of the ideals of love promoted by ecclesias.[101] They
uphold fidelity, chastity, temperance, moderation, honesty, humility, respect, and the "opposite of miserliness," "largesse," all of which are integral
to *amor Christianus*. From these, a detailed set of behavioral prescriptions
unfolds. Rules governing relations between the sexes, or moderation, or
largesse, always depending on one's condition, become essential to Andreas.
These include not only rules on gift-giving or deference but on the little
details of behavior: at dinner a man has to carve his lover's meat (for Andreas men are the only active seekers of love), offer her the best portions,
allow her to be first at drinking from the common cup. And through these
rules, Andreas ultimately delineates the care of body and mind that helps
transform the infrastructure of social relations of ecclesias into a fact that
admits no questioning.

In a way more intensely secular, Guillaume de Lorris's *Romance of the
Rose* (circa 1217) entails a similar intention.[102] The Romance tells the story
of a young man who struggles to win the heart of his beloved. Again, the
tale is concerned with spiritual and carnal love and probably as well with
the loss of virginity before marriage. It is written in allegorical form, the

story being a dream, the *dramatis personae* embodying the virtues, the vices, and the emotions Guillaume considered part of the experience of loving. The youth, having in his dream entered the garden of Mirth, looks at a magic fountain in which he perceives the image of the Rose. Wounded by the arrows of Sweet Looks, he falls instantly in love, and from then on, his life consists in trying to reach and, quite literally, to "deflower" his beloved. Fair Welcome, Franchise, and Pity help him reach his goal; Evil Tongue, Shame, Danger, and Fear protect the Rose from him. On the way he encounters the vices—Hate, Felony, Villainy, Covetousness, Avarice, Envy, Sorrow, Old Age, Pope Holy (a fairly blasphemous name for hypocrisy), and Poverty. And he encounters the virtues, represented as the court of the God of Love—Idleness (here presented as a virtue, for it makes a woman beautiful), Mirth, Courtesy, Gladness, Sweet Looks, Beauty, Wealth, Lady Largesse, King Arthur (who represents courage), Franchise, and Youth—joyfully dancing in the Garden of Mirth.

Guillaume's description of the vices and virtues involves a transposition similar to the one we observed in Andreas. Physical beauty, for instance, is seen as an extension of spiritual, divine beauty and consequently is provided with a decidedly ethical dimension. Thus Hate is depicted as

> A frenzied dame, with dark and frowning face
> And upturned nose, hideous and black with dirt.[103]

For the same reason, Old Age is defined as evil:

> Shrunken at least a foot from what her height
> Had been in youth. She scarce could feed herself
> For feebleness and years. Her beauty gone,
> Ugly had she become. Her head was white
> As if it had been floured. 'Twere no great loss
> Were she to die, for shriveled were her limbs—
> By time reduced almost to nothingness.
> Much withered were her cheeks, that had been soft;
> And wrinkled foul, that formerly were fair.
> Her ears hung pendulous; her teeth were gone;
> Years had so lamed her that she could not walk
> Four fathoms' distance without aid of crutch.
> . . . .
> No power she had, and no more force or sense
> Than yearling child, although she did appear
> Like one who in her prime was sage and wise;
> Henceforth she could be nothing but a sot.[104]

49

On the other hand, of Idleness Guillaume says,

> A man might travel to Jerusalem
> And find no maid with neck more fair and smooth
> And soft to touch. Her throat was white as snow
> Fresh fallen upon a branch. No one need seek
> In any land a lady daintier,
> With body better made or form more fair.[105]

She is the exact opposite of Hate and Old Age:

> All my companions call me Idleness;
> A woman rich and powerful am I.
> Especially I'm blessed in one respect:
> I have no care except to tress and comb
> My hair, amuse myself, and take mine ease.[106]

Idleness is leisure, and leisure, perceived as the opposite of what the lower classes do, is beauty.[107]

This is Courtesy:

> She was not overnice or overbold,
> But reasonable and wise; no insolence
> E'er hindered her fair words and fairer deeds.
> None misbespoken ever was by her;
> She held no rancor against anyone.
> A clear brunette was she, with shining face.
> No lady of more pleasant grace I know;
> Her form seemed that of empress or of queen.[108]

And the God of Love, "An angel seemed, descended from the sky."[109]

The moralizing element is evident in the permeation of a Christian ethics. Conceptions of good and evil that parallel those of courtoisie inform the characterization of the different vices and virtues. Moreover, the God of Love is unmistakably divine, while Courtesy comes second, fair as an empress or a queen. And the connection between the divine and manners is overtly implied; it is the God of Love who teaches the lover the rules of proper behavior. Here are some examples of what the God of Love taught the lover—the resonance with Andreas, or even Aquinas, is not fortuitous:

> Then guard yourself from telling what you hear
> That better were untold; 'tis not the part
> Of worthy men to gossip scandalously.
> . . . .

Be reasonable to men both high and low—
Companionable, courteous, moderate—
And when you walk along the street take care
To be the first with customary bow;
Or, if another greets you first, be quick
To render back his greeting, nor be mute.
. . . .
But elegance in manners is not pride;
He who is mannerly will realize,
Unless he is a mere presumptuous fool,
That one's most valued who most lacks conceit.
. . . .
Let no filth soil your body; wash your hands;
Scour well your teeth; and if there should appear
The slightest line of black beneath yournails
Never permit the blemish remain.
Lace your sleeves and comb your hair, but try
No paint or artificial aid-
. . . .
Let no one think that you are miserly,
For such a reputation causes grief;
It is most fitting that a lover wise
Should give more freely from his treasury
Than any common simpleton or sot.

These, in a most religious fashion, are presented as commandments, and the infringement of God's rules as heresy:

"Beware of Villainy, above all things;
I'll have no backsliding in this respect
Unless you wish to be a renegade,"
Said Love. "All those who Villainy admire
Should excommunicate and cursed be."[110]

But the romance goes one step further. It presents an approach to love that is not only moral in the conventional sense, but also, perhaps primarily, "psychological"in the most literally Foucauldian sense of the word, that is, as exemplary of the practices of normalization of the order to which it belongs.[111] Its theme is the lover, his internal struggles, his pains, his sorrows and his joys. It involves a dissection, greatly aided by the allegorical form, of the different forces that impinge upon the lover's emotions. The internal struggle of the hero is not only between good and evil, vice and virtue, but also between reason and passion,[112] religion and nature, the ideas of courtoisie and the carnal realities of everyday life. The romance becomes a study in guilt, and of the delicate balance of emotion, or unavoidable lack thereof, purported to bridge courtoisie and sexual desire. For courtoisie was an ideal that could not be reached, in perpetual conflict with the realities of everyday life, yet whose lure was difficult to resist: it promised honor in life, heaven in death. It implied a matter of choice, either of following one's impulses or, as we saw in the tales at the beginning of the chapter, of directing, by an act of will, one's behavior to the good as defined by ecclesias. To evade the choice, to succumb to one's desires without fighting, meant to be doomed to hell (a fate that, most probably, given the very real fear of damnation, most people sincerely believed in). To fail in the choice, to become aware of one's defeat, of one's impropriety, of the inability to reach towards God, on the other hand, meant to be at fault and to have only oneself to blame. That is the tension that Guillaume probes with the help of his allegorical characters, a tension that remains unresolved in the romance, yet—like the knowledge generated by psychology for Foucault—helps to define a condition of being as problematic and disabling, and points in the direction of its remedy.[113] For what is important is not the closure or open-endedness of the romance but the guilt and feelings of inadequacy and incompleteness that always accompany Guillaume's hero, along with the gist of the "therapy" needed to alleviate guilt and become a proper self—a therapy composed of practices of confession and of once again fashioning one's mind in the shape of the dominant order.

We see a similar transposition of the ethical into the normative in a work of a radically different character, the anonymous *Ordene de chevalerie,* a treatise on chivalry written about 1250.[114] This time it is the secular basis of power that is, in a way, absorbed by ecclesias, for the treatise describes in detail the ceremonial of dubbing, presenting all the minutiae of a knight's behavior as echoes of the Christian exemplar. Thus, for instance, the knight to be must take a bath: it is a bath of courtesy, recalling a child's baptism, cleaning the young man from all sin. He is taken to a fair bed: it is the symbol of paradise, the goal for which he should from now on fight. He is dressed with a scarlet cloak to remind him of the blood he will have to shed in the defense of God and His church. He has to wear a belt of white signifying virginity and make a vow of chastity, and so on.

The same transposition occurs in a work written around the third quarter of the twelfth century by Stephen de Fougères, a French clerk, chaplain of Henry II, not insignificantly called *Books of Manners.*[115] Fougères expounds upon specific prescriptions concerning the rights and duties of each order—and all privileges, all obligations, are once more seen as attributes of the collective, universal Self.

This varied, multifaceted codification of courtoisie into behavioral rules attests to the discursive deployment of ecclesiastical hegemony, to the spread of ecclesias through the discursive constructs of medieval culture. The codification is varied and multifaceted, yielding a multiplicity, not a homogeneity, of forms. Yet they all involve an extrapolation of what constitutes the collective self of ecclesias, the essence of the similar as defined and practiced by a Christian rationality, into the minutiae of deportment: how to talk, how to eat, how to dress, how and when to make a movement, how to come before one's superior—how, that is, to become one with "the similar," whatever form the connection might take. And through that multiplicity of forms, ecclesias in turn attains practical expression.[116]

It is clear, then, that the emergence of the first courtesy manuals—books in which the connection between manners and ecclesias is no longer taken for granted—points at the coming into dominance of a different infrastructure of social relations and at a decisive shift of power among European societies at that time. It also points at the simultaneous existence of a second, although less dominant up to the thirteenth century, infrastructure of social relations in medieval Europe, which complicates the picture sketched in the present chapter. A discussion of that parallel infrastructure and of the shift that ensues forms the core of the next chapter.

CHAPTER THREE

Courtesy, Detachment, and the Transformations of the Relational Order

> The text of Cervantes and that of Menard are verbally identical, but the second is almost infinitely richer. (More ambiguous, his detractors will say; but ambiguity is a richness.) It is a revelation to compare the *Don Quixote* of Menard with that of Cervantes. The latter, for instance, wrote (*Don Quixote*, Part One, Chapter Nine), ". . . truth, whose mother is history, who is the rival of time, depository of deeds, witness of the past, example and lesson to the present, and warning to the future."
>
> Written in the seventeenth century, written by the "ingenious layman" Cervantes, this enumeration is a mere rhetorical eulogy of history. Menard, on the other hand, writes, ". . . truth, whose mother is history, who is the rival of time, depository of deeds, witness of the past, example and lesson to the present, and warning to the future."
>
> History, *mother* of truth; the idea is astounding. Menard, a contemporary of Williams James, does not define history as an investigation of reality, but as its origin. Historical truth, for him, is not what took place; it is what we think took place. The final clauses—*example and lesson to the present, and warning to the future*—are shamelessly pragmatic.
>
> Jorge Luis Borges, *Pierre Menard, Author of Don Quixote*

B Y THE YEAR 1530, Baldesar Castiglione, a notable Italian gentleman, succinctly expressed the view on manners common to his days. "I hold that the principal and true profession of the [ideal] Courtier must be that of arms," Castiglione wrote.[1] The courtier had to be, therefore, first bold and faithful. But he also had to be dexterous and agile, and his body had to manifest the attributes of the good warrior: he had to be not too tall, nor too small; athletic, yet not too heavy; energetic, yet parsimonious. "But since one cannot always engage in . . . strenuous activities (moreover, persistence causes satiety, and drives away the admiration we have for rare things)," Castiglione explained, "we must always give variety to our lives by changing our activities."

> Hence, I would have our Courtier descend sometimes to quieter and more peaceful exercises. And, in order to escape envy and to enter agreeably into the company of others, let him do all that

others do, yet never depart from comely conduct, but behave himself with that good judgment which will not allow him to engage in any folly; let him laugh, jest, banter, frolic, and dance, yet in such a manner as to show always that he is genial and discreet; and let him be full of grace in all that he does or says.[2]

The key word is *grace,* for, according to Castiglione, in manners a courtier has to be above all "graceful": elegant, agreeable, refined, unaffected. Indeed, whenever he engages in social intercourse, he has to show complete mastery of aesthetic expression. It would be difficult to convey in more successful terms the extent to which the perception of social relations changed between the beginning of the thirteenth and the end of the fifteenth centuries. For what the quotation above suggests is not a mere refinement of manners, a straightforward perfection of the ways of courtoisie, but a shift of the referent from which manners are derived to begin with. To Castiglione, *sprezzatura,* "grace," constitutes the quintessence of decorum, and the vulgar (an aesthetic concept), not the villain (a moral character), embodies its opposite.[3] In effect, Castiglione no longer associates manners, at least not primarily, with religious virtue and moral goodness— referents whose behavioral expressions help give body to the practices of similarity and difference as defined by ecclesias. He relates manners to aesthetic virtuosity and technical excellence, referents whose expressions help substantiate an entirely different infrastructure of social relations—one giving body to a civil, as opposed to an ecclesiastical, power. As we shall see, "grace" involves not only the aesthetic element emphasized in the passage above but, simultaneously, a secular ethics and a secular politics, surmising the literal presence of a "pragmatics of grace" at the heart of this other infrastructure.

The Shifting Discursive Referent (Part 1)
The Anomalies of *Il Tesoretto*

Castiglione's book gives expression to a moment in the history of manners in which the shift from the ecclesiastical to the civil, from ecclesias to a *res civile,* from courtoisie to civility, that is, has already taken place. We must turn our attention first to the movement of infrastructural transition.

Clear indications of change are apparent as early as the year 1265, when Brunetto Latini, a Florentine citizen of vast repute, wrote what Julia Bolton Holloway has termed (a little hastily but not quite inaccurately) the first bourgeois courtesy book.[4] The book, *Il Tesoretto,* is actually more a hybrid than a courtesy book proper. In its first section it is like a morality book and, to a significant extent, the entire treatise does not seem much different from Guillaume de Lorris's *Romance of the Rose.* Yet subtle differences gradually emerge that bespeak a perception of propriety that is vastly different from courtoisie, although it is not yet "civility"; it is what I call "courtesy." The hybrid character of the book itself attests to its condition of liminality; it belongs neither to courtoisie nor yet to civility, but stands at the threshold of the shift.[5]

Latini himself seems to have been an exceptional person. He was well educated and seems to have known the basic treatises on politics and law well. He was well instructed in French, Spanish, Italian, and Latin and knew the major literary works in each language. He was born around 1220 in the Florentine state and early on became a civil servant. A notary by profession, a diplomat by avocation, a brilliant politician, Latini held the post of secretary of the Commune of Florence from August 15 to October 15, 1287. Like many of his fellow citizens, he was a member of the Guelph party, opposed to the Pope and the feudal aristocracy and in favor of freedom from the bondage of a strong central power. In 1260 he was sent on an embassy to the court of Alfonso the Wise, the newly elected Emperor, who sympathized with the cause of the Guelphs. Upon returning from Spain, Latini learned of the defeat of his party in the battle of Montaparti and exiled himself in France, where he wrote *Il Tesoretto.* After his return to Florence in 1266, he became Dante's preceptor.

It is interesting to learn that Dante sent his teacher to the Inferno to be punished among the Sodomites.[6] Little evidence that Latini was a homosexual exists, though, and the hypotheses attempting to explain Dante's harsh judgment of his master abound.[7] For some, Dante was chastising Brunetto because of blasphemy against the Italian language, Latini having written a second, larger book in French. Others argue that Dante was actually joking, just carrying out Latini's own will. Indeed, complaining that his book might fall into worthless hands, Latini implored,

> If that happens to [my book],
> I say: Let it be ripped apart,
> And the unbound leaves
> Be thrown into hell-fire.[8]

Most scholars suggest, however, that Latini was rudely chastised because of his blasphemy against ecclesias, because of his idolatry of Florence as a

Republic rather than of the Empire as the embodiment of Christianity. His sin was to have sought in his *Tesoretto* a treasure to be found on Earth rather than in Heaven. It was to have celebrated, and promoted, the emergence of the *res civile,* the civil, secular "thing."

In style and rhetorical structure *Il Tesoretto* is a true medieval product. Like the *Romance of the Rose,* it consists of a dream vision in which the dreamer, in this case the author himself, is instructed on the ways of the world by allegorical characters. First we meet Nature, who tells Latini about the Creation and the multiple things to be found in "her" midst: light, plants, water, animals and, of course, men and women, and the original sin. Then we meet Generosity, "gracious" Courtesy, Loyalty, and Prowess, all of whom teach about virtue and manners.

Nature's discourse—close to one-third of the book—is a hymn to God. It repeats, with extreme verbosity, the story of *Genesis,* hailing God's power and wisdom. In fact, it establishes the same principles of truth that we found in the books on courtoisie, all things ultimately being—for Latini as much as for Andreas Capellanus, Guillaume de Lorris, or Stephen de Fougère—but a partial expression of God's will. But when the narrative begins to discuss questions of goodness and evil with respect to behavior, *Il Tesoretto* manifests a visible departure from the principles governing courtoisie. Indeed, as I suggested before, *Il Tesoretto* appears to be two different books: its first section is an apologia of Christianity; its second, comprising the teachings of Courtesy and her companions, advances a completely different set of moral and behavioral parameters.

On the surface, *Il Tesoretto* does not appear particularly exceptional. The following, for instance, are some of Courtesy's instructions:

> To you, beautiful friend,
> First of all I say
> That in your speech
> You should have precaution:
> Do not speak too much,
> And think beforehand
> Of what you would say,
> For the word that is said
> Never comes back again,
> Just like the arrow
> That goes and does not return.
> . . . .

Do not be an initiator
Nor a repeater
Of what another person
Before you argues;
And do not use reprimands,
Or tell lies of another
Or slander anyone:
So that there is no one
Of whom you would suddenly
Say an ugly word.
. . . .
And if you go on horseback,
Watch for each false move;
And if you go through the city,
I counsel you to go
Very courteously:
Ride beautifully,
A little with bent head,
Rather than going unreined
With great wildness.[9]

Nothing in these quotations indicates a departure from the conventions of courtoisie. Moderation is there, faithfulness is there, respect for the other and the high value of aestheticism are there. The same ideals that inform the concept of courtoisie are advocated in *Il Tesoretto*. Moreover, a certain moralizing tone, if not intention, permeates Brunetto's writing. References to virtue and servitude to God, hospitality, kindness and largesse, liberality and love are to be found throughout the book. And yet, despite the parallels, anomalous interpretations of the known conventions slowly accumulate.

Quite predictably, Brunetto tells his readers,

Watch that you do not err
If you stand or move
With ladies or lords
Or with other great ones;
And although you may be their equal,
you should know how to honor them,
Each one according to his state.
And so be in this way mindful
Of the greater and the lesser.[10]

The reason advocated for that behavior, however, is most unconventional. According to Master Brunetto, as he is fond of calling himself, a person has to be polite with both the greater and the lesser "So that [he] do not lose control."[11]

"One should be astute" not to speak or laugh when others say absurdities, or speak nonsense, Latini has Courtesy teach us, and this time not only the explanation but the prescription itself is uncommon:

> Follow in their guise,
> And I counsel you beforehand
> That you follow their wrongness;
> For even if you should do well,
> You would not please them;
> Nothing will help you
> In saying good or evil.[12]

If everybody is a fool, be a fool; if everybody is evil, be evil, the master is telling us—so that you don't lose the esteem of others. In the same vein Brunetto suggests,

> When you go in company,
> Follow all the time
> Their way and their will,
> Since you should not wish
> Always to have your own way,
> Or make a division among them.[13]

That is, be careful not to be the source of discord. And with similar intention he advises,

> If in your company
> Is a man who appears to you
> To possess less wealth,
> By God, do not force him
> To do what he cannot afford;
> For if, through your encouraging,
> This one wrongly spends what he has
> And sinks into a worse state,
> You will be blamed for it.[14]

And again,

> In acts, do not be too bold,
> But gain for yourself from others
> To whom your deeds are pleasing.[15]

Indeed, a criterion of explanation that could no longer be associated with ecclesias and courtoisie emerges in *Il Tesoretto*. Brunetto speaks of pleasure-giving not in theological but in social terms. He speaks of situation management in a manner that reminds us more of Goffman than of courtoisie. He talks of control, control of self as much as control of the social juncture. Moreover, from the standpoint of courtoisie, some of *Il Tesoretto*'s precepts are utterly unethical—which, as I have suggested, reflects upon its author. Latini, in effect, advises people to hide their true intentions, to think in terms of social profit, to conduct their lives in terms of business. He advises them, in short, to make use of the mental frame of the merchant, not that of the courtois.

As both Elias and Foucault have suggested, the movement towards control, of self as well as of the situation, is of the utmost importance.[16] On this point, the following injunction, imputed this time to Prowess (also a woman) is most explicit:

> . . . courteously
> Carry yourself toward an enemy,
> And show him shrewd behavior;
> If you find him anywhere,
> Pretend to have honored him;
> If you find him in any place,
> With anger or with jest,
> Do not show any harshness
> Or fierce villainy;
> Give him all the road:
> Because self-control *[maestria]*
> Refines the ardor more
> Than does mere striking.[17]

And the same spirit transpires in all of Prowess's suggestions:

> . . . watch out always
> That you offer no injury
> Or violence to a living man,
> The more powerful you are,
> The more you must watch then,
> For the people do not delay
> In speaking evilly
> About a man who always is injurious.[18]

If wrong is done to you, don't react foolishly, hold on to your reason:

> I counsel you this well:
> That, if with a lawyer *[legisto]*
> You can help yourself out,
> I want you to do it,
> For it is the better deed
> To restrain madness
> With words sweet and slow
> Than to come to blows.[19]

If someone more powerful than you does you wrong, give up, Prowess advises. But if your shame and dishonor are too great, do not fear death. Never show fear: if you are found soft you will never achieve anything.

Avoid violence; consult; make use of the legal and political apparatus at your disposal; always weigh a situation of potential conflict; control yourself; appease your enemy; think constantly of the common good.

> And more, do not rush
> Into war or battle,
> And do not be a creator
> Of war or of scandal;
> But if it should happen
> That your city forms
> An army or cavalcade,
> I want you in that event
> To carry yourself with nobility.[20]

In a sense, Latini's treatise, foreshadowing Machiavelli, sounds like a book on political behavior. The political character of the book is highly visible and fits perfectly Elias's thesis regarding the role of the transformations of behavior in the formation of nation-states—although it suggests that we should date the beginnings of these transformations much earlier than Elias does.[21] What we are seeing in the *Tesoretto*, in effect, is the elaboration of a code of conduct that facilitates interaction between men of might: calming excesses, rationalizing emotions, urging the use of objectified legal instruments in the resolution of conflicts, providing, in short, the behavioral provisions for order among the multiplicity of polities in whose shape feudal power developed. We are seeing the emergence of a new awareness, what Marc Bloch called "a longing for peace,"[22] that grew increasingly urgent as the civil "thing" gained in substance.

Transformations of the Plane of Power

I should make clear that when I speak of the formation of a *res civile* in Europe during the thirteenth and fourteenth centuries, I am not speaking of the emergence of a new secular sphere of action or a new secularized type of power. Neither do I claim that with the formation of civility and the civil "thing," the religious spheres of action or ecclesiastical power disappeared. I speak, rather, of the transformation of the multiplicity of interwoven polities that characterize feudalism into a political unit, and of the coming into dominance of the secular spheres of power made possible by this transformation. Secular power had certainly been present in Europe before the thirteenth century, but it tended to be exercised by large numbers of individual rulers who claimed sovereignty over relatively small territories, and although their power was important in terms of their control over the "capital of physical force," they commanded little of the hegemonic force of ecclesias.[23] The genesis of the *res civile,* on the other hand, implied the conversion of feudal lords from a caste of independent oligarchs to a class of subjects subordinated to the rule of a monarch. It transformed the entirety of the secular plane of power of medieval societies and created the conditions for the infrastructural shift that we see fully expressed in Castiglione. But it involved only a change of dominance, not the sudden appearance of a new power or the definitive disappearance of the earlier one.

This transformation of the feudal polity is amply recognized and discussed in the vast literature on the genesis of nation-states.[24] The monopolization of the means of violence and coercion by an increasingly centralized government is one of the major changes leading to the emergence of nation-states. The elaboration of a code of conduct that reduced infighting among powerful lords and gave authority over the resolution of conflicts to the state is in turn seen as essential to that movement.

The example of vendettas is paradigmatic. Vendettas were common in medieval societies.[25] Death by murder required the death of the killer, and entire families (for vendettas were and still are essentially family affairs) engaged in the quest for "justice." Marc Bloch describes a number of these: the dispute between two noble families in Bourgogne at the end of the eleventh century that lasted for more than thirty years and claimed at least eleven lives after the first days of violence; the long quarrel that followed the murder of a father and two sons in Flanders at the close of the twelfth century; the "perdurable hatred" that entangled the Giroys with the Talvas in twelfth-century Normandy; the vendettas of the Lorrains against the

Bordelais.[26] Vendettas engaged not only the close relatives of victim and aggressor but their most remote relatives. An act of blood demanded retribution through blood, and when the guilty person could not be punished, a brother, an uncle, or a distant cousin, could well become the prey of vengeance.

Vendettas imply a dispersed rather than a concentrated or monopolized exercise of violence, and help constitute a polity in which the capital of physical force is itself dispersed. They facilitate the delineation of family ties, enhance clanlike solidarity, and anchor the capital of physical force in a multiplicity of polities grounded on interwoven lines of kinship. The emergence of practices leading to an assuagement of dispersed forms of violence, both through the establishment of a formal apparatus of law and through transformations in behavior, therefore involves a complete reconfiguration of the body politic and generates the conditions for the concentration of the means of violence conducive to the development of the modern nation-state.

I say assuage, not eradicate, for as long as the monopolization of the means of violence was not completed, kings maintained an interest in the division of their subjects.[27] Subjects, specifically noble subjects, were indeed a constant threat to the crown: they defended their traditional independence and demanded a share in power.[28] Moreover, and this is exactly the meaning of an incomplete monopolization of power, noble subjects kept relatively large armies—large enough to pit their united might against that of the king. Separately, however, no nobleman was strong enough to be a source of danger. It was in the interest of the monarch, then, to exploit divisions, to manipulate enmities, to feed, to a certain extent, potential sources of conflict. It was in his interest to maintain the dissensions provoked by the habit of vengeance. Nevertheless, the requirements of their own power pressed monarchs in the opposite direction. Monarchs needed control, not the chaotic entanglement of the vendettas.

Bloch summarizes well the terms of the formal apparatus introduced in the effort to define that middle ground. "The authorities," Bloch writes,

> sought to protect innocent people against the most flagrant abuses of family solidarity, and they fixed the period of grace. They also strove to draw a distinction between lawful reprisals and plain brigandage carried out under the pretext of justifiable vengeance. They tried sometimes to limit the number and nature of the wrongs which could be expiated in blood; in the Norman ordinances of William the Conqueror, only the murder of a father or a son was

so classified. . . . Above all, they laboured to bring the hostile groups
to reason, and sometimes to compel them to conclude treaties of
armistice or reconciliation under the arbitration of the courts. In
short, except in England where, after the Conquest, the disappearance of any legal right of vengeance was one of the aspects of the
royal "tyranny," they confined themselves to moderating the more
extreme manifestations of practices which they were unable and
perhaps unwilling to stop altogether. The judicial procedures
themselves, when by chance the injured party preferred them to
direct action, were hardly more than regularized vendettas.[29]

Not only were the scope and authority of the law limited, most of the
edicts were followed, if at all, with utmost reluctance, as a kind of nonbind-
ing ordinance, which highlights the importance of informal, behavioral
means of social control. Indeed, as Elias suggested, for the reconfiguration
of the body politic to take place, a frame of mind had to change, new
behavioral inclinations had to evolve, a different conception of self and
other had to emerge. A new habit of body and mind, marked by restraint,
self-control, reason, appeasement, and the like, had to develop. As Brunetto
beautifully put it:

Self-control crowns
Force and strength,
And makes vendettas be put off.[30]

As central as it is, however, the focus on the monopolization of the
means of coercion by the "state" only partially explains the movement from
"courtoisie" to "courtesy"—from a concept of propriety giving body to
ecclesias to one giving body to an inchoate form of the *res civile*. Pierre
Bourdieu's distinction between four types of capital—the capital of physical
force, economic capital, informational capital, and symbolic capital—expands our view of this transformation significantly.[31] Bourdieu explains how
the processes of concentration that began in Europe in the late twelfth
century involved the four types of capital, each producing a consolidation
of a different form of power. The concentration of the capital of physical
force in the institutions of the state produced the monopolization of violence that I discussed above.[32] The establishment of unified taxation yielded
a concentration of economic capital and economic power.[33] The development of mechanisms leading to the concentration of informational capital—in the form of the censuses, registries, the formulation of classificatory

systems, the monopolization of archival documentation in the hands of
state clerks, and so on—brought about a "theoretical unification" and imposed a dominant culture established and controlled by the state, especially,
according to Bourdieu, through the workings of a unified education system.[34] Finally, the centralization of the means by which social agents define
their fundamental categories of practice and perception, a consequence of
the concentration of the other three types of capital, led the state to become
"the site par excellence of the concentration and exercise of symbolic
power."[35]

In effect, we can view the movement from courtoisie to courtesy both
as a reconfiguration of the body politic and as a transformation of what
Bourdieu calls informational and symbolic capital. We must speak of transformation as we study the movement from courtoisie to courtesy, though.
We cannot speak only in terms of concentration or monopolization, as we
do (like Bourdieu) when we study the rise of nation-states. For however
effective the terms *concentration* and *monopolization* are in helping to explain the formation of modern polities, they do not shed adequate light
on the extent to which power *was* largely monopolized by ecclesias before.
Nor do they adequately express the extent to which the conceptual shift
that I am analyzing involved a transformation and a displacement of the
plane of power on which reality was anchored. Nor do they express the
extent to which the new plane was constituted in altogether different, discontinuous ways, yielding not only a different politics but, as I have suggested, a different pragmatics. Thus, when Bourdieu speaks of the concentration of informational capital during the thirteenth century as producing
a unification of culture and providing the basis for that culture's dominance,[36] we should understand it as the generation of a *new* unified culture.
We should see it as a complete change, as a reconfiguration of the mechanisms leading to theoretical unification and as a displacement of the site
in which symbolic power was concentrated and exercised. We should see
it as a complete transformation of the symbolic template that provided the
foundation for "culture." Using the concept of informational capital to
speak of the mechanisms of theoretical unification in the world of ecclesias
seems inadequate. For these mechanisms, in full congruence with the terms
that I discussed in chapter 1, seem to have been of an entirely different
order: theoretical unification was achieved in that world through the multiple practices of similarity discussed in chapter 2. The very possibility of
speaking of the new mechanisms in terms of informational capital indicates

the discontinuous nature of the transformations that we are exploring, for the emergence of informational capital was a characteristic of the infrastructure of social relations that emerged with the *res civile.*

The distinction between courtoisie and courtesy at the core of the present analysis conveys precisely the shifting nature of power in Europe during the late Middle Ages, and in particular the transformative, metamorphosing character of that shift. This focus on the metamorphosing character of the transformations that we are exploring sets the present study apart from the current literature on medieval courtesy, specifically from C. Stephen Jaeger's *The Origins of Courtliness* and Aldo Scaglione's *Knights at Court,* arguably the most important studies on the topic.[37] In many respects my study does not differ greatly from theirs. Indeed, both Jaeger and Scaglione trace much of the origins of courtesy to religious institutions and to the development of propriety among the episcopal clergy. They show how the central principles of courtoisie developed within the clergy and how these were in turn transformed as they entered the spheres of the secular and came in contact with principles of chivalry and courtliness. Moreover, like Elias, they clearly acknowledge the role of courtesy in the formation and consolidation of absolutism, thus linking its development to the evolving structures of power in Europe during the late Middle Ages. Yet, like the scholars who examine the concentration of power, neither Jaeger nor Scaglione convey adequately the extent to which the movement from courtoisie to courtesy involves a shift of power from ecclesias to the *res civile,* and how it marks the coming into dominance of a *different* order of things. Nor are they sensitive enough to the extent to which courtesy was part of the *displacement of the site* in which both political and symbolic power were concentrated and exercised.

Scaglione is fully aware of the tensions between what I call courtesy and courtoisie, yet he still attempts to identify an underlying commonality among them. "Much ink has been spilled on the presumed essence or unity of these ideals and, especially among German scholars, on the ethic of chivalry," Scaglione writes. "But, rather than a unitary ethical system, an ideal nomenclature, a philosophy, or an educational pattern, the common ground of all this literature is an underlying social reality which linked heterogeneous groups through a somewhat vague yet powerful ideology. The ideology existed in the form of a common mentality even without a unitary verbal expression of it."[38] I suggest that this vague commonality does not exist and that the absence of "essence or unity" of ethics, nomenclature, philosophy, and so on, is precisely that: an absence of essence and unity.

This suggests the existence of two orders, two sites, of political and cultural power. Thus, instead of searching for an imagined commonality, we should understand the shift from courtoisie to courtesy in terms of the changing relations of dominance between these two orders.

The different meanings that the same injunctions acquire in each order find little expression in Jaeger and Scaglione. For example, they see the injunction to "be pleasant" that marks courtesy and, later, civility, as equivalent to similar injunctions in courtoisie or, for that matter, in ancient Greece and Rome. They see it this way because such a concept of "pleasantness is not based on conformism and indifference to underlying moral issues: it is a necessary aspect of a way of life that takes into account the need to communicate and interact with others, in full respect for their feelings and interests."[39] But the point is that the symbolic and moral schemata from which the injunction to "be pleasant" takes its meaning vary, and that the form taken by "the need to communicate and interact with others" depends on the pragmatics inherent in any particular infrastructure of social relations. The passage from Borges that opens this chapter is relevant here: in the same way that exactly the same words have totally different meanings when written by Cervantes or Menard, the same injunctions have different meanings and implications in the traditions of courtoisie or courtesy—the injunctions belong, in each case, to different relational orders.

Indeed, the same principles that we identified in Latini appear in the frames of courtoisie. Moderation, for example, which was one of the central considerations of *Il Tesoretto,* was also one of the central values of courtoisie. We saw St. Thomas of Aquinas encouraging temperance, Guillaume de Lorris's hero torn between the opposing forces of passion and reason, the knight of the opening story, in his excesses, disowning the image of God. The conceptual framework inspiring restraint, however, was of a significantly different order. For St. Thomas, Guillaume, or the anonymous author of the *conte dévot,* moderation was a question of nobility of spirit, of moral beauty, of forgiveness and primordial goodness. For Brunetto it was primarily a practical matter tied to an ethics of public goodness.

What we are seeing is that in a very concrete sense courtoisie helped create the conditions of its own eclipse; for in stimulating a sense of social responsibility, it helped frame the contours of the new political order, furthered the impulse for the growth of formal rationalization, and promoted the emergence of a civic, public mentality. In its insistence on goodwill, brotherhood, and intellectuality, it fostered the formation of the political, cultural, and symbolic coherence that constituted the backbone of the civil order. Courtoisie, in effect, created within itself the grounds for its own transcendence.

The Self-Referential Properties of the Discourse on Manners

It would not be unreasonable to associate the ideas conveyed in *Il Tesoretto* with the interests of a specific class of people. After all, in Brunetto ideas and biography seem to coincide. His writings express a detachment of manners from the religious elements of courtoisie; his life exhibits a practical distancing from the political universe of ecclesias. The opponent of papal authority, unsurprisingly, lays the foundations for the emergence of a secular central power. The extent of the transformation must be fully realized, however, for the thrust towards a new definition of the social body is visible not only in the works of people in sympathy with the provisions of the civil world but also in the work of authors seemingly at odds with the increasingly dominant *res civile*.

Thomasin von Zerclaere's *The Italian Guest*, a long didactic poem written in German about 1215, is a notable example.[40] The date is significant, too, for it shows that the process that we observed in Brunetto was well developed fifty years before the composition of *Il Tesoretto*. Of Thomasin himself very little is known.[41] Most probably, he was born to an aristocratic family in the northern Italian province of Friuli, where he apparently received an intense and thorough education. As far as we can learn from his text, he had a fair knowledge of physics and astronomy and was acquainted with the ancient philosophers, the Latin authors of the Middle Ages, and the literature of his age. Of his occupation we know almost nothing. He became a cleric in his older age and died as a canon of Aquileja, but little evidence exists that he was committed to an ecclesiastic profession when the poem was written. The text suggests that Thomasin wrote *The Italian Guest* after the death of a dear wife, in deep retirement from the pleasures of life in which he seems to have been well versed.

One characteristic of Thomasin seems certain, though. He was a fervent supporter of the Pope. He affirmed ecclesiastical authority and advocated the unity of Christendom under the mantle of the church. An intensely religious person, his later cares seem to have been the fruit of a deep emotion. The rise of the city-states and the erosion of the old order of things, including the power of ecclesias as the power of the traditional feudal polities, caused him great anxiety. His book was in part a response to that state of affairs, an appeal to ecclesias and the feudal lords to restore their waning glory. He wrote it in German because its intended audience was composed primarily of German lords, the nobility of Friuli, a region adjacent to what today is Austria with an overwhelmingly German population.[42]

The differences between Latini and Thomasin could hardly have been more marked. While the first was overtly in favor of the substitution of the ecclesiastical order, the second was unambiguous in his support of traditional arrangements. One was a republican, a conscious partisan of the gradually prevailing civil spheres of conduct. The other was a Papist, devoted to feudal and canonical privileges. Yet, latently, subtly, *The Italian Guest* was as expressive of the growing civil order as was *Il Tesoretto*.

Thomasin instructs us on innumerable things: what to do with our hands when speaking; in what direction to stare while riding; how to place our legs when sitting; how to eat, with what hand to take our meat, and how to chew it; when we are allowed to talk, and to whom, and what language we should use; what our behavior should be as hosts, guests, masters, or pages; when, where and how to wash ourselves; what to wear and on what occasions we should change clothes; how to give and how to receive; to whom and from whom. He even instructs us on how to recognize a good from a bad physician:

> A physician who can cure well,
> He cures vigorously a sick man
> With thirst, with hunger, and with burning.
> He ties him up against a wall,
> He cuts and pricks him a very great deal.
> He tears another's beard
> And hair when he desires
> Him not to sleep too much.[43]

In a sense, *The Italian Guest* approximates better our own conception of a courtesy book. Unlike Brunetto, who gives very general indications concerning conduct, Thomasin touches upon the little details of manners—details of fashion and politeness, gallantry and ceremonial, food, drink, speech, and elegance. And here a most interesting transformation takes place: manners suddenly acquire a value in themselves. In contrast to the authors of morality books, who viewed manners as reflections of an absolute, Thomasin sees polite behavior as a path to virtue, as a precondition of morality. Once a corollary of God, of Truth, manners become axioms, little truisms that require no explanation. They are, for Thomasin, the attribute of good breeding:

When a strange guest comes to the Hall,
The young people shall do him great service,
The same as if he were the lord of all of them:
Such is the will and teaching of Good Breeding;
Let them speak choice words,
Seeing such is the treasure of Good Breeding.[44]

Ladies should not rest one leg over the other while sitting because "Good Breeding forbids all ladies / To sit with one leg over the other."[45] And he tells us the following regarding knights while riding:

Good Breeding forbids all knights
To look much at their legs
When they ride: I am much of opinion
That one is to look upwards.[46]

The authority of good breeding is echoed in all spheres of practice. Good breeding teaches that "one should honour the other" and that "none . . . shall at the door / Press before all others." Ladies should not leave home without a mantle, especially if they are not wearing their long upper gowns, for "that is quite against Good Breeding." "A younker and a knight . . . shall not swing his hands / Against a good man's teeth": he must keep them quiet. He should not place a hand on somebody's head, nor upon that person's shoulder: that is "good breeding." A host has to care for the food of his guests, and for his own behavior at table: he must touch nothing but his food with his hands; he should not drink or speak while eating; he should do without such food as his guests do not like. Then, and only then, will he bear himself with good breeding. And of course, good breeding requires of a woman "that she have not much artfulness, / If she is honest and noble."[47]

When manners are not the attribute of good breeding, they are the attribute of good sense—a concept that, as should be apparent, is certainly richer in meaning. Good sense dictates propriety of behavior in the realm of love, for instance. Beauty, friends, birth, riches, and love, Thomasin tells us, are worthless without sense.

In Greece over all the lands
[Helena] was a powerful queen.
She had much beauty and little sense,
Her beauty gained her great shame:
Beauty without sense is a weak security.[48]

Indeed, good sense makes women be "courteous and pliable, / And also have good gestures / With beautiful speech and a chaste mind."[49]

Foolishness, on the other hand, brings "unlove."

> Simplicity sits well upon women,
> Yet it is right that a woman
> Have that teaching and that sense
> That she may beware of un-love.[50]

Folly brings men to give too much, lovers to act like animals, lords to breathe cruelty, people in general to be uncourteous. Thomasin tells us:

> A man who is well balanced in his mind,
> When he begins to eat,
> He touches nothing but his food
> With the hand: that is doing things well.[51]

Courtesy becomes a terrestrial affair. Gone, indeed, is the moral referent, the deductive framework that gave behavioral norms an ethical sense in the world of courtoisie. Gone is the semiotic structure from which they acquired meaning. For Thomasin, good breeding and good sense acquire inherent meaning: they become perfectly self-referential. In *The Italian Guest* God becomes a passive observer of people's deeds—good and bad, evil and virtuous. He still is the Author and Creator of all things, yet, now, His presence has become unobtrusive. He does not prevent us from being unvirtuous, Thomasin tells us. He does not interfere with the Devil. He permits a bad man to do harm to a good one.[52] He does not tell us, either, what is the path to virtue. For Thomasin the relation between good breeding and good sense on the one hand and manners on the other is in effect perfectly circular. Manners derive from the inherent good attributed to good breeding and the inherent truth attributed to good sense. Yet the only evidence for the valuation of good breeding and good sense is provided by the positiveness of the behavior itself. A behavior is valued because it is the supposed consequence of good breeding; good breeding is valued because it implies behavior that is considered worthy in the first place.

The language that Thomasin uses in advancing his rules is most revealing, for it is highly conjectural and personalized, devoid of the moral authority that characterizes the moralists' speech. "As far as I can understand things," "so it appears to me," "if she will believe me," "that is my teaching," "believe ye that," "I truly tell you," Thomasin repeats again and again.[53] Indeed, he invokes an obscure and uncertain moral basis in constant need of rhetorical support. He no longer calls on the authority of God to justify action. Norms and decorum conform, now, to Thomasin's own observations of the world: if it seems to him that something is good, then it is. Although manners still generally conform to the principles of divine virtue, they are no longer deduced from those principles. Rather, integrated with the notions of good breeding and good sense, they become self-referential, truths in themselves.

As I suggested above, the shift of referent, the transference of manners into a different relational order, is of central importance. For, in a fashion that brings to mind Borges, the forms of the manners, as opposed to their meaning, do not seem to have changed to any significant degree. Forms of conduct that are prized in the world of courtoisie continue for the most part to be valued in *The Italian Guest.* Behaviors that are worthy of censure in the religious system are still, to a large extent, deemed vile and despicable. Yet, in Thomasin as in Brunetto, the interpretive framework used to make sense of the behavioral norms manifests a critical transformation. Removed from its ethical context—latently, unintentionally, indeed—the same pragmatic criterion that guides Brunetto pervades Thomasin's conception of manners. For it is the thrust towards moderation—a disposition justified in social, not theological, terms—that, as in *Il Tesoretto,* instructs Thomasin's poem. What we see taking shape is an urge to avoid potential sources of disorder—following a definition of disorder akin to that of the *res civile.* As we shall discuss in detail in the next chapter, the interpretation of propriety locates practice within the grounds of the civil "thing" and directs action towards its reproduction; the complex of behavioral instructions refers to and therefore helps frame interaction in a manner consistent with the terms of a civil, secular power.

What this new relational order consists in precisely—what this new system of social referents is—we cannot completely visualize in Brunetto or Thomasin. In their works we see the detachment from ecclesias and an initial assimilation of the precepts of courtoisie within the fabric of the growing civil world. But these works show us only the beginnings of the movement of assimilation, a movement that becomes fully visible only in Castiglione and the authors of civility books. As I suggested at the beginning of the chapter, Brunetto and Thomasin, and "courtesy" for that matter, represent a liminal stage in the shift from courtoisie to civility. The very self-referential properties of the discourse on manners suggest a condition of liminality. This is a moment in which the new power gradually takes over, transforms, indeed detaches manners—an embodiment and vehicle of symbolic power—from their social moorings. Yet it is simultaneously a moment in which the new power has not yet developed the instruments of symbolic self-affirmation, in which it has yet to bring its own definition of a collective self to maturity. We will observe a similar situation in the transition from civility to etiquette. The latter case, too, is marked by a liminal stage in which manners become detached from the powers that had given them their shape. Yet in that case the new power, unlike the power at the heart of civility, finds in the detachment of manners the very conditions of its self-affirmation. Compared to the earlier infrastructure of social relations, the one on which the aristocracy is to found itself is of an altogether different order. And indeed, as we shall see in the next chapter, the conditions under which the *res civile* developed were inimical to that detachment. In the territories of civility, propriety was to become reattached to a principle, "grace," endowed with the force of an ethics.

Before considering civility, however, we explore the condition of liminality beyond its discursive expressions, with regard to social practices and the plane of power on which these unfold.

The Shifting Grounds of Social Practice (Part 1)
Structural Displacements

Like courtoisie, courtesy was not and should not be limited to discourse. We should keep in mind that it was in the formation of an array of routines, in the institution of rituals and ceremonies, in the nurturing of practices of the body and of the mind, that ecclesias gave body to itself and projected its collective self, with its lines of similarity and difference, into others. The constant enactment of these practices made the world of ecclesias into a real, material presence for the men and women of the Middle Ages. And this constant enactment transformed its diverse elements, including courtoisie, into "truth." Courtoisie involved a merging of discourse and practice, neither being ultimately separable from the other.

The same was true for courtesy; the forms of the *res civile* evolved from a singular movement that involved both discourse and practice. Discourse and practice developed simultaneously, underwent similar transformations, and produced congruent formations. The discursive detachment of manners from their social referent was paralleled by the growth and consolidation of a realm of experience equally detached from ecclesias, a realm within which the practices that gave body to "grace," the concept through which the secular powers gave expression to their collective self, gradually developed. Indeed, accompanying the discursive shift, we observe a gradual displacement of the plane on which practice unfolds from the institutions of the church to the framework of monarchical power as embodied at its core by the person of the king.[54]

We see the growth of this secular, grace-bearing realm of experience in the changing character of jousts and tournaments, in the transformations of hunting and travel, in the construction of large, luxurious castles, and in the increasing scope and specificity of courtesy rules. As the routines for care of the body or for praying specific to courtoisie did for ecclesias, those activities afforded grounds of practice through which the *res civile* acquired its material, existentially significant forms.

The transformations of the practices of chivalry are in this sense exemplary. In the period extending from the middle of the thirteenth to the end of the fifteenth century, jousts, and especially tournaments, became increasingly ritualized activities.[55] Maurice Keen provides an example of this transformation when he compares the tournaments of Hem and Chauvency held in northern France at the end of the thirteenth century with the late medieval joust of the *Fontaine des Pleurs* staged at Chalon-sur-Saône in 1450.[56]

> The tournament at Chauvency [that for its days looked elaborate] lasted a week; the elaborate drama at Chalon was a year unrolling. There were real risks of fatal injury at Chauvency; no one was badly hurt at Chalon, and no one seems to have been in much danger of it. The ritual, moreover, had become much more complex and stylized in the later events. Neither at Chauvency nor yet at Hem, for all its elaborate Arthurian setting, do we hear of anything parallel to the ceremonious process of accepting challenge by touching shields which indicate the nature of the trial to be undertaken. Nor do we hear of any comparably careful process for the verification of the noble lineage of the contestants by expert heralds.[57]

The opulence and formalism exhibited in the later occasions could be dazzling. Champions were rewarded with golden weapons; banquets and festivities enhanced the *festes;* extravagant conventions preceded the jousts; decorations and dresses were extremely lavish and expensive; shields became increasingly symbolic.[58] A description of the Field of Cloth of Gold erected at the occasion of a grand Anglo-French tournament in Calais in June 1520 is most evocative:

> The main structure, about sixty paces in circumference, was supported by huge ship masts. Above the masts was stretched a canvas roof decorated on the inside with stars of gold foil and a painting

of the heavens. The exterior was covered with gold brocade deco-
rated with three circular stripes of azure velvet powdered with
golden fleurs-de-lis. A life-size gilt statue of St. Michel surmounted
the pavilion; in his right hand he carried a dart, and in his left, a
shield emblazoned with the arms of France. . . . The English had
built a huge temporary palace on the outskirts of Guisnes. . . .
Brick towers pierced with loopholes [reinforced its walls]. Wooden
statues of armed men defended the ramparts with hand guns,
stones, and cross-bows. At the entrance was a large gateway
adorned with images of ancient heroes such as Hercules and Alexander.[59]

The power dimension of these spectacles has been amply recognized
and discussed in the literature for some time now.[60] Their exuberance and
opulence, their enormity and meticulous attention to detail, their celebration of royalty, which positioned the monarch, or the prince, at the center
of the festivities, transformed, to quote Roy Strong's beautiful formulation,
"traditional forms of secular entertainment into a vehicle for dynastic apotheosis."[61] The elaboration of an imagery of the king as an embodiment
of splendor celebrated monarchical power, and the manipulation of the
dramatic intrigues of the spectacles by the men and women of the court
gradually became an instrument of political intrigue.[62] In the process, tournaments slowly became, in the words of Diane Bornstein, "a source for
social rituals and games that helped to create a sense of cohesion, separate-
ness, and superiority among the wealthy classes."[63]

Tournaments and other spectacles of the sort were certainly important
vehicles for the exercise of monarchical power. But they were more than
that: they helped give body to a concept of the similar determined, in apparently oblivious disregard of ecclesias, by all the powers at the heart of the
res civile, as an expression of *their* "essence." And as part of that collective
self, subtle lines of inclusion and exclusion emerged which, like the concentric lines of courtoisie, differentiated people into a continuous hierarchy of
"selfness" and "otherness."

The line setting the wealthier classes apart was the most obvious one
and might give the impression of a highly dichotomous differentiation of
society. But consider the activities of women during tournaments. Although
only men took part in the contests, women played an active role in the
more ceremonial aspects of the pageants. They participated in the banquets,
the *divertissements,* the glorification of the champions, and the ridiculing
of the losers, and their presence was perhaps more important in the rituals

and ceremonials preceding and following the competitions.[64] They also shared in the excitement of the feats of arms, watching—perhaps enduring—the action from especially constructed stands erected right beside, if not right over, the field of battle itself. The foregone exclusion of women from active participation in one of the central activities of the tournaments, the martial exercises, was of critical importance, for their roles were not only almost exclusively circumscribed to those of supporting or background characters; their exclusion from the feats of arms suggests the limits of their possible identification with the collective self of the civil powers.

Indeed, what we see burgeoning in this emphatically secular realm of experience is a complex of practices that melds the military element at the heart of the condition of the feudal nobility—an exclusively male element, that is—with the technologies of self-control and self-fashioning that mark the development of "courtesy." This merging of chivalry and gentility is actually well conveyed by Scaglione in the title to his book, *Knights at Court,* and is an inevitable element of any account of the transformations of social practices during the late Middle Ages. It is an unspoken premise in Castiglione: the combination of militarism and sociability had become so taken for granted by the early sixteenth century that it required no explicit formulation. It permeates Castiglione's book to its core. As the quotation at the beginning of this chapter indicates, to Castiglione the true profession of the courtier is that of arms, yet the profession is fashioned so that the courtier feels equally at home in the battlefield or the training camp and in the spheres of sociability. The "civilizing" element of manners spoken of in most of the literature on the topic refers precisely to this growing permeation of behavior by gentility, and more specifically to the domestication of violence that such a presence elicits.

But this phenomenon of "civilization," or domestication, represents only one aspect of the processes that we are studying. For these involve not just a permeation of otherwise "ungentle behavior" by gentility, but a real merging of the elements from which the collective self of the powers at the heart of the *res civile* develops. A perspective limited to the civilizing effects of courtesy tends to minimize the military, and eminently masculine, element in the civil definition of the similar that developed in Europe during the late Middle Ages. It therefore also tends to blur the lines of inclusion and exclusion that, for example, preclude women from ever fully developing the requisites of selfness, as well as the practices that define these lines.[65] Some historians have expressed perplexity, if not condescending amusement, at what they deem a continuation of obsolete forms of "chivalric" practices well into the sixteenth century and beyond.[66] But this perplexity is a result of a problem of perspective, of interpreting the changes in social practices at the time solely in terms of the domestication and transformation of violence. When we incorporate the martial aspect of the collective self of monarchical power, all the elements fall into place.

Surely, the military or martial constituent of the collective self of the *res civile* undergoes substantial transformations. For example, in terms of their usefulness for combat, the transformations in warfare would indeed render the chivalrous practices developed in the princely courts obsolete— although their continuation indicates that their significance lay elsewhere: in their embodiment of a collective self. More important, the actual blending of chivalry and courtesy transforms the technologies of the body in whose operations the military element takes shape.[67] For this element comes into being through the education and care of the body—through the cultivation and mastery of specific techniques of movement, exertion, hygiene, composure, recreation, pleasure, and the like—in which the traditional technologies of warfare and martial training and the skills of sociability merge. This is an element that attains equal measures of sport and deadliness yet maintains, or rather perpetuates, what Sydney Anglo calls a "delight in personal combat."[68] The term *delight* is appropriate, for the word nicely conveys, even though Anglo might not have meant it, the elation of self-affirmation, a sentiment that requires no external justification, that exists in and for itself.

In this light, tournaments involve a celebration and glorification of that collective self, or more properly, a self-celebration and self-glorification of and by that self. For they not only provide an arena in which the nobility can separate itself from the rest of society, they provide a site in which the secular powers can define themselves as "the essence" of the social, and in which the most powerful can establish, through the lines of inclusion and exclusion set by the actual practices, their higher affiliation with that self. To repeat Strong's formulation, tournaments are occasions in which that self, which receives its highest expression in the person of the prince himself but was not limited to the monarch, reaches, in all its glory, in its blinding radiance, a moment of apotheosis.

We can observe a similar transformation in the practices of hunting among the noble classes.[69] Combining elements of pastime, sport, and martial training, the chase had been one of the chief occupations of medieval noblemen well before the period covered in this chapter. It was also a useful occupation, for it helped to destroy wild animals (wolves in particular) and provided protein necessary for nutrition. Young men appeared to enjoy the headlong gallops through the fields, the combat with the creatures, and the prestige accorded to the bold and courageous. And all the while they engaged in natural training for war and for the endurance of long, exhausting campaigns.

The parallel between hunting and tournaments is striking. Like tournaments, hunting forays evolved into elaborate, sumptuous, sometimes solemn ventures. Their organization became increasingly costly and complex, and in time their pomp assumed as much importance as the hunt itself. Kings, princes, and other powerful noblemen not only pursued wolves and wild boars but executed complicated, magnificent routines designed to impress both their retinues and the peasants and other onlookers with a sense of their might. Like tournaments, the practices of hunting also attest to the civilizing trend of European societies at the time, the entire enterprise promoting the gradual domestication of violence. And as in tournaments, the military element did not disappear, although its expressions were significantly altered as the actual venture increasingly became an instrument of symbolic self-affirmation.

During the sixteenth and seventeenth centuries, a series of royal interdictions on hunting would be clearly designed to reduce the potential use of certain arms by still-powerful aristocrats. Thus they would become instruments in the process of monopolization of violence by the state that I discussed above. In France, for example, the first interdictions that touched the aristocracy came in the early seventeenth century, during the reign of Henry IV. These, according to Francis Rieupeyroux, were developed at least in part as a reaction to the power deployed by aristocratic families during the religious wars of the preceding century.[70] But these interdictions came later, when the provisions for the strengthening of royal power had consolidated. From the twelfth to the fifteenth century, during the period of liminality, royal as well as feudal interdictions targeted only commoners and were geared not towards the monopolization of violence by a central power but, Rieupeyroux suggests, towards the concentration of the means of violence and, more importantly for my argument, the guarding of the techniques of militarism by the diffused nobility of the times.[71] For it was not the game that was put off limits to the commoners—they maintained the right to use traps, nets, and baits—but the use of arms and the exercise of practices tied to militarism.[72] In that sense, the hunt itself became a site for the deployment of the feudal lords' fundamental military identity.

And as the experience of hunting gradually became the experience of the social gathering, the military elements of the hunt gradually merged with the provisions for sociability that mark the development of courtesy. This is precisely the kind of transformation in the technologies of the body that I have suggested above. The tendency towards self-control was manifest, for example, in the change in the techniques of killing; the slaying of animals became less brutal and more methodical. If still dangerous, chases nevertheless became increasingly harmless, the danger of an accident looming larger than the peril of combat with the beasts. In the chases at least, the major skill gradually changed from the actual handling of a weapon to the management of a pack of hounds.[73]

Two extended observations are in order. First, as the two examples that I have just given make explicit, the sphere of experience that we see here in the process of formation differed from that of ecclesias in one crucial respect. Whereas the practices that gave body to ecclesias pervaded the population at large, the practices in whose shape the *res civile* slowly acquired its objectified, existentially significant form were almost exclusively the preserve of the upper classes. Moreover, these practices not only developed among a reduced number of people but in a specific social space: where the new practices of power themselves were coming into being, namely, in the royal and princely courts.[74] As we shall see in the following chapters, this property of what I call the *res civile* will be simultaneously its greatest strength and its greatest weakness. It will be its greatest strength because the insularity of the court will contribute to the perpetuation of the collective self of the nobility and will serve as a protective layer around its center of power, the monarch. And it will be its greatest weakness because it will leave vast areas of social practice, uncontrollable by means of coercion, beyond the sway of monarchical hegemony.

This does not mean that the *res civile* did not spread beyond the confines of the courts. The pragmatics of grace did permeate life outside the courts, as we will see in the following chapters, after we gain a better understanding of this pragmatics. What we can see clearly at this point, however, is the awe that the loftiness of tournaments, hunting parties, and the like inspired among participants and onlookers alike: power thus spread itself through impression rather than permeation. The well-studied royal processions into the tournaments were specifically designed to inspire such impressions.[75] And royal expeditions, which gradually attained extraordinary proportions, had a similar effect. By the time of Castiglione, the king was in constant motion, and the men and women of the court—and a few others—followed him everywhere, constantly deploying the grandeur and might of the secular powers. Lucien Febvre, reconstructing life at the times of François I, gives us a vivid account:

> [They] followed him on the highway, through the woods, along the rivers and across the fields, more like a train of perpetual tourists [including twelve thousand horses, three or four thousand men, not counting the women (who were by no means all of the respectable sort)] than a court. Or, more exactly, it was like a troop doing a day's march. The advance party would move out ahead to set up "camp" before the king arrived: the quartermaster, the official charged with finding and allocating housing for everyone; and a whole tribe of cooks, specialists in sauces, roasts, and pastries. Riding old nags usually acquired through the generosity of the king, they hurried through the dawn to that night's stopping place. . . . Once the advance party had moved out, the body of the court began to leave also. First the king and his guards, officers and gentlemen of his household: as he passed through a village the church bells would ring, and the priests would come running to the roadside. The peasants who saw the royal cortege approach from the distance as they worked in the fields would run toward it. There, in the midst of a splendid group of mounted men, they saw the king. . . . [Behind] came the ladies of the court, ladies who did a day's march alongside the men. Following the example of the king, they too lived like soldiers on a campaign.[76]

For the peasants and townspeople watching the procession, the spectacle was indeed magnificent, although not as material, not as constitutive of their beings as were the practices of ecclesias—or as were the practices of the expedition for the men and women of rank accompanying the monarch. For to the latter, regardless of the length of their participation in the journey, the proceedings involved a routine totally subordinated to civil power. Moving on, walking all day, setting up camp, being part of the magnificence, inciting feelings of wonder among the peasants, *that* constituted their reality. And this reality, as we know, revolved almost uniquely around the figure of the king. It upheld his authority, transforming it into an unquestionable fact, and provided the infrastructure of social relations that gave the *res civile* a coherent structural center.

The idea of a structural center leads us to the second observation. Certainly I do not claim that all royal power was of a symbolic nature. Kings did exercise direct control over governmental matters, and their might was often of a coercive or more openly political nature—although the presence of other forms of power does not diminish the importance of cultural or symbolic power in the least. More important, neither do I claim that the exercise of symbolic power was the monopoly of the king and his court. In effect, what was true for the king and his social circle was also true for an array of other powerful noblemen and their own suites, as for the growing number of "new men" who would later compose what we know today as the bourgeoisie. Yet, what the first had very obviously and the second only somewhat less clearly, the third (with a very few exceptions) lacked almost completely. I refer here not to power in itself, power as a mere resource, decomposed to its fractional dimensions, but to a social space (in the case of the *res civile,* a space structured around the figure of the king) that enabled power, symbolic and otherwise, to be organized and exerted and a culture to be formed. I refer to the existence of a plane of practice on which a coherent praxis evolved—a plane simultaneously expressive and productive of the collective self of the powers at its core.

It is precisely this property that allows us to theorize the shift that we are studying in this chapter as a displacement of the plane of the organization of practice from the institutions of the church to the framework of monarchical power as embodied by the person of the king. This "civil" plane of practice, and of power, gives body to an infrastructure of social relations that, although appropriating many of the figurations of ecclesias—including its centeredness—is nevertheless unconnected to ecclesias. Here I speak deliberately in terms of "appropriation," for many of the practices of sociability that developed with courtesy originated in the confines of ecclesias. Yet, as the preceding discussion suggests, these were taken over and transformed in the social spaces of the *res civile,* generating an experience of self, including an experience of the body, that was of an altogether different order. This was an order attuned to the "essence" of the secular and, for the period covered in this chapter, still feudal powers.

Recall that the condition that we are witnessing in this chapter is one of liminality, of the secular powers gradually taking over, transforming, and detaching the practices of sociability, which were the embodiment and vehicle of symbolic power, from their social moorings in ecclesias. Yet it is simultaneously a moment in which the civil powers are still in the process of developing their instruments of symbolic self-affirmation, in which they have yet to bring their own definition of a collective self to maturity.

Individuation and the Changing Texture of Social Relations

The centrality of the displacement in the process of bringing to maturity the collective self of the *res civile*, as in the transition from courtoisie to courtesy in general, becomes all the more apparent when we consider that the growing importance of the civil did not imply the end of ecclesias. Ecclesias did not evaporate. Its modalities of thought did not stop kindling the imagination of men and women. Its routines did not lose their existential significance. If, in a way, ecclesias helped create the conditions of its own demise, it showed at the same time an extraordinary capacity for survival. For while its permanence depended on the perpetuation of ecclesiastical power, the perpetuation of that power in turn depended on the strength of its behavioral and mental practices—and this was considerable.

An analogy with the mechanisms of paradigmatic change in science— or rather the absence of change in science in spite of repeated anomalies— may help illustrate this capacity for survival. Imre Lakatos's description of what happens to a scientific theory when anomalous observations arise is most evocative. I quote at length.

> The story is about an imaginary case of planetary misbehaviour. A physicist of the pre-Einsteinian era takes Newton's mechanics and his law of gravitation *(N)*, the accepted initial conditions, *I*, and calculates, with their help, the path of a newly discovered small planet, *p*. But the planet deviates from the calculated path. Does our Newtonian physicist consider that the deviation was forbidden by Newton's theory and therefore that, once established, it refutes the theory *N*? No. He suggests that there must be a hitherto unknown planet p′ which perturbs the path of p. He calculates the mass, orbit, etc., of this hypothetical planet and then asks an experimental astronomer to test his hypothesis. The planet *p′* is so small that even the biggest available telescopes cannot possibly observe it: the experimental astronomer applies for a research grant to build yet a bigger one. In three years' time the new telescope is ready. Were the unknown planet *p′* to be discovered, it would be hailed as a new victory of Newtonian science. But it is not. Does our scientist abandon Newton's theory and his idea of the perturbing planet? No. He suggests that a cloud of cosmic dust hides the planet from us. He calculates the location and properties of this cloud and asks for a research grant to send up a satellite to test his calculations. Were the satellite's instruments (possibly new ones, based on a little-tested theory) to record the existence of the conjec-

tural cloud, the result would be hailed as an outstanding victory for Newtonian science. But the cloud is not found. Does our scientist abandon Newton's theory, together with the idea of the perturbing planet and the idea of the cloud that hides it? No. He suggests that there is some magnetic field in that region of the universe which disturbed the instruments of the satellite. A new satellite is sent up. Were the magnetic field to be found, Newtonians would celebrate a sensational victory. But it is not. Is this regarded as a refutation of Newtonian science? No. Either yet another ingenious auxiliary hypothesis is proposed or . . . the whole story is buried in the dusty volumes of periodicals and the story never mentioned again.[77]

It will eventually be mentioned again, after a new theoretical framework capable of explaining the anomaly is advanced. In that case, the identification of the phenomenon will be hailed as a clear victory for the new research programme. Now imagine what the result is when the interpretive system that makes sense of the world includes explanations in terms of miracles—when everything is thought to emanate from a power that is beyond understanding, and when people's routines constantly affirm the evidence of miracles and the existence of that power. The infrastructure of social relations of which that system is part would indeed show an extraordinary power of survival.

An infrastructure of that sort would weaken only after its interpretive system had gone through a period of disenchantment and new areas of experience, uncovered by its routines, had developed—that is, after the development of another power capable of establishing an alternative order of things, grounded on a different foundation. Neither the disenchantment with the interpretive grounds alone nor the mere presence of "other" still dispersed practices provides the conditions for the emergence of an alternative infrastructure. Disenchantment alone prompts a movement of renewal, of restoration, of a return to origins—as we shall witness in Erasmus and, with completely different consequences, Martin Luther.[78] A reality of dispersed practices, however antagonistic to the existing power, lacks the structural foundation that allows a power to anchor itself. And indeed, if ecclesias helped create the conditions for its own demise, it was in part because the gradual exhaustion and degeneration of its practices—as exemplified by the unscrupulous selling of dispensations—led to widespread disenchantment. More important, it was also because the behavioral norms of courtoisie helped generate the plane of practice on which the alternative order of things became established—because they helped generate the conditions for the displacement of the sites and the seats of power.

This irony is visible not only in the role of the moderating thrust of courtoisie in the transformations of the medieval polity but also in its effects on the change of texture of interactional orders of European societies during the late Middle Ages. One of the outstanding achievements of Elias's *The Civilizing Process* lies precisely in its identification and systematic analysis of that change, which requires little further investigation. Elias showed how the condition of social coalescence discussed in the previous chapter underwent a profound metamorphosis as behavioral norms slowly began to mirror the drive for restraint that originated in courtoisie. Norms as seemingly inconsequential as the directives not to exhibit in public the products of one's nose or the food one had been unable to swallow were, in effect, Elias showed, vehicles by which the thrust towards moderation attained explicit behavioral expression. These norms, which became prevalent during the fourteenth and fifteenth centuries, urged men and women to control themselves and thus led them to develop mechanisms of self-control. A "curve" (Elias's term) marked by an expansion and strengthening of the structures of inhibitions harnessing people's impulses seems to have characterized the transformation of manners throughout the period. Rules became more and more restrictive. Actions became gradually relegated to a private domain. Step by step, men and women were exhorted to wash more often and in greater seclusion, to refrain from exposing their natural secretions, to avoid paying attention to other people's soilures, to make use of increasingly personal effects to wipe their noses, clean their hands, comb their hair, and eat their food.

In the process, Elias revealed, the condition of social coalescence, the condition generative of a reality and an experience of interwoven selves, metamorphosed. What Elias portrayed in admirable detail was the process by which the material and psychological boundaries that gradually separated one person from another started to form. With the fading of behaviors rooted in practices of touching, of physical familiarity, of spontaneous intimacy, and with the evolution of behaviors rooted in practices of tactile distancing and corporeal insularity, Elias suggested, an individualized sensibility of body and self began to arise. People began to experience themselves as separate beings, each with his or her own body, each with his or her personal space. Very slowly, then, a complex of social relations constituted of interactions between increasingly well-defined monads, between people increasingly detached from one another, substituted for the reality of interpersonal coalescence.

In this process, the interactional foundation within which the power of ecclesias operated gradually disappeared. What formed instead, as Elias indicated, was an order of interactions embedded in the incipient reality of individuation and interpersonal detachment that established the grounds for the operation of power mechanisms of a very different order—one that attained full expression in the pragmatics and politics of grace described by Castiglione. Individuation and interpersonal detachment provided the fabric from which the terms of sociability constitutive of "grace" were to be fashioned. This was the fabric in and through which the *res civile* realized itself and in which, as we shall see next, its instruments of self-affirmation, as well as the entire relational order to which manners became attached, were woven.

The change from coalescence to individuation, still nascent during the period that we have discussed, was certainly an unintended consequence of the mechanisms set in motion by courtoisie: the initial disposition to moderate, to control, to create the conditions of order. On the surface, little seemed to have changed. Many of the old rules still applied, and new rules appeared as little more than extensions of the old. Under the guise of continuity, however, a completely new form in which to exist and experience the world emerged—a form that had become disconnected from its original sources of meaning and would be reconnected to a different infrastructure of order.

This process of reconnection is the subject of the next chapter. We shall see how Renaissance authors—Castiglione and Erasmus in particular—were to take the new experience of individuation to its utmost consequences while simultaneously searching for the enunciation of a new absolute to which they could attach the forms of the civil. In the following two chapters, as we study the consolidation of the infrastructure of social relations of the *res civile,* we will see how circumstances of a purely historical nature were to drive what I have called the civil "thing" in vastly different directions.

CHAPTER FOUR

Civility and the Politics of Grace

Truly, it is a new good and evil! Truly, a new roaring in the depths and
the voice of a new fountain!
> Friedrich Nietzsche, *Thus Spoke Zarathustra*

The Discomforts of Detachment

AN URGENCY TO EXPRESS yet at the same time overcome the ambiguities produced by the infrastructural change marks much of the literature on behavior during the Renaissance and the period immediately following it.[1] The metamorphosis in the ontological grounds of experiencing, the displacement of power and the reconfiguration of practice that it entailed, the precariousness of the link between behaviors and meanings that characterized the late Middle Ages all combined by the early sixteenth century to make of reality something rather fleeting and elusive. This perception, arguably, was one of the major forces at the core of the creative vivacity that we associate with the period. Yet it was also at the root of a feeling of perplexity and unease among the men and women for whom the new infrastructure had become, or was becoming, increasingly dominant.

Nowhere did this unease reveal itself better than in the new understandings of self prompted by the experience of interpersonal detachment and the feelings of existential freedom that came into being with the development of individuation. In this context, the specific form taken by the dramaturgical metaphor during the Renaissance and the period immediately following it is revealing. The conception of society as a stage and of the person as a role-player captured perfectly the problematics produced by the movement away from the reality of coalescence.

The concept of the person as a player of roles postulates the existence of a detached individual.[2] The idea involves more than simply complying with expectations, putting on appearances, or being constantly on a stage: it presupposes the reality of a person free to move from stage to stage. It implies the existence of an individual who exists outside of any specific play and who is therefore free to enact different, often incommensurable scripts. He or she is someone who does not belong just to the world of the play but

86

also, and more crucially, to the detached world of the author.[3] Interpersonal detachment and existential freedom are prerequisites for this form of conceiving the person.

But interpersonal detachment is not sufficient. The idea of role-playing as the enacting a multiplicity of scripts is also related to a certain moral attitude—what for lack of a better term we call "situational ethics"—and an ultimately relativistic perception of the world.[4] Only such an orientation allows people to enact scripts involving different, sometimes contradictory, normative systems without feelings of moral inconsistency. From this point of view, the role-player's behaviors become unproblematic, and reality can be experienced as something altogether "normal." In other words, role-playing involves a pragmatics that incorporates and gives expression to relativism, and this was completely absent from the world of civility. Within the confines of civility, practice did not give expression to a pragmatics of relativism but instead became reattached to a principle endowed with ethical force: grace.

The dramaturgical metaphor was in fact widely used during the Renaissance. We find it, for instance, in Cervantes, in a conversation between Don Quixote and his squire. "Hast thou never seen a play acted, in which kings, emperors, popes, knights, ladies and many other characters are introduced?" asks Don Quixote.

> "One acts the ruffian, another the sharper, a third the merchant, a fourth the soldier, a fifth the designing fool, and a sixth the simple lover; but, the play being ended, and the dresses laid aside, all the actors remain upon an equal footing." "Yes, I have seen all this," answered Sancho. "Then the very same thing," said the knight, "happens in the comedy and commerce of this world, where one meets with some people playing the parts of emperors, others in the characters of popes, and finally, all the different personages that can be introduced in a comedy; but, when the play is done, that is, when life is at an end, death strips them of the robes that distinguished their stations, and they become all equal in the grave." "A brave comparison!" cried Sancho, "tho' not so new but I have heard it made on divers and sundry occasions, as well as that of the game of chess, during which every piece maintains a particular station and character; but when the game is over, they are all mixed, jumbled and shaken together in a bag, like mortals in the grave."[5]

We find it in an epilogue by Ronsard,[6] in Calderón's *La vida es sueño*,[7] in Montaigne, in the essay "De l'inequalité qui est entre nous,"[8] and in

Shakespeare, of course. Jaques's well-known speech in *As You Like It* has become a favorite epigram among role theorists:

> All the world's a stage,
> And all the men and women merely players;
> They have their exits and their entrances;
> And one man in his time plays many parts,
> His acts being seven ages. At first the infant,
> Mewling and puking in the nurse's arms;
> Then the whining school-boy, with his satchel
> And shining morning face, creeping like a snail
> Unwilling to school. And then lover,
> Sighing like a furnace, with a woeful ballad
> Made to his mistress' eyebrow. Then a soldier,
> Full of strange oaths, and bearded like the pard,
> Jealous in honor, sudden and quick in quarrel,
> Seeking the bubble reputation
> Even in the cannon's mouth. And then the justice,
> In fair round belly with good capon lin'd,
> With eyes severe and beard of formal cut,
> Full of wise saws and modern instances;
> And so he plays his part. The sixth age shifts
> Into the lean and slipper'd pantaloon,
> With spectacles on nose and pouch on side;
> His youthful hose, well sav'd, a world too wide
> For his shrunk shank; and his big manly voice,
> Turning again toward childish treble, pipes
> And whistles in his sound. Last scene of all,
> That ends this strange eventful history,
> Is second childishness and mere oblivion;
> Sans teeth, sans eyes, sans taste, sans everything.[9]

In a slightly different form, the idea is repeated by Antonio in *The Merchant of Venice:*

> I hold the world but as the world, Gratiano—
> A stage, where every man must play a part,
> And mine a sad one.[10]

In *Hamlet* we are introduced to the image of the existentially detached person coping with the world. This is the image of a person conscious of the appearances of behavior, rejecting the hypocrisy of role-playing, while at the same time challenging the reality of authenticity. "Seems, madam?

Nay, it is. I know not 'seems,'" Hamlet tells his mother, refusing to quit his mourning:

> 'Tis not alone my inky cloak, good mother,
> Nor customary suits of solemn black,
> Nor windy suspiration of forced breath,
> No, nor the fruitful river in the eye,
> Not the dejected havior of the visage,
> Together with all forms, moods, shapes of grief,
> That can denote me truly. These indeed seem,
> For they are actions that a man might play,
> But I have that within which passes show;
> These but the trappings and the suits of woe.[11]

Still, authenticity seems no more than an illusion. The world is a "sterile promontory," life, "the quintessence of dust." The play within the play sensitizes both Hamlet and his audience to the fabricated nature of human action: the play seems real; the actors' emotions, authentic. Hamlet is shocked by the ostensible authenticity of the performers' feelings. The masquerade becomes confused with reality. Everything can be play, performance; and Hamlet, in a movement full of irony, slowly comes to define his own behavior in terms akin to the theatrical metaphor. Gradually, painfully, Hamlet becomes aware of the contradiction at the core of the reality of the role-player—of the simultaneity of oneself as "self," as a free person trying to express spontaneity, and of oneself as "actor," as a being merely reproducing a series of dramatic scripts.

In spite of the similarities, however, these passages do not signal the presence of a concept of role-playing as I defined it above. For the idea of the person that Don Quixote's conversation with Sancho, Jaques's speech, or Antonio's comment express is one of the person as *character* and not, as we might be led to infer, of the person as *actor*.[12] To Don Quixote, Jaques, and Antonio, life in the world compares to the life of characters *in* a drama, not to the life of actors *outside* of the play, of people freely changing the personae they enact, moving at will from role to role, from stage to stage. In Cervantes and in the Shakespeare of *As You Like It* and *The Merchant of Venice,* there is only one stage, the world, and every person performs only one part within the play, that of his or her character.[13]

One man in his times can play many parts, states Jaques, but "times" here refers to a person's entire life, and role-change is considered to follow the vicissitudes of the life-course, not the changing circumstances of the everyday.[14] We enter the drama of the social world as mewling and puking infants. We then become unwilling schoolchildren, then burning lovers, then soldiers, "Jealous in honor, sudden and quick in quarrel." Later we turn into justices, severe yet wise, and still later into shortsighted, pouched elders, to exit the stage of life "Sans teeth, sans eyes, sans taste, sans everything." In the course of our existence we enact many parts, but at any one age we are only one character. To use Malcolm Bradbury's phrase, we are "irretrievable within the play,"[15] like the pieces in a game of chess, each playing a definite role, each irrevocably tied to but one of many parts.

In *Hamlet* we do get an image of the wandering player of roles. As William B. Worthen has pointed out, *Hamlet,* among other things, is a play about taking a role.[16] Hamlet is an actor as much as he is a character— a person feigning, pretending, consciously imitating other people's ways in order to understand himself. But what we see now is, precisely, the difficulty of conceiving of such a person from within the mental frames of the *res civile.* Here, the condition of the detached individual is indeed presented as something unconventional, unusual—as something bordering on the insane. For Hamlet *is* mad, his mental alienation originating in the emptiness of existential freedom. Lost within the ambiguities of acting, questioning the reality of reality itself, shaping it, transforming it, Shakespeare's character—while driven by a clear sense of purpose—is unable to give proper meaning to his actions or properly to understand his condition, not because of any limitation of his own (or Shakespeare's), but because the structures of thought that help us to make sense of detachment and experience it as normal—amorality and relativism in particular—are not part of the dominant mental structures of the *res civile.* Insanity thus becomes the logical response to the growing awareness of existential freedom; role-playing becomes madness, and madness itself, in complete agreement with its own truth, becomes a role. "I essentially am not in madness, / But mad in craft," declares Hamlet, foreshadowing Goffman at his most perplexing. In fact, Hamlet is not alone in flirting with the insane in Shakespeare's plays. As A. C. Bradley remarked long ago, Jaques and Antonio also seem to be afflicted with what was then called "melancholy": Jaques by a "whimsical self-pleasing melancholy," Antonio by a "quiet but deep melancholy, for which," and this is most significant, "neither the victim nor his friends can assign any cause."[17]

It was as though a kind of insanity was being built within the structural frames of Renaissance societies. For, given the growing reality of detachment, existential freedom gradually became part of a historically specific condition of being,[18] a condition that—in the absence of a pragmatics that

90

allowed people to experience it as "normal"—was understood as madness, if not as a virtual monstrosity.[19]

The Ethics and Politics of Heroism
The Subjection of Existential Freedom

An analysis of the idea of the heroic as articulated during the late sixteenth and early seventeenth centuries gives us a unique view of the forms in which these feelings of perplexity and confusion were expressed within the infrastructures of social relations of the *res civile*.[20] The idea of heroism during that period represents an extreme, ideal-typical expression of the pragmatics of grace. It takes what we will identify as the foundational elements of grace beyond the pragmatically possible. It magnifies the practices at the core of the pragmatics of grace, accentuates the force of its principles, heightens their tensions, and celebrates the power at the heart of the *res civile,* making it visible in the process.

At the same time, the idea of the heroic provides an ideal perspective from which to begin studying the pragmatics of grace itself. It serves the same methodological function as the Arthurian romances or the *contes pieux* during the Middle Ages. It is not supposed to represent reality faithfully. Nobody is supposed to have followed its ideals to the letter. But like the idealized visions of the courtois in the medieval romance or the villain in the pious tale, the heroic conveys a sense of the conceivable, of what can be thought and done from within the infrastructure of social relations that gave body to the *res civile.* It conveys a sense of the cultural ordering within which representation takes place.

Indeed, the specific articulation of the idea of the heroic during the late sixteenth and early seventeenth centuries bears witness to the new awareness of individual autonomy—an autonomy that paradoxically becomes totally subjected to the authority of the king. Pierre Corneille's *Le Cid,* a tragicomedy first performed in 1637, provides the perfect example of this idea of heroism.[21] The drama unfolds as Rodrigue and Chimène, the play's central characters, are forced to choose between conflicting loyalties, each demanding total commitment. Deeply in love with each other, Rodrigue and Chimène are committed first to the devotions that follow passion. But then they also must maintain their honor. They have to protect their families' names, and the two commitments come inexorably to contradict one another in the play. Angered at being denied the tutelage of the royal prince, Chimène's father, don Gomés, slights his more fortunate rival, the elderly don Diègue, Rodrigue's father. Diègue prompts his son to defend his honor, and so the tragedy is set in motion: it is Chimène's love that is put in jeopardy, that seems forever lost as a result.

The depth of Rodrigue's tragedy is captured in the soliloquy at the close of Act I, which ends with the decision to avenge his father:

> My heart's o'erwhelmed with woe.
> A mortal stroke that mocks my tender trust
> Makes me avenger of a quarrel just,
> And wretched victim of an unjust blow.
> Though crushed in spirit, still my pride must cope
> With that which slays my hope.
> So near to love's fruition to be told—
> O God, the strange, strange pain!—
> My father has received an insult bold,
> The offender is the father of Chimène.
> 'Mid conflicts wild I stand.
> I lift my arm to strike my father's foe,
> But Love with mighty impulse urges "No!"
> Pride fires my heart, affection stays my hand;
> I must be deaf to Passion's calls, or face
> A life of deep disgrace.
> Whate'er I do, fierce anguish follows me—
> O God, the strange, strange pain!
> Can an affront so base unpunished be?
> But can I fight the father of Chimène?
> To which allegiance give!—
> To tender tyranny or noble bond?—
> A tarnished name or loss of pleasures fond?
> Unworthy or unhappy must I live.[22]

"Father, mistress, honor, love," reads at one point the original French text,[23] and indeed, "To which allegiance give?" All choice is "fatal," pain is unavoidable. To defend the father means to lose Chimène. To evade the duty of honor implies failure in the eyes of society, to become unworthy of *both* the father *and* the beloved. The decision seems therefore clear: if Chimène is "forever lost," then at least lose her in honor. And yet, how? How to face that "strange, strange pain"?

Rodrigue's conflict is paralleled, later, in Chimène. Rodrigue provokes and kills don Gomés: it is Chimène's turn to be confronted by the opposing powers of love and honor. She asks the king for justice and, after much grief, appoints a champion to fight Rodrigue. As the two men fight, Chimène, alone with her governess, gives free rein to her pain:

> Ah pity me, Elvire, my heart is torn!
> Between perpetual fear and feeble hope.
> No vow escapes me I would not recall;
> Repentance quickly follows every wish.
> Two rivals I have set to arms against me:
> The happiest result will cost me tears.
> Though fate has favored me, I must lament
> A father unavenged, or lover dead.
> . . . .
> My soul recoils from either choice. I fear
> The outcome of this combat more than death.
> Away with both revenge and love. No more
> Is either of these passions dear to me.
> And you, almighty fate, from which I suffer,
> Let neither win this combat. Let there be
> Neither a conquered nor a conqueror![24]

Like Rodrigue, Chimène is paralyzed by the impossibility of making a choice. The memory of the father and the life of the lover are equally vital, and mutually exclusive. The two "passions" cancel one another and lead to a sort of spiritual impotence, to a painful, frightening chilliness of the will: "Repentance quickly follows every wish," she says, "My soul recoils from either choice," and "No more / Is either of these passions dear to me."

The inner struggle, here, is between two passions or, perhaps, two reasons: a "*raison d'amour*" versus a "*raison d'état.*" The situation is radically different from the one that we observed in the *Roman de la Rose,* where the lover's emotions were divided between a commitment to an ideal and a response to his own passions. The conflict in *Le Cid* is not a conflict of good against bad; it is a conflict between two goods.

Love, in Corneille's play, involves an unquestionable sexual dimension.[25] But the love in question here is more sublimated than carnal. It is a passion leading to heroism, the highest achievement of virtue. It is an emotion, an enthusiasm, whose refining power gives rise to the fairest acts of nobility. For Rodrigue and Chimène to be unfaithful to "love" implies not only a negation of desire but a negation of integrity, the denial of a true source of moral excellence. And if love is a code of ethics, honor is a passion.[26]

Neither Rodrigue nor Chimène are moved by a simple sense of duty. The drive to fight for the insulted father or to claim revenge for the slain one arises from an emotion, from a pledge that goes far beyond mere obligation. It certainly involves compliance with a social law. But it also involves a desire for honor that cannot be explained by simple considerations of fealty. Even though released of all duty by the king, Chimène remains implacable in her demand for justice. She yields only after Rodrigue's glory, in a strange arithmetics of fervor and pain, exceeds the power of her dishonor.

In a sense, Rodrigue and Chimène portray the predicaments of the existentially detached individual. Theirs is an existential conflict, a conflict that places them outside of any single commitment that could orient their actions unequivocally. Neither love nor honor wins the inner struggle, and neither Chimène nor Rodrigue are given an indication of the path to follow. The sensation they are impressed with is not guilt, as it was for the lover of the *Roman de la Rose.* Guilt no doubt lingers on after they are moved to act, for then the feeling of betrayal is unavoidable. But at the critical moment of standing alone with their own volition, both Rodrigue and Chimène experience a "strange pain"—a pain that we, as did the translator of the English version, readily recognize as *anguish,* a pain that Corneille, however, does not interpret. "Whate'er I do, fierce anguish follows me" writes Florence Kendrick Cooper, the English translator;[27] "Whate'er I do, my pain is infinite [mon mal est infini]" reads, on the other hand, Corneille's text.[28] Infinite: boundless, terrible, unfathomable—the term conveys the same difficulty in interpreting the condition of the free-floating person that we observed in Shakespeare. Yet, while for Shakespeare existential freedom was madness, for Corneille it is a mystery, a strange, bitter, dreary mystery whose painful effects are eased, if not cured, by the intrinsic power of civil morality—by the force of a moral absolute whose practical expressions are integral to the hegemony of the *res civile.*

The Affirmation of Power

Indeed, if suffering finds no inner healing, and if, in Rodrigue and Chimène, honor and love cancel each other, in the play honor wins over love. It is a double triumph: first, because Chimène and Rodrigue, by an unaccounted movement of their own volition, always follow the *raison d'état* over the *raison d'amour,* always commit to the social over the personal cause; and second, because through the commitment to honor, love in turn triumphs. Despite their pain, Rodrigue fights don Gomés, and Chimène stays firm in her demand for justice. Yet it is precisely by showing such moral excellence that the lovers become worthy of one another. Virtue follows the path dictated by courage and social integrity, the path leading to distinction and dignity—and through the affirmation of the social order all conflict, all tragedy is finally resolved. The faith in God that provided the experiential basis of ecclesias is now replaced by a devotion to the sources of order and, by extension, to the collective self of the *res civile*. The very anxieties produced by the emerging experience of detachment evaporate in its midst.

As expressed in *Le Cid,* the heroic entails a blind allegiance to an idea of the state and to the power of the king, and it authenticates the substitution of the religious morality of ecclesias by a civil conception of the absolute. It is an absolute that comprehends all the elements of the collective self of the *res civile* that we discussed in the previous chapter. We see the military element at the heart of the condition of the nobility and its combination with the technologies of self-control and self-fashioning that mark "courtesy."[29] We see the exclusive focus in the civil plane of power and practice and the moment of apotheosis in the affirmation of the social order through an affirmation of the person of the king. In the parallel yet unequal positions of the active Rodrigue and the passive Chimène, we see the fine gradations of similarity and difference. And last but not least, we see the taken-for-granted character and the legitimation of a new relational order, one whose concentric circles revolve around the figure of the king and whose practical expression yields the pragmatics of grace.

This is an ideal, though, and must be understood accordingly. Rodrigue and Chimène are in effect as unreal, as pure and perfect, as simple and crystalline, as were Bors and Perceval. The situation in which they dwell and not, as in Hamlet, their psychological make-up provides the complicated, painful reality of the play. Like courtoisie, however, it draws the lines of a moral order in reference to which the men and women for whom the *res civile* had become dominant interpreted, judged, negotiated, subjected, opposed, and related their daily experiences. Like courtoisie, too, this order should not be confused with the entirety of the infrastructure of social relations at the core of the *res civile*. It was a constituent of that infrastructure, helping concretize its foundational tendencies, embodying the specific logic in whose terms people positioned themselves in relation to others and attributed similarity and difference among them. And as Michel Prigent remarked, this order is congruent and coincident with the political order.[30]

The two emerge simultaneously, as a consequence of the displacement of the plane of practice from one giving body to the power of ecclesias to one affirming the power of the secular authorities.

Moreover, as it subjects the detached person to a power outside of the self, heroism also points at the tension between the forces set in motion by courtoisie—individuation on the one hand, and the displacement of the plane of power from the church to the monarch on the other hand. For while they make one another possible, the experience of autonomy and the practices tied to the new absolute push in opposite directions: the first towards the affirmation of self, the second towards its negation. If in the midst of the new absolute the anxieties of role-playing evaporate, the experience of detachment itself becomes sublimated, diverted, transposed into a different impulse. It is moved into a different realm of being and therefore does not become part of the order of things. The difficulties in making sense of detachment, already burdened by the absence of applicable structures of thought, become unresolvable, and the entire infrastructure of social relations that ensues becomes mired in a chronic paradox.

The Manifold Discourses of the Renaissance

Such an idea of the heroic is certainly not unique to Corneille. Like courtoisie, it permeates vast literary spaces, taking a multiplicity of forms, deploying the collective self of the power at its origins. It is taken for granted in the imagined world of *La vida es sueño,* for example. The unquestioned allegiance to the legitimate monarch and the affirmation of a condition of "being-for-the-state" are taken as self-evident, framing rather than becoming a theme in the play.[31] And the major act of self-affirmation of the play's heroine, Rosaura, comes as she takes up arms and is ready to fight beside her prince—as she subjects herself not only to the civil state but to the masculine ideal. Then she becomes literally heroic. In Shakespeare's historical plays, the tension between individuation and state power comes into sharper view. The heroic becomes more ambiguous and more tragic. Yet, as I discuss in detail in chapter 6, the resolution of the tension takes in Shakespeare a similar form as in Corneille or Calderón. The transformation of the heroic from its medieval to its premodern forms is at the core of *Don Quixote.* It is his inability to understand and accept the transformation that makes Don Quixote such a pathetic, comical, and endearing figure.[32]

As was the case with courtoisie, the discursive expressions of heroism are varied and multifaceted, and yield heterogeneous forms. Not all expressions are categorically affirmative. Some are unavoidably oppositional, yet because of their very oppositional character, they still define themselves in terms akin to the dominant infrastructure of social relations and reproduce the power at its core. Marguerite de Navarre's *Heptaméron,* one of the few books written by a woman at the time, exemplifies this oppositional stance well.[33] The *Heptaméron* eschews the male-centered definition of self-affirmation and takes a stance that rejects the passivity with which the heroic fashions women—an effect that becomes visible in the contrast of Chimène and Rodrigue or in Rosaura's metamorphosis from passive to active subject as she embodies the masculine ideal. One of the strategies that Marguerite de Navarre uses to achieve that goal is to reverse the gender of the characters in well-known stories—the man of the source story becomes in the *Heptaméron* a woman, and the woman becomes a man. Thus it is the woman who becomes the active character, affirmative of her person or, given the licentious nature of most of the *Heptaméron*'s stories, her sexuality. Unlike Rosaura, the women in the *Heptaméron* do not transform themselves into men, however figurative or temporary that transformation might be. And yet merely reversing the characters' gender makes the affirmation of self of Marguerite de Navarre's women identical in form to that of men. To the extent that women become masters of their own sexuality, theirs is but the mirror image of men's sexuality. Ultimately, as the scholars who stress the oppositional character of the book recognize, the *Heptaméron* is as unequivocal as *Le Cid* or *La vida es sueño* in its affirmation of civil power and a civil order.[34]

Of course, the idea that the heroic permeates vast discursive spaces does not mean that it, or the practices of grace that it models, constitutes every aspect of what it permeates, or that nothing escapes its hegemonic grasp. Two characteristics of the Renaissance made the proliferation of relatively autonomous discourses at the time highly propitious.[35] First, in a very concrete sense the condition of liminality produced by the infrastructural shift that marked the late Middle Ages allowed the intellectual forces of Europe to search for new sources, new explanations, a new way to make sense of the changed experiential reality. Although never completely free from the hegemonic influence of ecclesias or impervious to the growing power of the *res civile,* a discursive space opened in which new ideas, however dispersed, could nevertheless burgeon and spread. Second, the particular characteristic of the workings of power at the heart of the *res civile,* its relative insularity, would in turn limit the force of its hegemony. Although the hegemony of the *res civile* would unquestionably reach beyond the courts, the discursive space would nevertheless remain substantially open and ultimately uncontrollable by the monarchical authorities called to curb the profusion of new, and sometimes dangerous, discourses.

One of the ways to understand the Renaissance is precisely as a widespread and manifold effort to give expression to the new experience of individuation and to integrate it within the confines of a normative regularity able to hold society together. The return to antiquity, the interest in philology and rhetorics, and the many reinterpretations of the Holy Scriptures represent as much the tip of a movement to free the intellect from the unconvincing ways of medieval scholarship as an unfolding of the kaleidoscopic possibilities kindled by the open discursive field. Indeed, the disposition to seek for and create new significations, or to reinterpret the old, led Renaissance men and women along remarkable paths. Rabelais made extensive use of nonsense to point out to his contemporaries the ethereal, problematic character of human knowledge and the arbitrariness of meaning. Leonardo hazarded a theory of the macrocosm in which the universe, compared to an organism, was governed by its own laws. Graphic and plastic artists rediscovered the human body and made nudity an expression of both the voluptuous and the chaste. Marsilio Ficino, while making Platonism available to Renaissance thought, also introduced the writings of Hermes Trismegistus and Zoroaster, and espoused certain forms of astrology and magic.[36] Thomas More created Utopia. Martin Luther revolutionized religion. Pontano rediscovered cultural relativism. Speaking of the diversity of human customs, he reasons, for instance,

> Why is this? Because peoples and nations, either by their very nature or by established custom and usage, approve and hold in high value what others elsewhere disapprove, and some are more taciturn and others, on the contrary, more loquacious. Boastful speech delights the Spaniards; colourful and complicated language the Greeks; the talk of the Romans was grave, that of the Spartans brief and rough, the Athenians fulsome and stilted, the Carthaginians and Africans shrewd and sly, as was said of their nature. Thus it happens that one kind of colloquy is more highly approved in one place and less so in another.[37]

The entire period was marked by an extraordinary movement of intellectual fervor eloquently described by Enea Balmas. "We are struck by the spiritual eagerness, by the urge to toil with everything new, to assimilate the most diverse ideas, to transform the given of thought; by the will to immerse the mind within all things and thoroughly examine it all," writes Balmas:

> It is an intensity of feeling partially aroused by humanism, yet is more comprehensive than humanism. There is optimism in such an original manner to approach reality, a certain reticence towards the traditional notion of sin, a new attitude towards nature; there is a sympathy, a true-hearted disposition towards Antiquity that overcomes and makes the opposite attitude of distrust and reticence towards the "poor Gentiles" look barbaric; there is like an impossibility to resort to the asceticism of old. . . . Moreover, an element that integrates and penetrates everything, a spiritual enthusiasm, a deepened interest for the life of the mind arises, which supposes a new-fashioned attention for questions that were irrelevant in the recent past. The exasperated religious formalism of the pre-Reformation . . . is indeed judged insufficient, and the mind turns towards a fresher and truer spiritual fare. . . . A desire for authenticity gives a very particular flavor to this spiritual season and helps to understand the extraordinary things that happened at its time and place.[38]

Other factors unquestionably contributed to this movement towards innovation. The invention of the printing press and the rapid development of the book industry, the foundation of state colleges, the growth of cities in general, provided the material conditions for the emergence and organization of a new culture of the mind.[39] The conquest of the Americas opened new perspectives of optimism and provoked, as Erich Auerbach's analysis of Rabelais showed, a real emancipation of the imagination.[40] Moreover, the wealth that flowed from the colonies contributed immensely to the general impression of expansion and progress that pervaded Renaissance societies. The regression of famines and plagues, the increased sense of security that followed the consolidation of royal power, or the conspicuousness of the rich also worked in the same direction. In the political realm, the periodic struggles between the civil and the ecclesiastical authorities gradually weakened the power of the Papacy, setting the ground for the enunciation of the revolutionary doctrines. This was compounded by the inability of the Church to respond to the deeper anxieties and aspirations of the population. The excessive use of relics and indulgences, the plurality of benefices, and the mediocrity of most clergymen made the personally significant, regenerating power of religious faith into something ordinary and meaningless.

To some extent, we can see heroism and grace as part of the profusion of vastly dispersed practices and discourses that developed during the period that we call the Renaissance—a period that varied from place to place and took different forms in different places. The dispersed character of Renaissance discourses is apparent in the very efforts of modern scholars to construct a coherent account of knowledge at the time. Attempting such a construction of philosophy alone, for instance, Charles B. Schmitt and Quentin Skinner, the editors of the massive *The Cambridge History of Renaissance Philosophy,* point not only at the broad range of topics that marked philosophical discourse during the sixteenth century but at the unwieldiness of providing a full account.[41] The very grounds for such an account seem to be lacking. What made the discourses of heroism and grace different, however, was the same element that I suggested made the power of the king and his court different from that of the bourgeoisie at the time: their inherence in a well-structured, dominant plane of power. Although they represented but a fraction of existing discourses, they were nevertheless central to the organization of the plane of power on which the *res civile* took shape and to the mechanisms of hegemony on which it rested. Moreover, unlike the other discourses, they did not emerge as a function of the opening of the discursive space that accompanied the infrastructural shift. They were foundational, integral to that shift, and as such they were part of the genealogy that helped produce the opening to begin with. The centrality of the shift itself in the discursive proliferation should not be minimized. None of the factors that I mentioned above, individually or *in toto,* reduces its significance. For if it was true that the displacement of power did not "cause" anything, the combination of the weakening of ecclesias and the insularity in which the new hegemony worked—a property that limited but, as the *Heptaméron* suggests, obviously did not halt its reach—still created the conditions that made the proliferation of other discourses possible.

Some of these other discourses were undoubtedly to gain importance as they were themselves taken over, co-opted, misused, distorted, or otherwise transformed by the established power or, alternately, as they were used or redirected in the generation of an alternative plane of power and practice. As the practices to which they were to become tied, that is, helped to generate a positive praxis—one able to give body to a different power, a different collective self, a different mode of being in the world—then the possibility of another genealogical shift would gradually emerge. The very shape that the infrastructure of social relations of the *res civile* was to take in different places, a theme I follow in the next chapters, itself depended on how these other discourses and practices were dealt with. It depended on how the local powers would take these discourses over and transform them, or how they would succeed, or fail, to coerce and silence them, and this in turn depended primarily on purely historical circumstances. The example of Protestantism, a discourse that ultimately implied an affirmation of individuation over royal power, is, in that regard, paradigmatic.

At this point, however, we should explore in detail the pragmatics of grace in terms of which these powers embodied themselves. For it was this pragmatics that provided the foundation in which the other practices and discourses became embedded as they were absorbed by the civil powers— providing at the same time the "theme," to use a musical image, on which the local infrastructures were variations. Baldesar Castiglione's *Il libro del Cortegiano,* a book first published in 1527; Desiderius Erasmus's *De civilitate morum puerilium,* first published in 1530; and Giovanni della Casa's *Galateo,* published posthumously in 1558, arguably the three most influential treatises on manners of the sixteenth century, afford, from three very different angles, a picture of the foundational modality of practice at the heart of "civility."

The Pragmatics of Grace
Technologies of the Body

In Castiglione's *Il libro del Cortegiano* the idea of grace receives its most explicit and comprehensive articulation, and reveals its simultaneously aesthetic, ethical, and political character the best.[42] To Castiglione, grace is not a trait associated only with graciousness in behavior or moral generosity. It is certainly both, but it is also associated with a political and social form of conduct. The meaning of grace is, simultaneously, behavioral, moral, and political.

The book is not what we usually conceive as a treatise on manners. It is a subtle, sophisticated, elegant book, fully aware of its own aesthetic value, and it has been widely regarded as a masterpiece of Italian literature. It was conceived as a series of fictional conversations held at the court of the Duke of Urbino, Castiglione's own lord, where some of the most renowned noblemen of Italy gathered from time to time. Castiglione has them "play"—in what today appears as an utterly boring game—at "setting forth all the conditions and particular qualities that are required of anyone who deserves [the name of Courtier]," as Frederico Fregoso, one of the supposed participants to the discussion, proposes.[43] Thus the book portrays, without establishing any precise set of rules, the qualities that the ideal courtier should possess—of which "grace," as we saw at the beginning of chapter 3, is the foundation. Castiglione has Fregoso and his companions converse on such diverse themes as the worth of vernacular languages; the virtues of art, literature, and music; and the abjectness of affectation or the importance of lineage; and in the process he delineates the image of the man, and to a certain extent of the woman, of perfect deportment. The book's reputation attained such heights that when François I, the king of France, wanted a book to improve the ways of his court, he turned to Castiglione's *Il libro del Cortegiano.* Translated into French in 1537 by Jacques Colin, it was soon to be the golden book of French nobility, among whom "knowing the *Cortegiano*" was to become proverbial.[44]

Grace appears first in its aesthetic guise, at the very beginning of the discussion. Castiglione has Count Ludovico da Canossa, the man assigned the task of setting forth the attributes of the ideal courtier, say, "I would have our Courtier born of a noble and genteel family; because it is far less becoming for one of low birth to fail to do virtuous things than for one of noble birth."[45]

> [But] besides his noble birth, I would wish the Courtier . . . endowed by nature not only with talent and with beauty of countenance and person, but with that certain grace which we call an 'air,' which shall make him at first sight pleasing and lovable to all who see him; and let this be an adornment informing and attending all his actions, giving the promise outwardly that such a one is worthy of the company and the favor of every great lord.[46]

The point is summed up by Cesare Gonzaga, another of the participants in the game. Besides setting the terms for the rest of the discussion, he suggests that more than simple aesthetics is involved—that grace is indeed concerned with a specific technology of the body:

> If I well remember, Count, it seems to me you have repeated several times . . . that the Courtier must accompany his actions, his gestures, his habits, in short, his every movement, with grace. And . . . you require this in everything as the seasoning without which all the other properties and good qualities would be of little worth. And truly I believe that everyone would easily let himself be persuaded of this, because, by the very meaning of the word, it can be said that he who has grace finds grace. . . . But as for those

who are less endowed by nature and are capable of acquiring grace only if they put forth labor, industry, and care, I would wish to know by what art, by what discipline, by what method, they can gain this grace . . . [since] you deem it to be so necessary.[47]

Grace, then, is the essential property of the courtier, the one quality that invests all others with value. In principle, it is a disposition bestowed by nature. Yet, Castiglione suggests, it can be acquired through hard work and a strict discipline. Castiglione repeatedly compares grace with art, its mastery drawing the admiration of a work of art, its schooling following the same processes and methods used in the culture of artistic skills. For grace is not learned in a conventional way. The courtier must acquire grace through observation and imitation, "stealing" this property, as Castiglione writes, "from those who seem to him to have it, taking from each the part that seems most worthy of praise."[48]

More important, as Castiglione is very careful to explain, grace cannot be simply possessed; it must be transformed into an integral element of oneself. It must become a habit, a quality so ingrained within one's character that it appears to be totally "natural." The courtier has to develop the naturalness of "a singer who utters a single word ending in a group of four notes with a sweet cadence, and with such facility that he appears to do it quite by chance." All his actions must have the quality of "a single line which is not labored, a single brush stroke made with ease and in such a manner that the hand seems of itself to complete the line desired by the painter, without being directed by care or skill of any kind."[49] The point, then, is to transform the language of bodily attitudes and gestures that constitute grace into a *habitu corporis*—into something equivalent to what Bourdieu called "habitus."[50] Indeed, according to Castiglione, grace has to become inscribed, as we would say today, in the courtier's body, its techniques becoming the techniques of the body itself. As Jay Tribby nicely put it, "The courtier's body was itself a repository for his social capacities—which, like a work of art, he displayed in what might well be conceived as a 'domestic museum.' "[51]

Many scholars have seen Castiglione's opening remarks about the innate quality of civility as being at odds with his subsequent, and more important, arguments about the procedures for attaining grace.[52] To some, this duality is the fruit of an intended irony, a rhetorical device by which Castiglione, rather than affirming the ways of court society, threatens its very foundations. Since in principle anyone can attain grace, the one quality that supposedly gives the aristocracy its uniqueness loses its capacity to differentiate. Aristocrats, therefore, can no longer claim distinction; they can no longer claim a special nature that makes them similar to one another yet different from all others. But that is only one possible interpretation, which assumes that the ontological foundations of court society exist outside of the practices that embody them. Yet, exactly as an episteme exists only in and through the thoughts that it makes possible, an ontological foundation exists only in and through the practices that *it* makes possible. Viewed from a perspective in which ontological foundations and the practices through which they come into being are inseparable, Castiglione's dual affirmation of inherence and apprenticeship takes on an entirely different meaning.

In that light, indeed, the *Cortegiano* becomes a medium for the expression, deployment, and fashioning of the collective self of the *res civile*, as for the self-fashioning of each of its members in its terms. The technologies of the body that Castiglione says the courtier must make part of his *habitu corporis*, make into attributes of his inner constitution as if they were natural to him, are those which define and realize the essence of the collective self of the civil powers. Learning and incorporating these technologies are precisely the means by which the "essence" of the collective self is brought into being. The discipline of the body does not threaten the foundations of court society, it contributes to their constitution.

This interpretation has the virtue of making sense of the enthusiastic reception of the *Cortegiano* in much of Europe throughout the sixteenth century—the significance of which has tended to be minimized, when not emphatically dismissed, by much of the recent literature attempting to present the book as an oppositional, or at least demystifying, text. Arthur Kinney's attempt to play down the popularity of the *Cortegiano* exemplifies this tendency. Kinney is well aware of the magnitude of the *Cortegiano*'s success. He notes its adoption at many European courts and quotes the comments written by Thomas Hoby, the translator of the English edition, in his epistle to Lord Henry Hastings: "You may see him [Castiglione] confirme with reason the Courtly facions, comely exercises, and noble vertues," Hoby wrote, "that unawares haue from time to time crept in to you and already with practice and learning taken custome in you."[53] Yet, to Kinney, both the enthusiasm at the courts and Hoby's comments are spurious. "[S]uch extravagant encomia, like the euphoric mood that prompts them," Kinney asserts, "seriously mislead. They are, like Pico's rhetorical praise of rhetoric, *self*-fulfilling prophecies. In protesting too much man's potentiality, they chart their own exposed uncertainty."[54] I would not contest that the responses to the *Cortegiano* work like self-fulfilling prophecies, or that they, or the book itself, expose their own uncertainties. Nor would I disagree with Kinney's suggestion, made two pages later, that the praise that Castiglione's characters dispense is essentially a self-praise, and therefore circular.[55] Rather than using those properties of the text to dismiss its public's response, however, I would suggest that they explain its popularity. For that is precisely what we would expect when we see the *Cortegiano* as a vehicle for the expression, deployment, and fashioning of the collective self of the *res civile*. The pragmatics of grace, in its entirety, is by definition self-referential, self-fulfilling, and self-celebratory. It is the modality of practice by which the aristocracy constructed and embodied itself within the confines of monarchical power.[56] The self-praise is precisely that, the praise of the affirmation of oneself. This perception fits Hoby's epistle perfectly. For Hoby's suggestion that the "Courtly facions, comely exercises, and noble vertues" have "crept into" Lord Hastings and "with practice and learning taken costume" in him conveys exactly the same idea that I introduced above. These qualities are not innate in Hastings, an aristocrat of unquestioned nobility. With practice he has absorbed them, made them part of his habitus—so that, indeed, they have "taken costume" in him. And all this Hoby is openly and publicly telling to none other than Lord Hastings himself, which indicates the extent to which what we take as problematic today did not seem to provoke any problem at the time.

For, in effect, nobility of birth and grace are not conceived as being synonymous. Although in principle someone can be naturally endowed with grace (even though, we slowly come to realize, this is so rare as to be almost impossible), this does not come from one's nobility of birth. To Castiglione, as presumably to Hoby and Lord Hastings, grace is a further, and separate, property of the courtier. It is something that Castiglione wants the courtier to have in addition to "his noble birth."[57] Like the relation between a work of art and the material of which it is made, or the quality of a musical instrument and the sound that it produces, noble birth is to be preferred to "low birth" because it allegedly endows a person with a substance better suited to be fashioned, or to use a term borrowed from Erasmus, "molded," into grace.[58] Nobility is seen as the material in which the technologies and codes that constitute grace can be most easily inscribed.[59] That these have "taken costume in" Lord Hastings indubitably attests to his nobility.

But we are dealing not with simple "fashioning" but with self-fashioning. Castiglione's courtier is not just someone to be fashioned; he must participate in his own fashioning. He is the one who through "labor, industry, and care" molds himself. He is the one who, through self-discipline, is called to carve and inscribe the forms of grace within himself. A perception of self in terms of self-fashioning was obviously not unique to Castiglione, as the actual practices of self-fashioning were certainly not unique to courtiership. As Stephen Greenblatt has shown, self-fashioning was highly characteristic of the Renaissance, at least as a concept, taking, as is typical of discourse in general, a variety of expressions.[60] It testifies to the emergence of a self that, because it is no longer the product of a condition of coalescence, because it is no longer the product of a condition of merging with its social environment, is seen as being in need of molding—grace being only one of the possible molds.[61] *To mold*, Erasmus's term, is in fact befitting, and conveys the same sense of self that I discussed at the beginning of the chapter. To mold, in effect, means to give a person a definitive shape according to a specific frame. It means to endow that person with a character as opposed to a shifting role—even if that character includes "performing in social life" to perfection. The process of molding oneself, as opposed to the process of being molded, in turn, points at the self-referentiality of grace and its practices. For at the same time that one molds one's self, at the same time that one embodies the techniques of courtiership, one fashions the molds in whose shapes he is cast. In fashioning one's self, that is, one simultaneously fashions the collective self that one comes to embody. The collective self exists only through the people who embody it. It has no existence outside that embodiment. The very method by which Castiglione suggests that one fashions oneself to acquire grace—a method that he specifies by extending to practice a principle of humanist rhetorics: *imitatio*—assumes self-referentiality.[62] For it is by imitating the people who have better internalized the behavioral codes of the courtier that the aspiring man of grace in turn comes to possess grace. By mirroring the people in whom the collective self of the *res civile* has become the most ingrained, the future courtier aligns his self with the practices of similarity at the heart of the infrastructure of social relations of the *res civile*.

Castiglione's discussion of the physical attributes of the courtier leaves little doubt that grace is first and foremost a property belonging exclusively to men.[63] For even though the technologies of the body that Castiglione wants the courtier to make part of his habitus must be modulated by the requirements of life at court, his physicality remains essentially masculine.

Elegance, parsimony of movement, decorum, moderation, sociability, and courtesy in general, are unquestionably attributes of courtiership. But the concern with virility, strength, physical fitness, agility, and the exercises associated with the education of the good warrior are equally central. The man of grace has to strike a middle ground between the two tendencies. The man who eschews elegance certainly lacks that "air" essential to grace. But the man who disregards the education of the body that renders him a "man" and applies himself only to parlor games lacks the magnetism that gives grace its power. Castiglione urges the courtier to train in the use of arms and in wrestling; to excel in horse-riding and all the forms of knightly exercises; to hunt, play ball, develop skills like vaulting on horseback, and so on. Failing to do so would make him "effeminate" and would disqualify him from ever becoming a man of grace.

The exclusion of women is, again, only partial, however. For although the masculine dimension of the technologies of the body advocated by Castiglione remains beyond them, women share fully in the skills that modulate the roughness of naked masculinity and generate the "air" indispensable for grace. Castiglione actually introduces some of these skills by celebrating and praising women—a device that should not be taken as an open affirmation of womanhood, however.[64] For these skills are not strictly feminine; they involve, as we shall see, a body language, a complex of behavioral strategies that allows to navigate the intricacies of court life and gain the "grace," or favors, of the prince. It is a body language available to men and women alike, none of its gestures being exclusively associated with one of the sexes. Men who eschew masculinity are taunted as effeminate precisely because this body language does not differentiate between the sexes. To fail at what renders one a man, therefore, is to become similar to women, to remain on the one side of grace within which women are fully included.

Politics and the Civil Absolute

The technologies of the body, however, are only one dimension of the pragmatics of grace and the infrastructure of social relations of the *res civile.* Grace, indeed, is not a purely aesthetic concept; it is also a moral concept. Castiglione's aesthetics is paralleled by an ethical principle—Horace's "golden mean," itself a derivation of the Aristotelian concept of *mesotes*— that endows grace with a clear moral quality.[65] Perfection of form and excellence of moral sentiment involve in fact congruent principles, and the two yield a similar disposition of body and mind. For to have grace means to have achieved the perfect balance between virility and the skills of sociability. It means to have the ability to avoid the extremes of behavior, to shy away from mannerisms and pretense alike. And it means, too, to realize in behavior the ideals of Horace's golden mean. As with courtoisie, the behaviorally perfect thus becomes the morally perfect, and vice versa.

The *Cortegiano* culminates in a Platonic discourse on love where goodness and beauty are overtly equated, giving final shape to the philosophical hybrid informing the concept of grace: an Aristotelian idea of ethics, and a Platonic idea of the unity between the moral and the aesthetic. "I say, then, that, according to the definition of ancient sages, love is nothing but a certain desire to enjoy beauty," Castiglione has Pietro Bembo, one of the major authorities on platonic love during the Italian Renaissance, assert, "and, as our desire is only for things that are known, knowledge must always precede desire, which by its nature turns to the good but in itself is blind and does not know the good."[66] "Outward beauty is a true sign of inner goodness," he writes later, and resorting to the same self-referential logic that I suggest characterizes the relation between birth and grace, he adds, "And this grace is impressed upon the body in varying degree as an index of the soul, . . . as with trees in which the beauty of the blossoms is a token of the excellence of the fruit."[67] This identity of beauty and goodness, of the technologies of the body of the courtier and a moral absolute, helps legitimize the collective self of the *res civile* at a higher level. Or rather, the evidence of its excellence and superiority lies in that identity of nature, in that congruence of beauty and goodness—something that we will observe to an even greater degree in Erasmus.

The fact that the *Cortegiano* is a conversation, that it is a *game,* is of considerable importance. As many commentators have noted, setting a very serious discussion in the context of play allows Castiglione to present a diversity of points of view—often contradictory, sometimes dangerous— and simultaneously defuse any threat of severe disagreement by simply dropping the controversial theme or, more typically, through the use of laughter.[68] Indeed, inevitably, as he deploys the collective self of the *res civile,* Castiglione also deploys its limits, its ambiguities, its tensions. Castiglione puts the players in a situation in which they have to reveal their own inconsistencies, in which they are forced to face the strains of their social order—a situation in which the self-portrait they are painting can at any moment self-destruct. As Thomas M. Greene put it, "If there is anything radically insecure or hypocritical, any area where norm and reality diverge too widely, it could be a destructive experience; it could confront the company with truths it might not be able to face."[69] The ludic character of the gathering therefore provides the group—and Castiglione—with an effective safety-valve, frequently blown open by laughter.

While *Il Cortegiano* is hardly an instrument of irony intended to subvert the foundations of the *res civile*,[70] neither is it an ideological tool, intended to conceal the realities of power in Renaissance societies. Quite the opposite, it is a manual that charts the infrastructures of social relations and power of the *res civile*. It unveils, rather than disguises, the inconsistencies and gaps—the hypocrisies, as Greene and others would say—of the dominant order of things. And it shows how these incongruities are absorbed, negotiated, and sometimes transcended in the universe of the taken-for-granted that follows, or constitutes, the very consolidation of civil power.

Disagreements concerning the traits of the ideal courtier indeed abound in the *Cortegiano*. Not even Canossa's remarks concerning nobility of birth are exempt. The paradox identified by some twentieth-century commentators as irony is, in effect, openly voiced in the book. Aren't many aristocrats, as is well-known to all, "ridden by vices," while many persons of humble birth, "through their virtue, have made their posterity illustrious?" another of the players, Gasparo Pallavicino, asks.[71] Isn't "fortune" as important as "nature" for achieving perfection? And indeed, as we have seen, the pragmatics of grace resorts to a self-referential logic of affinities to rephrase the connection between birth and grace and maintain the preeminence of nobility. Controversies occur, for example, regarding the courtier's language, or with whom he may engage in athletic competitions, or, more critically, the kind of relations he should entertain with his prince.

A potentially devastating controversy breaks out the second evening— the game having become so exciting that it lasts for (at least) four days— when a comment Castiglione attributes to Federico Fregoso causes a fracas. For, Fregoso suggests, in addition to the excellence of body and mind that was discussed earlier, a courtier should commit himself "to loving and almost adoring the prince he serves above all else, devoting his every desire and habit and manner to pleasing him."[72] The reaction is immediate. One player accuses Fregoso of sketching a flatterer; another retorts that the gap between Fregoso's ideal and reality is impossible to bridge, as only through presumption do people gain favors. The players come to doubt not merely the virtue of the courtier—they question the integrity of the rulers themselves. The very foundation of the social order that gives the courtier his reason of being is therefore challenged. Greene summarizes this situation well:

Here the players almost expose themselves to a perception of the corruption endemic to the system they live by, the perception of a courtier essentially passive, dependent on the whim of a master who may be evil and is likely to be a despot. A vision almost takes shape of the very condition of courtiership as potentially or inherently corrupting. The vision flickers briefly and obliquely but unmistakably, and for a while there is no laughter.[73]

Laughter, of course, safely returns, and the game, as though nothing has happened, regains its playful character. The subject is taken up again the fourth day, however, when the political dimension of grace comes into full view.

Fregoso's comment, in effect, points at the specific configuration of political and social relations in terms of which the *res civile* takes shape, and at the specific modalities of political and social behaviors that follow. It points at the structure of centeredness in which the monarch, or the prince, occupies the central position—and the courtier's behavior becomes fully and legitimately oriented towards his earning the "grace" of the prince. The moral, the aesthetic and, now, the political come together in the single word *grace* in a final, all-encompassing synthesis—a synthesis in which the moral and sensual goal-orienting behavior acquires a decidedly structural dimension.

For to Castiglione, grace is not only something to be attained, it is also something to be received and cherished. It is not only something to be learned and mastered, it is something to be earned from others—the prince, in particular.[74] Let grace, Castiglione has already told us through the voice of Canossa, "be an adornment informing and attending all [the courtier's] actions, giving the promise outwardly that such a one is worthy of the company and the favor ["*del commerzio e grazia*," reads the original[75]] of every great lord." Grace, that is, provokes grace, a grace that comes from a higher authority and legitimates the very existence of the courtier. It is a distinction, a mark of honor bestowed by a lord to his most deserving subjects. It is a gift that the lord distributes out of magnanimity and recognition—like God's loving mercy, which, according to the doctrines of ecclesias, endows mankind with primordial grace.

In a sense, the *Cortegiano* is a political manual. It is highly reminiscent of Brunetto's *Il tesoretto,* and more than passingly similar to Machiavelli's *The Prince.* It involves a recognition of the political structures and political realities of the *res civile.* As Daniel Javitch suggests, Castiglione's speakers recommend a model of behavior informed by an awareness of despotism, a model designed to secure the favors—or grace—of a whimsical ruler.[76] Love for the prince, blind commitment, and the willing bestowal of oneself, Fregoso is saying, are the attitudes necessary for achieving grace in the civil realm.[77] For only through total devotion to the lord does the courtier obtain his superior's grace; and only owing to this grace is he able to acquire the gracefulness of countenance, both moral and aesthetic, that his condition dictates. In this sense, then, the *Cortegiano* involves both an affirmation of a political system and a guide to survival in a world made of intrigues and arbitrary decisions for actual or would-be courtiers. It charts the configuration of centeredness in which the body of the prince becomes, literally, the axis of action. It unveils the modalities of interaction that the courtier must make his own in order to become part of "the system."[78] And as it deploys the forms of the *res civile,* it deploys its limits, ambiguities, gaps, and tensions. The logic is once again circular. The bestowal of grace by the ruler is a condition for the acquisition of grace by the courtier, yet only the graceful courtier gains the grace of his prince. Indeed, only that certain "air" called grace, to use Canossa's formulation, makes the courtier "lovable to all who see him," first and foremost to his own superior.[79] From this perspective, Machiavelli's *The Prince* and *Il Cortegiano* can be seen as two discourses emerging from the same infrastructure, each giving shape, albeit from different perspectives, to the structures of centeredness of the *res civile. The Prince* develops an instrumental discourse in which the prince and the courtier are portrayed as calculating, if not brutal. In *Il Cortegiano* the courtier is a man of "high ethical standards, able to guide through wisdom as well as strength."[80] Still, they express the same configuration of social relations.

The skepticism with which Fregoso's statement was received does not dispute the centeredness of the infrastructure. Quite the contrary, the players's reactions are fully informed by an awareness of centeredness and its realities. And the players question precisely the realities that follow from that configuration—realities that are obviously not singular or homogeneous. They highlight a second tension inherent in the *res civile* between the behavioral requirements that result from a secular definition of virtue and the realities of a social system based on principles of nobility and political despotism.[81] Neither the prince nor the courtier are exempt from imperfections, from a certain looseness of morals, yet the entire pragmatics of grace is oriented towards the affirmation of the prince's power and the maintenance of noble privilege, given the value of a moral absolute. And here, again, the path dictated by the higher rhetoric of grace provides Castiglione with a mechanism, inspired by Renaissance Humanism, able to salvage the *res civile* from its inconsistencies.

For Castiglione reserves to the courtier a higher goal intended to secure the self-sustaining properties of the *res civile*. Moreover, this goal will help transform the political, a most unreliable and capricious establishment, into a rational institution. Fittingly, Castiglione leaves the formulation of this goal for the last night of discussion,[82] after one of the speakers, in an extraordinary movement of self-criticism that exposes the troubling character of the game, is meant to point out the futility of courtiership. "Among the things which we call good," Castiglione has Ottaviano Fregoso, Federico's older brother, argue,

> there are some which, simply and in themselves, are always good, such as temperance, fortitude, health, and all the virtues that bring tranquility of mind; others, which are good in various respects and for the end to which they are directed, such as law, liberality, riches, and other like things. Therefore I think that the perfect Courtier, such as Count Ludovico and messer Federico have described him, may indeed be good and worthy of praise, not, however, simply and in himself, but in regard to the end to which he is directed.[83]

Many of the accomplishments that have been attributed to the courtier are but "frivolities and vanities, . . . deserving of blame rather than of praise," maintains Ottaviano; much of what has been claimed in the name of grace "often serves merely to make spirits effeminate, to corrupt youth, and to lead it to a dissolute life."[84] Unless directed to "a good end," courtiership is bound to remain a vain, even harmful pursuit.

Unquestionably, Ottaviano's comments involve an accentuation of the ambiguities revealed by his brother's earlier statement. Moreover, they represent the most threatening subversion that the game has to witness; for Ottaviano's censure of frivolity entails a repudiation of the game itself: unless courtiership is salvaged at a higher level of moral responsibility, Ottaviano is saying, the entire discussion cannot fail to be regarded but as an aimless exercise in self-indulgence.[85] At this point, the most explosive moment of the *Cortegiano,* the book attains its final unity of vision, for the ultimate goal that the author reserves for his courtier is nothing short of the moral and political education of his superior—which is to say, the creation of grace itself in the person of the prince. As Castiglione has Ottaviano assert,

To bring or help one's prince toward what is right and to frighten him away from what is wrong are the true fruit [*sic*] of Courtiership. And because the real merit of good deeds consists chiefly in two things, one of which is to choose a truly good end to aim at, and the other is to know how to find means timely and fitting to attain that good end—it is certain that a man aims at the best end when he sees to it that his prince is deceived by no one, listens to no flatterers or slanderers or liars, and distinguishes good [everything, that is, that follows the profession of *mediocritas*] from evil, loving the one and hating the other.[86]

The vision is thus finally rounded off and indeed becomes self-sustaining. The affirmation of order brings forth the affirmation of the good, of a secular good which in turn helps concretize the social and political arrangements that constitute that order. Grace represents a *telos,* a teleological scheme of the what-ought-to-be whose ultimate legitimacy derives from the legitimacy of the king himself and which instills action with a sense of direction—providing European societies, as we will see in the next chapter, with the experiential basis that helped transform the authoritarian ways of despotism into the political practices of absolutism.

The Pervasion of Grace

All the lines that Castiglione patiently draws to sketch the portrait of the courtier also come together, albeit in a very different form, in Erasmus's *De civilitate morum puerilium* (1530)[87] and Giovanni della Casa's *Galateo* (1558)[88]—two books that are very different from *Il Cortegiano*. Both are fully instructed by the pragmatics of grace, yet neither one shows any overt awareness of it. Both are ostensibly concerned with questions that would seem to be tangential, if not orthogonal, to grace[89]—yet both fully imply the pragmatics of grace. They deploy largely male-oriented, if not masculine, practices of behavior; they embody the same merging of aesthetics and ethics that we see in Castiglione; they present the same picture of the basic configuration of social relations—although their vision is not one of a singular system of concentric circles but of concentric circles within concentric circles organized in a type of Boolean logic. As such, the two attest to the permeation of the pragmatics of grace, or civility, outside of the confines of the court—in spite of the ways that the insularity of symbolic capital as it developed in the *res civile* limited the hegemony of the powers at its core.[90]

Compared to the *Cortegiano*—a subtle, sophisticated, elegant book—both *De civilitate* and the *Galateo* are small and rather sober treatises on manners. *De civilitate,* a manual intended for the education of young boys, presents in simple Latin the behavior that a well-reared boy should follow at church, at play, at table, at bed-time and, in general, in the company of grown-ups. It does not hesitate to study and to name, as Elias put it, "some functions of the body that our sensibility no longer permits us to discuss in public, much less in treatises of good manners."[91] It was until recently considered of minor value within the corpus of Erasmus's work, and to some, including a few of his contemporaries, it seemed inconceivable that the great Erasmus could devote himself to such trivial matters.[92] Still, the treatise rapidly became something like a best-seller. It was reprinted repeatedly,[93] was translated into most vernaculars (including Czech and Finnish) and was adopted by a large number of schools all over Europe as both a handbook on "morals" and a manual of Latin.

Its first section, "On the body," brings the merging of ethics and aestheticism central to grace immediately to light. I quote the first paragraph in its entirety.

> For the well-ordered mind of a boy to be universally manifested—and it is most strongly manifested in the face—the eyes should be calm, respectful, and steady: not grim, which is a mark of truculence; not shameless, the hallmark of insolence; not darting and rolling, a feature of insanity; nor furtive, like those of suspects and plotters of treachery; nor gaping like those of idiots; nor should the eyes and eyelids be constantly blinking, a mark of the fickle; nor gaping as in astonishment—a characteristic observed in Socrates; not too narrowed, a sign of bad temper; nor bold and inquisitive, which indicates impertinence; but such as reflects a mind composed, respectful, and friendly. For it is no chance saying of the ancient sages that the seat of the soul is in the eyes. Old pictures tell us that it was once a mark of singular modesty to observe with eyes half closed, just as among certain Spaniards to avoid looking at people is taken as a sign of politeness and friendship. In the same way we learn from pictures that it was once the case that tightly closed lips were taken as evidence of honesty. But the naturally decorous is recognized as such by everyone. Nevertheless in these matters too it is occasionally appropriate for us to play the polypus and adapt ourselves to the customs of the region. There are certain manners of the eyes which nature bestows differently

upon different men and which do not fall within our purview, save that ill-composed gesture often destroys the character and appearance not only of the eyes but of the whole body as well. On the other hand, well-composed gestures render what is naturally decorous even more attractive: if they do not remove defects, at least they disguise and minimize them. It is bad manners to look at someone with one eye open and one shut. For what else is this than to deprive oneself of an eye? Let us leave that gesture to tunnies and smiths.[94]

Like Castiglione, Erasmus engages in gradually drawing a picture, although the picture he seeks to draw is not that of a courtier but that of the man of quality or, more precisely, of the boy endowed with "a well-ordered mind." The passage opens with a statement of fact, and Erasmus devotes the rest of the section (indeed, the entire book) to articulating that "truth": that the well-reared boy has to reflect "a mind composed, respectful, and friendly." Composed, meaning calm, balanced, and under control; respectful, implying an affirmation of authority; friendly, denoting social sensibility and goodwill.

Erasmus sketches the qualities of the person of distinction in a series of carefully drafted images tending to emphasize the improper—images in which we can visualize some of Hieronymus Bosch's or Bruegel's more gruesome paintings. Posing, grimacing, acting like one were in constant astonishment, or always plotting, or in a state of perpetual irritability, Erasmus teaches through these figures, are the hallmarks of a mind ill-composed, disrespectful, and unfriendly. He makes extensive use of ridicule, largely by comparing the noxious to the behavior of animals—hedgehogs, bulls, peacocks, elephants, horses, dogs, storks, apes, pigs—or to the habits of grotesque people—scoffers and buffoons, idiots, blockheads, braggarts, charlatans, prigs, and last but not least, courtiers themselves. "The mouth should be neither tight-set, which denotes someone afraid of inhaling someone else's breath, nor gaping open like an idiot's, but formed with lips lightly touching one another," writes Erasmus in typical fashion, and adds ironically,

Nor is it very polite to be repeatedly pursing the lips as if making a clucking sound, although that gesture is excusable in grown-ups of high rank [i.e., courtiers] as they pass through the midst of a throng; for in the case of such people all things are becoming, while we are concerned in moulding a boy.[95]

"Moulding a boy"—I have already discussed the significance of that statement, although here it acquires a more clearly ethical dimension. Throughout the treatise, Erasmus associates the aesthetically negative with the immoral—the base, the abusive, the perverse, the treacherous—and through a virtual hammering of images combining the ludicrous, the ethically objectionable and, for that matter, the graceless, he communicates his vision of propriety. The same is true of the *Galateo*. Della Casa builds an argument using, in part, the same strategy of associating the aesthetically negative— people looking at the product of their noses "as if pearls or rubies might have descended from [one's] brain," or who "spray those near them in the face" as they sneeze[96]—with the immoral, thus drawing a parallel between propriety of form and propriety of substance. For these two authors, the rationale is similar to Castiglione's, for whom aesthetic balance follows directly from the ethical notion of *mediocritas*.[97] As in Castiglione, in both Erasmus and della Casa the concepts of the socially correct follow the principle of the happy medium, while the concepts of the perfectly shaped follow the principle of aesthetic balance—the one becoming a sign of the existence of the other, and the two producing the same impression, the same mode of perceiving the proper in social behavior.[98]

This does not amount to a concept of relativism. Somewhat in the spirit of Pontano, for example, Erasmus asserts from the outset that there are significant variations in human behavior, and that these must be fully acknowledged. But the proper, "the naturally decorous," he maintains repeatedly (twice in the first paragraph), "is recognized as such by everybody," regardless of place and possibly time. In bowing, for example, different standards have developed in different places, and all are perfectly acceptable:

> Some bend each knee equally, and there again, some do so while keeping the body erect, others while bowing slightly. There are those who, considering this to be somewhat effeminate, maintain the erect posture of the body but bend first the right knee and then the left, a gesture that is favoured among the English for the young. The French accompany a measured turn of the body with a bow of the right knee only. In such matters, where the various techniques do not conflict with "basic good taste," it will be permissible either to follow one's native fashion or comply with foreign practice.[99]

But whenever foreign fashions conflict with the "naturally tasteful," Erasmus is conclusive: "An oath," for example, "whether made in jest or in earnest comes ill from a boy's lips. For what is more distasteful than that custom among certain peoples where even the girls make every third word an oath: 'by the bread,' 'by the wine,' 'by the candle,' 'by anything at all' "?[100]

As a matter of fact, there is, most clearly in *De civilitate* but also in *Il Cortegiano* and the *Galateo,* an uneasiness with the idea of relativism that recalls our discussion at the beginning of the chapter. For in spite of all the openness of spirit, of a certain acceptance of the customs of other peoples, we can feel a reluctance about the foreign, a subtle uneasiness with the ways of others. Taking on outlandish demeanors, detaching oneself from what one is by virtue of birth and breeding, is, for Erasmus, abnormal and incongruous. Although it occurs, it is nonetheless beyond the bounds of the "natural." As he explicitly states in the first paragraph, to adapt to the customs of others, to become attached, however temporarily, to the habits of strangers means "to play the polypus": to be transformed into a sort of monster, into a creature affected by some abnormal growths over its spiritual tissue.

Neither Erasmus nor della Casa, however, incorporate the martially grounded physicality so central to Castiglione's courtier. Their books foster an experience of the body that, on the surface at least, relies exclusively on the cultivation of the civilizing elements of the pragmatics of grace. This difference might be explained by the authors' biographies. Of the three, only Castiglione pursued at one point in his life a military career; both Erasmus and della Casa engaged in primarily intellectual, religious pursuits and showed a deep antipathy for war and the deeds of arms. The remarkable success of their books suggests that the military element that I have stressed as foundational to the *res civile* might not have been as important as I claim. I would argue, however, that the absence of martial physicality embodies a more "bourgeois" version of the pragmatics of grace, one that fits precisely how we should expect to find it outside of the court—outside of the realm within which the self-referential "similar," within which power, that is, forms itself and operates. That is indeed how hegemony operates: as power, or, rather, its modalities permeate "others" without ever fully making them part of the similar. And most of the practices that I have associated with the pragmatics of grace emerge within the *Galateo* and *De civilitate* alike, helping fashion the practices of the newly forming middle classes yet at the same time foreclosing the possibility of their entering the circles of power.

Quite ironically, in spite of their authors' antipathy for and rejection of martial physicality, the *Galateo* and *De civilitate* engender a masculinity far more unauspicious to women than *Il Cortegiano.* For both Erasmus and della Casa focus exclusively on the civilizing dimension of grace, yet both eschew its feminine element—an element that presents no difficulties to Castiglione precisely because martial physicality provides him with such a clear line of gender differentiation. Erasmus's derision of courtiership by associating it with the most effeminate behaviors at court already suggests a strong disinclination for the feminine and, by extension, the presence of a marked masculinity.[101] The norms of the appropriate for men and for women are clearly different. The feminine becomes not simply inappropriate for men but, at least sometimes, a reason for mockery and contempt—feelings that we do not see in Castiglione. These tendencies take an even more radical expression in della Casa, whose comments often betray of misogyny. After condemning melancholy and distraction in appearance, he writes, for example,

> It is also not appropriate, especially for men, to be overly sensitive and fastidious, for to deal in this way with other people is called not companionship but servitude. There certainly are some who are so sensitive and easily hurt that to live or to be with them is nothing more than finding oneself surrounded by many fine glass objects, for they fear every little blow, and so they must be treated and respected like fine crystal. . . . Such sensitivity and such fastidiousness are best left to women.[102]

The association of the feminine with delicacy and the lack of strength is unequivocal, as is the desirability of their opposites, solidity and force, in men—the same dispositions that we observed in Castiglione. Misogyny aside, the image of the feminine that emerges is ultimately one of passivity—a passivity sometimes worthy of respect (the dominant tone in Erasmus), sometimes of contempt (the dominant tone in della Casa). For unlike Castiglione, for whom women make a positive contribution to the operation of the *res civile*, Erasmus and della Casa see women as eminently passive beings, objects of attention or derision rather than agents of civility, however partial, in their own right. Erasmus's only reference to women's behavior in his entire manual is to stress to boys the desirability of maintaining silence at table: "Silence is becoming in women but even more so in boys."[103]

The practices of centeredness that Erasmus and della Casa help nurture are consequently more male-oriented than in Castiglione. The permeation of the pragmatics of grace in the manners that Erasmus and della Casa advance is at its most marked as they incorporate and extend the practices of centeredness that bring into being the infrastructure of social relations of the *res civile.* The picture of a concentric hierarchy centered on the figure of the man of highest distinction emerges clearly from both *De civilitate* and the *Galateo,* as does the consideration of obtaining "the grace" of one's superior—even if neither of the authors uses the word.[104] Grace, after all, has too much of a religious connotation, and those who confer it are associated with the most exalted, if not with divinity itself. The word that Erasmus and della Casa use is *honor,* a far more appropriate word to denote the quality bestowed by anyone other than a prince and therefore more appropriate for the pervasion of grace outside of the court—the word, as we learn from Corneille, that would become the accepted term with which to speak of grace. The instruction is to honor one's superior, and to accept and cherish the honor that comes in return. Moreover, every person should aim for that honor, which, like Castiglione's grace, includes an ethical, an aesthetic, and a social, if not necessarily political, dimension. The merging of morals and countenance that we saw above becomes, as for Castiglione, integral to honor—an honor, I should add, that rewards women in proportion to their passivity.[105]

The configuration of social relations that results is also a function of the conditions for the deployment of grace, or honor, outside of the court. For if all hierarchical lines ultimately lead to the figure of the prince, when freed from the direct connection to the prince each person of "high distinction" becomes in turn a center from which honor originates. The structure is one of concentric circles within concentric circles: people of distinction form the circles at whose center is found the prince, yet each of them becomes a center within their own houses. And the people who encircle them become potential centers of still other circles, and so on, depending on the distinction they may themselves claim, or the honor they have themselves garnered.

In spite of the differences that follow from the provisions for the deployment of the pragmatics of grace in or outside of the court, the similarities between Castiglione, Erasmus, and della Casa are striking. The three express the same modality of practice, the same type of configuration of social relations, the same mode of relating to one another—their differences are variations of the same foundational infrastructure of social relations. Seen from within the infrastructure, their positions seem orthogonal to one another. Seen from the outside, however, their positions look like the fan-shaped heterogeneity of expressions typical of infrastructures of social relations in general.

Even the educational goal that Castiglione attributes to the courtier is present in *De civilitate* and the *Galateo*—though it is clearly given a different expression. The very aim of Erasmus's treatise represents a concretization of that goal.[106] Designed, perhaps, to teach the principles of propriety to children of all ranks, *De civilitate* is nonetheless explicitly intended for the instruction of boys of noble ancestry—first among them the future prince himself.[107] That the book is dedicated to the young Henry of Burgundy, the eleven-year-old son of Adolph, Prince of Veere, is of little significance, for Erasmus is merely following the conventions of his times. He is also obviously obeying certain rules common to his epoch when he writes that in being the son of a prince, raised in the best of company, educated by the best of teachers, Henry does not need his guidance. But the numerous references to the "well-born" and the frequent derision of behaviors followed at court indicate that Erasmus had in mind, first and foremost, the education of the boy of noble condition.

Erasmus's dedication in fact echoes Castiglione's philosophy of grace. The prince, Erasmus writes, has by virtue of his birth a grace in himself, already visible at a most tender age. But this grace, he also writes, must be shaped, developed through an education thoroughly informed by some high moral intention—a task that Castiglione reserves to the courtier, and Erasmus to the humanist. Moreover, by extending the principle of *mediocritas* to the realms of political behavior, the two authors, like Machiavelli and many others, come to embrace the same conception of the moral goal underlying the educational effort: the breeding of the rational prince. For if grace and civility denote a simultaneously aesthetic and moral disposition of the mind, the same principle governing the appreciation of beauty and the rules of rectitude should be assumed to mold the practices of political behavior. At dinner, at play, in bed, in whatever situation you find yourselves, Erasmus repeatedly tells his readers, do not let your whims take hold of you. Be as moderate in your judgment as you are in your manners and tastes; capriciousness in youth breeds injustice and viciousness in adulthood, he warns. This is the same message that Castiglione asserts through the voice of Ottaviano: only the higher goal of instilling the moderating properties of grace in the prince would salvage the *res civile* from falling into corruption and despotism.

The three books also express the tension between the new experience of individuation and the subjection of self that we analyzed at the beginning of the chapter, and to which the concept of heroism provides the ideal resolution—ideal, that is, from the point of view of the configurations of power of the *res civile*. And here, as we might expect, Castiglione's representation, the representation of the insider, incorporates a perception far closer to the ideal than either Erasmus or della Casa, whose representations, again, better fit the deployment of grace outside the realms of power of the *res civile.* Castiglione's call for total devotion to the prince, though he recognizes its perils, places the *Cortegiano* very near the position of heroism in a continuum of possible responses to the tension. Erasmus's prescriptions also demand a devotion intended to maintain the dominant order of social relations. "Even if the Turk (heaven forbid!) should rule over us," Erasmus writes in a most revealing passage, "we would be committing a sin if we were to deny to him the respect due to Caesar."[108] Yet this is a devotion that, throughout, Erasmus attempts to balance by nourishing a clear sense of self in his disciples: the sense of personal space, of a personal body, of the private experience of oneself to be made an object of self-identity—an act that ultimately embodies and deploys the tension itself. The *Galateo,* the most openly "bourgeois" of the three manuals, is the one that, fittingly, explicitly deploys the greatest resistance to the renunciation of self called for in the realms of the *res civile*—a position that underscores the existence and importance of the renunciation.[109]

Indeed, the development and hegemony of the pragmatics of grace varied from place to place depending on the extent to which the absolutist tendencies that it generated became institutionalized. No single, necessary line of development was followed by all European societies. Individuation continued to develop, and its pull continued to be felt. The experience of individuation continued to affect behavior and, overtly or latently, countered the constitutive hegemony of absolutism. However, the degree to which individuation received expression in the institutions and the social practices of European societies during the seventeenth century varied from place to place. As we will see in the next chapters, in some countries, as in France, the absolutist tendencies of the *res civile* become profoundly set, and the contradiction between the affirmation and the renunciation of self consequently grew deeper and deeper. In others, as in England, individuation received greater expression, slowly helped to undermine the hegemony of royal centrality and consequently produced a new displacement in the axis of organization of power—and a new shift of the plane on which reality is constituted. The advent of the concept of etiquette—a concept, we should recall, that appeared first in England, not France—embodied nothing short of that. I turn first, however, to an analysis of the French experience.

Honnêteté and the Consolidation
of Royal Centrality

Monsieur, dismiss all anxious fears. We live beneath a prince the foe of fraud—a prince whose eyes can penetrate all hearts; whose mind the art of no impostor can deceive. His great soul, gifted with a clear discernment, casts a straight glance on all things. In him no bias gains admittance, and his firm mind falls into no excess. He gives to righteous men immortal glory; but without blindness does he show his zeal; love for the truly good in no ways shuts his eyes to all the baseness of a hypocrite.

Molière, *Le Tartuffe*

Grace, Disgrace, and the Precariousness of Court Society

A S A LOGIC generative of practices of royal centrality, the pragmatics of grace yielded an infrastructure of social relations whose paradigmatic expression appeared in the palatial courts of Europe. After all, as we have seen, the courts were not just sites of power; they were sites in which power forged and established itself.

The following event, related by the Duc de Saint-Simon, arguably the major chronicler of everyday life in the court of France during the reign of Louis XIV, provides an exemplary view of that infrastructure—of both its solidity and its precariousness. The year is 1696, the place, Versailles, the palace of Louis XIV. The king had just asked Monsieur de La Rochefoucauld, a prominent nobleman, why he never attended the sermon:

[M. de La Rochefoucauld] said that he could not induce himself to go like the merest hanger-on about the Court, and beg a seat of the officer who distributed them, and then betake himself early to church in order to have a good one, and wait about in order to put himself where it might please that officer to place him. Whereupon the king immediately gave him a fourth seat behind him, by the side of the Grand Chamberlain, so that everywhere he is thus placed; the captain of the guard behind the King, the Grand Chamberlain at the captain's right and the first gentleman of the chamber at his left and nobody besides these three, up to this fourth that M. de la Rochefoucauld was able to get to himself, which is new, and that the King created for Guitry, killed during the crossing of the Rhine, whom M. de La Rochefoucauld succeeded. M. d'Orléans, the first chaplain, who has his place by the *prie-Dieu,* and nowhere else, had become used to place himself beside the Grand Chamberlain, and, since he is much loved and honored, he was allowed to do so without a word. This was the one that the King gave to M. de La Rochefoucauld. M. d'Orléans, who by dint of custom thought it was his, made a great ado, as though it really were his, and, not daring to quarrel with the King who had recently named him a Cardinal, quarrelled with M. de La Rochefoucauld, who, until then, had been one of his particular friends.[1]

The rift polarized the court, most of it siding with the offended party. The king intervened and tried to becalm Monsieur d'Orléans. La Rochefoucauld, "truly afflicted by the loss of his friend," did whatever, according to Saint-Simon, could be expected of him. Mutual friends interceded. Some of Monsieur d'Orléans closest acquaintances stepped in. All to no avail; the prelate "remained inflexible, and when he realized that all the scandal resulted in nothing but noise, he went to his diocese where he could pout at will."[2]

Saint-Simon is clearly not shy in laying bare his sympathies and antipathies. The *Mémoires* does not offer an objective assessment of the men and women who are its subjects, and much of its text reveals Saint-Simon's own preferences and weaknesses. But we have no reason to question the reality of the episode itself, or of its particulars.

To us, it all sounds inconsequential. The incident seems trivial. The behaviors of Monsieur d'Orléans and La Rochefoucauld seem, at best, childish. The gravity with which the two greet Louis XIV's action makes us raise questions about their intellectual capacities. The first, indeed, does not hesitate, because of a chair, to make a complete fool of himself. The second is content to lose a friend and to cause a commotion.

The seriousness with which Saint-Simon, an admittedly intelligent man, narrates the incident is baffling. Harold Nicolson echoes the view held until recently: "St. Simon may have been a difficult, tetchy little man; but he was certainly not stupid," writes Nicolson.[3] Yet the *Mémoires* are packed with inanities. The explanation would seem to be a simple one:

> Boredom brooded over Versailles like a heavy fog. "I am bored to death," wrote Mme. de Maintenon, "we gamble, we yawn, we have

nothing to do, we are jealous of each other, we tear each other to pieces." "What a torture," she wrote later about Louis XIV, "to be obliged to amuse a man who is unamusable." Inevitably in such circumstances questions of precedence assumed an importance devoid of all reality. Had they observed the look that the King gave Mme. de Torcy, wife of the Foreign Secretary, when she had the audacity to seat herself upon a tabouret reserved for a duchess? Who would be accorded the apartment vacated in the Château by the death of the Duc de Chevreuse? . . . Who was on the list of those to be invited next month to Marly? And was it true that the Chancellor on his last visit had been given the honour of the "*pour*"? The latter distinction was the most absurd of all; even Saint-Simon admits that it was foolish to attach such vast importance to so small a matter. For what did it amount to? Namely whether the intendant or billeting officer at Marly wrote the words "*pour M. le Duc de St. Simon*" in white chalk upon his bedroom door: or whether he did not.[4]

Yet the episode between Monsieur d'Orléans and La Rochefoucauld (like all the issues raised by Nicolson) seems to have been taken very seriously by the entire court, and not merely out of boredom. As an increasing number of scholars maintain, following the pioneering work of Elias and Emmanuel Le Roy Ladurie, neither the rituals of court life nor their consequences should be taken as mere trivialities.[5] Thus, as Saint-Simon tells it, to most people the king's action seems to have appeared dangerous and worthy of blame—as if something vital was being compromised.

We are indeed witnessing an agitation provoked by a real and weighty, even critical matter. To Monsieur d'Orléans, Louis XIV's decision to remove him from a position of privilege implied a disgrace of unsuspected proportions. To La Rochefoucauld, it provided a no less unsuspected social benefit, one that he could not possibly have refused. To the court in general, it was an indication of the vulnerability of the system. The king's measure had the potential to shake the assumptions of court society to its very foundations.

The story provides a telling glimpse into the infrastructure of social relations that, by the end of the seventeenth century, the *res civile* had attained in the one country where its absolutist tendencies developed the most: France. It draws attention to the force of the practices of royal centrality and to the power of grace and of its mirror image, disgrace. It reveals the extent to which the infrastructure had solidified into a complex of rigid behaviors that not even the king could break. Alternately, and as a direct consequence of its rigidity, it reveals the frailness of a system which any little deviation, any abuse of power alien to its pragmatics, can shatter.

Honnêteté
The Cosmological Metaphor

The emergence of a specifically French word for the behaviors associated with courtiership during the earlier parts of the seventeenth century, *honnêteté*, reveals the growing objectification of the pragmatics of grace in France at the time. Seventeenth-century French men and women indubitably subscribed to the notion that a person of note should first and foremost be of high civility. But it was not just civility, or grace, that the men and women of the court, or those pretending to belong to the court, sought. To them, perfection consisted in achieving *honnêteté*, and their deepest aspiration lay in becoming an *honnête homme* (or, we can assume, *une honnête femme*).

It was certainly no accident that one of the most popular books on the topic published in France during the first half of the century, and arguably the most influential, was called *L'honneste-Homme ou l'Art de Plaire à la Court* (1630).[6] Written by Nicolas Faret, a member of a bourgeoisie that seems to have been growing forever, the book appears to have spoken to the men and women of post-Renaissance France with particular force. According to Maurice Magendie, it was published at least six times between 1630 and 1640 and was regularly reedited up to 1681.[7] This last date is significant, for when the infrastructure attained its utmost rigidity by the end of the century, and a new pragmatics, oblivious of royal centrality, began to gain force, the fortunes of *L'honneste-Homme* were bound to change. It was to be strongly criticized, its vision of civility ridiculed, and its prescriptions deemed a paragon of falsehood.

On the surface, *L'honneste-Homme* would seem to be little more than an awkward copy of the *Cortegiano*. Extensive passages in *L'honneste-Homme* seem to have been copied from the Italian work, sometimes literally, sometimes with minor, irrelevant transformations. This is not surprising, for Faret's manual is a continuation of, not a departure from, Castiglione's. Faret's portrait of the *honnête homme*,[8] for example, derives almost completely from Castiglione's courtier. Like the ideal courtier, the *honnête homme* is to be of noble origins and, above all, a man of arms, strong and nimble yet not too big or corpulent—lest he be vulgar. He must honor women and serve his prince. And he must always act gracefully, avoiding affectation, leaving no trace of effort whatsoever. Grace, Faret writes, is the greatest human attribute. It is a gift that no art can teach. It is a virtue of such excellence that it shines like a beam of majestic glory.[9] Be moderate, wrote Castiglione; be moderate, writes Faret. Serve your prince, wrote the Italian; serve your prince, repeats the Frenchman.

And yet, if at times *L'honneste-Homme* seems no more than a rewording of the *Cortegiano* (a fact that did not pass unnoticed by Faret's contemporaries), the differences between the two books are nevertheless remarkably significant.

Consider the opening passage of *L'honneste-Homme*, in which the idea of royal centrality not only attains full metaphorical expression but, by virtue of being at the beginning of the book, sets the parameters for understanding the text as a whole:

> If ambition does not entirely shape the Courts of Princes, at the least we may say that it inflates them beyond all proportion, oftentimes making Sovereigns hate their own glory, and find the pomp that environs them intolerable. The natural desire which all men have to attain honors and riches engages them insensibly in this goodly confusion, and there are few [who] are wise enough to avoid being surprised by this agreeable disease amidst so many objects that transmit it. Princes and great men are around the king like goodly stars which receive all their splendor from him, but who confound all their brightness in this great light; and although their brightness does not appear but when they are remote from him, it is never vivid, nor full of glaze, but when this first fountain of glory spreads out and distributes into them like certain beams of its magnificence. The greatest part of the meaner sort consume themselves near this fire, rather than being warmed by it, and Fortune who takes delight to display upon this theater the most remarkable tricks of her malice and lightness, makes a sport at the ruin of a thousand ambitious men to raise only one to the top of the precipice, which she prepares for all those [who] suffer themselves to be blinded with her favors.[10]

The king, source of all splendor; center of the universe, around whom everyone circles; spring of light from whom all people receive their glow— royal centrality could hardly be expressed in more eloquent terms. The king is like a sun, Faret tells us years before Louis XIV is anointed as the Sun

King, the men and women of distinction turning like heavenly bodies around him. Noble people can come close to him and receive his grace. Others, unless helped by treacherous Fortune, burn up near him. All honor and glory derive from him, and from him, in a multitude of outreaching waves, social value spreads. And though he never replaces God as the ultimate source of goodness, he becomes God's sole mediator on Earth, his person combining both virtue and reason.

Now compare this perception of the king with Castiglione's view of an eminently human prince, of a person with weaknesses and shortcomings. And compare Faret's *honnête homme,* who receives all his grace from the king, with Castiglione's courtier, who, through his own grace, helps the prince to overcome his faults. The differences are indeed substantial and suggest the gradual consolidation and objectification of the absolutist forces at the heart of the infrastructure of social relations whose emergence we explored in the last two chapters. Their consolidation indicates that they have become increasingly dominant; their objectification means that, increasingly, they have acquired an objectlike existence, almost material in their solidity and inflexibility.

The stylistic differences between the books are suggestive. The *Cortegiano* is playful, elegant, literary, aristocratic in intention and spirit; in one word, it is "gracious." *L'honneste-Homme* is didactic, grave, artless, and though unquestionably well written, it is inspired by a rather practical spirit. Moreover, the *Cortegiano* was conceived as a series of conversations, as a game, a strategy that allowed Castiglione to discuss the most serious and potentially threatening subjects while maintaining the playfulness and subtlety of his text. *L'honneste-Homme* is a straightforward enunciation of behavioral principles interrupted only by regular yet never gratuitous digressions of a moral nature. As a consequence, Faret's text is devoid of the ambiguities that give the *Cortegiano* its unmistakable flavor. Constantly drawn into making clear-cut judgments, into making clear and coherent pronouncements on all topics of importance, Faret inevitably draws a more rigid picture of the infrastructure of social relations of court societies—a picture that seems to have appealed to his contemporaries, at least in France, with particular force.

Faret's transformed conception of the monarch thus attains the force of a logical premise.[11] It informs *L'honneste-Homme* throughout and constitutes the tenet in terms of which Faret in turn develops his conceptions of society and of the individual. The king, the center of the universe and sole source of light on earth, becomes as well the center of all order and of all action. The good of the *res civile*, Faret tells us, cannot be ;ived otherwise:

> When men unite their desires and wills in any one thing, there is great likelihood that they hope for support and advantage, and those things that they desire by common consent are most commonly such as they believe to be most noble, most perfect, and most useful. The consent they bring to obey one alone, is a sign that they hold this kind of government more excellent than all others: As in effect the true and lawful power of sovereigns is nothing but the tying and uniting of authority and justice for the preservation of the public good. And consequently, all those who have subjected themselves to this power aspire to approach it, and seek to maintain it with the hazard of their lives and fortunes. And therefore the good of the Prince is not separated from the good of the State, whereof he is the soul and the heart as well as the head: And the good of private men is not considerable in the general, but as it is profitable to the Prince, from whom alone they expect all the good and evil which is dispersed in the body of the monarchy.[12]

Then, echoing Castiglione, he adds,

> This being true, and it being likewise true that everything tends to an end as to the fullness of its perfection, what more worthy object can a wise courtier have, than the honor to serve his Prince well, and to love his interests more than his own. It is the only mark he should propound unto himself: All the rest are false and deceitful, and degenerate either into bareness or malice.[13]

There is no hesitation here: the service of the king and the good of the public form one unseverable unity. And this unity has come into being not only through an act of God, but because, as the most prominent political philosophers of the time argued,[14] such an arrangement embodies, in its own right, the best form of government. Men voluntarily defer their will to the authority of the king, Faret tells us in what we cannot fail to recognize as a prefiguration of the *Leviathan,* and the king voluntarily submits his to the needs of the "common good"—a good, that is, that receives its ultimate, organic expression in the person of the king.[15] Therefore, the most genuine desire of an *honnête homme,* Faret maintains, is to stand as close as possible to the mainspring of light. It is to receive and contribute to the radiance of the state, to serve and love his prince above all else. That should be his only goal, his only hope of reaching true perfection.

Hyperbole apart, Faret, like Castiglione, is articulating an infrastructure of social relations configured in terms of royal centrality. And like Castiglione, he spells out a pragmatics that gives shape to that infrastructure and provides it with its experiential grounds. In *L'honneste-Homme,* however, the reality that is still taking shape in the *Cortegiano* attains a fuller, more definite expression. Gone, indeed, are the ambiguities and open-endedness of the *Cortegiano,* its sense of danger and dialectics. Yet, if the subtleties of the earlier book are not to be found in *L'honneste-Homme,* it is because, by the first third of the seventeenth century, the subtleties, the plasticity, and the indeterminacy of Renaissance societies themselves seem, in effect, to have disappeared.

It is certainly no accident that the popularity of Castiglione's work started to fade during that period, at least in France. Translated twice, reprinted a total of eight times, the *Cortegiano* seems to have been a popular and, as its repute among the French suggests, influential book for most of the sixteenth century. Then, in 1592, the reprints stopped, not because Castiglione had ceased being relevant, but because thereafter his influence was to be felt only indirectly, as if something about the *Cortegiano*'s original formulations was no longer right—as if society had changed, and the book's ideas no longer applied with the same force. And indeed, as the *res civile* established itself, what was still forming during the 1530s had by the 1630s grown into a patterned and solid complex of social and political practices. What was a budding form of exercising power had become a system in full flower.

The Transformations of Violence

This change is visible in Faret's treatment of the principle of *mediocritas,* the golden rule that takes in *L'honneste-Homme* a structural, formal dimension absent in the earlier manuals. On the surface, again, little seems to have changed. Be not too much yet not too little, avoid the extremes of behavior, Faret advises, and nothing particularly new seems to emerge. Still, consider his admonition regarding quarrels:

> As there is no man which is not jealous of his reputation, especially in matters of his profession, how much more ought a gentleman be moved for that which concerns his Arms, which are the true marks of nobility? Herein he ought to be punctilious: For, as the honesty of a woman having been once tarnished with some blem-

ish, which can never be restored to its first purity: So it is impossible that the reputation of a soldier, having been once blemished with some base action, can never be well repaired, but there will remain something to reproach him: Likewise in occasions of honor, as in great commands at war, it is not permitted to err twice. But this point is so delicate, as most young men, either for want of experience, or by too much heat, and others either for want of judgment, or some capricious humor, lose themselves by this wretched course. Hereby we see daily that divine laws are profaned, that the authority of ordinances is violated, and that the clemency of our victorious monarch is sometimes forced to yield unto his justice.[16]

Now note the formalization of violence implied in Faret's advice:

The most healthful remedy that I can find for this mischief, which may be termed incurable hereafter, if this cure be not put in the number of the King's miracles, is in my opinion to learn the knowledge of quarrels in time, whereof they have made a kind of science by refining them much. Most of those which precipitate themselves into this brutish fury, do it most commonly for fear they should not do enough, in the ignorance and incertitude wherein they find themselves, whether they be obliged to come to this extremity or not: by being ignorant of the degrees of offense which deserve these bloody satisfactions, we see nothing but examples of extravagance in these quarrels, and not one beam of true honor which is the most precious treasure of Nobility.[17]

Faret speaks in these passages of the widely followed practice of dueling.[18] A person's honor, he tells us, cannot be tarnished even once without a definitive loss of social standing. Honor, that most estimable of goods, must be jealously defended, and resorting to arms—a sign of nobility, Faret makes patently clear—is the proper means to achieve satisfaction.

Faret's integration of loss of honor, reparation through arms, and nobility is important, for it highlights the extent to which duels involve an assault on a person's claims for inclusion within the collective self of the *res civile*. In situations leading to dueling, the dishonor does not come from an action of the king but from the action of another member of the collective self. Reparation through arms, therefore, involves a reaffirmation of self-worth through the successful use of the symbolic capital by means of which the aristocracy fashions itself. This martial dimension of the nobility is not, as many scholars have argued, a means for a useless and obsolete group of people who have lost all sense of meaning to "reinvigorate itself," as V. G.

Kiernan suggests regarding duels.[19] It is a means by which the civil powers constructed themselves, and in whose exercise they reproduced themselves as a collective. For an aristocrat to have his honor violated represents, as Faret is well aware, a challenge of the utmost consequence. The need of the offended to restate his filiation to the collective self becomes essential, and the use of arms, axiomatic.

This does not mean that the practice met with no reservation or resistance. To kings, it represented a double threat to their authority, and most monarchs outlawed dueling as early as the sixteenth century—without great success. Internal conflicts imperiled monarchical authority not only because they opened sites of aggression that eluded the control of the crown and escaped the well-oiled machinery of royal centrality; they also jeopardized royal authority by upsetting the monarchs' hold on symbolic power, because the reaffirmation of self inherent in a duel hindered a king's control of symbolic capital. To the aristocracy as a group, in turn, such conflicts were the seeds of the chaos that the *res civile* had managed to eliminate, and thus endangered its sense of collective self. Moreover, the act of personal affirmation represented a threat to the collective control of that self and, as for the crown, of symbolic capital. For, if disregarded, such acts of self-affirmation threatened to escape the fashioning powers of the collective: the collective was in danger of no longer shaping the expressions of the personal.

The formalization and ritualization of dueling to which Faret refers in the preceding passage follow from these multiple points of reservation. Faret is fully aware of its dangers and warns his readers of its potential consequences. Men sometimes provoke others for no good reason, he cautions, and quarrels develop where none is warranted. The justice of the king is then put in jeopardy, and honor, "the most precious treasure of Nobility," is inevitably tarnished and devalued. Nothing is more foolish and evil than the "senseless" and "capricious" recourse to violence, which should not be confused with the honorable practice of dueling. For, when justified, the practice was honorable, and as François Billacois shows, most aristocrats seem to have accepted it as a normal element of their way of being.[20] As Faret makes patently clear, duels are a form of violence exercised for a specific purpose, regulated by specific rules. They involve a "science," a doctrine based on a rationale that one has to learn and apply. This specifies the boundaries of offensive behavior, determines degrees of injury and, to each wrong, attaches a method of retribution. Dueling is proper only as a response to the most blatantly insulting acts, and both offended and

131

offender are compelled to follow the strictest of protocols.[21] In the process, the aristocracy spreads into the personal. In ritualizing the act of self-affirmation, the collective shapes that act and maintains control over symbolic capital. In the process, too, the act is kept within the confines of royal centrality, for it takes its place within an order of which the king is the center.

But the formalization and ritualization of violence also point at the formalization and structuration of *mediocritas*. They suggest the transformation of *mediocritas* from a flexible and highly malleable behavioral principle into one that, like the other aspects of the infrastructure of social relations in whose shape the *res civile* developed, becomes increasingly fixed, rigid, and objectlike. Such forms are external to any one person yet are formative of the inner self of every person. These forms remind us of Durkheim's "social facts,"[22] except that the phenomenon that I am examining suggests a historical understanding of "social facts," according to which social facts arise from the consolidation and objectification of an infrastructure of social relations. Whatever becomes "factual" is a consequence of a consolidation of power and embodies that power.

The Logic and Practice of Royal Centrality
The Behavioral Rationale of Royal Centrality

Following the thesis advanced by Maurice Magendie in 1925, most of the critical literature has tended to see *L'honneste-Homme* as a masterpiece of flattery whose only purpose is to teach how to deceive, how to manipulate others in order to gain favors. The idea is bluntly expressed by Jean-Pierre Dens in his study of the aesthetic aspects of *honnêteté*. "Faret's *honnête homme*," writes Dens,

> is above all an arriviste, a person who only seeks to climb the social hierarchy; his plebeian origins, his want of wealth compel him to please the king, hoping to gain some favors in return. It would be useless to look in this book, conceived as a vade-mecum, for a general discussion on the nature or on the principles of *honnêteté*; the concern for the immediate prevails over any sort of philosophical consideration. From this perspective the art to please is reduced to the art of getting on.[23]

Likewise, discussing the differences between Faret and Castiglione, Domna C. Stanton states, for example,

While he recognizes the importance of noble birth, Faret insists that a person of lowly origins can become intimate with the great. The military remains the only valid profession, but only because it can lead to honor, renown, and nobiliary status. . . . He gives lip service to disinterested learning and reduces the courtier's knowledge to those modish subjects which can further his social ambitions. . . . Although faithful to Castiglione's precepts on politeness, consideration, modesty, and adaptability, Faret ignores the art of conversation. And rather than a "perfect friend," this *honnête homme* will have a henchman or public relations man to pave his way at court.[24]

What was in Castiglione a delicate aestheticism, Stanton claims a few pages later, has been reduced by Faret to a mere "strategy of social arrivisme."[25]

Admittedly, the idea of monarchy that Faret presents in the opening lines of *L'honneste-Homme* may appear to be a piece of vacuous glorification, or pure, self-interested flattery. This impression is heightened when we consider some of the more concrete instructions set forth in the book: how to gain friends, or how to earn an entry to a ball, or to the following of a person of note, or to the palace—or why one needs to do all these things in the first place. Yet to argue that the book is no more than a manual on manipulation, or that Faret's opening image is sheer ideology, is to miss the extent of the consolidation of the infrastructure of social relations in general and royal centrality in particular. It is to miss the extent to which, at least in France, royal centrality had attained, among the higher classes, the same sort of solidity that ecclesias possessed for the men and women of the Middle Ages. It is to miss the extent to which the pragmatics of grace had come to mold, among the higher classes, people's experiences of self and other and had given form to what a moment ago seemed to us to verge on the absurd: their particular sense of themselves as subjects.

L'honneste-Homme is better understood as a book that answered real needs of real people—especially those belonging to the high bourgeoisie and the new *noblesse de robe,* the actual public of *L'honneste-Homme*—as these were defined in France during the first half of the seventeenth century.[26] The desire to succeed should not be confused with arrivism, and for the men and women of early-seventeenth-century France who could aspire to it, success in court was a source of prestige and power. To gain favors, to negotiate the intricacies of royal centrality, to learn how to define oneself in relation to others who occupied a precise position in the configurations of royal centrality and opened or foreclosed channels of status and power, were not only normal but necessary in order to succeed. Thus, when Faret tells a newcomer to seek

> a friend which is faithful, judicious and of experience, who may give us good directions and let us see, as in a picture, the customs which are observed, the powers which reign, the factions and parties which are in credit, the men which are esteemed, the women which are honored, the manners and fashions which are in course, and generally all the things which cannot be learned but upon the place,[27]

he does so because any other line of conduct would entail certain disgrace. In his own words, "These instructions are so much the more necessary, for that the errors which are committed in the beginning, are in a manner irreparable, and leave an opinion of us which many times is not forgotten until we are ready to retire both from the Court and the world."[28] The court is like a "stormy sea," radiant but dangerous, Faret warns, and like a good sailor, the inexperienced must show prudence and skill.[29] Therefore, too, the would-be courtier should know how to feign; for feigning allows a person to weather the storms and navigate through the dangers of the court. Whoever does not know how "to take his time, to press and defer to purpose, to yield and accommodate himself to occasions," Faret cautions, is often "injured." He becomes "a burden to all the world," and "makes himself insupportable unto himself."[30]

The book's opening passage perfectly expresses the behavioral rationale underlying the crystallization of royal centrality. The language is certainly exalted. From a late-twentieth-century perspective, Faret's formulation sounds definitely preposterous. Yet the borrowing of medieval imagery is not fortuitous; it expresses the appropriation of the hegemonic mechanisms of ecclesia by the machinery of civil power. The king has not merely become divine; he has come to occupy the place occupied by God in the cosmology of the Middle Ages. The king has become the center, concretely. A person's place in the social hierarchy has become a function of the distance that separates him or her from the monarch: of the number and caliber of the privileges that the king personally grants that person, or of the honor that attaches to him or her through the favors granted by people close to the king. It is no wonder, then, that, as the saga of Monsieur d'Orléans suggests, the people of the highest importance would vie for the most trivial favors of the king, for the honor of being closer to him, of sharing his intimacy, of being granted, however cursory, a smile.

This arrangement was, for the people of seventeenth-century France, or more precisely, for its nobility and high bourgeoisie, largely taken for granted. As is normal in every infrastructure of social relations, the system did generate its discourses of resistance.[31] Philibert de Vienne's *Le philosophe de court,* a book published towards the middle of the sixteenth century, for example, contained an ironic reading of the *Cortegiano* in which the pragmatics of grace was mercilessly mocked.[32] Many critics showed deep antagonism for its forms, and most people, including Saint-Simon, displayed a certain ambivalence towards it. Near the end of the seventeenth century, La Bruyère would deride its conception of the desirable. "The most honourable thing we can say of a man is, that he does not understand the court," he would write, "there is scarcely a virtue which we do not imply when saying this."[33] The fact that many did not recognize the irony in a text like Philibert's and took it, like Faret's, as perfectly sensible advice, suggests the extent to which royal centrality fashioned people's reality.[34] The very antagonism and irony suggest the force of the pragmatics of grace, for they reveal the extent to which its reality could not be ignored, and the extent to which it had to be opposed. Only when an alternative infrastructure of social relations, including a different concept of propriety, had gained enough weight would the antagonism and the irony become more than mere reaction. This alternative infrastructure, as I discuss below, was highly developed, though not dominant, by the time La Bruyère wrote his *Characters* and Saint-Simon composed his *Mémoires.*

The dominant infrastructure involved a network of social relations configured in terms of concentric lines of patronage. Both power and prestige circulated through these lines, and securing somebody's patronage—a tie that comprehended affective as well as instrumental dimensions—was essential in order to become part of the system.[35] The art of praise, as Bernard Bray has suggested, was an intrinsic element of patronage. It was taken totally for granted and was considered perfectly normal. And like the duel, it was governed by strict rituals.[36] A person rose and fell with his patron and the importance of patronage was beyond question: reality worked accordingly. Power and prestige did come from the strength of one's ties with one's patron, whose power and prestige in turn depended on ties with a person of higher prestige and power. Everything in turn attested to it: the splendor of the monarch, the daily routines of the court, the deepest desires of nobles and bourgeois alike, and the means by which prestige was obtained or advantages gained. The very organization of the cosmos proved it: the structure of the social was but an extension of the structure of the universe. And from all these, the men and women of the court developed a definite *raison d'être* without which absolutism itself could hardly have developed.[37]

The Formation of French Absolutism

The concept of absolutism denotes a dynamic reality, a tendency rather than a fixed structure of the practices of power as exercised in a certain place at a certain historical period. Indeed, the idea of a system in which the monarch exercises absolute authority has little connection with the political realities of European societies during the seventeenth century—and such an idea has become vastly discredited.[38] As Geoffrey Treasure put it, instead of a king or queen wielding complete control, the actual practices of power involved a ruler, surrounded by a small number of (relatively) loyal officials, trying to defend his prerogatives as best he could from crumbling under the weight of a powerful aristocracy. Instead of finding a nobility totally dependent on the king, we discover a class, however loose, working hard to maintain a measure of political autonomy. And this reality seems to have acquired a variety of forms in different places at different times. The concept of absolutism becomes useful only when applied to describe a condition in which the power-play between monarch and subjects favors the former, and only if this tendency attains certain institutional, although not necessarily fixed, expressions. In the words of David Parker, "Absolutism was always in the making but never made."[39] The importance of the pragmatics of grace in establishing and maintaining a balance in the king's favor is, I believe, evident.

The actual resolution of the power-play depended on purely historical circumstances, and it is on these grounds that we must understand the specific form the infrastructure took in different countries. The system that developed in France during the reign of Louis XIV came closer than any other to tilting the balance in favor of the crown—a system that, paradoxically, developed because of the original weakness, not the strength, of the king.

Louis was crowned King of France in 1654, at the age of fifteen, in a ceremony in which he committed himself to defend Catholicism and uphold the fundamental laws of France while receiving in return the power to cure by his touch those afflicted with scrofula.[40] One year earlier, for the traditional royal ballet of 1653, he had been dressed up as the Sun; an event whose meaning, twenty-three years after the publication of *L'honneste-Homme,* cannot be overstated.[41] For thereafter Louis was not only called the Sun-King but was treated as such by a legion of courtiers. He was represented so in a profusion of illustrations, and imagined as such in the lore of his subjects. Not until 1661, however, following the death of Mazarin, head of the French government since Louis XIII's death in 1643, did he begin to exercise the prerogatives and duties attached to his title.

As *L'honneste-Homme* attests, however, by the time that Louis XIV assumed power, absolutism was already highly developed. We may trace the formative lines of the absolutist state to the initial emergence of the *res civile,* back to the twelfth or thirteenth centuries, if not earlier. Not only did the monopolization of violence and the concentration of informational capital (the process leading to the emergence of a bureaucracy and a rational system of taxation) begin around that time, but the fashioning of symbolic capital, of a "civil capital," that is, and the struggle for its domination between the nobility and the monarch appear to have been already underway. Saint-Louis, king of France from 1236 to 1270, had already based his authority on an idea of divine will, and had placed himself at the center of any organizational principle.[42] Before the sixteenth century, however, the structures and practices of absolutism were in a largely embryonic state, like the infrastructure in general, and only during the sixteenth and seventeenth centuries, with the rest of the infrastructure, did these attain their full expression. As François Dumont put it, "French kingship was thus [during the late Middle Ages] absolute—in origin and in the way it developed— but it had to work to develop this character and realise its true nature."[43]

It was chiefly during the reign of Louis XIII (1610–1643), and more particularly during the government of Cardinal de Richelieu (1624–1642), Louis XIII's prime minister, that, as the infrastructure acquired the solidity reflected in Faret, the balance of power tilted in favor of the crown. For most of the second half of the sixteenth century, French royalty was a relatively weak institution.[44] Violence had diminished. The independent character of the feudal lords had been substantially curtailed. The social body was more of a unity than ever before. Civility had become an important element of the aristocratic mode of being in the world. Yet the major noble houses maintained considerable power, and large regions of the royal domain remained partially independent of the authority of the crown.[45]

The nobility remained divided, however. The so-called wars of religion that ravaged the country from 1562 to 1598, exacting a high toll both in lives and in financial capacities, were as much a struggle for power among contending factions of the nobility as a conflict over religious ideas. We cannot deny, however, the sincerity of the central figures in the strife regarding their faith. Antagonism between Catholics and Protestants had been growing steadily since the famed *affaire des placards,* in October 1534, when Parisian reformists mounted a sanguinary attack against the Catholic doctrine of the mass—an act that provoked a bloody repression from the Catholic authorities. Revulsion towards ecclesiastical patronage was unfeigned, and the spirit of the Reformation reflected unequivocally the state of mind of many people. But more than a collision over questions of principle, the wars of religion were an outgrowth of the power vacuum left at the royal court after the death of Francis I in 1547, and of the gradual monopolization and abuse of power by the Guise family under Francis's weak successors. This is not the place to recount the often turbulent events that led to the civil war. What should be stressed is that the political opposition against the Guises, deprived of the legitimate instruments of power, found in Protestantism—itself a target of governmental persecution—a movement in which their resistance could crystallize. Many aristocratic families that had been victimized by the Guises, including the Bourbon princes, joined the Huguenot cause, the "revolutionary cause," bringing to it both prestige and a considerable amount of material resources.

When the war came to a halt, there was no clear winner, however—except for the king. After more than thirty-five years of warfare, the noble houses were to find themselves financially and militarily exhausted. The cost of war, the inflation and the loss of productivity that it caused, combined to ruin many noble families and promote the growth of a new nobility composed mainly of the financial bourgeoisie on whose loans the embattled factions came to depend. The selling of offices, both by the crown and by poverty-stricken aristocrats, changed the composition of the nobility and created a *noblesse de robe,* a nobility of office-holders as opposed to the traditional, military-based nobility, or a *noblesse d'épée,* largely devoted to the king—a nobility for which the symbolic capital of the traditional nobility did not speak with the same force.

Once the king began to assert his power, the religious feud was rapidly settled, to the apparent satisfaction of all parties. Henry IV, the first of the Bourbon line to accede to the throne, was crowned in 1589. A Protestant, he was able to reclaim in a few years most of the territories controlled by the Catholic League. However, it was not until he abjured his faith that his authority was accepted by a majority of his subjects. Politically astute, the decision was to prove of the utmost importance. The Huguenots saw in Henry one of theirs; their claim for influence was legitimized in his person. And with the promulgation of the "Edict of Nantes" in April 1598, by which they gained the right to exercise their religion, much of the suspicion provoked by Henry's conversion was, in turn, overcome. The Leaguers, for their part, although never totally convinced of Henry's sincerity, secured for themselves significant political and economic privileges. More important, and of great symbolic import, they saw the king adopt their cause and the country pacified in accordance with the principles around which they rallied.

In terms of the constitutive relations of power, however, the king unquestionably gained the most. For the wars of religion weakened the old aristocracy, stimulated the emergence of a new nobility whose only allegiance was to the crown, and secured a growing concentration of resources around the king. This did not mean that the king's power became "absolute" in any real sense, or that the monarchy no longer manifested any sign of fragility—the events surrounding the Fronde should suffice to indicate the resistance to royal power among the aristocracy. But the outcome prompted the consolidation of royal centrality and the invigoration of its behavioral idiom, the pragmatics of grace: the infrastructural formations on which, as far as the struggle for power between the crown and the aristocracy was concerned, absolutism rested. All the honor that the ever-growing and increasingly important *noblesse de robe* could claim derived from an act of royal determination. No right of blood, no high descent warranted for these men and women any mark of distinction. For the high bourgeoisie, the new openness in the ranks of the aristocracy was a constant lure. Devoid of institutions able to give expression to its increasing power— influential, as it was, mostly at the local, not the national level—the bourgeoisie rallied around the figure of the king to gain a measure of self-importance. Finally, the closeness of the old aristocracy to the king gave it a way to assert its primacy over the multitude of new title-holders. It implied a higher claim of virtue and respect, a way to establish the proper boundaries between natural excellency and callow arrogance, between true honor and vulgar haughtiness.

And indeed, within the confines of the social elites—and *only* within those confines—royal centrality crystallized into a complex of practices that lent the entire system a feeling of authenticity. The king himself had an uncommon price to pay for it, however. "A prince can get everything he wants except the pleasures of a private life: only the charms of friendship and the fidelity of his friends can console him for such a great loss," wrote La Bruyère.[46] For if everyone revolved around him, he had to be always available for everyone to revolve around him; if grace derived from him, he had to be always ready to dispense it. The interests of the state passed before the interests of the king, or rather, the interests of state and king became one.

The King and the Court

The time and effort that the king spent on questions of protocol becomes fully understandable, for every one of his gestures was full of meaning, and was properly interpreted by the men and women crowding the palace. Who sat when, where, and in what kind of chair; who had priority over whom during processions; who was supposed to address him, and whom he was to address in given situations; how one was supposed to bow, when, and to whom; who accompanied the king, and at what distance one was sup- posed to stand from him—these were issues of major consequence for the people concerned, and any infringement of the rules, even when produced by royal decision, as was the case with M. d'Orléans, was taken as an offense of the gravest kind. We clearly understand the vexation of M. d'Orléans, then, as we understand the reluctance of La Rochefoucauld to forfeit his privilege.

The importance that Louis XIV came to give to these matters was con- siderable, and not merely to hold the attention of his courtiers, as is nor- mally argued,[47] but because they were essential in maintaining the solidity of the system as a whole. "Princesses of the Blood should not eat at the Grand Couvert," reports Saint-Simon. "After supper, they do not follow the King into his closet: such an honour is only for the sons, daughters, grandsons and grand-daughters of France. They are only invited on special occasions, wedding feasts in the royal family or other exceptional events."[48] To which Levron, for instance, echoing the opinion of Nicolson quoted at the beginning of the chapter, responds: "This rule was dated March 4, 1710. The Spanish War had brought France nothing but disappointment. The winter had been terrible, and the future was gloomy. At Versailles they froze in the galleries, and the silver plate was sent to the mint. Meanwhile, the greatest of Kings was deciding the precedence of the Princesses of the Blood."[49] The sarcasm of Levron's comment is not unusual, but, like Nicol- son's, it is certainly misplaced. True, the might of the kingdom was on the wane. The cold was relentless, and the grumbling of the people, not only at Versailles, was a source of disquiet. Surely, these were dangerous and inauspicious times. But to abandon the rigidity of protocol was as great a threat to the absolutist state as were the external situation or the discontent caused by the winter, for then the entire system in terms of which royal centrality took shape, an extraordinarily fragile system, would have been at stake.

This fragility is beautifully clear in the reaction of the court to the rift between M. d'Orléans and La Rochefoucauld. If anything, the reaction indicates that the court was not composed of a bunch of arrivists whose only goal was to please the king. Most of the court, in open opposition to the royal will, sided with M. d'Orléans. But the reaction also shows that the king, unlike a mighty despot, was bound to follow the statutes of his own making. "What God giveth, God taketh," goes the saying, but at least in this respect the king was no substitute to God. "What the king giveth, the king boundeth" would seem to be a more proper account of the realities of absolutism. For the king could hardly ignore his own law. The matter involved not simply letting go of rigid protocol, then. Any deviation, any serious lapse on his part tended to dilute the solidity of the hierarchical structure, to diminish its definitiveness, its presumption to truth, and would consequently weaken the people's faith in the system. It would shake the assumptions of court society to their very foundations.

Paradoxes of Royal Centrality
A New *Honnête Homme*

Like ecclesias, however, royal centrality contained the seeds of its own transcendence. Indeed, in a pattern that strongly resembles the fate of ecclesias, the same mechanisms that insured the strength of the system created the conditions for the development of a new infrastructure of social relations, one as alien to royal centrality and the pragmatics of grace as the *res civile* was to ecclesias. First, the insularity of the court, a phenomenon that allowed for the very definitiveness that I just discussed, left vast areas of social practice beyond the reach of monarchical hegemony—areas in which alternative discourses could flourish and a new infrastructure could develop and thrive. But the practices of court life also generated new ways of coming together, of defining oneself, and of relating to others. The very ontological grounds on which social relations were constituted seem to have undergone a new metamorphosis, yielding a foundation on which the aristocracy could redefine itself as a collective *exclusive* of royal centrality. The insularity of the court provided the spaces in which a new infrastructure could emerge, yet had no bearings on its essence. The new forms of coming together provided the ontological tissue that would constitute the new infrastructure.

We gain a first intimation of this new infrastructure in the unfolding of a new perception of *honnêteté* among the French aristocracy during the course of the seventeenth century, a perception that seems to escape the power of royal centrality altogether.[50] We learn about it in the writings of an aristocrat by the name of Antoine Gombaud, better known as the Chevalier de Méré, the person who was to become the most prominent herald of the new forms of the *honnête*. Méré introduces us to this new *honnêteté* in a short essay published in 1677 suggestively called "De la vraïe honnêteté," "On True *Honnêteté*," meaning, of course, that apparently there is a "false" *honnêteté*.[51] Genuine *honnêtes gens,* he explains,

> are those who possess a gentle Spirit and a sensitive Heart; they are dignified and civil; bold and unassuming, neither miserly nor ambitious, and are not eager to command, or to occupy the first place alongside the king: They have no other goal than to inspire happiness everywhere, and their main worry consists in no other thing than to deserve the respect of all, and to be loved by all.[52]

This, Méré makes clear, is indeed a new *honnêteté*. Although he recognizes the association made between *honnêteté* and the behaviors advocated by Faret (the association is implicit in the need to explain that the *honnêtes gens* are no longer those who "occupy first place alongside the king"), the word, he cautions, has developed a new meaning.[53] It is actually so new that only the French language has a word for it.[54] It refers to something still very tenuous and little known, so much so, he tells us, that the need arises to devote an essay to it.[55]

It so new and tenuous, in fact, that Méré is at pains to explain the substance of the new *honnêteté*. It consists in pleasing everyone equally, in instilling happiness in everybody, and in being loved by all—although "everybody," we can guess, does not necessarily mean "anyone." But Méré leaves its central element undefined, or rather, defines it as the undefinable, as a "*je ne sais quoi,*" which literally translated means "I don't know what." The *honnête homme* is that person endowed with a "*je ne sais quoi,*" and it is this *je ne sais quoi,* we are told over and over, that makes all the difference between true and false *honnêteté,* or between true worth and the admittedly essential yet insufficient mastery of politeness. We could be perfectly courteous, Méré tells us, but without a "certain something" that allows us to go beyond the merely urbane, we could never lay claim to true distinction.[56]

The distancing from royal centrality goes well beyond stating its irrelevance to the new *honnêteté*. Nothing, Méré asserts, no God, no king, should be placed between person and person. This further dimension emerges, for example, in the singular meaning that Méré gives to "happiness," about whose importance he leaves little doubt: it is, simply, "the end-goal of everything we undertake."[57] Anything that does not contribute to happiness, however worthy in appearance, entails a "false *honnêteté*." Even the virtues should be sought only in so far as they help to make us happy.[58] And what is happiness? Méré answers this question eloquently:

> It seems to me that at its most perfect honnêteté requires that we communicate with life, and even that we plunge into it, and I am convinced that we have to take the world into consideration in all our actions, including our minutest doings, as far as decency permits. That which languishes, doesn't gladden, and when nothing affects us, even though we are not, we always appear to be dead. The coming of winter saddens us, because it promises to extinguish so many enjoyable things that grow on earth; and the return of spring, which resuscitates them, seems to resuscitate us; and charms our senses.[59]

Happiness exists only in the gratification of the senses. It is a fruit of immediacy. To love and to be loved, to evoke feelings of sympathy, to be able to connect in a way that presupposes no mediation—that is, for Méré, the core of the *honnête*. Nothing, in effect, neither God nor king, should be placed between two individuals. Only the direct gratification of self and other is to be valued, and our main care should lie precisely in the cultivation of our "selves."

Here, in fact, Méré articulates an extreme version of an idea of self current among the French nobility at the time—extreme in two opposite ways.[60] On the one hand, Méré's *honnête homme* is a primarily sensual person for whom feeling and the discrete experience of the immediate determine the contours of being. As a concept, it conveys the idea of a self without social moorings, a self that not only can develop in different directions depending on the vicissitudes of one's biography but can take shifting, contradictory, multiple forms. This is the fictional self that authored the *Lettres Portugaises,* or the self consumed by immediacy represented, half a century after Méré, in the persona of Manon Lescaut.[61] In Manon, indeed, we have a person with an unquenchable desire to live, to feel, to enjoy to its utmost whatever life has to offer. Her behavior—inconsistent, unstable, multiple in the simultaneity of contradictory emotions it comprehends— is governed by a literal hunger for pleasure. Nothing comes between her cravings and her person, not even death, and for the narrator of the story, Manon's yearning becomes a value as powerful as any.

Yet this purely sensual being takes in Méré a determinedly positive expression. His *honnête homme* is, in a sense, a hedonist who has achieved perfect stability and coherence and merges fully with the surrounding society. He is a hedonist who channels his momentum into a new order of social relations, one in which the frames of the social body take a shape conducive to the constitution of a class. The rhetoric of love that pervades Méré's essays is significant, for this is a rhetoric that speaks, precisely, of an unmediated bond between people, of a merging of a plurality of individuals into one singularity.[62] The essence of the *honnête homme*, Méré says repeatedly, consists as much in loving as in inspiring love in others, a quality that he contrasts to the ideals of behavior of the old *honnêteté*. "As the world perceives it," writes Méré in an obvious allusion to the traditional conception of the *honnête*, "what is called *to be an habile homme* seems to be a quality that manifests itself only in the guise of power; yet it consists much more in finding the happiness of life, which depends greatly on being loved by the people we cherish."[63] People's practices, that is, should no longer be geared towards success in negotiating the centripetal webs of power. The oppositional and divisive pursuit of honor that characterizes the social in the absolutist society should be set aside. Instead, Méré urges, practice should affirm the unity of the group. It should promote fellow-feeling and, through the forging of emotional bonds, should breed a true sense of community and corporatism.[64]

Méré puts aside not only royal centrality, but the entire pragmatics of grace. For in the context of the new practices, the pragmatics of grace becomes irrelevant as a way of dealing with the world. Moreover, its terms are alien to the new practices. They are inconceivable as a way of acting from within the realities that the new practices generate—inconceivable in the most literal sense of the word. The pragmatics of grace engenders a centripetal web of social relations like the one at the core of absolutism. It exists by virtue of that engendering and is impossible outside of it. Outside of it, indeed, the pragmatics of grace becomes both unthinkable and existentially spurious—if not entirely absurd. No one has any reason to think in its terms, and no grounds for conceiving its terms.

Ontological Metamorphoses

The emergence of a new order of social relations among the French aristocracy becomes visible, for example, when we focus on the intensity of interaction that characterized court life. In purely spatial terms—living much of the time close to each other, sharing the same routines, meeting at almost every occasion, having to overcome, together, the very real boredom of life at court—the multitude of courtiers that crowded the king's palace were literally forced to bear one another's company for long periods of time. Moreover, the principal aim of a courtier was to be seen, to woo and be wooed. To be present was a must: "A man who leaves the court for a single moment renounces it forever," wrote La Bruyère; "the courtier who was there in the morning must be there at night, and know it again next day, in order that he himself may be known there."[65] These were certainly appropriate times for scheming, for concocting all kinds of intrigues that would hopefully yield a little grace for oneself, or much disgrace for a foe—behaviors that, reasonably enough for the interests of the crown, tended to maintain, not reduce, the divisions within the nobility. Yet at the same time, powerful and intricate networks of association developed, tying, to a certain extent, everybody to everybody else, creating a unique social frame in the shape of which the nobility as a class (a concept whose specific meaning I discuss below) attained a measure of concretizaton.

It is this particular body of social interactions that constitutes what we call "the court." And it is precisely this realization that allowed La Bruyère, the critic of court life, to identify court and theater as one. For to La Bruyère the role of the courtier is nothing else but to participate in the web of interactions that form the court. To him, life in the princely palace is little more than a vast, unchanging play:

> The world will be the same a hundred years hence as it is now; there will be the same stage and the same decorations, though not the same actors. All were glad to receive favours, as well as those who were grieved and in despair for boons that were refused, shall have disappeared from the boards; others have already made their entrances who will act the same parts in the same plays, and in their turn make their exits, whilst those who have not yet ap-

peared one day will also be gone, and fresh actors will take their places. What reliance is there to be placed on any actor?[66]

The metaphor is reminiscent of Cervantes and Shakespeare. Like Don Quixote comparing life and death with the entries and exits of the theater, like Sancho drawing a parallel between the world and a game of chess, like Jaques seeing in the course of a person's life as many representations as ages, yet always one at a time, La Bruyère sees the courtier as a dramatic character. Like the characters in Cervantes or Shakespeare, the courtier is someone enclosed by the reality of the play, enacting only one part—a part that is his only by virtue of a circumstantial coincidence. But there is one important difference between La Bruyère and the earlier authors: the essence of the play has changed. Whereas Shakespeare or Cervantes conceived the play in essentially substantive terms, La Bruyère conveys an image in which the formal qualities of social relations, in which the actual networks of social ties, that is, become the real core of the play. For in the theater of the court, La Bruyère suggests again and again, the content of one's role is not defined by what circulates through the networks—for example, grace—but by the very act of participating in them.[67] The play is equivalent to the nets of associations that people weave, and its plot consists of the acts by which these associations are woven.

La Bruyère thus gives expression to the same type of group formation and the same forms of coming together that we observed in Méré. Or, more correctly put, each develops a discourse that is very different from the other's, yet both originate in the same infrastructure of social relations and give expression to the same foundational properties. This is an infrastructure whose configuration takes the shape of a network of monads with no center, a network marked by the very dispersion of its elements. The absence of something that circulates from a central point precludes the possibility of a concept of centrality, and of a corresponding pragmatics. Instead, an infrastructure with multiple points of attraction and activity emerges, points that obviously are no longer held together by the same property that held the former system together—grace, again. Whatever it is that now ties the elements of the network together no longer derives from a source external to the network or the individuals themselves. In La Bruyère, the multiplicity of points is left devoid of any cementing property other than that inherent in the act of sociability itself, in the evanescent and ultimately unsubstantial moment of actual interaction. To Méré, however, this property is something that belongs to every single individual, to every single *honnête homme.* It is as evanescent and insubstantial as for La Bruyère, undefinable, yet something for which the rhetoric of love, a rhetoric of attachment *par excellence,* seems perfectly appropriate.

What emerges, in La Bruyère and Méré alike, is the conception of a group that exists mainly by virtue of the informal ties that develop among its members. It is a group without contents, without a clear notion of itself besides that of being distinct, of composing a unique, closed whole within which all its members are connected. That its expression hinged mostly upon this sense of difference should come as no surprise, then. For it was out of a feeling of social exclusiveness that the nobility delineated to itself a territory of meaning that clearly separated it from the rest of the population—from the wealthy yet despised bourgeoisie in particular. This phenomenon has been much discussed in the literature. It manifested itself in the uses of language, the guises of fashion, the forms of leisure, tastes in art, the general ways of deportment—traits that, besides, were common to the nobility of Europe as a whole.

Quoting from the *Letters* of Lord Chesterfield, which I discuss in chapter 7, William Doyle summarizes the point neatly. Doyle writes of the international character of the aristocracy and evokes, at once, both the structural and the cultural dimensions of noble exclusiveness. "Never before had the qualities expected of noblemen been so universally agreed on," he writes.

> Europe was dominated by an international aristocracy, whose passports were connections and good breeding. Travellers went armed with sheaves of letters of recommendation which opened up society along their route by introducing them to acquaintances of their acquaintances. The Bohemian nobility residing in Prague, wrote an early-eighteenth-century traveller, "are Polite and civil to Strangers, whom they know to be Persons of Quality." And a person of "quality" normally marked himself out, quite apart from the letters he carried, by certain standards of accepted conduct. "You may possibly ask me," wrote the earl of Chesterfield, "whether a man has it always in his power to get into the best company? and how? I say, Yes, he has, by deserving it; provided he is but in circumstances which enable him to appear upon the footing of a gentleman . . . good breeding will endear him to the best companies." Again, however, the criterion was a metropolitan one: . . . "There should be in the least, as well as in the greatest parts of a gentleman, *les manières nobles* . . . attend carefully to the manners, the diction, the motions of people of the first fashion . . . the language, the air,

the dress, and the manners of the Court, are the only true standard
. . . for a man of parts, who has been bred at Courts, and used to
keep the best company, will distinguish himself, and is to be known
from the vulgar, by every word, attitude, gesture, and even look."[68]

The intention was obvious: to establish a clear separation between gentility and *vulgus,* to promote a singularity of manner among the elite in order
to raise a tangible barrier between the *haut* and the *bas monde.* And in so
doing the nobility impressed itself with a profound sense of self, with an
exclusive bond of collective feeling, with a definite capacity to kindle experiences of an empathic nature. This is the context in which we must understand Méré's "love": as a cementing property that pertained to the aristocracy alone, and for whose actuality nothing but the very self of each
aristocrat was necessary.

The type of group that we see taking shape here is certainly not a social
class as Marx defined it. Nor is it simply a status-group as Weber formulated
that concept. Although the presence of a way of life exclusive to the aristocracy points at obvious affinities with Weber's status-group, the key structural characteristic of this type of group formation is closer to what Durkheim perceived as the basis of a solidarity structure.[69] What I call a "class"
refers indeed to the development of a specific type of solidarity structure,
of a specific way of coming together and relating to one another. This is
clearly not a solidarity based on relations of interdependence, and although
once again it is reminiscent of mechanical solidarity,[70] it once again involves, as we have just seen, something of a completely different order: a
coming together produced by participation in a network, a relationality
constituted by the series of links that compose the network.

Two characteristics of the social formation that ensues allow us to speak
of this particular solidarity structure in terms of a class. First, the suggestion
that its defining quality consists in its being a group in and for itself, and
that this quality in turn defines the identity of its members, points at the
cementation of the aristocracy, or more properly of the individuals who
compose the aristocracy, into a corporate body—into a unified albeit not
necessarily homogeneous or harmonious social entity that allows the aristocracy to organize and exert power independently of the king.[71] My use
of the word *cementation,* a word that conveys an act of attachment, is not
fortuitous. For here we are not witnessing a coalescence of bodies and psyches similar to the one we observed during the Middle Ages, a condition
for which questions of attachment are cognitively extraneous. We are seeing

a binding together of individual, separate selves, each with a relatively well-delineated corporeal and psychological space, whose attachment to one another becomes, therefore, an issue of practical consequences. Therefore, too, we see the importance and suitability of a discourse, like the discourse on love, able to give expression to a condition of total and unmediated attachment, yet one that at the same time does not nullify the personality of each individual.[72]

But as important as the cementation of the aristocracy into a corporate body for justifying a language of "class" is the suggestion that this particular way of relating and coming together provides, in the first place, a way for the aristocracy to realize its power. Indeed, as we shall see in detail in the next two chapters as I analyze the English case, just as the power of the monarch realizes itself in a structure of centeredness, the power of the aristocracy realizes itself, as a corporate body, in and through the very dispersion of elements at the core of the new infrastructure. And just as the power of the king is embodied in the practices and institutions of royal centrality, the power of the aristocracy will be a function of its success, as a corporate body, in giving practical and institutional expression to this dispersion. The term *class* is perfectly appropriate to denote the formation that ensues: I will indeed suggest that, provided with an economic rather than a fundamentally social character, the same infrastructure of social relations would be equally appropriate for the realization of the bourgeoisie as a social class.

We are no doubt also far from the emergence of a class like the one that we will see arising, about the same time, among the English aristocracy. But as we shall see, the difference between the two aristocracies can be attributed, precisely, to their differing success in giving institutional expression to this infrastructure. Inhibited by the strength of absolutism, in France the new infrastructure would remain long devoid of significant institutional expression. In England, however, the emergence of a class will take substantial form in the institutional frames of society, precisely because absolutism was weaker in England.

Institutional Insubstantiality and the New *Honnête Homme*

It is this absence of institutional substantiality among the French aristocracy that I suggest makes understandable the definition of the basic attribute of the new *honnête homme* in terms of a *je ne sais quoi*. At court, the new infrastructure coexisted with the old, men and women being in reality under the dual effects of grace and, however ethereally, class.[73] In a place like Versailles, the two incommensurable forms of coming together and relating to one another, royal centrality and the dispersed network of associations, were equally real and equally material in people's everyday lives. The shifting, contradictory, unstable self that we see portrayed in the literature of the time was also, in part, a consequence of such a duality of experience. But then not only the force and substantiality of royal centrality but also the practices that followed from the court's insularity were to make it impossible for the new infrastructure to attain any significant degree of institutional expression.

Guy Chaussinand-Nogaret's description of how the isolated character of the court worked as a protective layer around the king applies equally here. The isolation was certainly not physical. In material terms the court was open to almost everybody. To enter Versailles, it was enough to carry a sword, not too difficult a requirement, given that swords were leased at the palace gate.[74] But then one was a visitor at court. To belong, to be part of the intricate network of social relations in which the court was embodied was a different matter altogether, and only a small group of people really belonged. It was, to use Chaussinand-Nogaret's phrase, a "gilded ghetto," defusing all threats, helping to maintain the domination of the king and, by extension, inhibiting the materialization of any alternative to royal centrality.

> It was a frontier sealing off the crown from all contact with diversity, sheltering it from contamination, yet at the same time operating in a vacuum. It made the birth and development of opposition outside its own ambit ridiculous if not impossible. Opposition could only become effective at Court, and there everything was smothered, controlled, smoothed over. The Court of Louis XIV was a political edifice designed to neutralise any attempt to organise external opposition. It operated by centralising threats. Nothing must overflow. It was a system for neutralising dangerous forces which turned opposition into intrigue, a formula which turned bombs into squibs, political conflict into courtiers' games or harem conspiracies. The Court channeled, naturalised and neutralised opposition. The Crown watched over it, and was all the stronger in consequence.[75]

Under those conditions, the possibility of giving institutional form to the corporative tendencies of the aristocracy was virtually nil.

Outside of the court, at a distance from the reach of royal hegemony, the situation was different, yet the outcomes were still the same. Royal hegemony and the pragmatics of grace were obviously not confined to the court alone. Public spectacles and the living mythology of the king, for example, continued to impress in the collective consciousness of men and women throughout France a majestic image of the monarch, feeding the symbolic currency of the monarchy. And as we learned from Erasmus and della Casa, the pragmatics of grace was not limited to the palace or the presence of the king. "Sometimes people go to court only to come back again, so that, on their return, they may be taken notice of by the nobility of their county or by the bishops of their diocese," warned La Bruyère.[76] The very existence and popularity of Faret's treatise attests to the permeation and power of grace. Yet the insularity and sense of exclusiveness of the court limited the reach of royal centrality, and it was only within the court's confines, where the presence of the king helped substantiate its practices, that royal centrality attained concrete expression in people's lives.

In the multiplicity of spaces in which an alternative to royal hegemony could arise, however, the crown exercised power through coercion and censorship, and not only with regard to the new practices of the aristocracy but to any flurry of deviation from its authority. The crown regulated and controlled the press, publishing, artistic production, dress codes, food consumption, restaurants, coffee houses, civic gatherings, public spectacles, and so on. Thus it hindered the growth of any practice alien to its symbolic capital and, by extension, interfered, although not always successfully, with the development of alternatives to its power, symbolic or otherwise.

For even here the limits of royal power outside of the court became apparent. Take the example of itinerant players, an important source of cultural resistance in seventeenth-century France—an example that also helps illustrate the range of alternative practices fermenting at the time.[77] Since their performances were based for the most part on improvisation, there was no text that could be censored. Since they acted on improvised stages, there were no playhouses to close. And when the crown established a national troupe, the Comédie Française, that was given full monopoly over theater life, itinerant players overcame every single prohibition with a combination of wit and resourcefulness. When they were prohibited from performing real theatrical plays, they responded by staging representations made of unconnected *tableaux*. When they were forbidden to speak French during their performances—French had become the prerogative of the royal theater—the comedians reacted by using a jargon that could not be labeled French, yet was understood by everybody. When the crown banned all speech, the players produced out of their pockets banners with the written dialogue; those in the audience who were literate read the texts aloud, and everyone was able to follow the action.

Devoid of solid institutional structures that could be effectively regulated, however, it was in the many restaurants, bars, cafés and, most notably, in the erudite, fashionable salons presided over by aristocratic women, that royal control was at its weakest. The authorities could restrict the opening hours of restaurants and cafés. They could place interdictions or close them almost at will. They could limit what could be served, and how. They could, to a point, monitor conversation. Yet they could not regulate the forms of social intercourse of the aristocrats and bourgeois who frequented them. As for the salons, they remained virtually beyond any direct royal control. And there, as in the more private spheres in which the nobility used to socialize (at their parties, reunions, and retreats), the alternative infrastructure could freely flourish—freely, that is, as long as these sites remained with little formal structures over which the crown could exercise control.

Within the court, then, the power of royal centrality made the institutionalization of the corporative tendencies of the aristocracy virtually impossible. Outside of it the aristocracy could give expression to these tendencies, yet this expression was made possible, precisely, by the lack of institutionalization of the new forms of coming together and relating to one another.

Méré's definition of the basic attribute of the new *honnête homme* as an undefinable *je ne sais quoi*, I suggest, echoes the indefiniteness of the new collective self of the aristocracy. It is not difficult to characterize the idea of a *je ne sais quoi* as irrational, as a notion so unrelentingly opposed to discursive analysis that nothing can be said about it—for so it actually is, and that is how the men and women at the time seem to have understood it.

The person who came to closest to conveying the sense of the *je ne sais quoi* was actually not Méré but a churchman, Dominique Bouhours, better known as Père Bouhours, a man who despite his profession was one of the most exuberant and sought-after people of his day. And as Bouhours maintained, the *je ne sais quoi* is something that cannot and should not be explained.

Bouhours addressed the intangibility of the *je ne sais quoi* in his *Les entretiens d'Ariste et d'Eugène*, an extraordinarily popular book published in 1671, six years before Méré presented his more elaborate portrait of the new *honnête homme*, and to which Méré was clearly indebted.[78] At the beginning of the book's third chapter, Bouhours has his two characters, Ariste and Eugène, converse about the strong affection they feel for one another, bringing up the theme of love that would become so central in Méré. Theirs, notes Ariste, is a friendship that can be compared to love; for there is a *je ne sais quoi,* he tells his friend, that makes the sympathy that bonds them resemble the enchantments of love. At Eugène's request, Ariste explains what is, or rather what is not, this *je ne sais quoi:*

> It is something that is easier to feel than to know, answered Ariste. It would no longer be a je ne sais quoi if we were to know what it is: its nature is to be incomprehensible and inexplicable.
>
> Couldn't we say, asks Eugène, that it is an influence of the stars and a secret imprint of the astrological sign under which we were born?—We could certainly say such a thing, replied Ariste, and we can even say that it is the natural bent of the spirit, an instinct of the heart, an exquisite feeling of the soul for an object that moves it, a wonderful sympathy, like a kinship of the minds, to make use of the term of that lofty Spaniard, *un parentesco de los coraçones.*
>
> Yet by saying that and a thousand other things we say nothing. That secret imprint, that natural bent, that instinct, that feeling, that sympathy, that kinship are but beautiful words that the learned have invented to flatter their ignorance and deceive the others, after having first deceived themselves.[79]

The *je ne sais quoi* is indeed something beyond explanation, beyond language altogether. Its nature is mysterious, Bouhours tells us, and any attempt at describing it is doomed from the outset. Only its effects can be recognized and understood. This "certain something" is what makes, in the most literal sense of the word, the friendship between Ariste and Eugène: it is an inexplicable energy whose nature is to create a spiritual bond between equals. This too, the friends remark, is what gives *honnêteté* its fundamental character.[80] Bouhours extends the meaning of friendship to *honnêteté* and, as a consequence, *honnêteté* assumes an aspect similar to that of friendship. As later for Méré, it becomes a cementing faculty, an attribute invested with a *je ne sais quoi* that, although unintelligible, plays an unambiguous role in the formation of a social unit.

The tendency towards collectivism that we observed in Méré becomes more notorious; its vagueness, less ambiguous. The description of the concept as being entirely irrational is indeed on the mark. Like Faret's *honnête homme* in the same circumstances, from outside the new infrastructure the *je ne sais quoi* seems absurd. It appears at best as snobbism, at worst as an insidious stratagem of the aristocracy to keep its boundaries as impenetrable as possible. From the outside the corporative inclinations of the new *honnêteté* turn invisible, and all the talk about love, fusion, and "a wonderful sympathy" appears inane. Yet, seen from the inside, the imprecision of the new *honnêteté* has less to do with questions of rationality or irrationality, or with a will for closure, than with the imprecision at the level of reality itself. In a way we find in Méré and Bouhours the same type of ambiguity that we found, although far less markedly, in Castiglione—far less markedly because *Il Cortegiano* gave expression to a far more institutionalized infrastructure. In Méré and Bouhours we face an infrastructure that has not yet begun to solidify beyond the practices of sociability through which it has come into being and in the shape of which it exists. It exists in pure sociability, and this sociability, as Doyle surmised, becomes the essence of the new *honnêteté*, gradually replacing the military element in the collective self of the aristocracy.

An interpretation like Aldo Scaglione's, I suggest, projects this specific infrastructural modality over the entire development of social relations among the European elites in premodern Europe. It misses royal centrality almost completely and misrepresents the behaviors that follow it as abject and false. It is also bound to misrepresent the *je ne sais quoi,* for its role in the constitution of new infrastructure becomes, once again, invisible. Seen as a moment in a continuity, as a snapshot of something already formed, the *je ne sais quoi* indeed appears to be a simple strategy of closure, or plain snobbism—and so it will become when, during the late eighteenth and nineteenth centuries, it will be trumpeted as a sign of respectability and social excellence. But seen as an element of a discontinuity, of the emergence of something new, the significance of the *je ne sais quoi* becomes immediately visible. Its own indefiniteness fits the indefiniteness of the infrastructure of which it is a part, and which it helps generate.

Of course, with time the new infrastructure would gain substantiality and, given the force of French absolutism, would help produce a condition that was necessarily explosive. But this topic is beyond the scope of the present study. We turn now to an analysis of the English case, for this type of class-bearing infrastructure consolidated first in England, and there we can appreciate its practices. The contrast with the French case is indeed illuminating.

CHAPTER SIX

Paradoxes of the English Gentleman

There is nothing either good or bad, but thinking makes it so.
William Shakespeare, *Hamlet*

The Specificity of the English Experience

A VERY DIFFERENT development of the same infrastructural tendencies that we identified in Castiglione and Faret marked the genealogy
of social relations in England during the sixteenth and seventeenth centuries. As I suggested at the end of chapter 4, the infrastructure of social
relations that we saw emerging as a result of the affirmation of civil power
would develop in different directions and yield a number of alternative,
diverging futures. A future, even an ultimately discontinuous one, is always
a function of the conditions of possibility of a present; thus it always entails
a measure of continuity. To say that a future always involves a measure of
continuity, however, does not mean that all futures follow the same line
of development—nor, for that matter, that all futures are linear. Nothing
predetermines the actual forms into which an infrastructure consolidates.
These, it should become increasingly clear, depend on purely historical circumstances. And to the extent that a new power comes to affirm itself, the
linearity usually assumed to be a corollary of continuity in turn evaporates.

Neither the idea nor the pragmatics of grace were absent from the scene
of British civility. Although Faret's *L'honneste-Homme* had little influence
in England, Lorenzo Ducci's *Arte Aulica,* a book published in Italy in 1601
and translated into English six years later to great success, played in London
the role Faret's played in Paris.[1] Ducci's doctrine, the behaviors he advocated, his reasoning, were all similar to Faret's. Even more, in the *Arte
Aulica* the Castiglionesque became literally Machiavellian, and the world
that emerged from it was even more unambiguous than Faret's.[2] By the
beginning of the seventeenth century, England was governed by a well-
established monarchy, the heir of a long and, in contrast to the situation
in France, uninterrupted tradition of royal authority. The same power-play
between the crown and the aristocracy that we saw operating in France

operated in England, and the pragmatics of grace played an important role in the balancing act that ensued.[3] By the end of Elizabeth I's reign in 1603, the practices of royal grace had attained considerable importance, and their strict, parsimonious usage within and outside the court had become an effective instrument of power for the queen.[4] A century later the rituals of royalty were as present as ever, and as effective as ever in maintaining a mystique of exaltation among the masses. Yet as R. O. Bucholz's study of ceremonial during the reign of Queen Anne showed, their effects on the aristocracy had by then diminished considerably.[5]

Given the strength of royal centrality during the sixteenth and early seventeenth centuries, it is ironic that it was precisely an act of a powerful king, Henry VIII, that fostered the conditions for the future weakness of English absolutism. The decision to break with Rome, which during the 1530s made good political sense, was nevertheless to have some fateful, obviously unintended consequences. Lawrence Stone summarizes the positive effects of Henry's action for different sectors of the English population:

> [T]here is general agreement that the Reformation appealed to certain specific groups within sixteenth-century society. To princes, who found Lutheranism an ideal tool for state-building; to the more progressive urban oligarchs, who found the moralizing energy of Zwingli or Calvin a convenient instrument for the social control of their cities; to artisans and merchants in the newer trades who sought ideological support against an entrenched patriciate; to nobles seeking moral and religious justification for the transfer of church property to themselves and for taking over the administrative and ideological function of the clergy; to aristocratic wives, tormented by the futility of their idle and neglected lives, for whom the new doctrines at last seemed to offer some explanation for their existence; and lastly to the intellectuals, often minor clergy, monks, friars, or academics, who had lost all confidence in their role in the Catholic church and saw in the Reformed religion a more inspiring approach to the problem of salvation, and a faith with which they could make over the corrupt and worldly society in which they lived.[6]

Yet the decision was also to weaken the crown in altogether unpredictable ways. Carried out by dint of parliamentary statuses, Henry's decision had first the long-term effect of strengthening significantly the importance and legitimacy of the parliament—a political body that by definition was hostile to the absolutist tendencies of the crown. True, parliaments had played an active political role well before Henry, and not only in England. But the legitimacy that Henry's action conferred on the English parliament would become a powerful obstacle when, following the example of their continental counterparts, later British monarchs would try to strip the legislative assemblies of their powers.[7]

Moreover, the Reformation gave rise to a religious and political ideology that, once established, was to inhibit the independence of the monarchy and consequently thwart the movement towards absolutism. Usually associated with Puritanism, yet ultimately pertaining to Anglicanism as a whole, the central tenet of this ideology reclaimed for the Reformed churches the role of defenders of Christ.[8] It saw in the Protestant nations, and particularly in England, the army of the faithful waging the final battle against the Antichrist, incarnated in the person of the Pope. The monarch could lay legitimate claims to head this messianic army as long as he or she did not attempt to change the social order that grew out of the Reformation. Any attempt at change, especially if it was believed to challenge Protestant doctrine, was bound to turn the king or queen into an ally of the Antichrist—an accusation that in a period marked by religious ferment and unbridled fanaticism was not to be taken lightly.[9] Indeed, parliamentary opposition to Charles I was to crystallize during the 1630s around this ideology, reduced to its antipapist element, and under its banner, during the following decade, the population was to be mobilized.

But the full significance of this factor becomes visible only when we combine it with a third, which is from our perspective the most critical among the unintended consequences of Henry's shift to Protestantism. For the Reformation also promoted practices of multicenteredness and individuation evidently at odds with the provisions of royal centrality and grace. The two most salient doctrines advocated by Luther involved the idea of salvation by faith and the principle of priesthood for all believers. "A Christian man is the most free lord of all, and subject to none; a Christian man is the most dutiful servant of all, and subject to every one," wrote Luther in *On Christian Liberty* (1520), the work in which he formulated the essentials of his doctrine.[10] Luther sought to do away with the idea of mediation between believer and God underlying the corrupt practices of fifteenth-century Catholicism. In their relations to God, Luther asserted, men and women had to be conceived as individual beings, free from earthly interference, either ecclesiastical or civil. A person was subject only to God, and his or her one goal in life was to approximate Him, alone, through an individual act of faith. Only the gradations determined by faith existed in the cosmos; spiritual greatness was impossible without faith. Honor, glory, and grace, Luther preached, could neither be bought nor gained through good works. Nor could they be bestowed by an authority other than God. Honor was the fruit of faith, of the immanent presence of God in a person's being.

How such a doctrine fosters individuation is a question that needs no elaboration here. Starting with Max Weber and R. H. Tawney, the association has been amply discussed in the literature.[11] But Lutheranism also entailed a cosmology in which the unicentered, hierarchically mediated structure of the universe at the heart of the Castiglionesque definition of grace was replaced by a multicentered, unmediated vision. And since the world was a copy of the universe, society itself was conceived as multicentered. Its hierarchy had to answer to criteria other than princely grace. Any effort on the part of a monarch to move towards a stronger absolutism would collide with this newly found truth, and then the delicate balance that constituted the English system, and that made of every Englishman or woman a royalist, would crumble.

Along with the grace-exalting literature that came to England from the continent, then, we see the emergence of a distinctively English literature on civility, not necessarily Puritan, that gave expression in all its myriad multiplicity to this development towards multicenteredness and increased individuation. This included a large body of books of a Puritan bent, sometimes vastly unsympathetic to this development, of which John Bunyan's *Pilgrim's Progress* was the major exemplar. But it also included a vast secular literature more closely associated with civility per se, of which Henry Peacham's *The Compleat Gentleman* (1622) was arguably the most influential. It is interesting, and certainly no accident, that *The Compleat Gentleman* opened with an image of the universe that, in contrast to the first paragraph of *L'honneste-Homme,* contained no sun but a rather unstructured collection of stars—all equally important, all of equal worth.[12] And it was certainly no accident, either, that the majority of English manuals defined monarchical privilege in terms of priority, not of divinity, or advocated behaviors that revolved around the service of a whole, rather than the service of a prince.

The Ambiguous Discourse on Power

The tensions between the detached individual and the political complexions of the *res civile* yielded in England a discourse on power that in its ambiguities and resolutions was vastly different from the discourses of grace. For this was a discourse that, unlike the discourse of heroism that we analyzed in chapter 4, involved no unequivocal celebration of power and no absolute affirmation of monarchy. It was a discourse, rather, that pointed to an open discursive space—open not only in the sense that it allowed for the inclusion of a multiplicity of voices but in the sense that it affirmed neither monarchical nor aristocratic power, yet made possible the affirmation of either one. A comparison between the two central characters of *Le Cid*, the idealized representation of grace, and two characters of English literature, Shakespeare's Prince Hal and Falstaff, the hero and antihero of the *Henry IV* plays, is instructive.

Indeed, if amid Shakespeare's characters Hamlet represents (among other things) the predicaments of the free-floating person facing his or her detachment, Hal and Falstaff, like Rodrigue and Chimène, represent (among other things) the plight of the detached individual facing the political complexions of the *res civile*. Like Rodrigue and Chimène, Hal and Falstaff are in a continual struggle that pits a self-anchored value against the all-embracing values of civility. Like the characters of the French play, the English prince and his tutor are in a sense lost, and their difficulty in giving practical expression to their individuality breeds an anguish similar to that of Rodrigue and Chimène. Yet the heroes of Corneille instinctively align themselves with the requirements of grace, and in so doing their free will becomes inconsequential. The two *Henry IV* plays affirm the individual self and reconcile it with the velleities of the social whole—a whole, however, that as a consequence of this reconciliation is no longer defined solely in terms that relate and reduce everything to the person of the monarch.

Shakespeare delineates the problematics of detachment through Falstaff. We first meet Falstaff in the second scene of act 1 of *Henry IV, Part 1*.[13] A fat, quite grotesque personage, he is noisily sleeping on a bench when Prince Hal, the future Henry V, enters the stage. Falstaff is awakened by the Prince, and his first utterance sets the tone to his attitude throughout the plays: "Now, Hal, what time of day is it, lad?" he asks the future king (1.2.1). Hal's reply leaves no doubt about the sort of man that we have in front of us:

> Thou art so fat-witted with drinking of old sack, and unbottoning thee after supper, and sleeping upon benches after noon, that thou hast forgotten to demand that truly which thou wouldst truly know. What a devil hast thou to do with the time of the day? Unless hours were cups of sack, and minutes capons, and clocks

the tongues of bawds, and dials the signs of leaping-houses, and the blessed sun himself a fair hot wench in flame-coloured taffeta, I see no reason why thou shouldst be so superfluous to demand the time of the day. (1.2.2–11)

Of course, Hal is only partly serious, in a way tricking his tutor to an exchange of wit. The dialogue that ensues is in fact little more than a game. Hal hits and Falstaff hits back, with the same force and in an equal tenor, the two men mocking and belittling one another. But in Shakespeare no jest is just a jest. Hal's representation of Falstaff (as Falstaff's of Hal) underscores a real dimension of the old man's character. As the play unfolds, the impression that we receive from that first exchange gains strength. In Falstaff we detect (this is Northrop Frye's list) a coward, a braggart, a parasite, a comic butt, a vice, and, above all, indeed, a jester.[14] From the standpoint of Castiglione's grace, he embodies all that is wrong. He is the antithesis of moderation, courage, *sprezzatura,* princely subjection, and, as we will also learn, honor. To the grotesque, Shakespeare thus adds the vile, and Falstaff slowly becomes a synthesis of ugliness and baseness.

But that first dialogue also suggests someone endowed with a deep sensibility, as well as someone who is free—and like the first, this second impression only strengthens as the play unfolds. Falstaff displays genuine tenderness for Hal. His opening line, "Now, Hal, what time of day is it, lad?" suggests as much of irreverence as fondness, the concluding appellative transforming what could have been a prosaic question into an affectionate apostrophe.[15] Hal's answer hints at his tutor's freedom. "What a devil hast thou to do with the time of the day?" the Prince asks Falstaff, and indeed, Falstaff is a man who stands outside the bounds of time, of history itself.[16] As we gradually learn, he is beyond social constraints. His only guiding principle seems to be—quite like the new *honnête homme,* whom he slightly resembles—a passion for life. As Harold Bloom nicely put it, "Falstaff is *not* subject to a power that watches, discovers, and criticizes all his intentions. Falstaff, except for his single and misplaced love [for Hal], is free, is freedom itself, because he seems free of the superego."[17]

In a way, Hamlet and Falstaff represent the same person: a person overwhelmingly conditioned by the experience of detachment. Both Falstaff and Hamlet are detached from their respective worlds, free to move at their own discretion. Both see the world from a distance, ironically yet clearly, objectively. The two are actors. Hamlet feigns, role-plays, searches for truth and for identity in a world that has become shadowy, almost unreal. Falstaff also feigns, role-plays, and strives for an affirmation of self in a world that to him is absurd.[18] But Hamlet faces only himself, and the unreality of his world. In him, fact and imagination become confused, or rather collapse into a precarious, increasingly disembodied perception of the real. In Falstaff, in contrast, facts and imagination clash, provoking not a movement towards introspection but an explosion of intelligence. Falstaff is not a person facing himself. He knows exactly who he is and understands his own situation. It is not a disembodied but a hostile reality that he confronts: a reality inimical to freedom, a reality sustained, at least in part, by the powers of the absolutist state and the hegemony of grace.

Falstaff questions the sense of war and courage, reveals people's lies, and hints at the absurdity of life. But through his constant jibing, it is royalty itself, and the idea of honor that is so central to it, that agitates him the most. His denial of honor, exemplified by his monologue before the battle of Shrewsbury,[19] does not imply the denunciation of a merely abstract concept. It involves a full repudiation of royalty. If honor has become an abstraction for him, it is because he has severed it from its sources of meaning, because to him royalty itself has never attained any symbolic value. Here, the de-deification of the monarch that we observe throughout the Henriad gains full weight. Erich Auerbach noted how, suddenly, Shakespeare introduces us to a weary Prince, to someone who is more human than divine, someone unheroic yet deeply, touchingly alive.[20] Even before we meet Falstaff, in *Richard II,* Shakespeare had already raised questions regarding the nature of royal authority.[21] Richard had been deposed in a palace revolt, and his cousin, Bolingbroke, had been crowned king. Bolingbroke, the newly consecrated Henry IV, however, could not legitimately lay claim on a notion of divine right, for Richard, not he, was the lawful, God-anointed sovereign. Henry's struggle to establish a legitimate basis of authority becomes one of the central themes of the plays that bear his name.

With Falstaff, however, the earthly view of royalty achieves a new perspective. For Hal himself at moments takes on some of the characteristics of his tutor. Indeed, nudged by Falstaff, he becomes a liar, a thief, a profligate. And his participation in these acts is not that of a detached, somewhat reluctant auxiliary—in spite of his self-justifications.[22] What we see is the future King of England genuinely involved in lowly acts, enjoying himself and the freedom he experiences immensely. In so doing, the Prince becomes one more imperfect mortal—neither better nor worse than the average person.

Hal's journey from being a double of Falstaff to becoming first among equals represents to perfection the idea of civility that developed in England during the course of the sixteenth century.[23] The contrast with Falstaff is critical. For Falstaff's ultimate fall represents the exact reverse of Hal's rise to glory, the two outcomes having been set in motion from the very beginning of *1 Henry IV.*

The celebration of freedom is from the start accompanied by an ominous feeling of future downfall. "Farewell, thou latter spring; farewell, Allhallown summer," Hal tells Falstaff when they part company at the end of act 1, scene 2 of *1 Henry IV,* as though Falstaff were living on borrowed time. In act 2, scene 4, Hal is summoned in front of his father. Worried, the Prince asks Falstaff to help him prepare for the meeting. They roleplay, each in turn taking on the role of the king. As Hal plays the king and Falstaff plays Hal, it is only half in jest that he calls his tutor, using the voice of his future status and prefiguring a not too distant future, "That villainous abominable misleader of youth, . . . that old white-bearded Satan" (2.4.445–46). Falstaff defends himself impassionately:

> [T]o say I know more harm in him than in myself, were to say more than I know. That he is old, the more the pity, his white hairs do witness it; but that he is, saving your reverence, a whoremaster, that I utterly deny. If sack-and-sugar be a fault, God help the wicked! If to be old and merry be a sin, then many an old host that I know is damned. If to be fat be to be hated, then Pharaoh's lean kine are to be loved. No, my good lord, banish Peto, banish Bardolph, banish Poins; but for sweet Jack Falstaff, kind Jack Falstaff, true Jack Falstaff, valiant Jack Falstaff, and therefore more valiant being as he is old Jack Falstaff, banish not him thy Harry's company—banish plump Jack, and banish all the world. (2.4. 449–62)

Clearly, Falstaff here stands not only for himself but for what he represents: freedom, the fundamental condition of the detached individual. "[B]anish plump Jack," Shakespeare writes, "and banish all the world." Banish Falstaff and banish life. Banish the representation and banish the reality. Hal's response is chilling: "I do," he says, still playing a role, being something he is not yet. "I will," he immediately adds, dropping the game, taking over his real identity as crown Prince. Falstaff's fate, and by extension the fate of the detached individual, is sealed. Falstaff's downfall becomes imminent as *2 Henry IV* unfolds.

The final rejection comes as a logical outcome to Falstaff's ill-fated fortunes. Henry IV has died, and Hal has become king. Falstaff waits among the multitude to salute the new monarch. His emotion at seeing Hal is genuine, the banishment—long awaited, now certain—becomes as a consequence all the more poignant: "I know thee not, old man. Fall to thy prayers," Henry V begins his last address to Falstaff (5.5.47). It is an entire mode of being in the world that is condemned.

Order has finally triumphed over disorder. The monarchy has been reaffirmed. Hal, now king, becomes at last an example of virtue. The free-floating person finds no place in that order: the predicaments of the detached individual have been disowned by the necessities of power—doomed from the beginning. That Falstaff is disowned by a freedom-loving youngster turned king—or more tellingly, by a transformed reflection of his own image—is not accidental, for the triumph of order, if costly, is thus doubly affirmed.

But how different is this order from the one that emerges from the practices of grace. For although undisputed, power, in Shakespeare's two plays, is of a more fallible and ultimately more ambiguous nature. Two elements seem especially relevant.

We have already seen how the association of Hal and Falstaff problematizes the idea of royal perfection. But the contradiction between the inevitability of Falstaff's disgrace and the celebration of freedom that bursts in him points to a deeper problem. As an audience, we are simultaneously repelled by the man and moved to identify with him. His character drives us away from him; yet at the same time we aspire to what he represents. We are disturbed by his baseness, yet we long for him and wish we could raise him over his fate. We want more of him, of his promise of happiness, but we cannot subscribe to his person.[24] Although intrinsically good, then, power—monarchical power, the type of power at the heart of grace, that is—is also intrinsically bad. Gone is its unequivocally redeeming faculty, its capacity to solve all problems and cure all pain. Power might be doubly affirmed, but this double affirmation no longer entails an affirmation of everything else. In the Henriad the goals of monarchical power do not coincide with the totality of one's being. Monarchical power becomes vaguely unspiritual and morally ambiguous—and unlike the practices associated with an inherently worthy power, it must be endowed with the force of moral authority.

But there is a second sense in which order, in the Henriad, cannot be entirely reduced to the person of the king. In terms of a discourse and practice of civility, it is with Hal that one is invited to identify and whose example one is encouraged to follow. It is Hal who substantiates the spirit of perfection, however painful and ambiguous that perfection might be. He and his tutor can be seen as representing the ends of a continuum that helps to specify the terms of the desirable. At one end, Falstaff represents what one has to overcome. At the other, Hal represents what one has to strive for. The space in between, the space that real men and women are meant to occupy, comprehends the prince's transformational journey from a Falstaffian figure to an epitome of civility. For if one wishes to be civil, if one wants to become a true gentleman (or gentlewoman), one must learn to overcome the Falstaffian instincts and, like Hal, reconcile individuality with the service of "the whole." But this is a whole that can be defined in a multiplicity of ways, the very status of the king within it becoming an issue of fundamental importance. Unlike Rodrigue and Chimène, Hal does not transcend his individuality. He affirms it and integrates it within the whole and thus becomes an element of that whole. He might be the most important element of the whole, but he is still only one among many others. In this sense, again, the king is no different from others, and the possibility of defining an order in terms of the multiplicity of selves that compose the whole—in terms of multicenteredness, that is—remains open.

The Doctrine of the Public Weal

Of course, Shakespeare's Henriad does not exhaust the totality of political discourses in England during the late sixteenth and early seventeenth centuries, but it is helpful in two very different ways. From the perspective of the development of civility in England, it serves a function similar to the one that Le Cid served for grace. It identifies the foundational elements of English civility, focuses on its extremes, magnifies them, heightens their tensions, and makes fully visible the ambiguities implied in their resolution. In so doing, it draws the contours of a space of political discourses—some of affirmation, some of resistance, some coming from within the aristocracy, some from outside—in which the struggles between different powers, big and small, are played out.[25] The openness of the discursive space at the time is apparent, and marks a moment in the genealogy of the infrastructure of social relations in England in which neither the deepened experience of individuation nor the multicenteredness that marks its configuration had materialized to any significant degree, yet neither had the pragmatics of grace. It is a moment of open possibilities, a moment at which the monarchy seemed all-powerful yet at which, ultimately, the discourses on civility affirmed no power categorically.

The actual discourses of civility that developed in England during the sixteenth century gave expression to the same ambiguities, and the same openness, that we perceived in the Henriad. A highly theoretical, although admittedly less complex version is already found in Sir Thomas Elyot's *The Boke Named the Gouernour* (1531), a treatise on politics and civility—two domains, we understand clearly by now, that cannot be separated. The treatise, considered by many as the first genuinely British civility book, is dedicated to Henry VIII, and it is in the opening address to the monarch that Elyot defines the aim of his study: "[T]o describe in our vulgar tongue the form of a just public weal"—of a just "whole," I may add.[26]

The first chapter directly introduces us to the notion of a public weal:

> A public weal is a body living, compact or made of sundry estates and degrees of men, which is disposed by the order of equity and governed by the rule and moderation of reason. In the Latin tongue it is called *res publica,* of the which the word *res* hath divers significations, and doth not only betoken that that is called a thing, which is distinct from a person, but also signifieth estate, condition, substance, and profit. In our vulgar [English], profit is called weal; and it is called a wealthy country wherein is all thing that is profitable; and he is a wealthy man that is rich in money and substance. Public (as Varro saith) is derived of people, which in Latin is called *populus*.[27]

A "public weal" should not be confused with a "common weal." There is a very significant difference between *populus* and *plebs,* Elyot explains: *populus* means "public"; *plebs* means "commonality."

> And consequently there may appear like diversity to be in English between a public weal and a common weal as should be in Latin between *res publica* and *res plebeia.* And after that signification, if there should be a common weal, either the commoners only must be wealthy, and the gentle and noble men needy and miserable, or else, excluding gentility, all men must be of one degree and sort, and a new name provided: for as much as *plebs* in Latin and commoners in English be words only made for the discrepance of degrees, whereof proceedeth order, which in things as well natural as supernatural hath ever had such a pre-eminence that thereby the incomprehensible majesty of God, as it were by a bright leme [gleam] of a torch or candle, is declared to be blind inhabitants of this world.[28]

The thrust underlying Elyot's conception of order, as well as the entire idea of civility that we see evolving in England during the course of the century, including Shakespeare's, is by no means democratic. The weal of the public is not a wealth that belongs, or should belong, to the common people. It belongs to more than one person, or it would not be public; yet it is not owned by all. Chaos, Elyot tells us, would otherwise ensue.[29] The public weal is composed only of those whose purity of nature (read the nobility) endows them with a special gleam of excellence:

> [A]s the angels which be most fervent in contemplation be highest exalted in glory (after the opinion of holy doctors), and also the fire, which is the most pure of elements, and also doth clarify the other inferior elements, is deputed to the highest sphere or place, so in this world, they which excel other in this influence of understanding, and do employ it to the detaining of other within the bounds of reason, and show them how to provide for their necessary living—such ought to be set in a more high place than the residue, where they may see, and also be seen, that by the beams of their excellent wit, showed through the glass of authority, other of inferior understanding may be directed to the way of virtue and commodious living.[30]

The commoners are "the residue," whereas, unsurprisingly indeed, the nobility forms the body on which the social finds its substance.

Ironically, the ambiguities of power emerge at the point in which the *Gouernour* begins celebrating the monarch. The *Gouernour*'s second chapter, significantly titled "That One Sovereign Governor Ought to Be in a Public Weal; and What Damage Hath Happened Where a Multitude Hath Had Equal Authority without Any Sovereign," sets the theme of the relationship between monarch and aristocracy. Elyot here asserts the king's position at the top of the social hierarchy: the necessity of kingship is unquestionable. Power, Elyot maintains, has to be centralized, vested in one person; for its diffusion spawns chaos. Look at Athens, he writes, "where equality was of estate among the people, and only by their whole consent their city and dominions were governed."[31] There no authority existed, and each person represented but him or herself. And look at what happened: "[N]or never it was certain nor stable, and oftentimes they banished or slew the best citizens which by their virtue and wisdom had most profited to the public weal."[32] Elyot calls it a monster with many heads.

Yet, if one central authority is necessary, this one is, as for Shakespeare, fundamentally different from the one underlying the pragmatics of grace and the doctrine of the *honnête homme*. For instead of constituting a value in itself, and one from which the social body derives its own value, monarchical authority derives *its* value from the social body. In the *Gouernour*, authority becomes a trust placed in one person by the public weal itself. Elyot, it is true, never defines authority; he sees it as a precondition for the survival of society, and as such its sources are left undiscussed. It is part of the natural order of things, as "one sun ruleth over the day, and one moon over the night"; or as in a hive, in which "is left . . . by nature, as it seemeth, a perpetual figure of a just governance or rule, who hath among [the bees] one principal bee for their governor."[33] But the supreme governor, Elyot makes it clear, is only first among equals, and only because he is accepted as such.

Compared to the Henriad, the *Gouernour* is definitively less complex, at least as far as the existential uncertainties of power are concerned. But Elyot's treatise helps us to identify and follow the specific discourse in whose terms the lines through which power operates come to be defined. And in so doing, it begins to delineate the specific configuration in whose shape the English infrastructure of social relations, the "whole" whose future is still fully open, would indeed develop.

Not until Hobbes does the rationale of Elyot's argument receive an explicit formulation. Hobbes's distinction between an "author" and an "actor," as spelled out in chapter 16 of the *Leviathan*, indeed perfectly expresses what in Elyot is merely suggested. "Of persons artificial," Hobbes wrote, referring to a person who by virtue of his special position in society "represents" not himself but another person (e.g., lawyers), "some have their words and actions *owned* by those whom they represent. And then the person is the *actor*; and he that owneth his words and actions, is the AUTHOR: in which case the actor acteth by authority."[34] "Authors," that is all the members of the public weal, "own" their words and actions. They have inalienable control over their wills; they speak and act according to their personal inclinations. "Authority" is the right of doing any action. "So that by authority," writes Hobbes, "is always understood a right of doing any act; and *done by authority,* done by commission, or license from him whose right it is."[35] "Actors," thus, are the people who, in the form of a tacit contract binding both authors and actors, receive from the authors the license to represent and use their authority, to speak and act in their place. Princes are nothing but actors of this sort: artificial persons who represent a multitude of authors, thereby giving them unity. "For it is the *unity* of the represener, not the *unity* of the represented, that maketh the person *one*. And it is the represener that beareth the person, and but one person: and *unity,* cannot otherwise be understood in multitude."[36]

Writing towards the end of the period of liminality that I described in chapter 3, Elyot could be hardly expected to have expressed the ideas above with the clarity and logical perspicacity of Hobbes. But there they are, in the *Gouernour,* implicit in Elyot's entire conception of the social. They even inform the meaning that he gives to civility. For to Elyot, civility consists precisely in preparing people to become actors in Hobbes's sense of the word—a sense that clearly has nothing in common with the modern concept of the role-player.[37] It is a learned quality that makes some people worthy to represent a body of authors, to wield authority. And this is true not only for the small number of children in the royal family, but also for any child of note who might one day become an "inferior governor" or magistrate. As Elyot puts it in the title of the book's fourth chapter, most of the *Gouernour* is devoted to "The Education or Form of Bringing Up of the Child of a Gentleman Which Is to Have Authority in a Public Weal."

In the discourse of a "public weal" the provisions for multicenteredness and royal centrality are largely undifferentiated from one another. The postulate that not only the king is bound to become an actor is clearly not inimical to absolutism; witness the *Leviathan.* In Elyot as in Hobbes, king and nation become one, and at least in that respect these authors do not differ greatly from Faret. Thus the infrastructure can develop either in the direction of royal centrality or towards the affirmation of the aristocracy as a group. For if it is open to an affirmation of royal centrality, it is also open to the affirmation of the aristocracy as a corporate body. The lines through which power operates are not centered by definition. The possibility of having a multiplicity of centers defined by the body of each aristocrat, of each actor, is definitely present. Unlike the vision intrinsic in Faret's *honnêteté,* here there is finally no inherent difference between a person who is a king and one who is a magistrate. The fact that Elyot uses the same word, *governor,* to designate both kings and magistrates points to how similarly he perceives the nature of the positions. God does not invest the monarch, the supreme governor, with any particular amount of power. Power, by God's will, pertains to the nobility as a whole.[38] The authority of the monarch, we have already learned, comes from below, by virtue of a covenant between the king and the aristocracy. The difference between a chief and an inferior governor is, first and foremost, a quantitative difference that depends more on the amount of authority that the public weal confers on a person than on a primordial dissimilarity of character. A qualitative distinction is bound to result, for only the king represents the oneness of the weal; receiving only partial authority, no other governor can be said to embody the will of the people in its entirety. But this difference, again, is produced from below, by an eminently numerical cause.[39] Elyot does not see the tendencies towards absolutism and the affirmation of the aristocracy as a corporate group as merely coexisting side by side, though. To him, they are part of the same social formation, the public weal, and no real difference between the two exists. In the *Gouernour,* one naturally implies the other.

Civility itself consequently becomes something very different from what we observed in the realms of grace and the *honnête.* The education that Elyot advocates for the governor-to-be follows the best tradition of Renaissance humanism and is in this sense unexceptional.[40] As for any humanist, for Elyot learning should be a serious yet pleasant experience and should gradually include all the arts and sciences. Towards the end of his discussion, Elyot enjoins the future governor to deepen his study of the topic he deems the most important, moral philosophy, whose centerpiece is Aristotle's *Nicomachaean Ethics.* As for Erasmus and Castiglione, for Elyot the golden rule becomes the principle guiding everything.[41] All along, of course, Elyot enjoins the youngster to devote time and effort to nurturing the technologies of the body that are integral to the collective self of the civil powers.

But in Elyot an additional element emerges: understanding, he suggests, is not just a fruit of learning. Because governors are humans, because their understanding is always limited, learning should be always strengthened through practice.[42] Neither the causes of a public's "griefes" and "diseases" nor the means to cure them, Elyot tells us, can be known through learning alone. These, indeed,

> may neuer be sufficiently knowen of gouernours, except they them selfes wyll personally resorte and peruse all partes of the countrayes under their gouernaunce, and inserche diligently as well what be the customes and maners of people good and badde, as also the commodities and discommodities, howe the one may be preserued, the other suppressed, or at the leste wayes amended.[43]

This is knowledge of a different sort, Elyot explains. It is a "wysedome" attainable only through personal experience: through observation and, more importantly, through actual doing. The idea that Elyot conveys parallels Hal's journey away from his Falstaffian self and neatly rounds up the political and behavioral perception of the *Gouernour*. For Elyot suggests that in the process of becoming an actor, the future governor has to become, subtly albeit necessarily, all authors. He must learn how to serve as much as how to lead, for only thus can he gain the capacity to "understand" his inferiors. He has to know the roots of intolerance, infidelity, and ingratitude, and must have experienced the wrongs they cause. He has to know injustice and must have experienced its inequities. He has to know flattery and experience its seductions as well as its false promises. Only thus can virtue and moderation grow strong and lay deep roots in his character—stronger and deeper, as for Hal, than for any of the authors he represents. No real understanding and no real virtue is otherwise possible, Elyot suggests, neither for a magistrate nor, indeed, for a king.

The Compleat Gentleman and the Beginnings of Aristocratic Hegemony

By the first half of the seventeenth century, however, as the aristocracy gradually established its power and a pragmatics developed that was conducive to its operation (topics that I discuss in the next chapter), a trusting attitude towards multicenteredness became increasingly dominant among British authors of civility books. What came to be the dominant vision of society was composed of a multiplicity of centers, each representing the body of one aristocrat, brought together into a unity in the shape of the common weal—a vision fully prefigured in Elyot.

The opening passage of Peacham's *The Compleat Gentleman*, first published in 1622, less than a century after Elyot's, is indeed eloquent. For like *L'honneste-Homme, The Compleat Gentleman* opens with a cosmological metaphor of the social—a metaphor that, instead of portraying a central sun with the rest of the universe turning around it, depicts a myriad of stars and describes their key characteristic, simply, as "nobility." "If we consider arightly the Frame of the whole Universe and Method of the all-excellent Wisedome in her worke," writes Peacham,

> as creating the formes of things infinitely divers, so according to Dignity of Essence or Vertue in effect, wee must acknowledge the same to hold a Soveraigntie, and transcendent praedominance, as well of Rule as Place each over either. Among the heavenly bodies wee see the Nobler Orbes, and of greatest influence to be raised aloft, the lesse effectuall, depressed. Of Elements, the *Fire* the most pure and operative to hold the highest place; in compounded bodies, of things as well sensible as insensible, there runneth a veine

of Excellence proceeding from the Forme, ennobling (in the same kind) some other above the rest.[44]

To Peacham, there is not one central "orbe" but many "noble orbes," all more or less equal in purity and of equal excellence. It is the nobility as a whole that assumes the mark of recognition. Its value is "inherent and Naturall" and, like a "Diamond," has "lustre but only from it selve."[45] Value is not exclusive to the king; it is the heritage of all noblemen, of the "commonwealth" as a whole.[46] Princes, Peacham writes in an image that cannot fail to bring Hal to our mind, are the ones who, like the sun in the skies, "ought to out-runne the rest in a vertuous race, and out-shine them in knowledge."[47] Only this can place them in a position closer to God, the true source of the nobility's natural light.[48] Moreover, princes ought not to be just the first in the commonwealth; they must also be first in civility. Although no "meere naturall man," a king is nonetheless a natural person in Hobbes's sense of the word. His nature and function do not differ from those of any other member of the commonwealth. In *The Compleat Gentleman* princes and nobles are at the same level and are often mentioned together as having similar rights and duties, similar value, a similar need to master the fine points of civility—as though when dealing with the essential, their differences disappeared.[49]

Placed at the opening of the book, the metaphor, as was the case for Faret, acquires the force of a premise. Like the equation of king and sun in *L'honneste-Homme,* the vision of the aristocracy as the fountain of value informs *The Compleat Gentleman* throughout. It is the foundation from which everything else acquires meaning. The very claim that this value is "inherent and Naturall" and has "lustre but only from it selve" invests it with the force of a first proposition whose truth is beyond questioning. Of course, what the "it selve" means, most critically, is that the value—a largely underdetermined, flexible value able to change as the aristocracy redefines itself—is indeed a product of the practices by which the aristocracy creates and constantly recreates its collective self to begin with.[50]

The thrust becomes definitely oligarchic, not absolutist. What in Elyot was only a genealogical possibility becomes a certainty, and the concept of the gentleman elaborated by the English authors eventually translated this thrust into a practical philosophy of behavior. Most British manuals of the period carry a discourse on the prerogatives of the nobility that is absent from much of the continental literature. Peacham's first chapter ("Of Nobilitie in Generall: That It Is a Plant from Heaven; the Roote, Branches,

Fruit") ends, quite relevantly, with a catalog of the privileges of noblemen. These include not only questions of precedence, a theme universally debated, but also issues related to their position before the law, their freedom to hunt and hawk, or their demand to be consulted in affairs of state—topics almost never discussed in the Italian or French manuals.[51]

The idea of civility as a journey, the multicentered conception of the social, and the aristocratic definition of value permeate most of the major British manuals, puritanical and secular alike. Richard Brathwait, whose *English Gentleman* (1630) provides a highly puritanical view of politeness, speaks, for instance, of "perfection" as a gradual movement towards God to be pursued mostly during one's youth, when temptation is constant.[52] "No Perfection in this life is absolute, but graduall" he writes:

> Let us adresse our selves then to this Taske [of approaching perfection], and make this our ground, that as no man is simply good but God; so no man is absolutely *perfect* till hee be individually united to God; which on earth is not granted, but promised; not effected, but expected; not obtained, but with confidence desired, when these *few*, but *evill dayes* of our Pilgrimage shall be expired: yet is there a graduall *Perfection,* which in some degree or measure wee may attaine, becomming conformable unto him, whose Image we have received, and by whom we have so many singular graces and prerogatives on us conferred.[53]

"We" and "us," we know, do not include everyone. As Brathwait puts it most clearly in the book's subtitle, his advice concerns only the gentleman "of selecter ranke and *qualitie.*" Similarly, Owen Feltham, the author of the very moralistic, albeit not Puritan, *Resolves* (1628), defines privilege as a precondition of order, something that, by the grace of God, is part of the nature of the nobility. There is no idea of grace associated with the king, of a value that proceeds from an act of the crown. Glory, Feltham teaches, springs from the combination of nobility and the mastery of our passions.[54] Even a minor author like Thomas Gainsford does not fail to glorify the aristocracy and diminish the king, while simultaneously calling the monarch "Gods Lieuetenant" and bestower of virtue—a reason, perhaps, why his book never made it.[55]

The most notable exception to this trend is James Cleland's *The Institution of a Young Noble Man,* a book first published in 1607.[56] Considered one of the three most important books on civility published in England during the first half of the seventeenth century,[57] Cleland's does see the king as someone who is, by nature, qualitatively different from the nobility. Still, in Cleland's work, as in the rest of the British books, there is no idea of grace. To Cleland, the value of the nobility comes directly from God and is not mediated by the king. Service to the country does not coincide with service to the monarchy. And to Cleland, as to the other British authors, civility is above all a property related to the plurality of the whole, not the singularity of the monarch.[58]

Of course, to suggest that the multicenteredness or the affirmation of the aristocracy permeate most of the literature does not mean that other discourses did not exist, or that all discourses would be equally affirmative of the aristocracy. The same situation that we observed in chapter 4 regarding the discourses of grace certainly applies here. Puritan writings, of which Bunyan's *Pilgrim's Progress* (1678) is paradigmatic, would develop discourses extremely hostile to the aristocracy and promote a pragmatics ultimately irreconcilable with the pragmatics of systemic relationality, the pragmatics in whose terms, we will see in the next chapter, the infrastructure of social relations that unfolds with the power of the aristocracy finds its expression.[59] Much of this oppositional literature was even more affirmative of individuation than the literature on civility, some less. Some, like *Pilgrim's Progress,* would embrace the multicentered vision of the world, yet reject its aristocratic definition. For what Bunyan contests is the substance of the multicenteredness as expressive of aristocratic being. It is the lack of spirituality, the definition of a whole in material rather than spiritual terms. The pragmatics that he fosters is consequently a pragmatics grounded on faith and religious being and geared to the spiritual edification of the people who practice it.[60]

Some of these other discourses undoubtedly gained importance as they helped to substantiate an alternative plane of power and practice—witness *Pilgrim's Progress* and the power of the Puritan movement in England. But in terms of the present book, the existence of other discourses, even oppositional discourses, does not reduce the significance of multicenteredness or the aristocratic affirmation of being in the discourses of civility. For these other discourses involve only alternatives to the discourses of civility, and the fate of each discourse, in true genealogical fashion, follows the fate of the powers to which it gives expression.

The behaviors of the gentleman, at any rate, must conform to the requirements of the collective self of the aristocracy and the plurality of the whole. In terms of his political conduct, the gentleman is not seen as a mere counsel to the king, as was the case for the courtier. He is called to participate in the government of the commonwealth, to act for the good of the whole and therefore contribute to its "wealth."

"Wealth," here, means a number of things. It means first spiritual wealth, the sort that derives from the possession of a moral resource and the practice of a moral idea. This is the sort of wealth that justifies a nation's being and gives its people—or at least the people who partake of the collective self of the dominant group—virtue and grace. But "wealth" also means honor, knowledge, and, in total contrast to the courtier or any previous concept of propriety, the riches that derive from trade. For, as Peacham writes,

> If the owner of the *Earth, and all that therein is,* hath so bestowed and disposed of his blessings, that no one Countrey affordeth all things, but must be beholden not onely to their neighbours, but even the most remote Regions, and Common-wealths cannot stand without Trade and Commerce, buying and selling: I cannot (by the leave of so reverend judgements) but account the honest Merchant among the number of Benefactors to his Countrey, while he exposeth as well his life as goods, to the hazzard of infinite dangers, sometimes for medicinall Drugges and preservatives of our lives in extremitie of sicknesse; another, for our food or cloathing in times of scarcitie and want, haply for usefull necessaries for our vocations and callings: or lastly, for those . . . which the Almightie providence hath purposely, for our solace and recreation, and for no other end else created, as Apes, Parrots, Peacockes, Canarie, and all singing birds; rarest Flowers for colour and smell, pretious Stones of all sorts, Pearle, Amber, Corall, Cristall, all manner of sweete odours, fruites, infinitely differing in forme and taste: Colours of all sorts, for painting, dying, &c.[61]

Indeed, unlike the courtier, the gentleman should not limit himself to a career in the military. Provided that he does not betray his nobility, it is perfectly acceptable for him to engage in commercial activities or, more generally, in the production and exchange of earthly yet divinely created goods. He should care for his own estate and should make it flourish, Peacham instructs. He, not "a cheating Steward, or craftie Bailiffe," should manage the soil. He should not deem the plow too base or unworthy of his person. Nor should he labor only to conserve his state, Peacham insists. He should labor to augment it.[62] "Believe it," exhorts in turn Feltham,

"*Industrie* is never wholly unfruitfull. If it bring not *joy* with the *incomming profit*, it will yet banish *mischiefe* from thy *busied gates*."[63]

Elegance, a staple in the world of the courtier, has little room in the world of the gentleman. A property that serves mostly to "earn grace," to please one's prince, has no place in a doctrine that subverts the very meaning of the word, in a way restoring it to its original sense. Aestheticism is not to be enjoyed for its own sake, the British authors suggest, but used for the cultivation of the spirit alone, as a means towards the higher goal of spiritual wealth. Manners are important, of course, and a seemliness of garniture is always necessary. But elegance betokens immoderation, and an immoderate soul cannot serve the commonwealth well. The immoderate squanders his estate, makes a poor counselor, and endangers his friends.

Learning, which to the *honnête homme* serves mostly to ornament conversation, is for the English gentleman a condition for the fulfillment of duty. The use of learning to embellish discourse is given due importance, for sociability is indispensable.[64] But more than that, it is a tool by which the weal can be made prosper. Thus, mathematics attain in the educational program of the gentleman a prominence that makes little sense in a world that, like that of the *honnête homme*, emphasizes the political rather than the production of wealth.[65] Geography becomes not just a survey of places and peoples but a study of behavior: of the effects of climates on character, of architecture on mood, or of the soil on the shapes of the body. Natural history becomes useful for the study of organization. The study of law, a topic almost ignored in the education of a *gentilhomme*, becomes a necessity in the breeding of a gentleman.

Friendship also takes on a different meaning within the infrastructure of social relations at the core of the world of the gentleman. Lauded as a means to gain access to court, the view of friendship advocated by Faret is evidently alien to the gentleman.[66] To the English writers the value of friendship lies elsewhere: in the help that a friend provides in times of distress and in the counsel he affords in business. And both help and counsel are things one must seek always, although carefully. The more successful a gentleman and the larger his estate, Peacham tells his readers in a reversal of the role of the king in the world of the *honnête homme*,[67] the more advice he needs. And who can a man trust if not his friend?[68] Friendship must be measured by a person's capacity to increase his friend's wealth, and therefore the wealth of the whole. When difficult times arrive, though, a true gentleman should always help ease the misery of his friend to preserve the unity of the weal.[69]

CHAPTER SIX

Protestantism and the Doctrine of the English Gentleman

The affinities between the concept of the gentleman and both Protestantism and the constellation of attitudes associated with the bourgeoisie are obvious and strongly remind us of Weber's thesis on the Protestant ethic and the spirit of capitalism. The plane of power that forms in the complex of practices that affirm the aristocracy as a group, I would argue, is congruent with the provisions for the consolidation of the bourgeoisie as a social class. The conceptual foundations of Protestantism, in turn, help promote individuation and multicenteredness and foster a plane of practices compatible with—and in a sense, again, "congruent with" (a phrase that I define below)—the infrastructure of social relations in whose shape the power of the aristocracy unfolds.

The conceptual compatibility or congruence is visible not only in the vision of man and cosmos briefly discussed at the beginning of the chapter but also in the rationale underlying the idea of a commonwealth. For exactly as every free author is subject to the requirements of the commonwealth, every Christian man, so Luther's doctrine of servitude posits, is simultaneously free and subject to everyone. To Luther, this subjection does not arise from a social need, as it does in the doctrine of the gentleman, and the reason is eminently theological:

> Although . . . a man is amply enough justified by faith, having all that he requires to have, except that this very faith and abundance ought to increase from day to day, even till the future life; still he remains in this mortal life upon earth, in which it is necessary that he should rule his own body, and have intercourse with men. Here then works begin; here he must not take his ease; here he must give heed to exercise his body by fastings, watchings, labour, and other moderate discipline, so that it may be subdued to the spirit, and obey and conform itself to the inner man and faith, and not rebel against them nor hinder them, as is its nature to do if it is not kept under.[70]

Because of the original sin, Luther explains, man's body strives for lust and profligacy, and his spirit is driven to the forbidden. This contradicts the primordial design of becoming one with God; therefore, man must bring his compulsions under control. Good actions do not make a good person, Luther insists; this only faith can do. But in his desire to be pure, the good man must purify his body—and to that end, good actions, done

176

"out of disinterested love to the service of God," become essential.[71] Thus man becomes subject to everyone:

> Here is the truly Christian life; here is faith really working by love; when a man applies himself with joy and love to the works of that freest servitude, in which he serves others voluntarily and for nought; himself abundantly satisfied in the fulness [*sic*] and riches of his own faith. . . .
>
> Thus from faith flow forth love and joy in the Lord, and from love a cheerful, willing, free spirit, disposed to serve our neighbor voluntarily, without taking any account of gratitude or ingratitude, praise or blame, gain or loss.[72]

The gentleman is no Puritan, however. Despite Brathwait, most of the literature on the gentleman actually shows a deep antipathy toward the Puritan movement and the precepts that it advocates.[73] The idea of the gentleman is an aristocratic idea, self-contained and self-fulfilling. Its affinities with Protestantism, as the argument throughout the book suggests, are a consequence of the two, the theological and the social doctrines, involving different manifestations of the same conditions of possibility—those brought into being by individuation.

Although different in significant ways, the argument is clearly consistent with Weber's thesis of the effects of Protestantism on the rise of capitalism.[74] For if Weber did not see the two as manifestations of the same ontological conditions, neither did he suggest a causal relation, or even a strict correlation, between the religious and the social transformations. Weber did not claim that it was something about the substance of Protestantism per se that helped bring about capitalism. Capitalism was brought about by a combination of economic conditions and the development of rational patterns of action that followed the everyday practice of ascetic Protestantism. According to Weber, the key lay in the congruence (my word) or "elective affinity" (Weber's phrase) between these rational patterns of action and the type of economic activity, arrangements, and institutions necessary for the emergence of capitalism.[75]

Sociologists and historians have identified a number of difficulties with Weber's thesis.[76] Weber's readings of Puritan texts, for example, seem highly problematic, thus weakening the validity of his main source of evidence.[77] Similar ascetic doctrines arose among Catholic movements such as Jansenism and Rigorism, without the development of similar economic practices.[78] These two criticisms together significantly weaken Weber's claim of an elective affinity, understood as a correlation, between the outcomes of the daily practices of ascetic Protestantism and capitalism.[79] My own argument suggests that the patterns of practice that Weber saw as emerging from ascetic Protestantism started to form before the Reformation among people largely unaffected by its discourses.

Here, it is true, I shift my emphasis on the effects of Protestantism from its relevance to the emergence of rational patterns of action to its contribution to fostering a plane of practices marked by individuation and multicenteredness, one that is congruent with the practices of self-fashioning of the aristocracy as well as with the conditions necessary for capital-oriented economic action. The argument concerns Protestantism in general, not only its ascetic expressions, and indeed sees Protestantism as a manifestation, not a source, of individuation and multicenteredness. It does not deny the effect of Protestantism on rationalization, but sees it as indirect. I follow Simmel here in suggesting that the emergence of rational patterns of action is a consequence of individuation and multicenteredness, not of ascetic doctrines.[80]

Affinity or congruence is the result of the different discourses or patterns of action emerging from the common foundation. Such an argument of affinity has little to do with causality or correlation—nor does Weber's, for that matter. Neither Weber's concept of elective affinity nor my own concept of congruence relies on a causal logic. The processes of social formation that we see at work in the constitution of elective affinities or congruences are instructed by an analogic, human-mediated rationale rather than a causal, purely mechanistic one. An analogy involves, literally, "a similarity or likeness between things in some circumstances or effects when the things are otherwise entirely different."[81] An analogic rationale therefore refers to the processes by which outcomes of human activity attain a state of analogy. I use the geometrical concept of congruence rather than Weber's elective affinity to convey the types of structural analogies that I suggest follow from that process: the congruence between the multicenteredness (a characteristic of "mesostructures") or the interpersonal detachment (a characteristic of "microstructures") inherent, simultaneously, in Protestantism, in the doctrine of the Gentleman and the practices associated with it, and in an interactional order conducive to capitalism, for example.[82]

And indeed, the effects of Protestantism on the infrastructure of social relations in whose shape the power of the aristocracy takes form does not arise from any direct cause, but from its capacity to reinforce its ontological grounds—both practically, as the argument of congruence suggests, and conceptually.

As far as the role of religion in conceptually reinforcing the ontological grounds of a plane of power is concerned, my argument, again, does not differ greatly from Weber's. For Weber placed special stress on the role of Protestantism in changing what he conceived in terms of the psychological make-up of people. For capitalism to develop, he argued, the negative value given to wealth and the unproductive economic practices customary during the Middle Ages had to change. Only a religious ideology, he suggested, had, in late-medieval Europe, the power to elicit the commitment required to transform practice in so radical a way. Only a commitment grounded on faith could at the time endow the attitudes necessary for the emergence of a new, discontinuous set of economic practices with a force strong enough to be experienced as a "calling"—as an engagement whose meaning derives from the total identification that a person establishes with a cause, and which therefore remains beyond questioning.

For the purposes of the present discussion, it is inconsequential to agree or disagree with Weber's thesis of the calling. My own argument, again, suggests that the fundamental identification with a cause that we can see in the doctrine of the gentleman is one defined by the aristocracy itself and has nothing to do with Protestantism. Still, in terms of the mechanisms of infrastructural formation that we are examining, religion appears to play a role similar to the one Weber attributed to it, and for much the same reasons. For, as the discussions of the gentleman and the *honnête homme* suggest, religion seems indeed to have endowed the emerging infrastructures of social relations with discourses that help place them beyond questioning. In the world of the *honnête homme,* Catholicism helped make the centrality of the king into a practical certitude. In the world of the gentleman, I suggest now, Protestantism helps make multicenteredness and interpersonal detachment into a gospel of nature. Moreover, because of the divine sanction that follows their embeddedness in a religious discourse, the very logic of infrastructural formation become God's logic, and the respective grounds of practice become a reflection of God's will.

Religion is obviously not static. It responds and molds itself to changing political circumstances—which, again, does not mean that religion is "caused" by something else. It means that like any other element emerging from the same foundation, it simultaneously feeds and is fed by the whole, producing with the other elements something like a feedback mechanism, like a constant interpenetration mediated by human agency and human activity.

In both France and England religious discourses and their genealogy shifted in congruence with the shifting fortunes of the different secular powers in each country.[83] In England, as in the other reformed countries, the very rejection of Catholicism opened religious discourse in general to the formulation of a highly flexible, unstable, negotiable set of primary concepts. At least at the beginning, Luther's writings served mostly as an instrument to wrest political power from the Roman establishment or from a local administration controlled by a Catholic elite.[84] To Henry VIII or William of Orange, Protestantism was little more than that. Henry VIII took advantage of the schismatic character of Lutheranism to detach himself from the still strong if waning power of the Pope—an act that Henry's French counterpart, Francis I, his own autonomy secured by the Concordat of Bologna, did not need to undertake. For William of Orange, the Reformation helped affirm the independence of the Low Countries from the sway of imperial Spain. The Huguenots, as we saw in the preceding chapter, were primarily the fruit of a political coalition for whom the new faith provided both an identity and a catalyst. Indeed, the rejection of Catholicism was at first more nominal than real, and nothing prevented the separatist movements from stopping at that point. That was for instance the position advocated in England by Stephen Gardiner, Bishop of Winchester, who saw the withdrawal from Papal authority as the end-point of the Reformation.[85] Had his position prevailed, the Church of England might not have become more than a copy of the Roman church.

But nothing prevented the separatist movements from fostering their reforms, either, and their success in doing so was a function of the political circumstances and the power struggles within each country.[86]

The responses that William Tyndale's translation of the Bible provoked among British officials provide a nice example. Tyndale published his translation in 1525, in Germany, at a time when Britain was still officially tied to Rome. Largely influenced by Luther's teachings, it contained a number of overtly anti-Catholic formulations thoroughly inadmissible to the ecclesiastical authorities.[87] The very fact of the translation undermined traditional ecclesiastical authority. The English text allowed vast sectors of the population to discuss and reinterpret religious doctrine, depriving the clergy of one of its central mediating roles. Despite his own sympathies for the traditional doctrines, Henry VIII encouraged the use of Tyndale's Bible.

His motives were evidently political. His intention to use the new faith to break with Rome had to be accompanied by some concrete sign of good faith, and the endorsement of a Reform-spirited Bible served that purpose well. Now, the very act of challenging the authority of the Catholic church weakened the power of Catholic doctrine, making any opposition to change on the part of the clergy all the more difficult. The theologically grounded defenses against Lutheranism, the doctrine used as a pretext for the secession, became questionable. The claims of heresy on the part of a Church devoted to Henry VIII could not fail to sound mystifying. Henry's own interdiction of Tyndale's translation soon after could not be theoretically sustained.

Not only was the space for the emergence of Reformist discourses open, then, but Henry's decisions unintentionally fostered and condoned their dissemination. As they spread, they began to exert a significant influence on the shifting grounds of practice observable in England at the time. The popular adoption of Tyndale's bible, for instance, helped to challenge the concentric vision of the cosmos inherent in both Catholicism and the practices of absolutism. Its denial of a practice of interpretive mediation, in contrast, resonated with the interpersonal detachment and the multicentered definition of the cosmos inherent in its contemporary, Elyot's *Gouernour*. The discourses of Protestantism and the commonwealth would echo each other, and the practices connected to each would reinforce the other. Indeed, the congruence between Catholicism and absolutism on the one hand, and between Protestantism and the prerequisites for the aristocratically grounded plane of power on the other, was to be broadly recognized by seventeenth-century men and women. And as was so clear in France, the fortunes of the former would be tied to the fortunes of the latter.

Etiquette and the Constitution of Multicenteredness

What do we claim when we claim that we understand the semiotics means by which, in this case, persons are defined to one another? That we know words or that we know minds?

In answering this question, it is necessary, I think, first to notice the characteristic intellectual movement, the inward conceptual rhythm, in each of these analyses, and indeed, in all similar analyses [. . .]—namely, a continuous dialectical tacking between the most local of local detail and the most global of global structure in a such a way as to bring them into simultaneous view. [. . .] Hopping back and forth between the whole conceived through the parts that actualize it and the parts conceived through the whole that motivates them, we seek to turn them, by a sort of intellectual perpetual motion, into explications of one another.

Clifford Geertz, "From the Native's Point of View: On the Nature of Anthropological Understanding"

The Shifting Discursive Referent (Part 2)

THE ADVENT OF THE word *etiquette* during the second half of the eighteenth century marks the definitive anchoring of practice in the plane of power whose beginnings can be traced to the movement of self-expression among the English aristocracy. This plane was constituted first among the aristocracy but, as I have already suggested, not limited to it. The multicenteredness and interpersonal detachment that characterize it are in effect congruent with capitalism and the conditions of power of the bourgeoisie, and much of the eminently aristocratic doctrine of the gentleman can be easily identified as bourgeois.

The word was certainly not new. Its origins can be traced to the middle of the fifteenth century, to the time of Philippe le Bon, when it was used to designate the compendium of rules of protocol enforced in his court.[1] Soon after that the term disappeared, to reemerge only at the beginning of the eighteenth century in the correspondence of Madame de Maintenon. Given the extreme formality of everyday life at Versailles, the term, denoting an idea of ceremony, was apt, and Madame de Maintenon's movement to revive it was understandable. As used in the court of Philippe le Bon or in the letter of Louis XIV's companion, however, *etiquette* signified something quite different from what it came to signify in England. There its meaning moved from the formal to the informal, from the ceremonial to the everyday and, in a revealing reading of the French word, came to denote not just a system of protocol but, as we will see, *une petite éthique,* "a little ethics."

The concept of civility did not disappear. Yet, much like the concept of courtesy during the late Middle Ages, its meaning gradually changed, following what appeared to be a very similar pattern. The change was similar only in appearance, though, for although comparable in form, the concepts of civility and courtesy gave expression to phenomena of a completely different order. The idea of civility as we find it in a work such as John Locke's *Some Thoughts Concerning Education* (1693) or, later, in Lord Chesterfield's *Letters* (written between 1738 and 1765 and first published in 1774), was, like its predecessor, a fundamentally self-referential concept. But while the self-referentiality of the concept of courtesy represented a detachment from its infrastructural referent, it was an integral part of the concept of civility. The separation of manners from any external referent became one of its foundational characteristics.

To speak of a concept of civility as I do here is in a way misleading, for the picture presented in the last three chapters suggests the development of two divergent concepts of civility, one tied to the pragmatics of grace, the other to the doctrine of the gentleman. It is a complex picture that defies linearity by positing not only a vision of discontinuities but of varied lines of development and of different temporalities. The infrastructure of social relations that developed in England is often seen as a stage that followed a period of inarguable royal power. This is how the revolutions of the seventeenth century are usually understood. But the infrastructure that we saw developing in England in the last chapter does not "follow" the pragmatics of grace in any possible sense—except, perhaps, that the beginnings of the pragmatics of grace can be traced to an earlier period. The multicentered plane of power developed according to a completely different temporality, one that began after but partly coincided with the development of the pragmatics of grace in England. The key events of this temporality followed a completely different timing and involved, so to speak, a very different rhythm than the one that we saw in France.

This disjunction, this double meaning of the word *civility,* must be kept in mind throughout the following analysis.

Locke's Concept of Civility

The separation of manners and morals in the English concept of civility becomes explicit, perhaps for the first time, in Locke's *Some Thoughts Concerning Education,* a work published three years after his ground-breaking *Essay Concerning Human Understanding.*

Half-way through the treatise, Locke discusses the basic attributes that make a child into a gentleman. "That which every gentleman . . . desires for his son, besides the estate he leaves him," Locke writes, "is contained (I suppose) in these four things, virtue, wisdom, breeding, and learning."[2] Virtue consists in "imprinting" on one's mind "a true notion of God."[3] In line with what we observed in the previous chapter, Locke defines wisdom as the capacity of a man to "manag[e] his business ably, and with foresight, in this world."[4] Locke places learning last. To him, learning is but a complement to the other properties, for the study of books, although important, does not by itself produce a well-disposed mind: "Learning," he writes, "must be had, but in the second place, as subservient only to greater qualities."[5] Breeding, to which civility belongs, is, however, if only third to virtue and wisdom, one of the greater qualities. Locke adds a word of caution regarding these four concepts:

> I will not trouble myself whether these names do not some of them sometimes stand for the same thing, or really include one another. It serves my turn here to follow the popular use of these words, which, I presume, is clear enough to make me be understood, and I hope there will be no difficulty to comprehend my meaning.[6]

The caveat, which may appear as little more than a disclaimer aimed at circumventing the issue, is in fact highly significant, for it bears witness to the shifting character of the discursive referent at the time. Quite paradoxically, and perhaps intentionally, in the very act of refusing to discuss the issue, Locke calls our attention to it. Words that before used to stand for the same thing or include one another, Locke suggests, no longer do, or do only "sometimes." Or, put the other way round, things that were associated with one another and thus were semantically undifferentiated are now seen as belonging to different realms of practice. The semantic boundaries that helped define them as one have become problematic. Locke notes that this situation is reflected in popular usage, for present practices no longer coincide with prior ones. The discussion that follows, he insinuates, is to be limited to the present. He shall make no effort to explain the shifts in meaning—a most sensible position, given the eminently practical goals of his book. But Locke has made the point and properly warned his readers.

While they may appear to be the same as before, virtue, wisdom, learning, and breeding—and by extension civility—are then different, both in themselves and in their relations with one another. Locke defines breeding by reference to its contrary, ill-breeding—and on this point he reminds us far more of *De civilitate* and the books on grace, even of Brunetto's *Il tesoretto,* than of the English literature of the seventeenth century:

> There are two sorts of ill-breeding; the one, a sheepish bashfulness; and the other, a misbecoming negligence and disrespect in our carriage; both which are avoided, by duly observing this one rule, Not [*sic*] to think meanly of ourselves, and not to think meanly of others. . . .
>
> As the [first] consists in too great a concern how to behave ourselves towards others, so the other part of ill-breeding lies in the appearance of too little care of pleasing or showing respect to those we have to do with. To avoid this these two things are requisite: first, a disposition of the mind not to offend others; and secondly, the most acceptable and agreeable way of expressing that disposition. From the one, men are called *civil;* from the other, well-fashioned.[7]

The association between good breeding and eschewing offensiveness can be traced to Brunetto, if not earlier. To Brunetto, not to offend was the object of courtesy, and *Il Tesoretto,* a book written for adults, aimed to awaken such a consciousness in its audience. Erasmus went one step further. In insisting on an early education geared to create a reflex, he moved the behavior from the conscious to the unconscious. As for Castiglione, breeding was something that had to manifest itself naturally, effortlessly—or as Locke puts it, repeating exactly the same idea, it has to become a "disposition of the mind."

Locke continues:

> The latter of these [i.e., the principle of being well-fashioned] is that decency and gracefulness of looks, voice, words, motions, gestures, and all the whole outward demeanour, which takes in company, and makes those with whom we may converse easy and well pleased. This is, as it were, the language, whereby that internal civility of the mind is expressed; which, as other languages are, being very much governed by the fashion and custom of every

country, must, in the rules and practice of it, be learned chiefly from observation, and the carriage of those who are allowed to be exactly well-bred. The other part, which lies deeper than the outside, is that general good-will and regard for all people, which makes any one have a care not to show, in his carriage, any contempt, disrespect, or neglect of them; but to express according to the fashion and way of that country, a respect and value for them, according to their rank and condition. It is a disposition of the mind that shows itself in the carriage, whereby a man avoids making any one uneasy in conversation.[8]

Again, the passage seems to restate traditional notions of civility. Virtually nothing betrays the least departure from the traditional literature, yet the break is unmistakable. Locke does something that neither the continental nor, for that matter, the British authors did: he explicitly divides breeding into two parts, defining one of its parts, manners, as the translation of the other, civility. While all the earlier authors did to an extent imply a similar idea, none viewed it as fundamental to a perception of the civil. The translation of civility into manners was without exception a minor concern. Far more important was the translation of virtue into civility. If something translated some quality, it was civility that translated virtue, or wisdom, or both. It was that primary and by far more essential translation that was in turn expressed in the manners. Sometimes, as in Erasmus, good manners were even more than a simple translation of civility; they were its virtual concretization, its objectified expression in the world. Locke, however, displaces the idea of translation from a realm larger than breeding to the confines of breeding itself. He transforms civility from object to subject and thus severs the links connecting breeding and civility to the other "qualities of the mind"—the traditional notions of virtue in particular.

Indeed, in the *Thoughts* civility seems to stand by itself. Although there is a relation between civility and, let say, liberality, justice, or truthfulness, they are all at the same level, none implying a translation of the others. Rather, together they lay the foundations for what Locke calls, speaking of the character of a person, "good nature."[9] Religion, the foundation of virtue, has no bearing upon what will come to be known, a little later, as the "small virtues." We search in vain for a logical link between God and civility. As M. V. C. Jeffreys explains, "Locke's notion of religion was mainly intellectual and, although he regarded religion as the source and sanction of morality, religion for him seems to have had little inspirational connection with the education of moral character and conduct."[10] If there is some connection, it is primarily psychological, both the love of God and civility eliciting a similar disposition of humility and self-denial.

Problematically, and somewhat reluctantly, Locke thus elevates "good nature" into a primary value. Since religion is unable to provide a principle from which to deduce civility, he introduces the notion of good nature as a complement to religion. Good nature is not a derivative or attribute of religion; to Locke, good nature is juxtaposed to the love of God. Locke closes his discussion of virtue with an admittedly ambiguous statement:

> Having laid the foundations of virtue in a true notion of God, . . . the next thing to be taken care of, is to keep him exactly to speaking of truth, and by all the ways imaginable inclining him to be good-natured. Let him know, that twenty faults are sooner to be forgiven than the straining of the truth, to cover any one by excuse: and to teach him betimes to love and be good-natured to others, is to lay early the true foundation of an honest man; all injustice generally springing from too great love of ourselves, and too little of others.[11]

To this he abruptly adds, betraying a sense of inconsistency:

> This is all I shall say of this matter in general, and is enough for laying the first foundations of virtue in a child. As he grows up, the tendency of his natural inclination must be observed; which, as it inclines him, more than is convenient, on one or the other side, from the right path of virtue, ought to have proper remedies applied; for few of Adam's children are so happy as not to be born with some bias in their natural temper, which it is the business of education either to take off, or counterbalance: but to enter into particulars of this, would be beyond the design of this short treatise of education.[12]

Locke will of course elaborate on the particulars of these other "virtues." But in refusing to discuss them at this point, he avoids the problematic and rather dangerous task of defining their respective nature and value. The problematic character of the argument is obvious: good nature and truthfulness are to be understood as primary virtues, yet compared to religion they seem to be of inferior quality. In order to define them as less valuable, a criterion of comparison is needed, however, and this does not exist. In the traditional theories of the proper, the problem did not arise. Then all the "lesser qualities," including whatever Locke understands by good nature, were indeed deduced from a first principle. In Locke, however, good nature does not derive from the one, evident first cause, God—and there can be no other.

The idea that God entails the highest of virtues is inarguable. Locke makes it explicit in the first sentence of his concluding remarks on "virtue": the foundations of ethics lie in a true notion of God. The notions of good nature and truthfulness, on the other hand, appear to be afterthoughts— yet they are also foundational. The opening sentence of the conclusion's second paragraph leaves no doubt about it. Good nature and truthfulness must be foundational, for, even if they are of a lesser quality, they are virtues all the same. They are first causes in their own right. The inconsistency is too blatant, and Locke, fully aware of the danger inherent in resolving it, brushes it away as soon as he states it.

What makes good nature a first cause is the utilitarianism that informs the different "virtues" that compose good nature. As I mentioned above, according to Locke "good nature" is nothing in itself. It is a general term grouping all the "small virtues" into one category. It is the quality that results from the proper internalization of civility, liberality, justice, courage, and the like.[13] It is a composite of the small virtues, each having a value because of its social as well as its personal utility. Value, indeed, derives from each of the small virtues, not from the composite. Thus, Locke suggests, the value of civility does not come from its connection to a higher value. It does not translate or mirror anything else. Civility is a virtue because it helps to offset our natural inclination to dominate—an inclination that is both socially and personally negative. In developing within ourselves the disposition not to offend, Locke contends, we are developing the conditions necessary to exercise power—all the while cultivating a parallel disposition of good will within the social group at large.[14]

At times Locke's language resembles Méré's. He writes, for example, "To love and be good-natured to others is to lay early the true foundation of an honest man." And indeed, as was the case for Méré, it is through the cultivation of love and esteem that, according to Locke, one lays the grounds for the cementation of a cooperative whole.[15] And it is through the cultivation of love and esteem, Locke argues, that power should be exercised—a point that, given the largely ethereal character of the equivalent social formation in France at his time, was unavoidably absent from Méré.[16] The difference between England and France in the degree of substantiality of their respective social formations is fundamental. For whereas in Méré the practices that embody the affirmation of the aristocracy as a class remain confined to the surfaces of social intercourse, in the doctrine of the gentleman they become part of the institutional frames of the social. In Méré, the very idea of a class translates little more than the network of ties that form in the course of social interaction; in the doctrine of the gentleman it receives material expression in the workings of both political and economic institutions. Indeed, in their articulation as elements of a collective political body, the practices through which the aristocracy affirms itself as a class attain full political expression; in their definition as levers of a common economic wealth, they attain in turn definitive economic form. The notion of a *je ne sais quoi,* which in Méré expressed the insubstantiality of the social group, thus has no place among the British authors. To the latter, including Locke, the attributes of "love" have concrete causes and effects and so become socially substantial.

Civility derives its value from the chains of causes and effects that define its usefulness, both for the self as for the group. Although it is possible to associate the idea of the civil to one or more biblical precepts,[17] at bottom, it becomes something desirable, indeed necessary because of its utility.

Being an expression of civility, manners themselves thus become an expression of the useful. If the connection between civility and a higher morality fades, so by extension does the connection between manners and any possible moral absolute. Civility itself does not entail an absolute—at least not one of an ethical, as opposed to one of a social, nature. Locke has made patently clear that what "does not offend" is something that changes from place to place. Manners, as Locke stated in the passage quoted above, entail a language "which, as other languages are, being very much governed by the fashion and custom of every country, must, in the rules and practice of it, be learned chiefly from observation, and the carriage of those who are allowed to be exactly well-bred." Our reading of the passage is different now from our first reading. We can no longer mistake it for Erasmus. Erasmus's idea of the ever-adapting person as a "polypus," as a multiheaded monster, finds no echo in Locke. Locke's recognition of the variety of cultures is not qualified by an underlying ethical principle from which there can be no deviation, or which has to be concretized into a fixed character— the character of civility. As far as their foundation on an ethical absolute is concerned, both civility and manners have become genuinely relative concepts.

The transformation resembles the one that we observed in the transition from "courtoisie" to "courtesy." In both cases a sense of continuity masks a deep discontinuity. In both cases the existing concepts become disconnected from their moral underpinnings; the new concepts occupy, at least for a while, a dimension of self-sufficiency. But, as I suggested at the beginning of the chapter, a great difference also emerges. In contrast to what we saw happening during the Renaissance, the detachment from the ethical and the amorality that ensues now become part of the normal, and this normalization of detachment and amorality becomes an integral element of the infrastructure of social relations itself.

Not only does detachment come to be defined as normal, but because it becomes part of the very processes of thinking, it begins to be experienced as natural. The distinction is not spurious, for the change that we are witnessing is not uniquely, or even mostly, in the literal interpretation of detachment. It is not simply a question of whether detachment is good or bad, normal or abnormal. The change is in the nature of the experience of detachment; all experiences, including now the experience undergone in the very process of thinking, point to its positiveness. For the men and women of the eighteenth century, detachment becomes part of what is taken for granted; they come to experience it as something natural, not because one of the structures of their thought suddenly comes to express detachment, but because the complex of structures within which thinking takes place is itself constituted by, and therefore contains, the experience of detachment. It is because the very ground from which thinking arises, what Foucault called the "episteme," seems to have changed.[18]

We have to wait for the *Letters* of Lord Chesterfield before the new properties of civility that I have just discussed—the detachment from the ethical, the amorality, the emergence of a social as opposed to a moral absolute, the experience of detachment in thinking—receive expression in a system of practices. In Locke the discussion remains mostly theoretical and, truer to the spirit of the new civility, does not extend to a discussion of manners. Chesterfield is not concerned with theory but with practice, however, and in a discourse geared to effect practice, the invisible elements of Locke's civility become fully explicit. It is not surprising that when the *Letters* were published, they were assailed as the product of an immoral, corrupt mind—which did not prevent them from becoming a huge popular success.

The Shifting Grounds of Social Practice (Part 2)

But to what extent did actual practices follow the specific type of pragmatics deployed in the British literature? Three considerations seem important here, beyond the usual gap between theory and practice affecting all cases. First, as I argued in the previous chapter, we have to keep in mind that for most of the sixteenth and seventeenth centuries the infrastructure of social relations that developed among the British aristocracy was in a formative stage. Much like the discourses of grace during the sixteenth century, the traditional doctrine of the gentleman pointed at a tendency, not at a full-blown reality. Only towards the end of the seventeenth century did the multicentered plane of practice attain a solidity comparable to that attained by royal centrality in France during the early part of the century. Second, and inseparable from the first point, up to the end of the seventeenth century the pragmatics of grace continued to exert as strong an influence over behavior as the pragmatics of systemic relationality, the pragmatics instructing practice in the world of the gentleman. If we can identify a turning point in the genealogy of this aristocratic, class-bearing infrastructure of social relations, it would be marked by the fall of James II in 1688. For only then were the political conditions for the dominance of the multicentered definitions of practice definitely set—though, clearly, the hegemony of the aristocracy would remain always partial and, like the hegemony of the king under absolutism, would indeed be continually in the making. Third and last, there is in the doctrine of the gentleman, as in Locke, an assumption about the domestication of violence, of the body, and of social relations in general that is highly problematic—as if the roughness or the coalescence of bodies and psyches that characterized life in earlier times had totally disappeared. The point is most significant, for the domestication of violence, body, and social relations, and the concomitant process of individuation are necessary conditions, though not sufficient ones, for the pragmatics of systemic relationality to develop in the first place.

The pragmatics of systemic relationality is of an entirely different order than the pragmatics of grace or revelation. Although they can evidently exist side by side, separated from one another, as with the categories of Borges's imaginary encyclopedia, there is no possible common ground on which these three pragmatics could exist together. As Foucault argued regarding Borges's encyclopedia, the common ground on which these categories can stand together does not exist. The problem is not their lack of propinquity; it is the absence of a foundation that can include them all.[19] The contiguity suggests the coexistence of incommensurable foundations, not the commensurability of the different pragmatics.

The pragmatics of revelation is grounded on a reality founded on the circulation of belief. The parameters of the experiential are established in practices that sustain and are sustained by theism. Truth, rightness, and truthfulness, the perception and experience of the world, society, and self respectively, the "ordering of things" in general, are a function of engagement in the practices of divination—in discovering hidden meanings and essences assumed to originate in divine or some other supernatural power. Rationality itself is defined in terms of divination, and knowledge produced on some other basis, like the modern-day principles of science, defies comprehensibility.[20]

The pragmatics of grace is founded on the circulation of honor along relational lines centered in the figure of the monarch. Truth, rightness, and truthfulness follow from an engagement in practices of royal centrality and the preservation of the mechanisms by which honor circulates. As faith is the essence of symbolic capital in the pragmatics of revelation, honor is the symbolic currency, so to speak, that gives the pragmatics of grace its essence.

The pragmatics of systemic relationality is grounded on a multicentered reality whose major currency is the very allegiance to the multiplicity of points that constitute its essence: "the group" itself. I have called this a pragmatics of systemic *relationality* to suggest that the generation of and engagement in practices of relationality—relationality to self, to others, and to the whole—is, precisely, the fundamental form of practice in this pragmatics. I have called it a pragmatics of *systemic* relationality because the practices of relationality are best conceived in systemic terms. Systemic terms allow us to conceive of a complex unit (in this case "the group") formed of many diverse parts, simultaneously independent and interrelated (the body of each aristocrat), the whole serving as origin and purpose for each of its parts. A pragmatics of systemic relationality suggests that the practices of relationality that people engage in yield a system of this type, the formation of the system being the reason and the goal of the practices to begin with. Perceptions of truth, rightness, and truthfulness themselves follow a systemic logic. As we shall see, for example, the very model of the cosmos used to interpret the relation between individual and society ceases to be conceived in terms of centrality or of a scattered cluster of stars, as was the case in the doctrine of the gentleman. An increasing number of authors, including Locke, begin to turn to Newton's model of order—or more properly, to "import" Newton's model, as Gay writes in his analysis of Locke—to develop their own understandings of society and individual.[21] Or, as we shall also see, honor does not disappear, but its essence changes. Honor is no longer a currency that circulates as a function of grace; it becomes a property, an element of character, embodying one's engagement within and one's allegiance to the group.[22]

The funneling of violence and aggression through channels that do not disturb the proper functioning of the system is indeed a precondition for its development.

Incongruences of Everyday Life

A look at the practices of everyday life in England during the second half of the seventeenth century helps put the development of the pragmatics of systemic relationality into perspective. Take the testimony offered by a diary like Samuel Pepys's, perhaps the most genuine of all diaries written at the time.[23] Pepys recounts his everyday life in detail, describing personal as well social events, writing down his thoughts with little or no reservation. Virtually any entry gives us the flavor of the entire diary. "Lay in bed, being Lords day, all the morning talking with my wife, sometimes pleased, sometimes displeased"; he wrote, for instance, on Sunday 19 February 1665, a relatively calm day for Pepys,

> and then up and to dinner. All the afternoon also at home and Sir W. Batten's, and in the evening comes Mr. Andrew and we sung together; and then to supper, hearing by accident of my mayds their letting in a rogueing Scotch woman that haunts the office, to help them to wash and scour in our house, and that very lately, I fell mightily out, and made my wife, to the disturbance of the house and neighbours, to beat our little girle; and then we shut her down into the cellar and there she lay all night. So we to bed.[24]

The next day was a normal working day. Since 1660 Pepys, a man of relatively low origins, had been one of the highest ranking civil officers of the Navy Board, a position he obtained through his patron, Edward Mountagu, first Earl of Sandwich, Vice-Admiral of the Kingdom.[25] The entry for 20 February is typical:

> Up, and with Sir J. Mennes [the comptroller of the Navy] to attend the Duke [of York, Lord High Admiral]; and then we back again and rode into the beginnings of my Lord Chancellors new house near St. James's, which common people have already called Dunkirke house, from their opinion of his having a good bribe for the selling of that town. And very noble I believe it will be. Near that is my Lord Berkely beginning another on one side, and Sir J. Denham on the other. Thence I to the House of Lords and spoke with my Lord Bellases; and so to the Change and there did business; and so to the Sun Taverne—having in the morning had some high words with Sir J. Lawson about his sending of some bayled goods

to Tanger; wherein the truth is, I did not favour him. But being conscious that some of my profit may come out, by some words that fell from him; and to be quiet, I have accommodated it. Here we dined, merry; but my club and the rest come to 7s. 6d., which was too much. Thence to the office and there found Bagwells wife, whom I directed to go home and I would do her business; which was to write a letter to my Lord Sandwich for her husband's advance into a better ship as there should be occasion—which I did; and by and by did go down by water to Deptford yard, and then down further and so landed at the lower end of the town; and it being dark, did privately entrer en la maison de la femme de Bagwell, and there I had sa compagnie, though with a great deal of difficulty; néanmoins, enfin je avais ma volonté d'elle. And being sated therewith, I walked home to Redriffe, it being now near 9 a-clock; and there I did drink some strong waters and eat some bread and cheese, and so home—where at my office, my wife comes and tells me that she hath hired a chambermaid, one of the prettiest maids that ever she was in her life, and that she is really jealous of me for her—but hath ventured to hire her from month to month. But I think she means merrily. So to supper and to bed.[26]

Quite obviously, Pepys was not short of stamina. Usually he rose around four o'clock in the morning, worked at his office, met with a dozen people or so, had lunch with friends, went to visit a few personalities, worked at his office, had dinner at home, often along with some guests. Then he returned to the office and worked until late. He finally went back home and, as he put it, to bed with his wife, where they regularly "made merry." It was not unusual for him to go to see a play, or, in the company of friends of both sexes, to have long dinners lasting until two or three in the morning. Nor was it unusual for him to make an escapade or, at times, openly indulge in the touch of a woman's body.[27] His advances were not always welcome, as the first lines of the entry for 21 February 1665 indicate: "Up, and to the office (having a mightty pain in my forefinger of my left hand, from a strain that it received last night in struggling avec la femme que je mentioned yesterday), where busy till noon."[28]

Pepys wrote his diary in a special shorthand, both to expedite its composition and to hide its contents from potential readers, chiefly from his wife. Its more delicate passages were further shrouded in a lingo composed of bad French, bad Spanish and, whenever Pepys was short of French or Spanish, bad English. It is not clear why Pepys started to write a diary. According to Robert Latham, the editor of the diary, one of the reasons might be connected with his love for order and neatness. Indeed, Pepys diary was neither a vehicle for introspection nor the fruit of a casual reporting of everyday events; "fully and regularly kept," Latham suggests; it rather "had the effect of imposing a factitious order on the succession of often random events that made up each day's experience."[29] Little or nothing was left out of it. Pepys admitted not only his infidelities but dutifully recorded his moral weaknesses, his financial dishonesties, his jealousies, his fits of bad temper. He did not hesitate to speak out his mind, writing ill of his superiors, simultaneously recognizing the hypocrisy manifest in his own behavior. He commented on public affairs, repeated the gossip of the day, noted his impression of a play, of a meeting, or of the people he met. All the while, he recorded the routines of the everyday, from the moment he woke up to the moment he went to sleep. Pepys diary is a unique document indeed: unaffected, intimate, unsparing. Even the hygienic wants of his wife were chronicled. After telling of the strain in his forefinger following the struggle "avec la femme que je mentioned yesterday," Pepys wrote, "[M]y wife being busy in going with her woman to a hot-house to bath herself, after her long being within doors in the dirt, so that she now pretends to a resolution of being hereafter very clean—how long it will hold, I can guess—I dined with Sir W. Batten and my Lady, they being nowadays very fond of me."[30]

The comment is not without interest. At the very least, it reveals the still relatively poor hygienic practices of Pepys days.[31] At a deeper level, more relevant to our concerns, it speaks directly to the third of the considerations above: the relative limits of the domestication of violence, body, and social relations at the time—as well as the limits in the process of individuation itself. The severe beating and ruthless punishment inflicted to a maid amiable enough for Pepys to call her, as we read in the first quotation, "our little girle"; the silence on the incident the next day, which indicates either a total absence of remorse or the normalcy of such an occurrence, or both; Pepys's ill-concealed brutality in his affair with "Bagwell's wife"; the nonchalance and naturalness of his attitude towards the act; the very relation to cleanliness, to begin with; all these, and more, which we learn about in the space of little more than two entries, point at a reality at odds with the rhetoric of civility that characterizes English literature during the seventeenth century.[32]

Pepys's descriptions of the bubonic plague of 1665, of the Great Fire of London the next year, or, returning to more mundane matters, of his frequent socializing, reveal a similar complex of sensibilities. The comprehensible awe that he feels seeing the many dead from the plague, for example, is suggestively colored by the surprise that his emotions arouse in him.[33] His account of the four-day fire in September of 1666 vividly conveys the chaotic mood of the city, the ravage, and the despair of the population. Yet the narrative remains silent on any sense of lasting pain, as though nobody had been affected, or, more probably, as though the losses and suffering had been rapidly absorbed, and life had resumed its course as soon as the flames subsided.[34] And on his socializing, consider the following passage. Pepys has just attended the wedding of Lady Jemima Montagu, the daughter of Lord Sandwich, his patron. It was an illustrious event and to Pepys a notable honor, an unparalleled occasion to rub elbows with the highest ranks of the aristocracy.[35] Here the process of individuation is put in perspective.

> At night to supper, and so to talk and, which methought was the most extraordinary thing, all of us to prayers as usual, and the young Bride and the bridegroom too. And so after prayers, Soberly to bed; only, I got into the bridegroom's chamber while he undressed himself, and there was very merry—till he was called to the bride's chamber and into bed they went. I kissed the bride in bed, and so the curtaines drawne with the greatest gravity that could be, and so good night. But the modesty and gravity of this business was so decent, that it was to me, endeed, ten times more delightful then if it had been twenty times more merry and Joviall [which incidentally hints at what was the usual practice then]. Whereas I feared I must have sat up all night, we did here all get good beds—and I lay in the same I did before, with Mr. Brisband, who is a good scholar and sober man; and we lay in bed, getting him to give me an account of Rome, which is the most delightful talk a man can have of any traveller [picture to yourselves the scene!]. And so to sleep—my eyes much troubled already with the change of my drink.[36]

Other diaries from the period, men's and women's alike, show a similar combination of urbanity and roughness, a similar pattern of physicality, a similar complex of boundaries between bodies and between psyches.[37] "Before I was out of my bed did I pare off the tops of the nails of my fingers and toes," writes on 22 February 1676 a very old Lady Anne Clifford, for example, "and when I was up I burnt them in the chimney of my chamber, and a little after in this same chamber of mine did George Goodgion clip off all the hair of my head, which I likewise burnt in the fire, and after supper I washed and bathed my feet and legs in warm water, wherein beef had been boiled and brann. And I had done none of this to myself since the 13th of December that George Goodwin cut my hair for me in this chamber of mine. God grant that good may betide me and mine after it."[38] Anne Clifford's diaries are extraordinary documents attesting to her struggles as a woman in seventeenth-century England and, by extension, to the patriarchal realities of British society in general. They are touching, deeply felt texts that reveal a woman of strength and sophistication. Compared to Pepys, Clifford shows a much greater awareness of and sensibility about the care of her body, and yet the same elements that we discussed above are, however less markedly, present in the passage just quoted.

Clearly, the condition that we see in this literature has little in common with the one that we observed during the Middle Ages. But in spite of the immense differences from the reality of the Middle Ages, we still perceive a situation in which the practices outlining the boundaries of the normal are largely incongruous with the pragmatics of systemic relationality. Our discussion of Chesterfield, which will give us a much clearer picture of this pragmatics, will clarify this point properly. But the consequences of such a situation for the consolidation of class-bearing structures, structures that, as we began to visualize in Locke, depend on a reduction of aggression within the "group" and its rechanneling towards subjects or certain aspects of subjectivity that do not violate the integrity of the "group," begin to become apparent. And the consequences of such a situation for the development of multicenteredness itself also come into view. For the development of multicenteredness depends as much on the integrity of the whole as on the integrity of any of its focal points.

It is true that Pepys is not an aristocrat and that, according to my own argument, we should expect the conditions for the development of the pragmatics of systemic relationality to have emerged among the aristocracy, and among the aristocracy alone. And it is also true that among aristocrats we find a greater awareness of and a greater sensibility to the domestication of the body and its concomitant, individuation—witness Clifford's diaries. But if the sensibility is greater, the final situation does not seem greatly different.

The diary of John Evelyn, a member of the cultivated gentry, a man widely respected and generally considered one the finest minds of his times, is illuminating.[39] Evelyn was one of the founding fellows of the Royal Society, served on its council fifteen times, and wrote over thirty books on subjects as varied as the techniques of tree-planting and the art of mezzotint engraving. He was a regular at court, too, and unlike Pepys—whom he knew well and came to befriend dearly—he did not need to be invited to a wedding to socialize with the best of society.

His diary is a highly civilized, controlled, solemn and, at least externally, thoroughly compassionate document. Its descriptions of the 1665 plague or the 1666 fire, while far from being arresting, are filled with impressions of humanity and grief that can hardly be overlooked. Its civility, too, shows everywhere, almost to excess, suggesting an author of deep moral sensibilities and rare rectitude. But we should be wary of its external forms, for Evelyn wrote his diary to be read, and actually rewrote extensive passages with his readers in mind.[40]

Yet, precisely because of its fabricated character, little revelations appear in Evelyn's diary that underscore the peculiar configuration of sensibilities of the times. Thus, for instance, Evelyn devotes a mere six lines to the death of a newborn son, and is more concerned with accusing the nurse of having killed the child, a claim for which he has no foundations, than with mourning him.[41] The paucity of that entry takes on particular significance when we consider that one of the diary's longest entries is entirely devoted to the story of a girl ("a plain, ordinary, silent, working wench, somewhat fat, short, and high-colored") who, as if by a miracle, regularly has a pattern of red crosses appear on her arm.[42] In the same vein, it is noteworthy that, given all that Evelyn leaves out of the diary, the only thing he sees fit to report in a period of over a month is that he went to see "a tall gigantic woman who measured 6 feet 10 inches high, at 21 years old, born in the Low Countries."[43]

Evelyn's picture of life at court, despite all the refinement and glitter, is also marked by a certain coarseness of behavior that seems to us bizarre and incongruous. Here is his description of the banquet on St. George's day, 1667:

> The King sat on an elevated throne at the upper end at a table alone; the Knights at a table on the right hand, reaching all the length of the room; over-against them a cupboard of rich gilded plate; at the lower end, the music; on the balusters above, wind music, trumpets, and kettle-drums. The king was served by the Lords and pensioners who brought up the dishes. About the middle

of the dinner, the Knights drank the King's health, then the King, theirs, when the trumpets and music played and sounded, the guns going off at the Tower. At the Banquet, came in the Queen, and stood by the King's left hand, but did not sit. Then was the banqueting-stuff flung about the room profusely. In truth, the crowd was so great, that though I stayed all the supper the day before, I now stayed no longer than this sport began, for fear of disorder. The cheer was extraordinary, each Knight having forty dishes to his mess, piled up five or six high; the room hung with the richest tapestry.[44]

Whether or not Evelyn intended the last remark to be ironic, we do not know. Judging by the humor that runs through the diary, it was most probably meant to provide a nice, cultured closing touch to the entry as a whole. The one thing we can safely assume is that the tapestry must have been substantially enriched, especially since the same "sport" had taken place the day before.

As we can expect, the salience of this dimension of everyday life would tend to increase as we move along the social spectrum, from the higher to the lower estates, or from the cities to the countryside. Everyday attitudes that we might hardly notice in Pepys, Evelyn, or Clifford regularly emerge in the diaries of people of humbler conditions. The almost obsessive concern with the weather that a man like Ralph Josselin, a clergyman in a small town near Colchester, displays throughout his diary, or his recurrent reportage of accidents and offenses, major and minor, illustrate, for example, the very real impact of the natural elements and the coarse character of people in the rural areas at the time.[45] But even someone as enlightened as John Locke displays a perplexing attitude to violence, at least as long as it concerns children in poverty. "If any boy or girl, under fourteen years of age, shall be found begging out of the parish where they dwell," wrote Locke, for example, in 1697 in a plan to revise the Elizabethan Poor Law, "they shall be sent to the next working school, there to be soundly whipped and kept at work till evening, so that they may be dismissed time enough to get to their place of abode that night."[46]

The impression regarding the solidity of the infrastructure of social relations that we gain when we read the literature on the gentleman is also blurred. For the consequences of the partial domestication of violence that we are witnessing extend to the realities of the institutions that form within and help give body to the infrastructure, including the state, throwing doubt upon the very frames of what is taken for granted. Consider just one episode, taken from Pepys's diary. It is dated 23 February 1665, the same week as the first entries:

> Up, and to the office, where busy all morning. At noon to the Change, where I hear the most horrid and astonishing news that ever was yet told in my memory—that De Ruiter [the commander of a Dutch fleet sent to West Africa to reclaim Dutch dominance for the area], with his fleet in Guinny, hath proceeded to the taking of whatever we have—forts, goods, ships, and men—and tied our men back to back and thrown them all into the sea—even women and children also. This a Swede or Hamburger is come into the River and tells that he saw the thing done.[47]

Pepys relates the event clearly and concisely, and records his reaction in the same fashion. Given the nature of the news, his reaction seems somewhat exaggerated but nonetheless most sensible. After all, the news implies a brutality that goes well beyond anything Pepys approved of. But his profound annoyance involves something more than horror at an act of piracy that, though appalling, was not uncommon for the time. What makes the news particularly shocking is not the fact of its alleged occurrence, but the suggestion that its violence proceeded from a most unexpected source: the high command of the Dutch navy. This is no simple act of piracy, but an act of brutality allegedly committed by the machinery of the Dutch state, by an organism for which the assumed domestication and rationalization of violence is supposed to have attained its highest level.

Now, it is not the act itself that points at the fragility of the taken-for-granted. As Pepys would learn a couple of days later, the stranger had fabricated the story in its entirety. What reveals the fragility of the taken-for-granted is the readiness with which Pepys, as well as the entire London elite, believe in the story. For the unquestioned acceptance of the word of the stranger, a meager and not very creditable source of evidence, points at the ease with which the assumption of a well-domesticated weal guided only by principles of instrumental rationality can be shaken. The assumption is fully premised in the doctrine of the gentleman, and is equally shared by Pepys and his peers. Nothing in Pepys's diary suggests otherwise. What we are witnessing is the difficulty of sustaining such an assumption, as well as the difficulty of acting according to the principles of the pragmatics of systemic relationality in general, not their nonexistence. After it is discovered that the story is actually a lie, Pepys, this time in full congruence with his definition of the appropriate, approvingly tells of the stranger's punishment: "At noon to the Change; where just before I came, the Swede that had told the King and the Duke so boldly this great lie, of the Dutch flinging our men back to back into the sea at Guinny, so perticularly and readily and confidently, was whipped round the Change—he confessing it a lie, and that he did it in hopes to get something."[48]

The Duality of Social Practice

Adding to the difficulty of bringing the pragmatics of systemic relationality into operation, we have the continuing presence of the pragmatics of grace. A look at the perceptions of hierarchy and the practices of relationality in the different diaries reveals a combination of dispositions, sometimes very clearly separated, sometimes largely blurred, guided as much by a logic of centeredness as by a logic of multicenteredness. Pepys's diary unmistakably reveals the vigor with which social distinctions are held at the times. The examples are numerous: the delight he shows at the sympathy of Sir W. Batten and his wife; his feeling of honor at being invited to the wedding of Lord Sandwich's daughter; the almost universal respect that he manifests, even in the intimacy of his diary, for the men and women of rank. The arrogance and insolence that he displays with those that he deems his inferiors, especially the women (Ms. Bagwells is by no means unique), represent the flip side of the same hierarchical spirit. The gradations are finely tuned, and Pepys shows an intuitive grasp of differences: "[T]o Whitehall [the royal palace], where the House full of the Dukes going tomorrow;" writes Pepys on 22 March 1665, a few days after the Duke of Albemarle was named to head the English fleet in the war against Holland,

and then

> to St. James, wherein these things fell out:
> 1 I saw the Duke. Kissed his hand. And had his most kind expressions of his value and opinion of me, which comforted me above all things in the world.
> 2 The like from Mr. Coventry, most heartily and affectionately.
> 3 Saw, among other fine ladies, Mrs. Middleton, a very great beauty I never knew or heard of before;
> 4 I saw Waller the Poet, whom I never saw before.[49]

In both textual and practical terms, Pepys presents people in a descending order of distinction. First in the list is of course the Duke. Pepys does not only convey respect for him, he displays a turn of mind that cannot be described but as an earnestness of subjection, as a spontaneous willingness to affirm his subordinate condition. The language is obsequious yet simultaneously proud, dignified, and, we cannot fail to observe, self-congratulatory. Then Pepys writes of Mr. Coventry. Coventry was a member of the gentry, Secretary to the Lord High Admiral, a man who was soon to be knighted by Charles II. Here, a great deal of respect remains, even a clear awareness of Pepys's lower status. But little of the submissive bent is left. Instead, in both the behavior and its textual rendering we sense a familiarity that is totally incompatible with a practice of submission. Ms. Middleton, a woman of Pepys's condition, remarkable because of her beauty, is just a "fine lady," someone Pepys treats as an equal. The reference to Waller the Poet, finally, reveals a haughtiness and acerbity of form that echoes Pepys's belief in his own superiority. He is not a fine gentleman or simply a gentleman, to be called Mr. or whatever. He is, quite pejoratively, "Waller the Poet."[50]

Here we see a pattern that we find often among the subordinate classes.[51] For the attitude that Pepys displays towards the members of the aristocracy seems closer to the pragmatics of grace than the pragmatics of systemic relationality—although in its fundamentals Pepys's behavior is very different from that of Faret's *honnête homme* (I shall return to this idea briefly below). Still, each aristocrat appears to be a center of grace, which Pepys, like other people of his status, would seek and value, and from which they would derive a sense of worth.[52] In the multicentered reality that we are studying, each center has its own radius of concentric circles. Once again, only in the relationships among the centers, among the aristocrats themselves, should we expect the pragmatics of systemic relationality to have become a reality.

What do we see in Evelyn, then? First, that both the hierarchical definition of the world and the pragmatics of grace are even more forcefully marked than in Pepys. Second, that in spite of the strong presence of the pragmatics of grace, the pragmatics of systemic relationality is more fundamental and dominant.

The first point is evident, for instance, in the manner Evelyn speaks of the notables above him. When he does not refer to them by their official titles, they are always "their graces." His tone, although seldom obsequious, is often self-aggrandizing—as though by the contact of his social superiors, in a manner that reminds us of Faret, he had really become "more." "I went to thank the Treasurer, who was my great friend and loved me," he wrote, for instance, on 29 February 1671. "I dined with him and much company, and went thence to my Lord Arlington, Secretary of State, in whose favour I likewise was upon many occasions, though I cultivated neither of their friendships by any mean submissions."[53]

The passage is remarkable, and not, as Evelyn perhaps would have liked it, because it shows its author's greatness, but because it betrays, as I suggested above, an almost Faretian perception of the social. The language, not merely the event, is important here: the use of the word "favour," and Evelyn's suggestion that "favour," as *L'honneste-Homme* teaches, is something to be "cultivated." Evelyn resorts to similar language, with similar connotations, a number of times. Despite his disclaimers, we see him "making court" to the people of importance,[54] or "being graced" with an unexpected invitation or visit.[55] Clearly, because he was himself a man of distinction, his use of such a vocabulary is not frequent. Besides the king and the Duke of York, whom Evelyn always calls "their Majesties," there are very few people to whom he grants such distinctive marks of honor. But the allusion to a hierarchy in which value is distributed along clearly delineated lines, all of which start in the person of the king, is unquestionably there.

The more Evelyn takes us inside the court, the greater the signs of the pragmatics of grace.[56] At times we might think ourselves in the midst of Louis XIV's court: "I visited my Lady Arlington, Groom of the Stole to her Majesty, who being hardly set down to supper, word was brought her that the Queen was going into the park to walk, it being now near eleven at night; the alarm caused the Countess to rise in all haste, and leave her supper to us."[57] That Evelyn was in no way perturbed by the extravagance of Lady Arlington's title indicates that such titles were common. This impression is reinforced by the fatalism that pervades his remarks on the incident: "By this one may take an estimate of the extreme slavery and subjection that courtiers live in, who had not time to eat and drink at their pleasure. It put me in mind of Horace's 'Mouse,' and to bless God for my own private condition."[58]

That last sentence warns us not to jump to conclusions too fast, however. For if the presence of the pragmatics of grace is quite evident, Evelyn's comment substantiates its limited appeal. To Evelyn, indeed, the honor that derives from the king is not all. Something that cannot be reduced to the person of the king and whose logic does not respond to the terms of royal centrality, namely, the complex of mechanisms that give factual expression to the pragmatics of systemic relationality, is also at work. There is little doubt in Evelyn that this is something that originates in the aristocracy, understood in its most comprehensive sense, as a social class. And there is little doubt that its logic responds to terms conducive to an affirmation of the aristocracy as a group. In Evelyn, the image of the aristocracy as a social and political body, with its own logic and exigencies, with its own machinery of significances and valuations, emerges as clearly as the image of a society governed by grace and royal centrality. Evelyn's is in fact an image of duality, one in which the two pragmatics exist side by side, sometimes in accord, sometimes in disaccord with one another, and together yield a duality of planes of power and practice. This is quite different from the image that we see in Pepys, where we do not find a duality of planes of practice. We find one plane whose practices are reminiscent of the pragmatics of grace yet are simultaneously very different—both because they are oriented to a multiplicity rather than one central point and because they derive their meanings from the machinery of significances of the aristocratic commonwealth rather than that of monarchical power.

Pepys's description of his first encounter with Charles II is most revealing. The passage, dated 17 April 1665, deserves to be quoted in its entirety.

Up, and to the Duke of Albemarles, where he showed me Mr. Coventry's letters; how three Dutch privateers are taken, in one whereof Everson's son is Captaine. But they have killed poor Capt. Golding in the *Diamond.* Two of them, one of 32 and the other of 20 odd guns, did stand stoutly up against her, which hath 46, and the *Yarmouth,* that hath 52 guns, and as many more men than they—so that they did more then we could expect, not yielding till many of their men were killed. And Everson, when he was brought before the Duke of Yorke and was observed to be shot through the hat, answered that he wished it had gone through his head, rather then been taken. One more thing is written: that two of our ships the other day appearing upon the coast of Holland, they presently fired their Beacons round the country, to give notice. And news is brought the King that the Dutch Smirna fleet is seen upon the back of Scotland; and thereupon, the King hath wrote to the Duke that he doth appoint a fleet to go to the Northward to try to meet them coming home round—which God send. Thence to Whitehall; where the King seeing me, did come to me, and calling me by name, did discourse with me about the ships in the River; and this is the first time that ever I knew the King did know me personally, so that hereafter I must not go thither but with expectation to be Questioned, and to be ready to give good answers. This day was left at my house a very neat Silver watch, by one Briggs, a Scrivener and Sollicitor; at which I was angry with my wife for receiving, or at least opening the box wherein it was, and so far witnessing our receipt of it as to give the messenger 5s. for bringing it. But it can't be helped, and I will endeavour to do the man a kindness—he being a friend of my uncle Wights.[59]

What is extraordinary about the passage is that the encounter with the king, Pepys's first, seems to have been nothing extraordinary. To Pepys it is certainly less important than the battles being waged in the war against the Dutch, an issue that directly affects the well-being of the common-wealth. It even seems barely more consequential than his wife's blunder at accepting the watch from Mr. Briggs. Compared with the joy and distinc-tion he felt when invited to the wedding of Lord Sandwich's daughter, Pepys's reaction to meeting the king and to being called by his name, a distinction of immense proportions in the world of grace, is decidedly sober. The objectivity with which he conveys the meeting contrasts with the en-thusiasm that colors the description of the battles. The casualness that he displays in moving from the account of the encounter to that of the watch, not a single comment or transition separating the narratives, makes the two matters seem to be of the same order. No feeling of being honored, let alone of being graced by the king, shows up. Pepys's attitude resembles more that of a school-child striving not to get caught without knowing his lesson—the only peculiarity being the capital letter with which he distin-guishes the questions of the king from, we might assume, the questions of any other mortal.

But in Evelyn we do see a duality of planes of practice and mechanisms of power that affect individuals differently and produce two different modes of experiencing the world, and two different attitudes towards society and the political institutions of the state. This duality of attitude—and I mean duality, not hypocrisy, or simulation, or anything of the sort—was most evident when the actions of the crown departed the most from the interests of the nobility as a class. The major conflicts occurred when the king, in an effort to gain power, attacked the central ideological component of the doctrine of the gentleman, namely, its Protestantism. This happened most forcefully twice in the history of seventeenth-century England, first during the reign of Charles I (1625–1649), then during the reign of Charles's second son, James II (1685–1688). In both cases the monarchs did not just flirt with the idea of moving towards a more absolutist-oriented Catholic faith but pushed towards the institution of Catholicism as the religion of the state.[60] They made their moves more or less subtly. Charles adopted Arminianism, a variety of Protestantism that was so close to Catholicism—or at least was perceived to be so close to Catholicism—that most people failed to see any difference between the two.[61] James, more openly, converted to Catholicism and appointed Catholics to some of the most important offices of government.[62] The reaction was identical in the two cases. The connection between Catholicism and absolutism being widely recognized, the moves were understood as attempts to weaken the ideological pillar on which the power of the Parliaments rested, and the power of the social class whose interests the Parliaments served. Aided by the extreme anti-Papism that I mentioned at the beginning of chapter 6, in both cases the Parliament toppled the monarchy, the first time most violently but briefly, and the second time in less violent and radical fashion but far more decisively.

For Evelyn, as for a majority of his peers, the issues were not as clear-cut as they might appear, however, for the duality of dispositions produced by the two planes of practice evoked a plurality of incompatible feelings. Thus, for instance, when in Evelyn's eyes James II went too far in his turn to Catholicism, he could not bring himself to accept the transformed system of practices.[63] Yet neither could he conceive an alternative to what he considered to be the natural state of affairs.[64] His disaffection did not result in a rejection of royalty or, more important, of the practices of royal centrality. Rather, his attitudes became marked by a continual ambivalence that eventually led him, overcome by a genuine sense of loss, to retire from public life.

Evelyn's decision to withdraw from the public was by no means typical, though. Both his sympathy for the monarchy and his attachment to the pragmatics of grace were stronger than what seems to have been the norm.[65] This distinctiveness is relevant in two different ways. First, although admittedly extreme, it nonetheless highlights a duality of disposition that to differing degrees was shared by many members of the aristocracy at the time— the time before and during which the definitive displacement of the plane of power from the monarchy to the aristocracy was taking place. Second, because Evelyn's attitude is extreme, it also suggests the growing presence of the pragmatics of systemic relationality—a presence whose importance increases as the displacement of the plane of power takes place. Evelyn's genuine grief after the revolution of 1688, his sincere regret for what he believes to be a bygone world, is revealing, for it does not express a simple fit of nostalgia. Rather, it hints at the erosion of an entire domain of practice, of a way of life, of a mode of being that the revolution made imminent and would unquestionably precipitate. It indeed points at a shift of planes, at a new balance, or more accurately, at a new imbalance in the relative power of each set of forces that constitute reality. The certainties of a unicentered reality, the practices and dispositions that follow from a centralized power, gradually evaporate,[66] depriving the English aristocrat of an integral element of his being. The mode of existence sparked by the practices of royal centrality stop making sense, and many of the experiences to which they give rise become, quite literally, impossible within the pragmatics of systemic relationality.

The diaries of Anne Clifford give us yet another perspective on the realities of seventeenth-century England—one that again reminds us that a single infrastructure always gives rise to a multiplicity of experiences. The diaries tell of Clifford's political, social, and psychological struggles as she faces the hostility of a patriarchal world that she defies, although it is at the same time irrevocably hers. They tell of a woman and her equivocal, mystifying position within an infrastructure, or rather two infrastructures, that by virtue of her class are effectively hers, yet by virtue of her gender are not; like all women of her class, she is called to exist simultaneously within and outside of them.

Clifford's story is indeed exceptional. The heiress of a very substantial estate, still a very young woman, she resists the pressures of her husband and of almost everyone else, including the king, to force her to give it to him. What ensues, poignantly told in the diaries, is a story of psychological violence, social ostracism, and personal solitude. It is the story of a woman who resists and defies yet wants to belong, wants to be accepted, and painfully realizes the impossibility of her desires. Her position has nothing in common with the dualism of Evelyn, for it is the same regarding the two planes of practice. Both place the same demand on her, and both are willing to accept and celebrate her only if she submits to the male-centered and male-defined order of things. Both deprive her of honor, and both exclude her from their social universes. She exists within both infrastructures, yet she does not fully participate in the collective self of either one: both demand that she surrender her integrity, a trait whose importance within the pragmatics of systemic relationality I discuss below, to become part of those selves. Maintaining her integrity, as the diaries unmistakably show, implied her unrelenting exclusion. Only as she grows older and her husband has been long dead does she fully regain her place in society.

Etiquette and the Pragmatics of Systemic Relationality
Chesterfield's Concept of the "Little Ethics"

But what, exactly, is the pragmatics of systemic relationality? We learn this, better than anywhere else, in the letters of Lord Chesterfield, written between 1738 and 1765. Through Chesterfield's letters we gain the best access to the multicentered plane of power, now fully established, and they give us a clear view of the techniques and mechanisms that anchor practice in the social space constituted by the aristocracy, which has now become dominant.

Chesterfield was a diplomat by career and was often away from home. He resorted to letter-writing to teach his only son, who was then just six years old, about the ways of the world. He continued to write until his son was thirty -three, when he considered the young man's education either complete or, as it turned out, hopeless.[67] Although they were obviously meant to be read, Chesterfield did not intend his letters to be published, and they were kept private for as long as he lived, first by his son, then, after young Philip's death in 1768, by Philip's wife, Eugenia. Following the Earl's death in 1773, Eugenia sold them to a London publisher. The first edition of the *Letters* appeared in 1774 and, despite many unfavorable, often vitriolic criticisms, became an immediate success.[68] In their first year alone the *Letters* were printed five times. These were followed by many more printings and, copyright laws being nonexistent, by many plagiarized editions over the years.

The letters, intended to be private, were not written for commercial reasons, or with intention to please, or to achieve fame. Their aim was to instruct and to communicate, as genuinely as possible, a way of life, a practical philosophy, a perception of practice in everyday life. Thus the letters contain an unadulterated representation of Chesterfield's perception of society,[69] a representation as truthful as he could convey so as to provide his son with the information he would need to prevail, and thus succeed, in the world.

The disparate reaction to their publication points, on the other hand, to the deeper significance of that representation—at what the word *etiquette,* coined by Chesterfield to speak of the new forms of propriety, came to convey. For the large readership seems to indicate that many shared the view of society at the core of the letters. Had they not been so well received, we could have dismissed them as the expression of a single subjectivity, representing little more than the idiosyncrasies of their author. But that was not the case; the content of the letters seems to have resonated with considerable force among many of Chesterfield's contemporaries. The vitriolic critiques that the book provoked, on the other hand, indicate that there was something deeply disturbing in Chesterfield's representation of the social. "Take out the immorality," wrote with typical cynicism Samuel Johnson of the letters, "and the book should be put in the hands of every young gentleman."[70] The *Gentleman's Magazine* called them a "lurking poison" and denounced their author as "an awful and profligate father."[71] To the poet Cowper, Chesterfield had become the "Grey-beard corrupter of our list'ning youth."[72]

The accusation of a lack of morality was certainly on the mark. Yet we must understand that what was so disturbing, what caused so much moral outrage yet rang so true, was precisely the disconnection of behavior from any stable morality that I argue is at the core of the word *etiquette*—a peculiarity that could receive full expression in the letters because they were not meant for publication. Chesterfield, I suggest, found himself moved to invent the word *etiquette* because no existing word expressed the condition that he was attempting to convey. Obviously, the idea was not that the dissociation of manners from ethics had created a condition of anarchy, that because behavior was no longer tied to morals, people had become free to do whatever they wanted. Had that been the case, there would have been no need for the letters to begin with. The idea was that the *criteria* guiding manners were no longer connected to morals, that the principles instructing manners were now of a different order and could no longer be derived from debates in moral philosophy. The idea was that the moral conclusions reached in metaphysics, theology, or political theory no longer applied to the interpretation of behavior in society. Like Locke, Chesterfield felt that manners constituted their own ethics, albeit an admittedly minor, a "smaller" ethics. Now, if we take into consideration that during the eighteenth century speaking in French was a sign both of education and of chic, and that Chesterfield was not only a well-educated person and a genuine snob but a francophile and deep admirer of French culture and manners, we are in a position to understand why he was moved to concoct a word in French to embody his perceptions. *Etiquette* indeed stood for *une petite éthique,* "a little ethics."[73]

Chesterfield established the distinction between higher and lower morals very early, painstakingly explaining to his son the autonomous nature of the second regarding the first. When Philip Jr. was barely seven years old, his father wrote, for instance,

> [A]s learning, honour, and virtue are absolutely necessary to gain you the esteem and admiration of mankind, politeness and good-breeding are equally necessary to make you welcome and agreeable in conversation and common life. Great talents, such as honour, virtue, learning, and parts, are above the generality of the world, who neither possess them themselves, nor judge of them rightly in others: but all people are and consider themselves to be judges of all the lesser talents, such as civility, affability, and an obliging, agreeable address and manner; because they feel good effects of them, as making society easy and pleasing.[74]

Here, it is true, Chesterfield does not speak of *morals* but of *talents,* contrasting the properties of the virtues, which supposedly make humankind a better race, to those of politeness, whose function is to bring easiness into the world. But he soon makes the association of civility and morals explicit, the lesser talents becoming, literally, little virtues. "Great talents and great virtues (if you should have them)," wrote Chesterfield in a letter dating from late 1749,

> will procure you the respect and the admiration of mankind; but it is the lesser talents, the *leniores virtutes,* which must procure you their love and affection. The former, unassisted and unadorned by the latter, will extort praise; but will at the same time excite both fear and envy; two sentiments absolutely incompatible with love and affection.[75]

As for Locke, for Chesterfield civility is not the product of a translation. To him the civil virtues are, as they are to Locke, of an order that cannot be deduced from the higher virtues. Their essences emerge from two different realms of practice, and their effects are complementary rather than linear. From the higher virtues people gain respect and admiration; from the smaller, love and affection.

It thus follows that whatever earns affection is to be positively valued and carefully nurtured—regardless of its "moral" content. In one of his most revealing letters, Chesterfield writes (and here we can understand the scandal that the *Letters* provoked): "A man of the world must, like the chameleon, be able to take every different hue, which is by no means a criminal or abject, but a necessary complaisance, for it relates only to manners, and not to morals."[76] To him the most important principle of behavior is, simply, not to be different. "Avoid singularity," he tells his son over and over, for being different makes you seem awkward, even offensive, and never earns you esteem. At table do not hold your knife, fork, or spoon differently from other people; don't wear clothes that are different; don't make movements that are uncommon; in short, don't make yourself ridiculous.[77] "Take, rather than give, the tone of the company you are in," he advises; "Above all things, and upon all occasions, avoid speaking of yourself, if it be possible."[78] Always, always conform to others, he enjoins.

What we see taking form here is in fact more than a simple disconnection between behavior and morality. For, as I suggested, the conceptual change that we observe in Chesterfield (and Locke) represents only the tip of a much larger transformation. Note, indeed, the normalization of amorality that the above implies, or the plasticity, rather than the relativism, manifest in the principle of nondifference.

Chesterfield's injunction not to be different involves a completely circular concept. What is proper and what is improper, Chesterfield explains, is defined solely by the members of a group, as a consequence of their own behavior. It is only in the midst of good company that the best manners and the best language are learned, Chesterfield writes, "for they establish and give the tone to both, which are therefore called the language and manners of good company, there being no legal tribunal to ascertain either."[79] Or in other words, good manners become such because they are the manners of the group, and the group becomes good company because the people in it have good manners. What is proper in one company, Chesterfield often reminds us, may be improper in another.[80] In this sense, manners become a language, a formal property through which the group takes shape. To Chesterfield, their only point is to allow for the continuity of the social unit.[81] Knowing one's manners brings the acceptance of the group, and the promise to be successful within it. That is why Chesterfield does not condemn hypocrisy: as long as it serves both the group and the individual, hypocrisy is, like any other mode of action, fully compatible with the small virtues.[82]

The Social Absolute and the Plasticity of Substance

A kind of radical relativism seems to inform Chesterfield's conception of the social, the abstraction at its basis admitting, in theory, a multitude of different definitions of the proper, each embodying a different combination of ethical and behavioral practices. To him, the substance that circulates within the networks of relationality is of little importance. What is important is that something circulates and that this something sustains the networks of relationality. But Chesterfield's stance should not be confused with relativism. For what he is conveying is a situation marked by a plasticity of substance, not its complete irrelevance, a property that endows the infrastructure of social relations itself with a quality unlike anything that existed before and provides "the group" with one of its primary devices of exclusion.

Chesterfield's relativism is, at best, a mixed relativism. In full agreement with the social moorings of the infrastructure in the power of the aristocracy, Chesterfield comes to accept relativism only in its moral, not in its social guise. "Good company," Chesterfield asserts, "is composed of a great variety of fashionable people, whose characters and morals are very different, though their manners are pretty much the same."[83] Good company, that is, can assume a variety of moral properties yet admits only one behavioral norm. This is the aspect of Locke's philosophy of behavior that reveals itself only when the theoretical is translated into the practical, when the discussion of civility becomes a discussion of manners. For then we find some behaviors that by definition are good, others that by definition are bad; groups that by definition are fashionable, others that by definition are vulgar. And we already know which group is considered to be genuine, and which is not: the one genuine group, as even a person as enlightened as Locke took for granted,[84] is the aristocracy; the rest, simply, are worthless. This was so obvious that Chesterfield never saw any need to mention it, and it did not seem to have posed any problem to the book's audience.

While the idea of a *moral* absolute disappears, then, the idea of a *social* absolute becomes forcefully marked—and this becomes a constitutive element of the mechanisms of power of the group. The social formation that the practices of everyday life affirm is obviously not just "the group." It is a group whose boundaries are clearly defined and whose attributes, whose "substance"—a plastic, changeable substance—are given the force of an absolute.

The plasticity of the substance through which the aristocracy defines and realizes itself indeed operates as a perfect mechanism of closure. Because it is nearly impossible for anyone outside of the elite to follow the transformations and therefore "be," this plasticity helps keep "the group" closed to outsiders and insures the integrity of its boundaries. The study and identification of mechanisms of closure is nothing new in the sociological literature. Weber, Elias, Bourdieu, and Frank Parkin, to mention only the most visible, have made these mechanisms central interpretive and explanatory tenets of their theories.[85] Their presence in etiquette should be neither surprising nor deserving of much discussion. Two characteristics of the mechanisms of closure as we find them within the realms of etiquette are noteworthy, however. First is the proposition that the mechanisms consist precisely in the plasticity of substance, not in its contents. Existing theories attribute closure for the most part to a difference in the quality of the substance of a group, or to the specificity of its symbolic capital: the substance that circulates forecloses entrance into the group. Here, the absence of any stable substance keeps the group closed. Chesterfield again resorts to a French expression, to Méré's *je ne sais quoi,* to speak of this unstable substance defining aristocratic being—although, of course, as always happens when a concept is displaced into a different discursive universe, the meaning of the phrase changes completely. To Chesterfield the *je ne sais quoi* no longer reflects the insubstantiality of an emerging social class. To him, it is a perfect expression to describe the indefiniteness of etiquette: the "thousand nameless little things, which nobody can describe, but which everybody feels, conspire to form that *whole* of pleasing."[86] The second characteristic of the mechanisms of closure at work in etiquette that is worth mentioning is the transformation they imply from earlier forms of closure. Earlier mechanisms depended on the circulation of a stable substance—grace, faith, or whatever. What marks the new mechanisms is, again, the unstable nature of whatever circulates.

An infrastructure and a pragmatics that make instability of substance into part of reality thus develops. Instability of substance or, rather, the detachment from any stable substance, fashions reality and with it, people's experiences, as well as their experience of experience. I speak not only of "experience" but of people's "experience of experience" to convey the sense in which, to the experiencer, that is what experiencing *is.* To this experiencer, the detachment from any stable substance is constitutive of, and in this sense prior to, experience itself—including, as I suggested earlier, the experience of thinking. For the very experience of thinking is constituted by that fundamental experience of detachment. As one attempts to think of one's experiences, as one "experiences one's experiences," the thinking is pre-predicated on, and therefore both substantiates and reproduces, the experience of detachment. It becomes part of the habitus in Bourdieu's sense of the term: a prereflective, prelinguistic experiential pattern underlying behavior at its most fundamental.

I do not want to give the impression that with the advent of etiquette all discourses linking behavior to morals disappeared. Clearly, the popularity of the *Letters* did not imply that people stopped reading other manuals of behavior. Highly puritanical books in which the fusion of behavior and ethics was an unquestioned truth continued to achieve considerable success for most of the eighteenth century—even though, significantly, most of them were written during the 1600s. John Bunyan's *Pilgrim's Progress,* for one, was one of the most widely read books in England during the eighteenth century. But two points are worth noting in this regard. The first concerns the history of this literature: while its influence during the 1700s cannot be denied, its relevance decreased drastically as the century came to an end. Towards the beginning of the nineteenth century, much of it had actually disappeared—while, not accidentally, the message of Chesterfield's *Letters* seems to have become part of the taken-for-granted.[87] But, as I have argued repeatedly, the existence of this literature should not blind us to the emergence of something different. The significant point is that etiquette itself came into being. The advent of etiquette indicates the emergence of something different, something that did not exist before, and this point of difference, not the lines of continuity, is what must be explained. The continuation of older and soon to be superseded concepts of behavior does not diminish, let alone refute, the importance of the new.

Clearly, too, most existing theories of social change—ranging from functionalism to Marxism and to all kinds of neo-Weberian approaches— would advance their own explanations for the separation of ethics and behavior that I claim lies at the core of the emergence of the concept of etiquette. It would not be difficult, for example, to see the separation of behavior from ethics as part of a wider process of cultural differentiation related to and explained by the growth of secularization in Western societies. The very existence of two parallel literatures on behavior, one religious, one secular, would come to support that contention. The unfolding of two parallel systems of norms would, in this case, be explained by a trend towards increasing differentiation and specialization, as a product of the division of labor and the multiplication of social spheres, or as an extension of the separation of church and state that characterizes the development of modernity in the West in general.[88] It becomes possible then to see an end to the practice of defining propriety in terms of a moral absolute, as part of a larger process of rationalization, or as an outcome of the emergence of nation-states, or as a by-product of capitalism itself—of the new centrality of capital in the constitution of social reality at its different levels, including the cultural. None of these explanations is implausible.

Yet none of these potential explanations seem to capture adequately two key elements of etiquette. The first concerns the extent to which the breakdown of manners and morals involves a shift of the plane on which "the meaningful" is anchored, of the patterns of social relations in terms of which people develop an understanding of themselves in relation to others. The second concerns the extent to which this transformation in turn implies a shift in power, the substitution of one set of hegemonic practices for another—the very separation of ethics and behavior, the very substitution of a social for a moral absolute being one of its primary mechanisms. None of the explanations sketched above can account for these shifts adequately. Weber's theories concerning changes in types of action and domination, his discussion in the essay *Politics as a Vocation* in particular, are the best that anyone has done to capture the kind of transformation that Chesterfield's analysis suggests.[89] But again, to speak of changes in types of action or types of domination is very different from speaking of changes in planes of practice and an embedded complex of hegemonic practices. The phenomena that the second language calls our attention to cannot be subsumed under the terms of a variation among four ideal types of action or three ideal types of domination. The replacement of one set of hegemonic practices by another involves a fundamental transformation in the techniques of domination, and it is precisely in and through the consolidation of a new complex of techniques that a new plane of action, that is, a new foundation for behavior, forms. This complex of techniques shapes people's experiences, prompts certain attitudes towards self and other, makes people act in certain ways and not in others, regardless of their "type." And the experience of this complex of techniques, not a mysterious sense of "a calling," as in Weber, is at the root of people's commitment to, or identification with, a cause—the cause of the people whose power the practices come to affirm.

The substitution of a social for a moral absolute provokes more than a reorientation of behavior geared uniquely to the production and reproduction of the social group, rather than to the circulation of a stable substance, that is, faith or grace. It changes the nature of the principles according to which social relations and power operate, that is to say, the pragmatics in whose terms relationality unfolds.

The extent to which the social definition of order attains in Chesterfield the force of an absolute is unmistakable. The preeminence of the social in the definition of propriety has been visible in earlier writers. It occupies a central place in Peacham's *Compleat Gentleman* and, implicitly, takes full shape in Locke. But only in Chesterfield does the social group acquire the force of an absolute, of a foundational fact to which everything must be related and which therefore constitutes the ultimate or final referent of everything. Indeed, in Chesterfield the group attains the same properties that were before attributed to God and to the monarch. True, Chesterfield's understanding of the group does not include a notion of divinity, and therefore its properties are defined as being "smaller." But, like God or the monarch, the group in Chesterfield becomes a source of value, in and by itself, and through their participation in the group, people not only gain prestige but achieve, quite literally, meaning in their lives. To Chesterfield, the group demands the same sort of belief in its primary value as did God and the monarch. Its truth becomes a doctrine of faith, a reality whose authenticity is beyond questioning and from which people derive an existential sense as genuine as they did when truth was in the domain of divinity.

A belief in the authenticity of "the group," in its primordial truth value, becomes, thus, one of the cornerstones of the infrastructure of social relations that we see in Chesterfield's *Letters*. It is simultaneously a condition for the operation of the pragmatics of systemic relationality and a function of its operation. For as one engages in actual practices informed by systemic relationality, the reality of the group they sustain expands, and its "truth" gains strength. And as the "truth" of the group strengthens, as it attains the dimension of a distinct ontological reality, one's belief in its primary value and one's engagement in its practices in turn grow stronger. Chesterfield indeed takes the authenticity and righteousness of the group for granted, affirming its primacy and integrity almost incessantly—a stance, again, I insist, that seems to have posed little problem to the book's audience. This is not difficult to understand, for once one becomes engaged in practices of systemic relationality, its realities do gain the force of evidence. We have already seen this in the diaries of Pepys and Evelyn, and the testimony offered by other journals is, in this regard, overwhelming.

Honor becomes a function of one's engagement in the group, not a product of the circulation of grace.[90] To act honorably means to commit oneself to upholding the integrity of the group, and to maintain that commitment. To the members of the group, to the aristocrats in this case, worth is not something they have to gain. They do not have to seek it from a source located outside of themselves. Worth is a property that belongs to them: it is inherent in their nobility—"inherent and Naturall," to use Peacham's formulation. Honor is a collective good, and one's claim to honor depends on one's contribution to upholding the integrity of the collective. I use the word *integrity* in two senses: to refer first to the wholeness or organic unity of the collective, and second to its trustworthiness. In this sense, to act honorably means to act in such a way that nothing in one's behavior disturbs the organic unity of the collective, and nothing one does violates its claims of authenticity and trustworthiness. It means that nothing in one's actions violates the principles on which the collective self of the group rests; nothing in one's behavior will violate the integrity of the collective. To have honor, as opposed to acting honorably, means, on the other hand, to be perfectly aligned with the collective self of "the group."

This is the type of honor that, for example, Steven Shapin analyzes in his study of civility and science in early modern England.[91] Shapin analyzes practices of truth-telling, standards of credibility, and techniques of laboratory work in England during the seventeenth century and shows the central role played by "trust," in the sense that I have just described it, in the making of scientific knowledge. Shapin actually studies how the character-traits associated with being a gentleman and how the practices of honor called to sustain the integrity of the group provided then the conditions for interaction on the grounds of trust. Credibility and truth-telling depended on the trustworthiness of the person making a claim, and these, according to Shapin, followed the social practices established in civility as much as objective standards established in science. And of course, I might add, as scientists engaged in practices that both depended on and helped reproduce the ontological reality of "the group," the entire infrastructure of social relations that we have been studying gained strength.

This infrastructure, we should not forget, is marked as much by multi-centeredness and individuation as by the making of the collective, or the multiplicity of centers, into an organic whole. In a way, the practices of engagement in the group produce solidarity between the multiple centers in Durkheim's sense of the term—although, again,[92] this is neither a typically mechanical nor a typically organic type of solidarity. The relations of inter-dependence that ground organic solidarity for Durkheim have nothing in common with the connectedness between multiple centers that we have been discussing here. The division of labor itself, Durkheim's fundamental variable in the transformations of solidarity, has no role in the structures of relationality among these multiple centers. Neither are the practices producing solidarity among the multiplicity of centers a function of similarity. Quite the opposite, it is these practices, like all the practices by which the power of the group realizes itself, that produce similarity in the first place. Still, the practices of engagement and group formation in general bring the different centers together, cement them, and help make them into a functioning whole. The practices of engagement involve not simply an engagement in, and therefore a commitment to, the group; they involve an engagement and a commitment to the multiplicity of centers that are the group.

These practices help to embody a multiaxial plane of social organization in which multicenteredness takes shape. And indeed, the realities of etiquette can be best understood in terms of a multiaxial plane of practice. Compared to the centered organization of reality at the core of the pragmatics of grace (and by reality I mean both the action of people as well as the structures of the social, in this case the social spheres of the aristocracy), the mechanisms that we see at work in Chesterfield involve a positioning of self within the realms of a plane constituted by multiple axes of organization. The world of etiquette, the social space constituted by the group, includes not one but a multiplicity of focal points—namely, the body of each of the members of the group—around which action is oriented and in terms of which the group takes shape. It is a space constituted of multiple lines and nodes of action and structuration, decentering action and spreading its focus all over the space. Self-understanding no longer develops as a function of one's relation to the one center, or of the social networks organized around and leading to that center, but in terms of a multiplicity of relations to a multiplicity of focal points. And it is precisely by making those points the focus of practice that, I have suggested, the hegemony of the group, of the aristocracy in Chesterfield's times, operates.

The appeal of a systemic model of order in interpreting the relations between individual and society as well as the relations between individuals in society thus becomes understandable. For such a model is fully congruent with the patterns and practices of relationality that we have seen taking form in England since the mid-seventeenth century, if not earlier. I use the term *congruent* as I defined it in the previous chapter. To say that the patterns and practices of relationality and a systemic model of order are congruent is to say that they are structurally analogous, that they share a similarity of form, whereas they are otherwise entirely different.[93]

Locke's "importation" of Newton's mechanistic model of the cosmos, an otherwise problematic strategy for developing an understanding of social life, is in this sense perfectly legitimate. As a branch of the physical sciences, mechanics deals with energy and forces and their relation to the equilibrium, deformation, or motion of bodies. A mechanistic model of order is one that conceptualizes a universe of bodies, physical or social, individual or collective, in terms of the forces that put them in motion, that determine their interrelationships, that lead to their equilibrium or disequilibrium; together they form a machine–like whole in constant movement.[94] Such a model of order provides an interpretive apparatus fully compatible with the multicenteredness, the individuation, the affirmation of the group, and the ultimate self-referentiality of etiquette. And it does so by adducing a formal yet dynamic conception of things. To Locke, at least to the Locke of the *Thoughts,* practice indeed gives way to a systemic, functional whole whose major characteristics, like those that we see in the *Letters* of Lord Chesterfield, are primarily formal, not substantive.

As Shapin's study illustrates, the plasticity of substance involves a second aspect, however—one paradoxically capable of undermining the power of the aristocracy. Shapin's study shows how the doctrine of the gentleman and the pragmatics of systemic relationality permeated other, non-aristocratic sectors of the population.[95] It shows how the infrastructure of social relations that developed among the aristocracy could give rise to a multiplicity of groups, in Shapin's example a scientific community. For what the infrastructure brings about with its emergence are the conditions of possibility for the fashioning of a multicentered collective as a group—of any multicentered collective, that is, as any group. The provisions of the infrastructure are indeed formal, not substantive, and the same property of the plane of practice that allows for the plasticity of substance as it regards the aristocracy, allows for the eventual expression of any substance. The same property that is one of the key mechanisms of power of the aristocracy then becomes one of its major weaknesses. For from the moment that another group grows strong enough, or independent enough, to develop and deploy its own symbolic capital, its own substance, the hegemonic reach of the aristocracy is bound to weaken considerably and become eventually ineffective.

It is noteworthy, then, that in spite of the plasticity of the infrastructure itself, the hegemony of the aristocracy was left largely uncontested for much of the eighteenth century. Precisely after noting the strength of the hegemonic power of the aristocracy, John Cannon, the British historian, calls the eighteenth century an "aristocratic century." For, as he remarks, despite all the internal divisions, or the unequivocal prosperity of the bourgeoisie, eighteenth-century England seems to have been characterized by a "massive consensus, based upon the widespread acceptance of aristocratic values and aristocratic leadership."[96] To Cannon, the central question regarding the century is not how the bourgeoisie came to control the structures of power but why that did not happen before the end of the eighteenth century. "The remarkable thing," he observes speaking of the bourgeois, "is not their assertiveness but . . . their strange submissiveness, their acquiescence in aristocratic rule. The essential problem is not how a capitalist development grew up inside a bourgeois regime, which is what one would expect, but the paradox of a developing capitalism within the framework of a non-capitalist order."[97]

Of course, in terms of the arguments above, neither the submissiveness of the bourgeoisie nor the paradoxical development of capitalism within the infrastructure that we have seen emerging are very puzzling. The first is clearly a function of the aristocratic character of the substance that circulated at the time. For although the actual contents of the substance was irrelevant, and although the fact of its plasticity made it impossible to grasp, it still was an aristocratic one—produced, controlled, transformed, and deployed by the aristocracy. It was the aristocracy that fashioned the definitions of the social absolute, and on that point, as we saw and as Cannon reminds us, its authority was seldom seriously challenged. The second is a function of the congruence, not the contradiction, between the plane of power that we see forming in the complex of practices affirmative of the aristocracy as a group and the provisions for the consolidation of the bourgeoisie as a social class. As I have suggested, the hegemonic mechanisms that the concept of etiquette helped constitute were not necessarily or uniquely aristocratic; they were akin to class relations and class politics in general. A complex of practices capable of giving substance to the bourgeoisie, that is, was already in place.[98] In this sense, the "rise of the bourgeoisie" did not involve a discontinuous transformation of the plane of practice but the introduction and circulation of a different substance within the existing plane.

But this is clearly an issue that I cannot address here. The chain of transformations that I have been studying in this book is indeed endless, and so, consequently, is the "story" that I have been sketching. Our own reality at the dawn of the twenty-first century is neither the beginning nor the end of anything beyond itself. It is, like the realities of ecclesias or the *res civile,* a reality that begins and ends with itself, to be transcended by the emergence of a new foundation, the fruit of new powers as they are embodied in their collective selves.

Foundational Metamorphoses

Τ HIS BOOK HAS ANALYZED changes in the logics governing interpersonal relations among the English and French higher classes over
a period of three hundred years, and in the pragmatics through which these
logics find expression in practice. It identifies three logics, and by extension
three pragmatics, each a function and instrument of the power of a different
group. First it examines a logic and a pragmatics of revelation, a function
and instrument of the power of the medieval church. Then it turns to the
study of a logic and a pragmatics of grace, in whose terms monarchically
centered power operated. It ends with a probe into a logic and a pragmatics
of systemic relationality, in whose terms the power of a multicentered aristocracy took shape. And from each emerged altogether different infrastructures of social relations, not totally unrelated yet nevertheless incommensurable with one another.

Indeed, two of the most critical characteristics of these logics, and among
the most far-reaching in their implications, concern, first, their apparently
impossible combination of relatedness and incommensurability and, second, their inherence in the processes by which a powerful group fashions
its collective self and therefore constructs itself.

Relatedness and Incommensurability

The combination of relatedness and incommensurability comes most
clearly into view when we consider the chain of transformations that link
the infrastructures of social relations together. For, as we have seen in the
course of this study, the chain of transformations is neither simply continuous nor unqualifiedly discontinuous. Each new infrastructure is a function
of the conditions of possibility of a former infrastructure, yet each is at the
same time more than a simple continuity. The argument, for instance, that
the new plane of action that emerged with the rise to power of the aristocracy was itself made possible by the previous formation of detachment suggests a concept of history that does not do away completely with an idea
of continuity. Indeed, integral to the argument of this book is the suggestion that without the previous constitution of corporeal and psychological

boundaries as described by Elias, the conceptual detachment fundamental to the hegemony of the aristocracy, or later of the bourgeoisie, could not have formed. In this sense, then, each new plane of practice could be seen as involving a transformation—for example, the breaking of the connection between manners and ethics—of something already existing, that is, as a function of the conditions of possibility of a former plane. Etiquette, then, would appear as one chapter in the history of social detachment in the West. And yet, at each breaking point in the history of detachment, whenever a transformation like the one at the core of the advent of etiquette takes place, the entire infrastructure of social relations underlying experience re-constitutes itself differently. Points of reference, orientations to action, and meanings change. The very substance that circulates within the networks of relationality changes. And even though all these new things are functions of the previous infrastructure, they could not have been predicted, they could not even have been imagined, from within the reality of the former infrastructure. And within the new realities they generate, new phenomena, with altogether unintended consequences, in turn emerge.

The transformations that we observe from infrastructure to infrastructure do not only involve a reconstitution of elements into a new pattern, something like what happens with the pieces of a kaleidoscope after we move the instrument. They involve a change in the essence of these elements, as if every time that we turn the device, the pieces of the kaleidoscope undergo a chemical reaction, giving birth to new substances, derived from yet totally different from the originals. In this sense, each infrastructural transformation can be seen as a metamorphosis of the very foundations on which social relations rest. For the shifts from faith to grace to honor, or from coalescence to individuation, we have seen, change the nature of the elements in whose substance social relations unfold and in whose texture they take shape, and therefore change the grounds of what is possible and what is not possible at its most fundamental. The very detachment of manners and morals at the core of etiquette, to give only one example, is impossible within a pragmatics of faith. To make it possible, a social currency that derives its value from a source outside morals has to emerge—as does honor in the realities that follow from practices of systemic relationality, which derives its value from a social absolute as defined by "the group."

Theoretically, then, what emerges from the present study is a nonessentialist perception of changing foundations of being: of partial, relatively stable, incommensurable grounds of social practice succeeding one another as a function of political shifts of power. The foundations are partial, for as this study has shown repeatedly, the practices they make possible neither permeate everything completely nor prevent other practices, alien to them, from emerging. Even within what is arguably the most hegemonic of the infrastructures of social relations that we have studied, the medieval infrastructure associated with ecclesias, practices like magic arose and thrived—dispersedly and on the defensive, yet still resistant to the generative power of the church. The stability of the foundations is therefore only relative, for although the specific logic of practice that marks each foundation remains stable, each is nevertheless in constant ferment. Each yields, within itself, a multiplicity of practices that oppose, and clash, and change constantly—yet still reproduce, as did magic in relation to the pragmatics of faith, the same foundational logic.

Analytically, the idea of incommensurable foundational logics in turn points at the impossibility of formulating broad sociological categories to explain the development of infrastructures of social relations. In effect, and in full agreement with the perspective developed by Foucault, the idea suggests that we can find no constant force that drives the genesis and growth of all infrastructures. Not even the transformation of detachment that I just alluded to can be considered such a category, for the development of detachment at any specific point in time lays down conditions of possibility for the emergence of another infrastructure—it does not drive the change; it does not cause anything. Moreover, other lines of relatedness and discontinuities gain and lose importance (e.g., the change from centeredness to decenteredness). New infrastructures involve the emergence of new social substances, and what undergoes metamorphosis, therefore, changes from transition to transition.

The processes that bring an infrastructure of social relations into being are historical in character, specific to a place and time. The differences between the French and the English infrastructures that I analyzed in the last chapters are instructive. For in spite of clear similarities in the political structures of France and England during the sixteenth century, the infrastructures that developed were ultimately very different. The differences between the two, as we have seen, were the result of historical events and their largely unintended consequences. These events affected the balance of power between the crown and the aristocracy differently in each country, affecting in turn the terms and the substance of each infrastructure. In each country a different collective self constructed itself in the shape of its particular infrastructure of social relations.

However, we should be careful not to make the opposite mistake. For the suggestion that there are no broad sociological categories able to explain the emergence of infrastructures of social relations or to describe the pragmatics at their core does not mean that sociological categories are entirely irrelevant. What it means is that sociological categories are themselves historical and that the study of their formation and transformation becomes, as for instance Bourdieu has suggested, a topic of research in itself.[1] This is what we saw with the formation of different forms of capital in chapter 3, or with the formations of individuation and decenteredness, or with the changing structures and mechanisms of power. All these refer to sociological formations with explanatory power within the infrastructures in which they emerge, or within those that are taken over by a different power, where they are transformed—although in the second case their operations acquire completely different effects, and whatever it is that they explain changes as a consequence.

Collective Self-Fashioning

The changing meanings of honor and the changing practices that embody them provide a useful example of how the infrastructures of social relations and the pragmatics associated with them are the outcome of processes of collective self-fashioning. We can identify a concept of honor in all three infrastructures that we studied. In the world of courtoisie, as symbolized in Bors's story, honor is a function of service to God. Bors gains honor by being graced with adventures and being therefore allowed to serve God. He becomes a chosen one, and the glory of God radiates in him. The knights who have no adventures live in a sort of disgrace, wandering aimlessly in search of never-to-be-found glory. In the world of grace, honor is taken over by the civil powers and transformed to signify proximity to the monarch. Honor becomes the currency that follows from monarchical grace, its circulation helping shape the concentric networks of social relations through which absolutist power operates. The new meanings and the new practices of honor develop as monarchical power develops, and monarchical power constructs itself, among its multiple mechanisms, in the shapes of the transformed honor. In the world of systemic relationality honor is taken over again, this time by the aristocracy, and is once again transformed into something entirely different—something through which the aristocracy fashions itself as a group. For there, as we saw, honor helps to give substance to the multiplicity that constitutes the group, simultaneously as multiplicity and as a whole, and helps define the multiplicity and the whole as the *raison d'être* of action. The aristocracy forges itself as an operating body and literally becomes something it was not before: an entity in its own right, formed of a substance entirely its own, expressive of its own multiaxial relational configurations.

Honor is not "something," a stable substance passed from one infrastructure to another. Honor is an instrument of collective self-affirmation, a mechanism taken over and transformed to operate within the confines of a new infrastructure—or rather, to help construct the new infrastructure and to help fuel its operations. What honor is as a "thing" depends on the specific configuration of social relations that it helps bring into being—a configuration through which a powerful group of people fashions its own net of associations. The variety of forms that honor can take is equivalent to the variety of infrastructures that might be possible. Eiko Ikegami's study of honor in Samurai culture calls our attention to the diversity of forms that the concept can take, a diversity that goes well beyond the forms analyzed in this study.[2] Ikegami shows beautifully how the Samurai concept of honor embodies a combination of individuality and sociality largely alien and largely incomprehensible to Western modes of thinking and acting. And she shows how this combination gives practical expression to the relational configurations of Samurai society, helping to fashion the collective self of one of the dominant elites of the Japanese past. Ikegami suggests, in consonance with the arguments that I am advancing, that new versions of these configurations still mark Japanese society today and to a significant extent account for the difficulty that Western men and women have in understanding Japanese culture.

The success of a group of people in establishing and exercising power, what I have referred to throughout as the force of their hegemony, depends on two conditions. It depends, first, on the extent to which the pragmatics at the core of their infrastructure permeates a multitude of "others," the differentiations between them becoming, in themselves, a function of the pragmatics. But it also depends, as the contrast between France and England makes patently clear, on the extent to which they can forge the institutions of society "in their own image," as a projection of their collective self.

The idea of permeation comes the closest to a concept of cultural hegemony, a concept that refers to the degree to which the categories of thought and the logic of practice of a dominant group fashion the preconscious of the dominated.[3] As a social phenomenon, permeation is not simply a source of domination in the straightforward sense of the word. It is ironic and insidious, turning the dominated into the instruments of their own domination. It is true that permeation is variable, always partial, never fashioning the "other" in his or her entirety. But it is also true that permeation does not only mean that "others" internalize, however partially, the pragmatics of the dominant groups and act accordingly, by which they therefore reproduce the foundations of the power that dominates them. It also means, as I have just suggested, that they adopt, however partially, the practices of differentiation of the dominant group, use them to differentiate among themselves, and therefore reproduce the mechanisms that cause their very definition as "others" in the first place.

"Otherness" itself is variable, and fluid. Poststructuralist perspectives make a point about the fallacy of thinking in terms of dichotomies and show how the practice helps generate conditions of oppression. Yet many of these perspectives do not pay adequate attention to the variance in the incidence of otherness. As a consequence, they run the risk of unwittingly reproducing the type of dichotomous perception they so persuasively condemn. "Otherness," like its mirror image, "selfness," is a function of the degree of participation of a person or group in the collective self of the dominant group. Both the people in power and the dominated use the gradations of selfness and otherness to locate themselves and others in a network of social relations, according to the principles by which boundaries are constructed in a given infrastructure. Otherness follows the values attributed to the concentric circles in the worlds of ecclesias and grace; in the former, it further varies according to the degree of religiosity and the signs of God's love; in the latter it also varies according to the degree of military and feminine attributes—attributes whose combination fluctuates and therefore renders the practices of assigning similarity and difference fluid and unstable. In the world of etiquette otherness acquires a more dichotomous nature: the very multicenteredness of the infrastructure makes the fine gradations of a centered world difficult. Yet even here, otherness is not strictly dichotomous. Although excluded from any possibility of gaining "honor" in the sense established by the logic of systemic relationality, aristocratic women participate in many of the practices that make the aristocracy into a class—practices that belong as much to them as to aristocratic men. Aristocratic women see themselves as sharing much of the collective self that gives the aristocracy in the eighteenth century its social substance and define all others as "other," as one singular "other" by which "otherness" becomes in effect dichotomous—and thus reproduce the very mechanism that defines them as part of a singular "other" to begin with.

But the fashioning of a collective self and its permeation among the multitude of "others" is clearly not sufficient for a group, however dominant culturally, to consolidate its power. Whether we look at the effectiveness of the power of the king compared to that of the nobility or the incipient bourgeoisie in the confines of the *res civile,* or we contrast the success of the English to that of the French aristocracy during the seventeenth and eighteenth centuries, or we consider the force of the hegemony of ecclesias, we see that the consolidation of the collective self of the dominant group of people in a complex of economic, political, cultural, or any other type of institutions becomes instrumental for the exercise of their power. For it is in the guise of these institutional settings that the otherwise largely insubstantial formations made of slippery and ephemeral social relations, as was true of the French nobility during the height of absolutism, stabilize and acquire a degree of solidity. And it is in these institutions—the medieval church with its mechanisms for the deployment of centeredness and faith, the structures of absolutism organized around the figure of the king, the type of representative political formation able to embody the multiplicity of centers of the English aristocracy—that the power of the dominant group itself consolidates and becomes dominant. Through them, power—symbolic and otherwise—is organized and exerted. Through the channels established in them, the social currencies in whose substance power takes shape circulate. And because a group is able to forge new institutions in its own image, oblivious of existing formations (as the civil powers did during the fifteenth and sixteenth centuries), its power becomes effective. In their absence, indeed, the group remains a largely ineffectual formation, like the French aristocracy in and around Versailles, or like the bourgeoisie before they developed the economic institutions on which their power would rest.

The entire notion of collective self-fashioning conveys a second sense in which the arguments of this book defy linearity. For it is not only a conception of discontinuities that emerges from the present study. Complementing an idea of discontinuities, the notion of collective self-fashioning suggests a logic of social formation that is eminently circular, and by extension an equally circular vision of social reality. The idea of historical discontinuities, even in the weak version that I introduce here, begs the question of how something "new," incommensurable with what existed before, is possible to begin with. If there are no continuities, how can we conceive the "new"? The ideas inherent in a notion of "genealogy" of the Nietzschean or Foucauldian type, and the elaborations of a concept of "creativity," whether conceived in terms of pragmatism or as a philosophy of praxis, as in Gramsci or more recently Castoriadis, have been among the most fruitful efforts in this direction.[4] Yet what is certain is that however we conceive "newness," the "new" is something that contains itself, that includes within itself the seeds of its own emergence. The vision of reality that ensues is therefore always circular—and this book is no exception. In a view largely akin to Saussurian structuralism, the book views practices as constantly reinforcing one another and existing only by virtue of another. Like language, social reality becomes circular, self-referential.

The book suggests that the process of self-formation of a group and the subsequent institutionalization of these new formations can best explain the genesis of such circularities—of new infrastructures of social relations, of their pragmatics, and of the logics of relationality that constitute them.

Chapter One

1. *The Oxford English Dictionary,* 1930 edition, s.v. "etiquette."

2. Oscar Bloch and Walther von Wartburg, *Dictionnaire étymologique de la langue française* (Paris: Presses Universitaires de France, 1968), s.v. "étiquette."

3. *Grand Larousse de la langue française* (Paris: Librairie Larousse, 1971–78); Paul Robert, *Dictionnaire alphabétique et analogique de la langue française* (Paris: Société du Nouveau Littré, 1960), s.v. "étiquette."

4. Norbert Elias, *The Civilizing Process: The History of Manners, and State Formation and Civilization* (Oxford: Basil Blackwell, 1994). For a detailed analysis of Elias, see Stephen Mennell, *Norbert Elias: Civilization and the Human Self-Image* (New York: Basil Blackwell, 1989).

5. In spite of Elias, or perhaps because of Elias, broad studies on the history of manners remain rare. Most general surveys of the history of manners in the West date from before the publication of *The Civilizing Process* in the mid-seventies. These include Esther Aresty, *The Best Behavior: The Course of Good Manners—from Antiquity to the Present—as Seen through Courtesy and Etiquette Books* (New York: Simon and Schuster, 1970); John E. Mason, *Gentlefolk in the Making* (New York: Octagon Books, 1971); Harold Nicolson, *Good Behavior* (Boston: Beacon, 1960); and Joan Wildeblood and Peter Brinson, *The Polite World: A Guide to English Manners and Deportment from the Thirteenth to the Nineteenth Century* (London: Oxford University Press, 1965). The major exceptions are two multivolume collections published in the last ten years in France, both on topics far wider than manners per se: Philippe Ariès and Georges Duby, eds., *A History of Private Life,* vols. 1–4 (Cambridge: Harvard University Press, 1987–91), and Jean Poirier, ed., *Histoire des moeurs* (Paris: Gallimard, 1990–91). I cite individual volumes and other literature limited to specific periods as appropriate.

6. Edmond Huguet, *Dictionnaire de la langue française du seizième siècle,* 7 vols. (Paris: Librairie Ancienne Edouard Champion, 1925), s.v. "civilité."

7. "That among Christians may be a common shew of religion, and among men may be man-like civilitie," T. Norton tr., Calvin's Inst., 1561; *The Oxford English Dictionary,* s.v. "civility."

8. This I discuss in chapter 4.

9. In particular, Michel Foucault, *The Order of Things: An Archaeology of the Human Sciences* (New York: Vintage, 1970); and *The Archaeology of Knowledge* (New York: Pantheon, 1972). This book, I should note from the outset, clearly takes both Foucault and Nietzsche in a direction they might have objected to. Both were antifoundationalists, and to theorize

social reality in terms of changing historical foundations, as I am about to do, violates the tenets of antifoundationalism. On this point, however, my position is not dissimilar to Foucault's own position regarding Nietzsche. Responding to the many critics who questioned his interpretation of Nietzsche, Foucault wrote, "For myself, I prefer to utilize [rather than comment on] the writers I like. The only valid tribute to thought such as Nietzsche's is precisely to use it, to deform it, to make it groan and protest. And if commentators then say that I am being faithful or unfaithful to Nietzsche, that is of absolutely no interest." See the interview with J.-J. Brochier, "Prison Talk," in Michel Foucault, *Power/Knowledge: Selected Interviews and Other Writings, 1972–1977,* ed. Colin Gordon (New York: Pantheon, 1980), 37–54. The quotation is from pp. 53–54.

10. A selected list of studies and commentaries on Foucault follows: Jonathan Arac, ed., *After Foucault: Humanistic Knowledge, Postmodern Challenges* (New Brunswick, NJ: Rutgers University Press, 1988); Timothy J. Armstrong, ed., *Michel Foucault, Philosopher* (New York: Routledge, 1992); Deborah Cook, *The Subject Finds a Voice: Foucault's Turn Toward Subjectivity* (New York: P. Lang, 1993); Hubert L. Dreyfus and Paul Rabinow, *Michel Foucault: Beyond Structuralism and Hermeneutics* (Chicago: University of Chicago Press, 1983); Lois McNay, *Foucault and Feminism: Power, Gender, and the Self* (Boston: Northeastern University Press, 1993); Todd May, *Between Genealogy and Epistemology: Psychology, Politics, and Knowledge in the Thought of Michel Foucault* (University Park, PA: Pennsylvania State University Press, 1993); and Jana Sawicki, *Disciplining Foucault: Feminism, Power, and the Body* (New York: Routledge, 1991). Two very different biographies of Foucault have been published lately: Didier Eribon, *Michel Foucault* (Cambridge: Harvard University Press, 1991); and James Miller, *The Passion of Michel Foucault* (New York: Simon and Schuster, 1993). Gilles Deleuze's *Foucault* (Minneapolis: University of Minnesota Press, 1988) is in a category of its own.

11. This concern with modalities of being squarely locates the present monograph within the growing concern for ontological issues noticeable in sociology today. For a discussion of the revival of ontological preoccupations in sociological theory, see Piotr Sztompka, "Introduction: The Return of Grand Theory," in *Agency and Structure: Reorienting Social Theory,* ed. Piotr Sztompka (Amsterdam: Gordon and Breach, 1994), ix–xvi.

12. Emile Durkheim, *The Elementary Forms of the Religious Life* (New York: Free Press, 1965). See especially pp. 21–25, 169–73, 479–87.

13. "This book," writes Foucault, "first arose out of a passage in Borges, out of the laughter that shattered, as I read the passage, all the familiar landmarks of my thought. . . . This passage quotes a 'certain Chinese encyclopaedia' in which it is written that 'animals are divided into: (a) belonging to the Emperor, (b) embalmed, (c) tame, (d) sucking pigs, (e) sirens, (f) fabulous, (g) stray dogs, (h) included in the present classification, (i) frenzied, (j) innumerable, (k) drawn with a very fine camelhair brush, (l) *et cetera,* (m) having just broken the water pitcher, (n) that from a long way off look like flies.' In the wonderment of this taxonomy, the thing we apprehend in one great leap, the thing that, by means of the fable, is demonstrated as the exotic charm of another system of thought, is the limitation of our own, the stark impossibility of thinking *that.*" (Foucault, *Order of Things,* xv).

14. Durkheim, *Elementary Forms*, 486.

15. Thomas Kuhn, *The Structure of Scientific Revolutions* (Chicago: University of Chicago Press, 1970).

16. Foucault showed, for instance, how a system of classification informed by a logic of resemblance produces a different order of knowledge, a different modality of thought, and a different experience of thinking than, let us say, a system grounded on a logic of signification (see *Order of Things*, 50–63). In a logic of resemblance—the type of logic that Foucault saw, for example, as constitutive of European Renaissance thought—associations are made by identifying affinities among things, by establishing relations of "sympathy" among the essential character given to things by God (as Foucault claimed sixteenth-century men and women believed) at the moment of creation. Thinking through resemblance therefore involves a continual and infinite act of searching for "some sort of kinship, attraction, or secretly shared nature" between things, and knowledge takes the form of "drawing things together," of making lists of things whose characters are "in sympathy" with one another (55). A logic of signification, on the other hand, is informed by a principle of discrimination and comparison, according to which things are related to each other through a common unit or sign that allows us to measure and order them in a hierarchical sequence. Thought, in this case (which Foucault identifies with seventeenth-century classicism), consists in establishing relations of equality and inequality between things and in arranging differences "according to the smallest possible degrees" (53) of discriminating one thing from another in terms of admittedly arbitrary signs. The sign, the instrument of thought and organizing principle of knowledge, thus becomes a tool of analysis, a mark of identity and difference, and the basis for establishing taxonomies, the form taken by knowledge in classical thought (58).

17. To my mind, Pierre Bourdieu's large body of work includes the major effort to theorize an idea of conditions of being, or to use his word, of *existence*. His concept of the "habitus," indeed, in some ways affords a more elegant and flexible understanding of social practices—including practices of thinking—than the one that I derived from Foucault, and in that sense affords a more versatile heuristics for theorizing "conditions of being"; see, for example, Rogers Brubaker, "Comments on Pizzorno," in *Social Theory for a Changing Society*, ed. Pierre Bourdieu and James S. Coleman (Boulder, CO: Westview, 1991), 234–38. The concept of infrastructures of social relations, however, conveys a dimension of reality that Bourdieu's corresponding concept of "schemata" does not. The term *schemata* refers to the "mental and bodily" practices of classification "that function as *symbolic* templates for the practical activities—conducts, thoughts, feelings, and judgments—of social agents." See Pierre Bourdieu and Loïc J. D. Wacquant, *An Invitation to Reflexive Sociology* (Chicago: University of Chicago Press, 1992), 7; emphasis in the original. For a definition of *habitus*, see Pierre Bourdieu, *The Logic of Practice* (Stanford: Stanford University Press, 1990), 53. Like the concept that I propose, then, schemata involve particular modalities of thinking and acting that instruct practice at its most general. The idea of infrastructures of social relations, however, places special stress on the *logic* in terms of which we constitute modalities of thinking and acting in the first place. In this sense infrastructures of social relations

would involve a second order of schemata—the same infrastructure, that is, making possible many different schemata and habituses. The difference is important, for it implies not only that multiple habituses are produced by one infrastructure (a point that is perfectly consistent with my discussion of the heterogeneity of infrastructures of social relations above) but that transformations in a habitus, as Bourdieu describes it, do not necessarily involve a discontinuity. Indeed, as long as the habitus deploys the same infrastructure of social relations, there is no real transformation.

18. Truth, rightness, truthfulness, and comprehensibility are the four validity claims, each associated with a different domain of reality, that are specified by Habermas. See in particular Jürgen Habermas, "What Is Universal Pragmatics," in *Jürgen Habermas: Communication and the Evolution of Society* (Boston: Beacon Press, 1979), 1–68.

19. The phrase *epistemological field,* signifying the language of "grounding," is Foucault's; see his *Order of Things,* xxii.

20. Again, I develop this notion in analogy to Foucault's notion of the impossibility of thinking certain things, as expressed in Borges's bestiary. For a parallel formulation in Foucault see the preface to *The Order of Things,* xxii.

21. In spite of the large number of practices and experiences that the infrastructure makes possible (which to the insider appears to contain all of what can be experienced and thought), we should keep in mind that an infinite number of other practices and experiences, the product of other infrastructures, remain outside of the realm of a particular infrastructure.

22. The idea that knowledge exists through its practices is obviously not unique to Foucault. Although specifics vary from author to author, a similar perception is shared, for example, by Clifford Geertz, Erving Goffman, Kuhn, and Bourdieu. See, in particular, Clifford Geertz, "The Way We Think Now: Toward an Ethnography of Modern Thought," in *Local Knowledge: Further Essays in Interpretive Anthropology* (New York: Basic Books, 1983), 147–63; Erving Goffman, *Frame Analysis: An Essay on the Organization of Experience* (Cambridge: Harvard University Press, 1974); and Kuhn, *Scientific Revolutions.* For Bourdieu, see Pierre Bourdieu, *Outline of a Theory of Practice* (New York: Cambridge University Press, 1977); *Distinction: A Social Critique of the Judgment of Taste* (Cambridge: Harvard University Press, 1984); *Logic of Practice;* and Bourdieu and Wacquant, *Reflexive Sociology.* For Durkheim see *Elementary Forms,* book 3.

23. Geertz's formulation is worth quoting: "What connects Victor Turner, shuffling through the color symbolism of passage rites, Philippe Ariès, parading funeral images of death or schoolhouse ones of childhood, and Gerald Holton, ferreting out thermata from oil drops, is the belief that ideation, subtle or otherwise, is a cultural artifact. Like class or power, it is something to be characterized by construing its expressions in terms of the activities that sustain them" (Geertz, "The Way We Think Now," 152).

24. Max Weber, *The Protestant Ethic and the Spirit of Capitalism* (New York: Scribner's, 1958).

25. A beautiful example is his description of the break at the heart of reason in *Madness*

and Civilization, the constitution of the boundary between reason and nonreason lasting for the entire period that we know as the Renaissance. In *The Order of Things* Foucault describes the formation of a new episteme as taking several decades. The same is true in his later work, neither the emergence of the Panopticon nor the deployment of confession (like, incidentally, the birth of the clinic) being a matter of a few years. See Michel Foucault, *Madness and Civilization: A History of Insanity in the Age of Reason* (New York: Vintage, 1965); *The Birth of the Clinic: An Archeology of Medical Perception* (New York: Random House, 1975); *Discipline and Punish: The Birth of the Prison* (New York: Vintage, 1977); and *A History of Sexuality,* vol. 1, *An Introduction* (New York: Vintage, 1978).

26. The objects it generated, as the chapter epigraph from Nietzsche suggests, are taken over and transformed by the new power.

27. For Foucault's reading of Nietzsche, see his "Nietzsche, Genealogy, History," in *The Foucault Reader,* ed. Paul Rabinow (New York: Pantheon, 1984), 76–100. My (mis)use of Nietzsche is obviously different from Foucault's.

28. This is the case for anyone defined as an "other"—women; religious or ethnic minorities; the people in the lower estates of society or at its margins—who therefore escape to some extent the constitutive hegemony of the infrastructure. My double allusion to Gramsci, in my use of the word *hegemony* and in my reference to "the people at the margins," is certainly not fortuitous. Foucault's beautiful and appropriately poetic description of the "ship of fools" in chapter one of *Madness and Civilization* is an example of these marginal people during the Middle Ages. Note, also, that hegemony is a variable, not a constant. For Gramsci's concept of cultural hegemony see, in particular, the sections on "State and Civil Society" and "Americanism and Fordism" in Antonio Gramsci, *Selections from the Prison Notebooks,* ed. and trans. Quintin Hoare and Geoffrey Nowell Smith (New York: International Publishers, 1971). See also Carl Boggs Jr., "Gramsci's 'Prison Notebooks,' Part 1," *Socialist Revolution* 10 (winter 1971): 79–118, which contains what is arguably the best introduction to Gramsci's cultural hegemony.

29. This proposition has little in common with the idea, to use Goffman's formulation, of a multiplicity of loosely coupled social orders at the core of much of contemporary sociological theory. Bourdieu's concept of the "field" is an example of this way of thinking. According to Bourdieu, indeed, societies are constituted of a multiplicity of somewhat autonomous fields, each involving its own practices of power and structuration, each embodying a different "order," and each following its own dynamics of development. As powerful as Bourdieu's formulation is in explaining the constitution and diffusion of practices within given institutional fields, it does not fare as well in explaining the "trans-" or "infra-field" processes that keep the development of a society from unfolding in completely different directions. Like the argument of second-order schemata, my approach suggests a notion of second-order fields that might help us understand precisely that point. For an elaboration of a very similar argument, see Jorge Arditi, "Geertz, Kuhn, and the Idea of a Cultural Paradigm," *British Journal of Sociology* 45 (December 1994): 597–617. For a further elaboration of Bourdieu's thought in the direction that I have just sketched, see William H. Sewell

Jr., "A Theory of Structure: Duality, Agency, and Transformation," *American Journal of Sociology* 98 (1992): 1–29. For a discussion of this point in the context of sociological theory, see Derek Layder, *Understanding Social Theory* (Thousand Oaks, CA: Sage, 1994).

30. This also points at the impossibility of constructing a conventional, linear theory of social change, and therefore the impossibility of identifying such a theory in the present study. Any attempt to do so runs against the basic argument of the book.

31. For a similar argument that deals with a quite different reality from the one I study here, see Eiko Ikegami, *The Taming of the Samurai: Honorific Individualism and the Making of Modern Japan* (Cambridge: Harvard University Press, 1995).

32. Michele Lamont has taken a similar position in her study of contemporary manners in France and the United States; see Michele Lamont, *Money, Morals, and Manners: The Culture of the French and American Upper-Middle Class* (Chicago: University of Chicago Press, 1992).

33. In periods of transition, however, etiquette books, as we shall see, are useful to an emergent power in clarifying its own standards.

34. Baldesar Castiglione, *The Book of the Courtier,* translated by Charles S. Singleton (Garden City, NY: Anchor Books, 1959), 47.

35. In the following chapters I make a distinction between the terms *courtoisie* and *courtesy*. By *courtoisie* I mean the moral concept taking definitive shape during the twelfth and early-thirteenth centuries; I use *courtesy* to refer to the secular version of the concept that began to become dominant at the end of the thirteenth century and acquired full expression by the fifteenth and early sixteenth centuries. The distinction is important because, as I discuss in chapter 3, it accounts for the interpretation of medieval propriety that I present, which differs significantly from that of C. Stephen Jaeger, whose study of early medieval courtliness is arguably the most comprehensive to date. See C. Stephen Jaeger, *The Origins of Courtliness: Civilizing Trends and the Formation of Courtly Ideals, 939–1210* (Philadelphia: University of Pennsylvania Press, 1985).

36. The paradox, of which almost anyone attempting to interpret the past—including historians, literary critics, and social scientists—is well aware, is beautifully expressed by Borges (again) in the epilogue to his story "Averroes' Search." Borges's account of the genesis of the text is as fictional as the story itself.

> I remembered Averroes who, closed within the orb of Islam, could never know the meaning of the terms *tragedy* and *comedy*. I related his case; as I went along, I felt what that god mentioned by Burton must have felt when he tried to create a bull and created a buffalo instead. I felt that the work was mocking me. I felt that Averroes, wanting to imagine what a drama is without ever having suspected what a theater is, was no more absurd than I, wanting to imagine Averroes with no other source than a few fragments from Renan, Lane, and Asin Palacios. I felt, on the last page, that my narration was a symbol of the man I was as I wrote it.

See Jorge Luis Borges, *Labyrinths: Selected Stories and Other Writings,* ed. Donald A. Yates and James E. Irby (New York: New Directions, 1964), 155. For a discussion of this point in literary theory, see Hans Robert Jauss, "The Alterity and Modernity of Medieval Literature," *New Literary History* 10 (1979): 181–230. For a fascinating collection of essays on the problematics of reading the Middle Ages, see M. Perrin, ed., *Dire le Moyen Age: Hier et aujourd'hui* (Paris: Presses Universitaires de France, 1990).

Chapter Two

1. An English translation of the text is found in books 13–17 of Sir Thomas Malory, *Le Morte d'Arthur* (London: J. M. Dent, 1906). For a modernized version in English, see P. M. Matarasso, *The Quest of the Holy Grail* (London: Penguin, 1969). For reasons that I explain below, I am quoting from Malory's translation, pp. 221–24. A version of the thirteenth-century French text appears in O. Sommer, *The Vulgate Version of Arthurian Romance* (Washington, DC: Carnegie Institution, 1910). For a translation into modern French see *La quête du Saint Graal*, trans. Emmanuèle Baumgartner (Paris: Honoré Champion, 1979). For some relevant studies on the *Quest* and medieval French romance in general, see Emmanuèle Baumgartner, *L'arbre et le pain: Essai sur "La queste del Saint Graal"* (Paris: SEDES, 1981); Matilda Tomaryn Bruckner, *Shaping Romance: Interpretation, Truth, and Closure in Twelfth-Century French Fictions* (Philadelphia: University of Pennsylvania Press, 1993); E. Jane Burns, *Arthurian Fictions: Rereading the Vulgate Cycle* (Columbus: Ohio State University Press, 1985); Dennis H. Green, *Irony in the Medieval Romance* (Cambridge: Cambridge University Press, 1979); Douglas Kelly, *Medieval French Romance* (New York: Twayne Publishers, 1993); Jacques Ribard, *Du philtre au Graal: Pour une interprétation théologique du "Roman de Tristan" et du "Conte du Graal"* (Paris: Champion, 1989); and Anne Wilson, *The Magical Quest: The Use of Magic in Arthurian Romance* (Manchester: Manchester University Press, 1988).

2. See Nigel Bryant's introduction to *The High Book of the Grail* (Ipswich: D. S. Brewer, 1978).

3. Malory, *Le Morte d'Arthur*, 221–22.

4. Ibid., 223–24.

5. For a study of Malory, see P. J. C. Field, *The Life and Times of Sir Thomas Malory* (Cambridge: D. S. Brewer, 1993). For an analysis of Malory's transformations of the French text, see Sandra Ness Ihle, *Malory's Grail Quest: Invention and Adaptation in Medieval Prose Romance* (Madison: University of Wisconsin Press, 1983).

6. As a very short example of the evidence of Bors's courtoisie to his contemporaries and of his facility in conveying it, here is how a lonely hermit reacted after having seen and heard him for a short moment:

> So rode they [Bors and the hermit] together till that they came to an hermitage. And there he prayed Bors to dwell all that night with him. And so he alit and put away his armour, and prayed him that he might be confessed; and so they went into the chapel, and there he was clean confessed, and they ate bread and drank water together. . . . And then he took him a scarlet coat, so that should be instead of his shirt till he had fulfilled the quest of the Sangreal; and the good

man found in him so marvellous a life and so stable, that he marvelled and felt that he was never corrupt. (Malory, *Le Morte d'Arthur*, 220).

7. For a recent study on courtoisie and villainy as forming a hierarchical opposition, see Kathryn Gravdal, *Vilain and Courtois: Transgressive Parody in French Literature of the Twelfth and Thirteenth Centuries* (Lincoln: University of Nebraska Press, 1989). Curiously, however, Gravdal engages in a critique of the idea that *courtois* was always associated with nobility and *vilain* with peasantry, a position that only the most crude interpretations of the period would support. Her book, then, shows how these categories could not be easily related to social classes. Her conclusion is part of the assumptions of the present study.

8. A version of the original French text, in verse form, can be found in Etienne Barbazan, ed., *Fabliaux et contes des poètes francois des 11e, 12e, 13e, 14e, et 15e siècles* (Genève: Slatkin Reprints, 1976), 1: 208–42. I quote from the modernized version in Felix Lecoy, ed., *Le chevalier au barisel: Conte pieux du XIIIe siècle* (Paris: Champion, 1955); reprinted in Jean-Claude Aubailly, ed., *Fabliaux et contes moraux du Moyen Age* (Paris: Poche, 1987). A condensed, modernized version of the tale appears in A. Perier, ed., *Fabliaux et contes choisis du Moyen Age* (Paris: Hatier, 1948), 49–66. The translation is my own.

9. Lecoy, ed., *Le chevalier*, 153–54.

10. Ibid., 154.

11. Ibid., 161–62.

12. Ibid., 165.

13. Ibid., 169–70.

14. While close in form and tone to the more secular and irreverent *fabliaux,* the *contes pieux* tell stories of tragedies and moral struggles. A greedy, unfaithful and unthankful forester loses a fortune; a hermit kills a woman who was sent by the Devil and with whom he had sinned; a mother kills her son. Though often of ancient origins, they were always adapted to the mentality of the times. Their recurrent themes were faith and, as in the present tale, the power of repentance to transform the person. See, for instance, Perier's introduction in *Fabliaux et contes choisis,* and the brief discussion of the tale by Aubailly in *Fabliaux et contes moraux,* pp. 211–13; see also Jean-Charles Payen, *Littérature française,* vol. 1, *Le Moyen Age* (Paris: Arthaud, 1984), 151–54. I discuss the *fabliaux* briefly below.

15. Payen, *Le Moyen Age,* 151.

16. Barbazan, *Fabliaux et contes,* 1: 236, lines 835–40.

17. Thus, for instance, in the *Quest:*

When Sir Gawaine was departed from his fellowship he rode long without any adventure. For he found not the tenth part of adventure as he was wont to do. For Sir Gawaine rode from Whitsuntide until Michaelmas and found none adventure that pleased him. So on a day it befell Gawaine met with Sir Ector de Maris, and either made great joy of other that it were marvel to tell. And so they told every each other, and complained them greatly that they could find none adventure. Truly, said Sir Gawaine unto Sir Ector, I am nigh weary of this quest, and loth I am to follow further in strange countries. One thing marvelled me, said

Sir Ector, I have met with twenty knights, fellows of mine, and all they complain as I do. (Malory, *Le Morte d'Arthur*, 213)

The explanation of this is given by a hermit, whom Sir Gawaine asks to interpret one of his dreams:

Sir, said the hermit unto Sir Gawaine, the fair meadow and the rack therein ought to be understood the Round Table, and by the meadow ought to be understood humility and patience, those be the things which be always green and quick; for men may no time overcome humility and patience, therefore was the Round Table founded; and the chivalry hath been at all times so by the fraternity which was there that she might not be overcome; for men said she was founded in patience and humility. At the rack ate an hundred and fifty bulls; but they ate not in the meadow, for their hearts should he set in humility and patience, and the bulls were proud and black save only three. . . . And the three bulls which were white save only one that was spotted: the two white betoken Sir Galahad and Sir Percivale, for they be maidens clene and without spot; and the third that had a spot signifieth Sir Bors de Ganis, which trespassed but once in his virginity. (Ibid., 217)

The same is true of Lancelot who, because of his sins, is unable to see the Grail when it appears before his eyes.

18. For a short yet incisive discussion of the concept of *ecclesias*, see Walter Ullman, "The Medieval Origins of the Renaissance," in *The Renaissance: Essays in Interpretation,* ed. André Chastel et al. (New York: Methuen, 1982), 33–82.

19. For the original formulation of this argument, see J. Ncalc Carman, "The Symbolism of *Perlesvaus*," *P.M.L.A.* 61 (March 1946): 42–83; see also Ribard, *Du philtre au Graal*.

20. For arguments in this direction, see, for instance, Bruckner, *Shaping Romance;* Gravdal, *Vilain and Courtois*.

21. Johan Huizinga, *The Waning of the Middle Ages* (Garden City: Doubleday Anchor Books, 1954), 67, 190.

22. Marc Bloch, *Feudal Society* (Chicago: University of Chicago Press, 1961), 82.

23. Robert Delort, *Life in the Middle Ages* (New York: Crown, 1983), 63–64.

24. The most notable example of this trend is the volume devoted to the Middle Ages in the collection on the history of everyday life cited in chapter 1, from which, but for a few exceptions, religion is almost absent. See Georges Duby, ed., *Revelations of the Medieval World,* vol. 2 of *A History of Private Life,* ed. Philippe Ariès and Georges Duby (Cambridge: Harvard University Press, 1988). The major exception, ironically, is Duby's own contribution to the volume.

25. Maurice Keen, *Chivalry* (New Haven: Yale University Press, 1984). A similar perception instructs most of the books on Arthurian romance listed above.

26. Bruckner, *Shaping Romance*, 3–4.

27. The exemplar in this case is Emmanuel Le Roy Ladurie, *Montaillou: The Promised Land of Error* (New York: Vintage, 1979).

28. Besides the literature already cited, for everyday life in the Middle Ages, see also Yvonne Bellenger, ed., *Le temps et la durée dans la literature au Moyen Age et à la Renaissance* (Paris: Nizet, 1986); Jean Chapelot and Robert Fossier, *The Village and House in the Middle Ages* (Berkeley: University of California Press, 1985); Christopher Dyer, *Everyday Life in Medieval England* (London: Hambledon Press, 1994); Joseph Gies and Frances Gies, *Life in a Medieval City* (New York: Thomas Crowell, 1969); Hans-Werner Goetz, *Life in the Middle Ages: From the Seventh to the Thirteenth Century* (Notre Dame: University of Notre Dame Press, 1993); Christiane Klapisch-Zuber, ed., *A History of Women in the West*, vol. 2, *Silences of the Middle Ages* (Cambridge: Harvard University Press, 1992); Paul Lacroix, *France in the Middle Ages: Customs, Classes, and Conditions* (New York: Ungar, 1963); Jacques Le Goff, *La civilisation de l'occident médiéval* (Paris: Arthaud, 1967); Marie-Thérèse Lorcin, *Façons de sentir et de penser: Les fabliaux français* (Paris: Honoré Champion, 1979); Angela M. Lucas, *Women in the Middle Ages: Religion, Marriage, and Letters* (New York: St. Martin's, 1983); and Erika Uitz, *Women in the Medieval Town* (London: Barrie and Jenkins, 1990).

29. Delort, *Life in the Middle Ages*, 68.

30. For a paradigmatic study of space and everyday life, see Raymond Ledrut, "L'homme et l'espace," in *Histoire des moeurs*, vol. 1, ed. Jean Poirier (Paris: Gallimard, 1990), 59–114.

31. See Georges Duby and Philippe Braunstein, "The Emergence of the Individual," in *Revelations of the Medieval World*, ed. Duby, 622.

32. Ibid., 627–29, for example.

33. Bryan S. Turner, *Medical Power and Social Knowledge* (London: Sage, 1987), 26–27.

34. See Erich Auerbach's splendid essay "Figura," in *Scenes from the Drama of European Literature* (Gloucester, MA: Peter Smith, 1973). See also Eugene Vance, *Marvelous Signals: Poetics and Sign Theory in the Middle Ages* (Lincoln: University of Nebraska Press, 1986); Jean-Claude Schmitt, *La raison des gestes dans l'occident médiéval* (Paris: Gallimard, 1990), chap. 2.

35. I dealt with Foucault's discussion of resemblance in chapter 1.

36. Auerbach, "Figura."

37. The phrase "undifferentiated experience" is from Michel Foucault, *Madness and Civilization: A History of Insanity in the Age of Reason* (New York: Vintage, 1965), ix.

38. Richard Kieckhefer, "The Specific Rationality of Medieval Magic," *American Historical Review* 99 (June 1994): 813–36. See also his *Magic in the Middle Ages* (New York: Cambridge University Press, 1989); Valerie I. J. Flint, *The Rise of Magic in Early Medieval Europe* (Princeton: Princeton University Press, 1991); and Sophie Houdard, *Les sciences du diable: Quatre discours sur la sorcellerie* (Paris: Cerf, 1992).

39. Nicole Oresme, *Nicole Oresme and the Marvels of Nature: A Study of His 'De causis mirabilium,'* tr. and commentary by Bert Hansen (Toronto: Pontifical Institute of Mediaeval Studies, 1985), quoted in Kieckhefer, "The Specific Rationality," 821.

40. On this point Flint's *Rise of Magic* is invaluable.

41. Kieckhefer, "The Specific Rationality," 821.

42. Ibid.

43. It is interesting to note here the parallelism between the lives of saints and sorcerers during the Middle Ages and after, the second representing the mirror image of the first. See Houdard, *Les sciences du diable,* 126 ff. The type of sorcery I refer to, I should add, was a specifically medieval, European form of magic, grounded on a Christian, medieval definition of the demonic in which Satan, that ever-present figure, played the central role.

44. Bloch (*Feudal Society,* 81 ff) remarked upon this a long time ago. Christianity in the Middle Ages was indeed characterized by a vagueness of dogma and a plasticity of norms that in practice produced, so to speak, a "multiplicity of Christianisms."

45. Flint, *Rise of Magic;* see especially chapters 8 and 9.

46. Exorcism provides an example of legitimate incantation as defined by medieval Christianity.

47. Kieckhefer, in "The Specific Rationality," writes: "Much of the unofficial ritual practiced by medieval laity and lower clergy was tolerated, however grudgingly, as nonmagical, provided their rituals appealed to the same spiritual forces that orthodoxy recognized as legitimate" (831).

48. Flint, *Rise of Magic,* 233 ff, 290 ff.

49. On the association of negative magic and women, see Flint, *Rise of Magic,* for example, pp. 231 ff. See also the collection of articles edited by Brian P. Levack, *Witchcraft in the Ancient World and the Middle Ages* (New York: Garland, 1992); and in particular, although it refers to a later period, Anne Llewellyn Barstow, *Witchcraze: A New History of the European Witch Hunts* (San Francisco: Pandora, 1994).

50. Ernst Cassirer, *The Individual and the Cosmos in Renaissance Philosophy* (New York: Barnes and Noble, 1963), 9. See also Malcolm Barber, "The Medieval World View," in *The Two Cities: Medieval Europe, 1050–1320* (New York: Routledge, 1992), chap. 16.

51. Cassirer, *Individual and Cosmos,* 9–10.

52. During the Middle Ages, thinking in terms of centeredness, the practice of arranging "things" in concentric circles, was not the sole domain of cosmology. Literary theorists of the time, for example, developed a concentric model of relationships between signs to explain literary composition and genre—a model obviously instructed by the semiotics of revelation that I discuss above. See Gravdal, *Vilain and Courtois,* 1 ff.

53. On this, see Georges Duby's splendid *The Three Orders: Feudal Society Imagined* (Chicago: University of Chicago Press, 1980). See also Huizinga, *Waning of the Middle Ages,* chap. 3.

54. Karl Marx, "Contribution to the Critique of Hegel's *Philosophy of Right:* Introduction," in *The Marx-Engels Reader,* ed. Robert C. Tucker (New York: Norton, 1978), 54.

55. Duby, *Three Orders,* especially pt. 2; Huizinga, *Waning of the Middle Ages,* 56–59. Huizinga writes, for instance, "That which, in medieval thought, establishes unity in the very dissimilar meanings of the word, is the conviction that every one of these groupings [the clergy, the nobility and the "third estate"] represents a divine institution, an element of the organism of Creation emanating from the will of God, constituting an actual entity, and being, at bottom, as venerable as the angelic hierarchy" (58).

Now, if the degrees of the social edifice are conceived as the lower steps of the throne of the Eternal, the value assigned to each order will not depend on its utility, but on its sanctity—that is, its proximity to the highest place.

56. Edith Rickert, in her introduction to *The Babees' Book: Medieval Manners for the Young* (New York: Cooper Square, 1966), gives a nice example:

> Serving was a profession in which every rank, except royalty itself (if indeed this is to be omitted . . .), might honourably wear the livery of a man of higher rank. Indeed, under the system of entail, this was, in time of peace, the only possible livelihood for a gentleman's younger son, unless he had a special aptitude for law or the Church. Debarred from all trade, he could only offer his services to some great man who was compelled by his estate to keep up a large household, and so earn his patronage to provide for the future. . . . Among rich men it was the custom to receive a number of boys for training in this way. In the household of Lord Percy there were nine young "henchmen" who served him as cup-bearers and in various other capacities. To these he allowed servants, one for each two, unless they were 'at their friend's finding,' in which case they might have one apiece. Likewise, in his household, his second son was carver, his third, sewer. (xviii–xx)

57. Duby, *Three Orders,* 68, 74.

58. Shulamit Shahar, *The Fourth State: A History of Women in the Middle Ages* (New York: Routledge, 1990). Shahar's expression is particularly evocative in conjunction with the remarks on magic above, for it brings powerfully to view the extent to which women were defined as "other" in medieval societies. For other studies of women in the Middle Ages beyond the literature already cited, see Edith Ennen, *The Medieval Woman* (Oxford: Basil Blackwell, 1989); Gloria K. Fiero, Wendy Pfeffer, and Mathe Allain, eds., *Three Medieval Views of Women* (New Haven, Yale University Press, 1989); Julius Kirshner and Suzanne F. Wemple, eds., *Women of the Medieval World: Essays in Honor of John H. Mundy* (New York: Basil Blackwell, 1985); Mary Beth Rose, ed., *Women in the Middle Ages and the Renaissance: Literary and Historical Perspectives* (Syracuse: Syracuse University Press, 1986); and Michel Rouche and Jean Heuclin, eds., *La femme au Moyen Age* (Paris: J. Touzot, 1990). For a collection of essays on the historiography of medieval women, see Susan Mosher Stuard, ed., *Women in Medieval History and Historiography* (Philadelphia: University of Pennsylvania Press, 1987).

59. Duby, *Three Orders,* 68.

60. See Bloch, *Feudal Society,* chap. 24.

61. Duby, *Three Orders,* 69.

62. See, for instance, the *Ordene de chevalerie,* a book that exemplifies beautifully the permeation of ecclesias into the feudal.

63. Le Goff, *La civilisation,* 402. Alexander Murray, in *Reason and Society in the Middle Ages* (Oxford: Clarendon Press, 1978), chapter 16, makes an even more forceful argument

NOTES TO PAGES 38–42

in claiming that saints became "classless," that is, people who could socialize equally with anybody, regardless of background or class. Saints thus become the exact opposite of heretics.

64. Delort, *Life in the Middle Ages,* 134–35.

65. Le Goff, *La civilisation,* 387 ff.

66. Ibid. For noblemen, the form of punishment depended, as with all other groups, on the proportion of the fault. Noblemen, however, because of their particular position in society, tended to be absolved of many crimes for which other people would have been severely punished. Thus an act committed against a superior or a group as a whole was readily sanctioned, while "lower sins" were rapidly pardoned.

67. We should be careful not to generalize the ontological condition of coalescence, which is specific to the European Middle Ages, to "traditional" or "premodern" societies. Although other societies may show properties that remind us of coalescence, they may also include other characteristics that are different from coalescence. For some description of these, and a suggestion of how they differ, see the essays in Clifford Geertz, *Local Knowledge: Further Essays in Interpretive Anthropology* (New York: Basic Books, 1983).

68. Nigel Bryant, ed. and trans., *The High Book of the Grail: A Translation of the Thirteenth-Century Romance of Perlesvaus* (Ipswich: D. S. Brewer, 1978), 151–52.

69. R. Howard Bloch, in *The Scandal of the Fabliaux* (Chicago: University of Chicago Press, 1986), cautions against a reading of medieval literature in terms of representation and instead advocates a poetic reading of *fabliaux*. According to Bloch, my approach to interpretation in this chapter is erroneous. Reading *fabliaux* we learn nothing about actual practices, only about certain discursive techniques of power and resistance. I have addressed the issue of frame in my discussion of the *Quest,* and I address it further at the beginning of the section titled "Discursive Deployment of Ecclesiastical Hegemony."

70. Huizinga, *Waning of the Middle Ages,* 24.

71. Ibid.

72. See in particular the chapters by Georges Duby, Dominique Barthélemy, and Charles de la Roncière, "Portraits," and by Dominique Barthélemy and Philippe Contamine, "The Use of Private Space," in *Revelations of the Medieval World,* ed. Duby. See also Delort, *Life in the Middle Ages;* Chapelot and Fossier, *Village and House;* and Goetz, *Life in the Middle Ages.*

73. On this point, see Annik Pardailhé-Galabrun, *The Birth of Intimacy: Privacy and Domestic Life in Early Modern Paris* (Philadelphia: University of Philadelphia Press, 1991). Pardailhé-Galabrun traces the beginnings of intimacy, at the earliest, to the late sixteenth century.

74. See in particular Le Goff, *La civilisation;* and Goetz, *Life in the Middle Ages,* chap. 1.

75. Le Goff tells, for instance, the story of two brothers who, at the beginning of the thirteenth century, controlled a wide area in the forest of Sadlno, in Silesia, terrorizing the population and preventing the lord of the territory from exercising power; see *La civilisation,* 171.

76. Delort, *Life in the Middle Ages,* 98 ff; Philippe Ariès, *L'homme devant la mort* (Paris: Seuil, 1977). For a critical discussion of Ariès's book, which nevertheless does not falsify the points that I am highlighting, see Arno Borst, "Three Studies of Death in the Middle Ages," in *Medieval Worlds: Barbarians, Heretics, and Artists in the Middle Ages* (Chicago: University of Chicago Press, 1992), 215–43.

77. Georges Duby, *Guillaume le Maréchal, ou le meilleur chevalier du monde* (Paris: Fayard, 1984).

78. Norbert Elias, *The Civilizing Process* (Oxford: Basil Blackwell, 1994), 69–70.

79. Ibid., 69.

80. On this, see Duby's section on solitude in Duby and Braunstein, "The Emergence of the Individual," 509–33.

81. Emile Durkheim, *The Division of Labor in Society,* introduction by Lewis A. Coser (New York: Free Press, 1984), especially book 1, chaps. 1 and 2.

82. This is best exemplified by Ferdinand Tonnies's concept of *Gemeinschaft.* Durkheim's point in *Division of Labor* was precisely to show that with the emergence of modernity and the development of the division of labor, solidarity, a "natural" state in premodern societies, does not disappear, as generally perceived during the nineteenth century, but changes in its forms. For Tonnies's formulations, see his *Community and Society* (New York: Harper, 1957).

83. On this, see Lewis Coser's introduction to Durkheim's *Division of Labor,* xxiv.

84. Malory, *Le Morte d'Arthur,* 220. This also implies that none of the other Knights of the Round Table, with the exception of Galahad and Perceval, is, indeed, supposed to be chaste.

85. Duby, *Guillaume le Maréchal,* 15.

86. Here the story related by Elias of the Greek princess who had the "impudence" to use a fork in eleventh-century Venice—although the utensil was clearly in use in her country of origin—and was as a consequence beheld as a terrible sinner is exemplary. See Elias, *Civilizing Process,* 68–69.

87. In this respect it is interesting to hear how the medieval text justifies Perceval's vengeance: "God commanded in the Old Law and in the New that we should exercise justice on murderers and traitors, and so shall I on you; never shall his commandment be broken" (Bryant, ed. and trans., *High Book of the Grail,* 151).

88. The emotional nature of medieval men and women, a feature clearly related to the uninhibited character of their society, is by no means unique to this period. It seems, indeed, to have been a characteristic of Western societies in general up to modernity. See, for instance, Erich Auerbach, *Mimesis: The Representation of Reality in Western Literature* (Princeton: Princeton University Press, 1953).

89. Malory, *Le Morte d'Arthur,* 269.

90. For this interpretive line regarding medieval romance, see Bruckner, *Shaping Romance;* Burns, *Arthurian Fictions;* Gravdal, *Vilain and Courtois;* and especially Green, *Irony in the Medieval Romance.* For an argument about *fabliaux* as involving a poetics of subversion, see Bloch, *Scandal of the Fabliaux.* Such an approach to medieval literature in general

was first formulated in D. W. Robertson Jr., *A Preface to Chaucer: Studies in Medieval Perspectives* (Princeton: Princeton University Press, 1962).

91. Kelly, *Medieval French Romance*, 125–27 and, for a more extensive critique of the orientation above, 134–37.

92. Short catalogs of manners, especially regarding behavior at table, were composed and circulated within and among monasteries at the time. In those compilations, however, the connection between manners, courtoisie, and ecclesias did not require explicit expression. I elaborate on this point as I discuss Jaeger's *The Origins of Courtliness* in the next chapter.

93. The phrase is Elizabeth Keiser's; see "The Festive Decorum of *Cleanness*," in *Chivalric Literature; Essays on the Relations between Literature and Life in the Later Middle Ages*, ed. D. Benson and John Leyerle (Kalamazoo, MI: Western Michigan University Press, 1980), 65.

94. Ibid.

95. Andreas Capellanus, *On Love*, trans. P. G. Walsh (London: Gerald Duckworth, 1982); and Andreas Capellanus, *The Art of Courtly Love*, trans. John Jay Parry (New York: Columbia University Press, 1941). The title preferred by Parry is somewhat misleading, for the term *courtly love* is a nineteenth-century invention that refers to a wide variety of different forms of love. On this last point, see Edmund Reiss, "Fin'Amors: Its History and Meaning in Medieval Literature," *Medieval and Renaissance Studies* 8 (1979): 74–99. I ground much of my interpretation on P. G. Walsh's introductory chapter to his translation of Capellanus.

96. See, for example, Robertson, *Preface to Chaucer*. For a discussion of this approach regarding *On Love*, see P. G. Walsh, "Introduction," 5–7, 13–5.

97. P. G. Walsh, "Introduction," in Capellanus, *On Love*, 6; he is paraphrasing C. S. Singleton's argument in his study of Dante.

98. Ibid., 13. The condemnation of homosexual love at the outset of the treatise also points in the direction of religious acceptability argued by Walsh; see Capellanus, *On Love*, 35.

99. On reactions to Andreas, see ibid., 13–14.

100. Ibid., 15.

101. Capellanus, *On Love*, 117. These include the following:

1. Avoid miserliness as a harmful disease, and embrace its opposite.
2. You must maintain chastity for your lover.
3. When a woman is appropriately joined to another in love, do not knowingly try to seduce her.
4. Be sure not to choose the love of a woman if natural modesty forbids you to join marriage with her. [Here the allusion is clearly to one's social status.]
5. Remember to avoid lying completely. [Although people obviously do].
6. Do not have too many privy to your love.
7. Be obedient to mistresses' commands in all things, and always be eager to join the service of Love.
8. In the granting and receiving of love's consolations there should be the utmost modesty and decent restraint.

243

9. You must not be foul-tongued.

10. You must not expose lovers.

11. Show yourself civilised and chivalrous in all things. [The word for "civilised" used in the Latin version is "urbanum," which is important, given my argument that "civility" emerged much later; see ibid., 116].

12. When practising the consolations of love do not go beyond the wish of your lover.

These are followed at the end of the discussion on love per se by thirty-one "less important precepts," which Andreas uses to summarize his major arguments [ibid., 283–84]. These mostly recapitulate the same intentions of the twelve rules above.

102. Guillaume de Lorris, *Romance of the Rose,* trans. Harry W. Robbins (New York: E. Dutton, 1962). I refer throughout to this edition. This work is also mentioned as one of the exemplars of irony. For a review of interpretations, see Heather M. Arden, *The Romance of the Rose* (Boston: Twayne Publishers, 1987), chaps. 2 and 3.

103. Lorris, *Romance of the Rose,* Ibid., 6.

104. Ibid., 9–10.

105. Ibid., 13.

106. Ibid.

107. It is interesting to note that for Andreas, too, working people are mostly described as ugly and unworthy—without a hint of cynicism.

108. Lorris, *Romance of the Rose,* 25.

109. Ibid., 19.

110. Ibid., 45–47.

111. For a study of the romance as involving a psychological dimension, see Daniel Poirion, *Le roman de la rose* (Paris: Hatier, 1974).

112. Reason, here, is "embedded" in ecclesias. I am using the idea of "socially embedded rationalities" as developed by Tom R. Burns and his colleagues. For a theoretical statement of the idea, see Tom R. Burns, "Two Conceptions of Human Agency: Rational Choice Theory and the Social Theory of Action," in *Agency and Structure: Reorienting Social Theory,* ed. Piotr Sztompka (Yverdon, Switzerland: Gordon and Breach, 1994), 197–250.

113. On the open-endedness of medieval texts in general and the subversive potential that ensues, see Burns, *Arthurian Fictions.*

114. A detailed description of this book is found in Keen, *Chivalry,* 6 ff.

115. A description of this book is found in Duby, *Three Orders,* 205 ff.

116. As I have mentioned, although it would be unquestionably important, a systematic analysis of that multiplicity is beyond the scope of this book.

Chapter Three

1. Baldesar Castiglione, *The Book of the Courtier,* trans. Charles S. Singleton (New York: Anchor Books, 1959), 32.

2. Ibid., 39.

3. For an analysis of the concepts of "grace" and "sprezzatura" in Castiglione, see Eduardo Saccone, "*Grazia, Sprezzatura, Afettazzione* in the *Courtier*," in *Castiglione: The Ideal and the Real in Renaissance Culture,* ed. Robert W. Hanning and David Rosand (New Haven: Yale University Press, 1983), 45–67; and J. R. Woodhouse, *Baldesar Castiglione: A Reassessment of The Courtier* (Edinburgh: Edinburgh University Press, 1978), 76 ff and *passim.* I analyze these concepts in detail in the next chapter.

4. Brunetto Latini, *Il tesoretto,* ed. and trans. Julia Bolton Holloway (New York: Garland, 1981). Holloway's statement is from p. xxiv of her introduction. For studies of *Il tesoretto,* see, in addition to Holloway's introduction, Bianca Ceva, *Brunetto Latini: L'uomo e l'opera* (Milano: R. Ricciardi, 1965); Marcello Ciccuto, "Introduzione," in *Brunetto Latini, Il tesoretto,* ed. Marcello Ciccuto (Milano: Biblioteca Universale Rizzoli, 1985), 5–54; Julia Bolton Holloway, *Twice-Told Tales: Brunetto Latino and Dante Alighieri* (New York: Lang, 1993). For a comprehensive, annotated bibliography on Latini, see Julia Bolton Holloway, *Brunetto Latini: An Analytic Bibliography* (London: Grant & Cutler, 1986).

5. The relevance of Latini for understanding medieval Italian literature and culture has been recently defended by, among others, Hans Robert Jauss in "The Alterity and Modernity of Medieval Literature," *New Literary History* 10 (1979): 181–230. Jauss goes as far as to argue for the inclusion of Latini in the Italian literary canon.

6. See Canto 15 of *The Inferno.* No less interesting is the real fondness that Dante shows for his master in that same piece. "Had I all my wish," Dante tells Brunetto,

> you would not yet be banished from the world
> in which you were a radiance among men,
> for that sweet image, gentle and paternal,
> you were to me in the world when hour by hour
> you taught me how man makes himself eternal,
> lives in my mind, and now strikes to my heart;
> and while I live, the gratitude I owe it
> will speak to men out of my life and art.

(Trans. John Ciardi [New York: Mentor, 1954], 138)

7. For a short survey, see Holloway's introduction to *Il tesoretto,* xiv.
8. Latini, *Il tesoretto,* 7.
9. Ibid., 81, 83, 91.
10. Ibid., 91.
11. Ibid., 90. The Italian version reads: "Che tu non perde freno."
12. Ibid., 89.
13. Ibid., 91, 93.
14. Ibid., 85, 87.
15. Ibid., 85.
16. Indeed, the development of self-control is seen by both authors as perhaps the most important transformation leading towards individuation and rationality, and therefore away from the conditions of being of the Middle Ages. See Norbert Elias, *The Civilizing Process*

(Oxford: Basil Blackwell, 1994); and Michel Foucault, *Discipline and Punish* (New York: Vintage, 1977).

17. Latini, *Il tesoretto*, 103, 105.

18. Ibid., 100–101.

19. Ibid., 101.

20. Ibid., 107.

21. As developed, in particular, in the second volume of Elias, *Civilizing Process.*

22. Marc Bloch, *Feudal Society* (Chicago: University of Chicago Press, 1961), 410.

23. Here I am following Bourdieu's distinction between four types of "capital": "the capital of physical force," "economic capital," "informational capital," and "symbolic capital." Bourdieu uses this classification to point at the limitations of most approaches to understanding the formation of nation-states, which focus almost exclusively on the concentration of the first two forms of capital, and on the concentration of the capital of physical force in particular. I discuss Bourdieu's arguments briefly below. See Pierre Bourdieu, "Rethinking the State: Genesis and Structure of the Bureaucratic Field," *Sociological Theory* 12 (March 1994): 1–18.

24. Among the most prominent of contemporary figures in this literature is Charles Tilly, whose work for the last twenty years has reshaped the debate on the topic. His major statement is *Coercion, Capital, and European States, A.D. 990–1990* (Oxford: Basil Blackwell, 1990). The thesis was originally formulated by Max Weber in volume 2 of *Economy and Society*, ed. Guenther Roth and Claus Wittich (Berkeley: University of California Press, 1978), and in the essay "Politics as a Vocation," in H. H. Gerth and C. Wright Mills, *From Max Weber* (New York: Oxford University Press, 1946), 77–128.

25. See Bloch, *Feudal Society*, 125–30; for general historical background, see Georges Duby, *The Chivalrous Society* (Berkeley: University of California Press, 1977); and *Le Moyen Age: De Hugues Capet a Jeanne d'Arc* (Paris: Hachette, 1987). Two recent studies on vendettas, albeit covering a later historical period, are Edward Muir, *Mad Blood Stirring: Vendetta and Factions in Friuli during the Renaissance* (Baltimore: Johns Hopkins University Press, 1993); and David Nicholas, *The Van Arteveldes of Ghent: The Varieties of Vendetta and the Hero in History* (Ithaca, NY: Cornell University Press, 1988). Muir's book in particular presents an understanding of vendettas that follows Elias's thesis almost to the letter.

26. Bloch, *Feudal Society*, 126–27.

27. For a discussion of this point, see Leopold Genicot, *Contours of the Middle Ages* (London: Routledge & Kegan Paul, 1967), 210 ff; and *Le XIIIe siècle Européen* (Paris: Presses Universitaires de France, 1968), 147 ff.

28. Indeed, we must conceive the exercise of monarchical power as a constant struggle between monarchs and aristocracy, even under conditions of "absolutism." I discuss this relationship in detail in chapter 5.

29. Bloch, *Feudal Society*, 128. Although recent scholarship has vastly refined and expanded on Bloch's theses, the essentials remain remarkably valid. See, for example, André Gouron and Albert Rigaudière, eds., *Renaissance du pouvoir législatif et genèse de l'état* (Montpellier: Société d'Histoire du Droit, 1988).

30. Latini, *Il tesoretto*, 105.

31. Bourdieu, "Rethinking the State."

32. Ibid., 5.

33. Ibid., 5–7.

34. Ibid., 7–8.

35. Ibid., 9.

36. Ibid., 7.

37. C. Stephen Jaeger, *The Origins of Courtliness: Civilizing Trends and the Formation of Courtly Ideals, 923–1210* (Philadelphia: University of Pennsylvania Press, 1985); Aldo Scaglione, *Knights at Court: Courtliness, Chivalry, and Courtesy from Ottonian Germany to the Italian Renaissance* (Berkeley: University of California Press, 1991). Scaglione's book is an expansion of Jaeger's and owes much to the earlier study. Elias does not study the origins of courtesy. As I mentioned in the introduction, *The Civilizing Process* is confined to "civility," and the same problem of historical perspective that I claim limits his study with regards "etiquette" exists with regard to "courtesy"—the first leaves out a study of the future of civility; the second, of its past.

38. Scaglione, *Knights at Court*, 6.

39. Ibid., 255.

40. Thomasin von Zerclaere, *The Italian Guest*. A translation of significant portions of the work is found in *Queene Elizabethes Achademy*, ed. Frederick J. Furnivall (Early English Text Society, Extra Series 8, 1869; reprint, New York: Kraus Reprint, 1981), part 2. All subsequent quotations are from this edition. For the original German, see *Der Waelsche Gast*, ed. H. Ruckert (Berlin: de Gruyter, 1965).

41. Biographical material on Thomasin is from E. Oswald's introductory note in Furnivall, ed., *Queene Elizabethes Achademy*, and from Mary Paul Guetz, *The Concept of Nobility in German Didactic Literature of the Thirteenth Century* (New York: Ams Press, 1935).

42. For background information on Friuli, see Muir, *Mad Blood Stirring*, and Giovanni Francesco Palladio degli Olivi, *Historie della provincia del Friuli*, Bologna, Forni, 1966.

43. Zerclaere, *Italian Guest*, 134. Indeed, Thomasin seems to have been well versed not only in physics and astronomy but also in the biological sciences.

44. Ibid., 114.

45. Ibid.

46. Ibid., 115.

47. Ibid., 113 ff, 119.

48. Ibid., 118.

49. Ibid., 119.

50. Ibid.

51. Ibid., 116.

52. Ibid., 126, 128.

53. Ibid., 115, 116, 124.

54. The classical study on the almost literal embodiment of monarchical power in the person of the king is Ernst H. Kantarowicz, *The King's Two Bodies: A Study in Mediaeval*

Political Theology (Princeton: Princeton University Press, 1957). See also Alain Boureau, *Le simple corps de roi: L'impossible sacralité des souverains français, XV–XVIII siècle* (Paris: Les Editions de Paris, 1988). For a study of ecclesias in its relation to Christ's body, see Sarah Beckwith, *Christ's Body: Identity, Culture, and Society in Late Medieval Writings* (New York: Routledge, 1993). The movement from a pragmatics anchored in Christ's body to one anchored in the king's body perfectly conveys the idea of displacement that I am advancing.

55. Jousts involved a contest between two individuals fighting on horseback; tournaments, "a contest between two teams using sharp weapons in a *melée*[;] simulating, in other words, the procedures of warfare." For the definitions, see Juliet Vale, *Edward III and Chivalry: Chivalric Society and Its context 1270–1350* (Woodbridge, Suffolk: Boydell Press, 1982), 5. For studies of medieval tournaments other than Vale, see Richard W. Barber and Juliet R. V. Barker, *Tournaments: Jousts, Chivalry, and Pageants in the Middle Ages* (Woodbridge, Suffolk: Boydell, 1989); Juliet R. V. Barker, *The Tournament in England, 1100–1400* (Woodbridge, Suffolk: Boydell, 1986); and for brief historical overviews, see William H. Jackson, "Tournaments and the German Chivalric *renovatio:* Tournament Discipline and the Myth of Origins," in *Chivalry in the Renaissance,* ed. Sydney Anglo (Woodbridge, Suffolk: Boydell, 1990), 77–91; and Helmut Nickel, "The Tournament: An Historical Sketch," in *The Study of Chivalry: Resources and Approaches,* ed. Howell Chickering and Thomas H. Seiler (Kalamazoo, MI: Medieval Institute Publications, Western Michigan University, 1988), 213–62. For general reference, see Bradford B. Broughton, *Dictionary of Medieval Knighthood and Chivalry: Concepts and Terms* (New York: Greenwood, 1986).

56. These two tournaments are described in detail in Vale, *Edward III.*

57. Maurice Keen, *Chivalry* (New Haven: Yale University Press, 1984), 202-3

58. Ibid., 200 ff.

59. Diane Bornstein, *Mirrors of Courtesy* (Hamden, CT: Archon Books, 1975), 13–14. For a further description of this tournament and a detailed analysis of a later one, see *The Great Tournament Roll of Westminster: A Collotype Reproduction of the Manuscript,* with an introduction by Sidney Anglo (Oxford: Clarendon Press, 1968).

60. The classic studies remain Roy Strong's two books, *Splendour at Court: Renaissance Spectacle and Illusion* (London: Weidenfeld and Nicolson, 1973), and *Art and Power: Renaissance Festivals, 1450–1650* (Berkeley: University of California Press, 1984), which, in spite of referring to a later period, are nevertheless valid for the argument at hand. Besides the bibliography cited above, see also A. G. Dickens, ed., *The Courts of Europe* (London: Thames and Hudson, 1977).

61. Strong, *Splendour at Court,* 22–23.

62. On this last point, see in particular Susan Frye, *Elizabeth I: The Competition for Representation* (New York: Oxford University Press, 1993).

63. Bornstein, *Mirrors of Courtesy,* 17.

64. Keen, in *Chivalry,* gives some examples of the latter:

> Anthony, bastard of Burgundy, at his *pas* of the *Femme Sauvage* in 1470 made play with notions of primitive life, and with the sort of allegory that the *Roman of the Rose* had popularized: his "champion of the Joyous Quest" had been cured

of wounds by the *Femme Sauvage* as he left the land of *Enfance* for that of *Jeunesse,* and entered the lists surrounded by a troop of her "wild women." . . . The champions whom Duke Louis of Orleans assembled at Sandricourt in 1493 threw themselves with exuberance into the Arthurian mode, riding out into the woods near the castle (the "Waste Forest"), accompanied by their maidens, to seek "chance" encounters with challengers. (204)

Here, indeed, we see women becoming part of the rituals, of the enactment of allegories, of the whole imaginative apparatus of the tournaments. At the least, women participated in the rituals of championing and of glory. See also Nickel, "The Tournament," 234–38.

65. In the next chapter I discuss some of the contemporary arguments for the inclusion of women within what I have called the *res civile.*

66. See, for example, Michael Foss, *Chivalry* (London: Michael Joseph, 1975), chapter 7.

67. The language of technologies of the body received its classic formulation in Marcel Mauss, "The Techniques of the Body," *Economy and Society* 2 (February 1973): 70–88. For a reader of classical texts on the social study of the human body, see Ted Polhemus, ed., *The Body Reader: Social Aspects of the Human Body* (Harmondsworth: Penguin, 1978). Jean-Claude Schmitt, *La raison des gestes dans l'occident médiéval* (Paris: Gallimard, 1990) contains the most comprehensive study of the body during the Middle Ages. For other studies with a sociohistorical perspective, see Jan Bremmer and Herman Roodenburg, eds., *A Cultural History of Gesture* (Ithaca, NY: Cornell University Press, 1991); Michel Feher, ed., *Fragments for a History of the Human Body,* 3 vols. (New York: Zone, 1990); the collection *Le corps humain: Nature, culture, surnaturel,* Actes du 110è Congrès National des Sociétés Savantes (Paris: CTHS, 1985); and Patricia Curran, *Grace Before Meals: Food Ritual and Body Discipline in Convent Culture* (Urbana: University of Illinois Press, 1989), which is especially helpful as a means of comparing the technologies of the body that developed in the princely courts to those dominant in a culture like that of ecclesias,.

68. Sydney Anglo, "How to Kill a Man at Your Ease: Fencing Books and the Duelling Ethic," in *Chivalry in the Renaissance,* ed. Anglo, 9.

69. Francis Rieupeyroux, *La chasse en France de la fin du Moyen-Age à la révolution* (Poitiers: CRDP, 1984). See also Broughton, *Dictionary of Medieval Knighthood,* 260–65; Urban T. Holmes, *Medieval Man* (Chapel Hill: University of North Carolina Press, 1980), 157 ff; Joseph Strutt, *The Sports and Pastimes of the People of England* (Detroit: Gale, 1968); and Marcelle Thiebaux, "The Medieval Chase," *Speculum* 37 (1962): 260–74.

70. Rieupeyroux, *La chasse,* 6–7, 20–21, 31–32.

71. Rieupeyroux, *La chasse.*

72. Although again, we should conceive of "others" as a heterogeneous group, or rather, as many groups with different degrees of selfness and otherness. Here, again, the case of women is instructive, for women did sometimes actively participate in hunting (e.g., in hawking). But consider the limitations of women's participation in chases, for although they often rode with the men, most of the evidence—ranging from paintings from the times to their hunting garments—suggests that they rode sidesaddle, which hindered their maneuverability and demanded a different range of participation and a different technique

of the body. See Rieupeyroux, *La chasse;* on hawking, see Delort, *Life in the Middle Ages* (New York: Crown, 1983), 216.

73. For these points, see Raymond Carr, *English Fox Hunting: A History* (London: Weidenfield and Nicolson, 1976), chap. 1.

74. For an explicit discussion of this point, see Sergio Bertelli and Giulia Calvi, "Rituale, cerimoniale, etichetta nelle corti Italiane," in *Rituale, cerimoniale, etichetta,* ed. Sergio Bertelli and Giuliano Crifo (Milano: Bompiani, 1985), 11–27.

75. See, for example, Lawrence M. Bryant, *The King and the City in the Parisian Royal Entry Ceremony: Politics, Ritual, and Art in the Renaissance* (Genève: Droz, 1986); Bernard Guenée and Françoise Lehoux, *Les entrées royales françaises de 1328 à 1515* (Paris: CNRS, 1968).

76. Lucien Febvre, *Life in Renaissance France* (Cambridge: Harvard University Press, 1977), 15–16, 18. For a full account of the transformations of travel during the Middle Ages, see Margaret Wade Labarge, *Medieval Travelers: The Rich and Restless* (London: Hamish Hamilton, 1982).

77. Imre Lakatos, "Falsification and the Methodology of Scientific Research Programmes," in *Criticism and the Growth of Knowledge,* ed. Imre Lakatos and Alan Musgrave (Cambridge: Cambridge University Press, 1970), 100–101.

78. Here, the work of Robert Bellah and his associates, and the entire communitarian movement in American intellectual circles, comes to mind regarding our contemporary disenchantment with "modernity." I discuss Erasmus in chapter 4; Luther, in chapter 6. For the thesis of disenchantment in the contemporary world, see Robert N. Bellah, Richard Madsen, William M. Sullivan, Ann Swidler, and Steven Tipton, *The Good Society* (New York: Knopf, 1991).

Chapter Four

1. The use of the term *Renaissance* has always been problematic. There is no absolute consensus of what the Renaissance consists of, or of the period it is supposed to cover. I suggest, at times, that the Renaissance may have started as early as the beginning of the thirteenth century, with Thomasin, or perhaps even before, with the very first manifestations of the *res civile,* while ending with the institutionalization of absolutism. At other times, however, I use the term to encompass a much shorter period that, though still ending with the rise of the absolutist state, began only at the moment when the infrastructural transition discussed in the previous chapter attained its turning point—a moment that actually changes from place to place. The first definition of Renaissance becomes in fact synonymous with what I have called the *res civile;* I use the term here in its more restrictive sense. A comprehensive overview of the problem as manifested in historical studies can be found in Denys Hay, "Historians and the Renaissance during the Last Twenty-Five Years," in Andre Chastel et al., *The Renaissance: Essays in Interpretation* (New York: Methuen, 1982), 1–32. For more recent discussions of the concept of the Renaissance, see Charles Trinkaus, "Renaissance Ideas and the Idea of the Renaissance," *Journal of the History of Ideas* 51 (1990): 667–84, and the opening chapter, "What Is the Renaissance?" in C. Black, M. Greengrass,

D. Howarth, J. Lawrance, R. Mackenney, M. Rady, and E. Wech, *Atlas of the Renaissance* (London: Cassell, 1993).

2. For a definitive discussion, see Malcolm Bradbury, Bryan Heading, and Martin Hollis, "The Man and the Mask: A Discussion of Role Theory," in *Role,* ed. J. A. Jackson (Cambridge: Cambridge University Press, 1972), 41–64. See also Jorge Arditi, "Role as a Cultural Concept," *Theory and Society* 16 (1987): 565–91; Rose Laub Coser, *In Defense of Modernity: Role Complexity and Individual Autonomy* (Stanford, Stanford University Press, 1991); and John Hewitt, *Dilemmas of the American Self* (Philadelphia, Temple University Press, 1989), 115–21.

3. On these distinctions see Bradbury, Heading, and Hollis, "The Man and the Mask," 46–47.

4. For an extended discussion see Arditi, "Role as a Cultural Concept."

5. Miguel de Cervantes, *Don Quixote de la Mancha,* trans. Tobias Smollett (New York: Farrar, Straus and Giroux, 1986), 484–85.

6. I quote in the original French, from E. Curtius, *European Literature and the Latin Middle Ages* (London: Routledge, 1953), 140:

> Ici la Comédie apparaît un example
> Ou chacun de son fait les actions contemple:
> Le monde est un thêàtre, et les hommes acteurs.
> La Fortune qui est maîtresse de la scène
> Apprête les habits, et de la vie humaine
> Les cieux et le destin en sont les spectateurs.

For a brief discussion of this and other examples, see Elizabeth Burns, *Theatricality: A Study of Convention in the Theatre and in Social Life* (London: Longman, 1972).

7. Calderón de la Barca, *La vida es sueño,* with an introduction by Alberto Porqueras-Mayo (Madrid: Espasa-Calpe, 1978). As Porqueras-Mayo notes in the introduction to the cited edition (pp. 14–5), the theme of the *theatrum mundi* is the "fundamental theme" of *La vida es sueño,* and one of Calderón's preferred motifs throughout his oeuvre.

8. Michel de Montaigne, *Les Essais* (Paris: Presses Universitaires de France, 1985) chapter 52, book I.

9. William Shakespeare, *As You Like It,* 2.7.139–66, in The Complete Works, ed. Stanley Wells and Gary Taylor (New York: Clarendon Press, Oxford University Press, 1988). All references are to act, scene, and lines, and are to this edition.

10. William Shakespeare, *The Merchant of Venice,* 1.1.77–79.

11. William Shakespeare, *Hamlet,* 1.2.76–86.

12. On this distinction, see again, Bradbury, Heading, and Hollis, "The Man and the Mask," 46–7.

13. The most comprehensive analysis of the uses of the dramaturgical metaphor in Shakespeare remains Thomas F. Van Laan, *Role-Playing in Shakespeare* (Toronto: University of Toronto Press, 1978). The book's title is actually misleading, for except for literal role-playing, as when a character plays a role in a play within the play, all the other forms of

"role-playing" that Van Laan identifies indeed correspond to the conception of the person within the play as a character, not the actor assumed by the modern understandings of the term.

14. It is interesting to note that in the vast majority of cases the quotations of this passage in sociology books reproduce only the first four lines of Shakespeare's text. The impression they provoke without their context is evidently different. See, for example, Michael Banton, *Roles: An Introduction to the Study of Social Relations* (New York: Basic Books, 1965), 21–22; Lewis A. Coser, *Masters of Sociological Thought* (New York: Harcourt Brace Jovanovich, 1977), 576; William C. Levin, *Sociological Ideas: Concepts and Applications* (Belmont, CA: Wadsworth, 1984), 177; Jonathan H. Turner, *The Structure of Sociological Theory* (Belmont, CA: Wadsworth, 1991), 411. Bruce J. Biddle and Edwin J. Thomas, *Role Theory: Concepts and Research* (New York: John Wiley, 1966), 3, arguably the most influential theoretical discussion of the concept, opens with a quote of the first five and a half lines of Jaques's speech.

15. Bradbury, Heading, and Hollis, "The Man and the Mask," 46.

16. William B. Worthen, *The Idea of the Actor: Drama and the Ethics of Performance* (Princeton: Princeton University Press, 1984), 26.

17. A. C. Bradley, "Shakespeare's Tragic Period—*Hamlet*," in *Twentieth-Century Interpretations of Hamlet,* edited by David Bevington, Englewood Cliffs, NJ: Prentice-Hall, 1968), 14. And I should note that Don Quixote is also mad. For two interpretations of Shakespeare that point in a similar direction, see David Margolies, *Monsters of the Deep: Social Dissolution in Shakespeare's Tragedies* (Manchester: Manchester University Press, 1992); and Molly Smith, *The Darker World Within: Evil in the Tragedies of Shakespeare and His Successors* (Newark: University of Delaware Press, 1991), especially chap. 2, "Evil as Nonbeing: Physical and Mental Fragmentation."

18. This is one of the central points of Georg Simmel's sociology. The association of detachment, existential freedom, and (for that matter) alienation and the understanding of the historical specificity of this association form the backbone of his analyses of individuality. See the collection of Simmel's work, *On Individuality and Social Forms,* ed. Donald N. Levine (Chicago: University of Chicago Press, 1971), and *The Philosophy of Money,* trans. Tom Bottomore and David Frisbie (London: Routledge, 1978), chaps. 4 and 6.

19. On the negative perception of acting and the theater in general at the time, see Worthen, *The Idea of the Actor;* and Joseph Lenz, "Base Trade: Theater as Prostitution," *ELH* 60, no. 4 (winter 1993): 833–56.

20. I speak here only of forms within the infrastructure. Outside of the realms of the pragmatics of grace, the same feelings were addressed in a variety of forms, some of which I consider below.

21. On Corneille and heroism, see Serge Doubrovsky, *Corneille et la dialectique du héros* (Paris: Gallimard, 1963), esp. 87–132; Michel Prigent, *Le héros et l'état dans la tragédie de Pierre Corneille* (Paris: Presses Universitaires de France, 1986); Peter H. Nurse's introductory notes to his edition of the original 1637 French text, *Le Cid: The Text of the Original Edition*

(1637) (Baton Rouge: Louisiana State University Press, 1978); and, in particular, Paul Béni-chou, *Morales du grand siècle* (Paris: Gallimard, 1948).

22. Pierre Corneille, "The Cid," in *Six Plays by Corneille and Racine,* edited and with an introduction by Paul Landis (New York: The Modern Library, 1959), 13.

23. Corneille, *Le Cid,* ed. Nurse, 81.

24. Corneille, "The Cid," ed. Landis, 58–59.

25. Rodrigue, for instance, speaks of "pleasures forever lost," of "flames betrayed;" Chi-mène, of a renunciation "To the sweetest promise of my possession." On this, see Doubrov-sky, *Dialectique du héros,* 101. The translations are mine.

26. This point is forcefully argued by Antoine Adam in *L'age classique. I, 1624–1660* (Paris: B. Arthaud, 1968), 265 ff.

27. Serge Doubrovsky speaks of "a total and *anguishing* opposition between two values." *Dialectique du héros,* 101; emphasis added.

28. Corneille, *Le Cid,* ed. Nurse, 81.

29. On the centrality of the image of the armored male body in the idea of the heroic, see Jeffery C. Persels, " 'Qui sommes tous cassez du harnoys' or, the *Heptaméron* and Uses of the Male Body," in *Heroic Virtue, Comic Infidelity: Reassessing Margurite de Navarre's Heptaméron,* ed. Dora E. Polachek (Amherst, MA: Hestia Press, 1993).

30. Prigent, *Le héros et l'état,* 28–9.

31. Following Goffman, I am using the concept of frame as a way to denote the constitu-tive figurations of the organization of experience. See Erving Goffman, *Frame Analysis: An Essay on the Organization of Experience* (Cambridge: Harvard University Press, 1974). I took the expression "being-for-the-state" from the introduction in Polachek, ed., *Heroic Virtue,* 15–16.

32. See Erich Auerbach's classic account of *Don Quixote* in *Mimesis: The Representation of Reality in Western Literature* (Princeton: Princeton University Press, 1953), chapter 14.

33. For an analysis of the oppositional character of the *Heptaméron* with regard to the heroic, see Patricia Francis Cholakian, "Heroic Infidelity: Novella 15," and Carla Freccero, "Unwriting Lucrecia: 'Heroic Virtue' in the *Heptaméron,*" in *Heroic Virtue,* ed. Polachek, 62–76 and 77–89 respectively.

34. See, for example, Freccero, "Unwriting Lucrecia."

35. I say "relatively autonomous" because the degree of autonomy varies from discourse to discourse to an extent that must be evaluated separately for each, and its causes differ from case to case. A systematic exploration of that variability is beyond my intentions here and unnecessary for my argument.

36. On this last point, see Thomas Moore, *The Planets Within: Marsilio Ficino's Astrolog-ical Psychology* (Lewisburg, PA: Bucknell University Press, 1982); and Giancarlo Zanier, *La medicina astrologica e la sua teoria: Marsilio Ficino e i suoi critici contemporanei* (Roma: Edizi-oni dell'Ateneo, 1977). For the classic account of Ficino's philosophy in general, see Paul Oskar Kristeller, *The Philosophy of Marsilio Ficino* (New York: Columbia University Press, 1943).

37. Quoted in Charles Trinkaus, "Themes of a Renaissance anthropology," in *Renaissance,* ed. Chastel et al., 86.

38. Enea Balmas, *La Renaissance: II, 1548–1570* (Paris: B. Arthaud, 1974), 29–30; my translation.

39. On the history of the book and its effects, see Roger Chartier, *The Order of Books: Readers, Authors, and Libraries in Europe between the Fourteenth and the Eighteenth Centuries* (Stanford, Stanford University Press, 1994).

40. Auerbach, *Mimesis,* ch. 11.

41. Charles B. Schmitt and Quentin Skinner, eds., *The Cambridge History of Renaissance Philosophy* (Cambridge: Cambridge University Press, 1988), 3.

42. The standard translation is Charles S. Singleton's in Baldesar Castiglione, *The Book of the Courtier* (Garden City, NY: Anchor Books, 1959); subsequent citations are of this edition. Sir Thomas Hoby's translation, dating from 1561, appears in a new edition by J. H. Whitfield (London, J. M. Dent & Sons, 1974), who also writes a penetrating introduction. Critical books on *The Book of the Courtier* include Virginia Cox Balmaceda, *The Renaissance Dialog: Literary Dialog in its Social and Political Contexts, Castiglione to Galileo* (New York: Cambridge University Press, 1992); Valeria Finucci, *The Lady Vanishes: Subjectivity and Representation in Castiglione and Ariosto* (Stanford: Stanford University Press, 1992); Antonio Gagliardi, *La misura e la grazia: Sul Libro del Cortegiano* (Torino: Tirrenia Stampatori, 1989); Robert W. Hanning and David Rosand, eds., *Castiglione: The Ideal and the Real in Renaissance Culture* (New Haven: Yale University Press, 1983); Arthur F. Kinney, *Continental Humanist Poetics: Studies in Erasmus, Castiglione, Marguerite de Navarre, Rabelais, and Cervantes* (Amherst: University of Massachusetts Press, 1989), chapter 3; Richard Lanham, *The Motives of Eloquence* (New Haven: Yale University Press, 1976), chapter 7; Carlo Ossola, ed., *La corte e il "Cortegiano,"* vol. 1, *La scena del testo* (Roma: Bulzoni Editore, 1980); Wayne A. Rebhorn, *Courtly Performances: Masking and Festivity in Castiglione's "Book of the Courtier"* (Detroit: Wayne State University Press, 1978); and J. R. Woodhouse, *Baldesar Castiglione: A Reassessment of "The Courtier"* (Edinburgh: Edinburgh University Press, 1978).

43. Castiglione, *Book of the Courtier,* 25.

44. On this last point, see Yves Giraud and Marc-René Jung, *La Renaissance, I: 1480–1548* (Paris: Arthaud, 1972), 26. For a study of François I and Castiglione's concept of courtiership, see Cecil H. Clough, "Francis I and the Courtiers of Castiglione's *Courtier,*" *European Studies Review* 8, no. 1 (1978): 23–70. Although the meanings of the *Cortegiano,* as we shall see, are hotly debated, its influence is undisputed. Indeed, even though Arthur Kinney attempts to minimize the practical importance of *Il Cortegiano,* he mentions that the book established the "style of Henri's Paris, of Philip's Escorial, and of Elizabeth's Whitehall" (*Continental Humanist Poetics,* 89).

45. Castiglione, *Book of the Courtier,* 28.

46. Ibid., 29–30.

47. Ibid., 40–41.

48. Ibid., 43.

49. Ibid., 47.

50. For the language of *habitu corporis,* see Peter Burke, "The Language of Gesture in Early Modern Italy," in *A Cultural History of Gesture,* ed. Jan Bremmer and Herman Roodenburg (Ithaca, NY: Cornell University Press, 1991), 76.

51. Jay Tribby, "Body/Building: Living the Museum Life in Early Modern Europe," *Rhetorica* 10, no. 2 (1992): 139–63. Whether intended or not, Tribby's reference to the courtier in the masculine is appropriate. The courtier, as we already know, is not a gender-neutral construct.

52. Kinney, *Continental Humanist Poetics,* especially chapter 3. For the argument with regard to the literature of aristocratic conduct in general, see Susan Staves, "The Secrets of Genteel Identity in the Man of Mode: Comedy of Manners vs. the Courtesy Book," *Studies in Eighteenth-Century Culture* 19 (1989): 117–28.

53. Kinney, *Continental Humanist Poetics,* 89.

54. Ibid.; emphasis in the original.

55. Ibid., 91.

56. For a similar point, see, for example, Cox Balmaceda, *Renaissance Dialog,* 26—although she does not speak of a "pragmatics of grace." This, I should note, is a very different process from the one associated with etiquette by which the aristocracy constructs itself as a unique group.

57. Castiglione, *Book of the Courtier,* 29.

58. In *De civilitate morum puerilium* Erasmus uses the verb "to mold" to speak of the process by which the attitudes and gestures that constitute civility become embodied—a fairly conventional idea in Renaissance humanism.

59. I say "most easily inscribed," and not a "precondition for its inscription," for low birth in itself is not an obstacle to grace—one can still produce beautiful music with an instrument that is not of the finest quality.

60. Stephen Jay Greenblatt, *Renaissance Self-Fashionings: From More to Shakespeare* (Chicago: University of Chicago Press), 1980.

61. Although, again, what distinguishes grace from other "molds" is its association with an established power, its participation in the infrastructure of social relations of the *res civile.* I should note that the discourse of grace is not one of the self-fashionings studied by Greenblatt.

62. See Cox Balmaceda, *Renaissance Dialog;* Kinney, *Continental Humanist Poetics,* 94.

63. For a study of the permeation of military ideas in *Il Cortegiano* see J. R. Hale, "Castiglione's Military Career," in *Castiglione: The Ideal and the Real in Renaissance Culture,* ed. Robert W. Hanning and David Rosand (New Haven: Yale University Press, 1983), 143–64. For an excellent summary that also shows the recurrence of Castiglione's ideas at the time, see Woodhouse, *Castiglione,* 75–76. Although many authors tend to minimize the importance of the masculine element in *Il Cortegiano,* as they do nobility of birth, the essential "virility" of the courtier is nevertheless, and paradoxically, amply accepted. See, for example, Rebhorn, *Courtly Performances,* 20.

64. See Dain A. Trafton, "Politics and the Praise of Women: Political Doctrine in the

Courtier's Third book," in *Castiglione,* ed. Hanning and Rosand, 29–44. Valeria Finucci suggests that even this element is primarily masculine, and that the positive representations of women in *Il Cortegiano* are themselves "male representations of femininity." See Finucci, *The Lady Vanishes,* 15 and *passim.* Analyzing the hierarchical position of women in *Il Cortegiano,* Giuseppa Saccaro Battisti brilliantly shows how the relation of women to society is always mediated by their relations to men. See Giuseppa Saccaro Battisti, "La donna, le donne nel *Cortegiano,*" in *La corte e il "Cortegiano,"* ed. Ossola, 219–49. My argument is actually weaker than either Finucci's or Saccaro's.

65. For a discussion of this point, see Eduardo Saccone, "*Grazia, Sprezzatura, Affettazione* in the *Courtier,*" in *Castiglione,* ed. Hanning and Rosand, 54 ff.

66. Castiglione, *Book of the Courtier,* 336.

67. Ibid., 342.

68. See, for instance, Thomas M. Greene, "*Il Cortegiano* and the Choice of a Game," in *Castiglione,* ed. Hanning and Rosand, 1–15.

69. Ibid., 5.

70. The degree of foolishness that this argument attributes to the people of the European courts, including the monarchs, who so overwhelmingly embraced the book is, in my view, both condescending and untenable.

71. Castiglione, *Book of the Courtier,* 30.

72. Ibid., 110.

73. Greene, "Choice of a Game," 10.

74. On this, see Saccone's excellent discussion in, "*Grazia, Sprezzatura, Affettazione,*" esp. 47 ff.

75. Ibid., 51.

76. Daniel Javitch, "*Il Cortegiano* and the Constraints of Despotism," in *Castiglione,* ed. Hanning and Rosand, 17–28. See also Trafton, "Politics and the Praise of Women."

77. As love of God, commitment to the church, and the willful bestowal of oneself to the practices of Catholicism were necessary to achieve grace in the religious realm.

78. A number of scholars, most prominently Sidney Anglo, have seen in the practices that follow the structures of centeredness as described by Castiglione the grounds for arrivism and systematic immorality. I address this issue in the next chapter when discussing Nicolas Faret's *L'honneste-Homme ou, L'Art de Plaire à la Court.* See Sidney Anglo, *The Courtier's Art: Systematic Immorality in the Renaissance,* an Inaugural Lecture delivered at the University College of Swansea, 1983.

79. In the next chapter I analyze in detail the patron-client relationship that develops from this dimension of the pragmatics of grace. Like Sharon Kettering, I argue that questions of honor and civility—questions of grace—are definitive characteristics of early-modern European patronage. See Sharon Kettering, "Patronage in Early-Modern France," *French Historical Studies* 17 no. 4 (1992): 839–62. For an incisive discussion of flattery as a characteristic of what I call the infrastructure of social relations of the *res civile,* see Bernard Bray, "Praise: A Requirement of Courtesy and Epistolary Practice in the Seventeenth Century," *Dix-septième Siècle* 42, no. 2 (1990): 135–53. For an overview of debates on the topic, see

Ronald G. Asch and Adolf M. Birke, eds., *Princes, Patronage, and the Nobility: The Court at the Beginning of the Modern Age, c. 1450–1650* (New York: Oxford University Press, 1991).

80. For an argument along these lines, which includes the passage quoted, see Lauri Huovinen, "Renaissance Ideals of Personality" (originally in Finnish), *Historiallinen Arkisto* 70 (1975): 46–60; see also Eva Vigh, "Court and Courtiers in Sixteenth-Century Italy" (in Hungarian), *Vilagtortenet* 1 (1987): 3–15.

81. The first is the tension between the heightened awareness of self and its subjection to royal power that I discussed above, and to which I return below.

82. The *Cortegiano,* it should be noted, is left open-ended; further discussions are a real possibility. This strategy helps Castiglione to underline the unlimited scope of his subject as well as the inexhaustiveness of the book itself.

83. Castiglione, *Book of the Courtier,* 288.

84. Ibid., 289.

85. See Greene, "The Choice of a Game," 12.

86. Castiglione, *Book of the Courtier,* 290.

87. The text of *De civilitate,* in a translation by Brian McGregor, can be found in *The Collected Works of Erasmus,* ed. J. K. Sowards, vol. 25 (Toronto: University of Toronto Press, 1985), 273–89. This text differs in a number of important ways from the current French translation by Alcide Bonneau (Paris: Editions Ramsay, 1977), particularly in questions of vocabulary. I have done my best to quote passages on which the two translations agree. Studies of Erasmus's treatise appear in the introductions to both translations; see also Franz Bierlaire, "Erasmus at School: The *De civilitate morum puerilium libellus,*" in *Essays on the Works of Erasmus,* ed. Richard L. DeMolen (New Haven: Yale University Press, 1978); Herman de la Fontaine Verway, "The First 'Book of Etiquette' for Children," *Quaerendo* 1 (1971): 19–30; Jacques Revel, "The Uses of Civility," in *A History of Private Life: Passions of the Renaissance,* ed. Roger Chartier (Cambridge: Harvard University Press, 1989), 167–205; and, of course, much of part 2 of volume 1 of Norbert Elias, *The Civilizing Process* (Oxford: Basil Blackwell, 1994).

88. Giovanni della Casa, *Galateo,* translated, with an introduction and notes, by Konrad Eisenbichler and Kenneth R. Bartlett (Toronto: Centre for Reformation and Renaissance Studies, 1986). Subsequent citations refer to this edition. For the Italian original, see Giovanni della Casa, *Galateo,* edited and with an introduction by Giuseppe Prezzolini (Milano: Rizzoli, 1985).

89. They are indeed often interpreted as such; for a major example, see Revel, "Uses of Civility," 190–92.

90. On the permeation of civility, see Revel, "Uses of Civility," 167–205.

91. Elias, *Civilizing Process,* 1: 78.

92. Franz Bierlaire reports, for example, the reaction of the French humanist Guillaume Budé to the publication of *De civilitate:* "[A]nd, great gods," Budé wrote in a letter to Erasmus, "you will tell me again that you corrected the little Cato . . . and that you do not regret the short day's work devoted to that trivial task; as if so many little books do not risk tarnishing the brilliancy of your name." Erasmus's reply was most typical of

the man and, for that matter, most evocative of the spirit of the book itself: "In the domain of belles-lettres," he answered, "there is nothing on earth, even the most vulgar, which is to be scorned, and especially not these verses of the pseudo-Cato that so adorn the Latin language and serve as the means to good manners. . . . For whoever may seek to render service only and not to attract attention, the brilliancy of the material is less important than its utility. I will not reject any work, not even that scornfully wretched *Catunculus,* if I determine that it is useful in bringing about progress in studies. I do not write for Persius nor Laelius, I write for children and for the unlettered" (Bierlaire, "Erasmus at School," 239). Among modern scholars, despite Elias, *De civilitate* has not fared much better. It is rarely mentioned in monographs on Erasmus, in which the religious reformer and the humanist shadow the teacher of manners to the point of invisibility; for example, *De civilitate* is virtually absent from Bruce Mansfield's massive, two-volume exploration of interpretations of Erasmus through history, and in most biographies the little manual takes, at best, a paragraph. See Bruce Mansfield, *Phoenix of His Age: Interpretations of Erasmus, c. 1550–1750* (Toronto: University of Toronto Press, 1979); and *Man on His Own: Interpretations of Erasmus c. 1750–1920* (Toronto: University of Toronto Press, 1992).

93. Twelve times in its first year, an estimated thirty times up to Erasmus's death in 1536. See McGregor, "Introduction," in *Collected Works of Erasmus,* ed. Sowards, 272; Richard L. DeMolen, "Introduction to *Opera Omnia Desiderii Erasmi,*" in *Essays on the Works of Erasmus,* ed. DeMolen, 43.

94. Erasmus, *De civilitate,* 274.

95. Ibid., 275.

96. Della Casa, *Galateo,* 6–7; see in particular the discussions towards the end of the book, 53–61.

97. For a discussion of this dimension of the *Galateo,* see Eisenbichler's and Bartlett's introduction to *Galateo,* xvi–xx.

98. In Erasmus, at least according to Johan Huizinga's interpretation, this attitude would seem to reflect the very personality of the man. According to Huizinga, Erasmus was a person striving for a strict balance of opinion in all things, a person showing strong displeasure not only for the violent and extravagant but for anything denoting a passionate spirit— including the choruses of Greek drama. He was supposed to be in a constant search for harmony, purity, simplicity, gentleness, and rest. Huizinga describes Erasmus's ideal of the good life, as he himself did in one of his *Colloquia,* as a literal incarnation of the golden mean, as an idyllic situation marked by an aloofness from earthly concerns and a healthy contempt for all that is sordid. Living thus, one could find an easy post of honor and live in perfectly safe mediocrity, free from judgment, both of things and of men. See Johan Huizinga, *Erasmus and the Age of Reformation* (Princeton: Princeton University Press, 1984), chapters 12 and 13, especially 104 ff.

99. Erasmus, *De civilitate,* 278, quotation marks added.

100. Ibid., 287.

101. Erasmus, *De civilitate,* 276–78.

102. Della Casa, *Galateo,* 16–17.

103. Erasmus, *De civilitate,* 284. For an analysis of Erasmus's attitude to women, see Barbara Correll, "Malleable Material, Models of Power: Women in Erasmus's 'Marriage Group' and 'Civility in Boys,'" *English Literary History* 57 no. 2 (1990): 241–62.

104. Della Casa has a concept of grace very similar to Castiglione's, but only regarding the moral and aesthetic dimensions of the term; see *Galateo,* 53–54.

105. Honor should not be confused with virtue. Virtue refers to a personal property which, all three authors maintain, can be equally attained by men of high and low birth—although the first have a clear advantage over the second. Honor refers to a social property tied to a person's position in the social hierarchy, and to a currency that circulates along the networks connecting every person to a center.

106. For the *Galateo,* see della Casa's explanation of how the manual was allegedly conceived (7–9). Della Casa tells how the treatise was inspired by a minor fault committed by an aristocrat of the highest distinction, a man of almost impeccable grace, and tells of the extraordinary gift that teaching him to avoid his fault entails.

107. Here I am following Bierlaire's argument in "Erasmus at School," 240–41.

108. Erasmus, *De civilitate,* 286.

109. See Christian Bec, "La Politique de Giovanni della Casa," *Pensiero Pol* 7, no. 3 (1974): 362–78.

Chapter Five

1. I am quoting from two sources: Louis de Rouvroy, Duc de Saint-Simon, *The Memoirs of the Duke of Saint-Simon on the Reign of Louis XIV and the Regency,* trans. Bayles St. John (London: George Allen & Company, 1913), 1: 86, and my own translation from Saint-Simon's *Mémoires* (Paris: Gallimard, 1983), 1: 285–86. For a review of critical analyses of the *Mémoires,* see the introductory chapter in Guy Rooryck, *Les "Mémoires" du Duc de Saint-Simon: De la parole du témoin au discours du mémorialiste* (Genève: Droz, 1992), which includes a comprehensive bibliography. As a historical document, the *Mémoires* is usually seen as portraying the realities of a society in decay, as presenting a canvas of life under Louis XIV that unmasks its degeneration and exhibits a gallery of "monstrous creatures, the perfect product of absolutist rottenness" (Rooryck, *Mémoires,* 27). My interpretation is far less caustic. While I clearly see the *Mémoires* as revealing the tensions and ambiguities of French court society under Louis XIV, I am less inclined to see the men and women of the court as monsters, as products of their society's decadence.

2. Saint-Simon, *Mémoires,* 284.

3. Harold Nicolson, *Good Behaviour* (Boston: Beacon Press, 1960), 173.

4. Ibid., 173–74.

5. Norbert Elias, *The Court Society* (New York: Pantheon, 1983); Emmanuel Le Roy Ladurie, "Auprès du roi, la cour," *Annales ESC* 40 (1985): 21–41, and "Système de la cour," in *Le territoire de l'historien* (Paris: Gallimard, 1978), 2: 275–99. For a critique of Elias's *Court Society* particularly hostile to its sociological project, see Jeroen Duindam, *Myths of Power: Norbert Elias and the Early Modern European Court* (Amsterdam: Amsterdam Univer-

sity Press, 1994). Since most of Duindam's criticisms do not apply to the approach that I develop in this monograph, a detailed discussion of the book is unnecessary.

6. Nicolas Faret, *L'honneste-Homme ou, L'Art de Plaire à la Court* (Paris: Chez Toussaincts du Bray, 1630). A reprint of the 1634 edition was published by the Presses Universitaires de France in 1925; see Nicolas Faret, *L'honneste-Homme ou, L'Art de Plaire à la Court,* ed. Maurice Magendie (Paris: Presses Universitaires de France, 1925). The book was translated into English by a certain F. G. in 1632 as *The Honest Man: or, The Art to Please in Court;* I follow this translation partially, to which I have made substantial changes. Page numbers in the quotations follow the pagination of the original 1630 edition. The classic study of *L'honneste-Homme* is Maurice Magendie, *La politesse mondaine, et les théories de l'honnêteté, en France au XVIIè siècle, de 1600 à 1660* (Genève: Slatkin Reprints, 1970), esp. 355 ff. See also Magendie's introduction to the 1925 reprint. For an elaborate study of sociability in France up to the French revolution, see Daniel Gordon, *Citizens without Sovereignty: Equality and Sociability in French Thought, 1670–1789* (Princeton: Princeton University Press, 1994).

7. Magendie, "Introduction," ii; see also Jean-Pierre Dens, *L'honnête homme et la critique du goût: Esthétique et société au XVIIè siècle* (Lexington, KY: French Forum Publishers, 1981), 11.

8. When referring to the title of Faret's book I write *L'honneste-Homme; honnête homme* refers to the character that Faret portrays.

9. See Faret, *L'honneste-Homme,* 32–33.

10. Ibid., 1–3.

11. On this point, Claude Michaud, in *L'Europe de Louis XIV* (Paris: Bordas, 1973), writes, "It is with Louis XIV that the identification of king and God attains its utmost point" (76).

> Louis XIV is God incarnate, a living image of divinity. The religious and intellectual currents of the time combine to prove that belief. . . . The idea appeared under Louis XIII and blossomed under Louis XIV. On 18 May 1643, Omer Talont, a member of the Parisian Parlement, addressed the young king: "The seat of Your Majesty embodies the living throne of God." Later, Bossuet was to exclaim: "Oh king, you are like the gods." The king does not participate just [in] divine authority, but also [in] its omniscience: "Occupying in a way the place of God, we believe that we participate [in] His knowledge, as well as [in His] authority," noted the king himself. (76)

12. Faret, *L'honneste-Homme,* 76–78.

13. Ibid., 78–79.

14. Jean Bodin, in particular, whose treatise, *Six Books of the Republic* (1576), is considered as the first and most important French theory of absolutism. See Julian H. Franklin, *Jean Bodin and the Rise of Absolutist Theory* (Cambridge: Cambridge University Press, 1973); and Simone Goyard-Fabre, *Jean Bodin et le droit de la république* (Paris: Presses Universitaires de France, 1989).

15. *Leviathan* was first published in 1651, twenty-one years after *L'honneste-Homme.* For

a work comparing Hobbes and Bodin, see Preston T. King, *The Ideology of Orders: A Comparative Analysis of Jean Bodin and Thomas Hobbes* (New York: Barnes & Noble, 1974).

16. Faret, *L'honneste-Homme,* 17–20.

17. Ibid., 20–21.

18. For some recent studies on dueling, see François Billacois, *The Duel: Its Rise and Fall in Early Modern France* (New Haven: Yale University Press, 1990); V. G. Kiernan, *The Duel in European History: Honour and the Reign of Aristocracy* (New York: Oxford University Press, 1988); and Robert A. Schneider, "Swordplay and Statemaking: Aspects of the Campaign against the Duel in Early Modern France," in *Statemaking and Social Movements: Essays in History and Theory,* ed. Charles Bright and Susan Harding (Ann Arbor: University of Michigan Press, 1984), 265–96.

19. Kiernan, *Duel in European History,* chap. 9, esp. 152–53.

20. Billacois, *Duel,* chap. 11.

21. Compare the battle between Don Rodrigue and Don Diègue in *Le Cid* with that between Romeo and Tybalt in *Romeo and Juliet.* The first is a duel, the fighters having followed the prescribed rules, and is condoned by society. The second is a fight, and Romeo has to escape to save his life.

The rules specified, for instance, that offended and offender should not cross arms at the moment of the challenge. First they had to exchange cartels, discuss seconds, choose weapons, and select a field of battle. Then the battle itself followed a ritual, depending on the choice of arms and the conditions of the field. The ritualization did not stop the killings, but that was not the intention. Death estimates, as reported by French diarists and visitors, were enormous. Pierre de l'Estoile assessed at seven or eight thousand the number of noblemen killed between 1589 and 1609, as did Tavannes. The Comte de Montmorency-Bouteville, a reputed duelist, was reported to have participated in twenty-two fights. A Venetian ambassador advanced a three-year figure of twenty-five hundred deaths. Another cited eight thousand in ten years—a number that, even if inflated, indicates a most serious situation. See Schneider, "Swordplay and Statemaking," 276–78.

22. See Emile Durkheim, *The Rules of Sociological Methods,* edited and with an introduction by Steven Lukes (New York: The Free Press, 1982).

23. Dens, *L'honnête homme et la critique du goût,* 11–12.

24. Domna C. Stanton, *The Aristocrat as Art* (New York: Columbia University Press, 1980), 20–21.

25. Ibid., 44. See also Gordon, *Citizens without Sovereignty,* 121–22. Gordon includes in this pattern Antoine de Courtin's *Nouveau traité de la civilité qui se pratique en France parmi les honnêtes gens,* and Eustache de Refuge's *Traité de la cour.* His comments on Courtin are interesting. After noting that Courtin was unable to present a moral rationale in his manual, Gordon writes, "[Courtin] also failed to offer a clear definition of the courtier as a character ideal and took the form of a list of rules to be observed at court—simply because they happened to be the rules at court" (122). Gordon's one sentence comprises all the misunderstandings that I have discussed in the last two chapters, beginning with the search

for a specific type of "character ideal" and ending with a failure to recognize the circularity at the heart of any established power.

26. Although referring to a later period, on this point see also Micheline Cuénin, "Evolution and Revolutions in the Pursuit of Happiness in France from 1688 to 1750," in *Culture and Revolution,* ed. Paul Dukes and John Dunkley (London: Pinter Publishers, 1990). Cuénin's brief article is also useful in reminding us of the differences between the cities and the country. In the country, most people were happy just to survive.

27. Faret, *L'honneste-Homme,* 87–88.

28. Ibid., 88–89.

29. Ibid., 87. "Everyone trembled at the thought of committing a blunder," writes Jacques Levron, discussing life at Versailles during the reign of Louis XIV, "and one understands why all noise ceased as soon as the ushers had shouted from afar 'Gentlemen, the King.' . . . Such attention to minute detail in the most commonplace activities required an application to which everyone submitted with good grace. The slightest mistake drew endless comments and was the subject of infinite discussion"; see *Daily Life at Versailles in the Seventeenth and Eighteenth Centuries* (New York: Macmillan, 1977), 38–39.

30. Faret, *L'honneste-Homme,* 166, 167.

31. On the multiplicity of discourses on the topic, Gordon's *Citizens without Sovereignty* is invaluable.

32. Philibert de Vienne, *Le philosophe de cour,* edited and with an introduction by P. M. Smith (Genève: Droz, 1990).

33. Jean de La Bruyère, *The Characters of Jean de La Bruyère,* trans. Henri van Laun (New York: Brentano's, 1929), 183.

34. On the misinterpretation of Philibert, see Sidney Anglo, "The Courtier: The Renaissance and Changing Ideals," in *The Courts of Europe: Politics, Patronage, and Royalty, 1400–1800,* ed. A. G. Dickens (London: Thames and Hudson, 1977), 51 ff. Strictly speaking, Anglo refers of the translation of *Le philosophe de cour* into English, pointing out with amazement that the English version missed all ironies, as though the translators did not recognize their critical dimension. To the translators, Anglo notes, books like Philibert's were "regarded simply as sensible advice on how to succeed within a competitive society" (51). It is clear, however, that the oddity of the English public becomes so only when viewed from the perspective of an outsider to the group. From the perspective of the insider, the seriousness with which these books were received makes complete sense and attests to their affinity with the insider's definitions of the significant, not to an insufficiency of interpretative skills on the part of the English.

35. See Sharon Kettering, "Brokerage at the Court of Louis XIV," *Historical Journal* 36, no. 1 (1993): 69–87; "Patronage in Early-Modern France," *French Historical Studies* 17, no. 4 (1992): 839–62; and *Patrons, Brokers, and Clients in Seventeenth-Century France* (New York: Oxford University Press, 1986).

36. Bernard Bray, "Praise: A Requirement of Courtesy and Epistolary Practice in the Seventeenth Century," *Dix-septième Siècle* 42, no. 2 (1990): 135–53.

NOTES TO PAGES 136–137

37. This does not mean that *honnêteté* and the pragmatics of grace are "causes" of absolutism. Causality has nothing to do with the processes at work.

38. On this, see the short but excellent discussion in Geoffrey Treasure, *The Making of Modern Europe, 1648–1780* (London and New York: Methuen, 1985), 181–90. See also Nicholas Henshall, *The Myth of Absolutism: Change and Continuity in Early Modern European Monarchy* (New York: Longman, 1992).

39. David Parker, *The Making of French Absolutism* (New York: St. Martin's Press, 1983), xvi.

40. On Louis XIV, see François Bluche, *Louis XIV* (New York: Franklin Watts, 1990); Peter Burke, *The Fabrication of Louis XIV* (New Haven: Yale University Press, 1992); Ragnhild Hatton, "Louis XIV: At the Court of the Sun King," in *The Courts of Europe: Politics, Patronage, and Royalty, 1400–1800,* ed. A. G. Dickens (London: Thames and Hudson, 1977); Levron, *Daily Life at Versailles;* and Andrew Lossky, *Louis XIV and the French Monarchy* (New Brunswick: Rutgers University Press, 1994).

41. The association between the king and the sun was definitely not new. Roland Mousnier provides a brief survey of this association in "Le Roi-Soleil," in Georges Mongrédien et al., *La France au temps de Louis XIV* (Paris: Hachette, 1965):

> The sacred character of the king had taken, according to an old French tradition, an allegorical, symbolical, mythological form, that of the Sun-King. The Roman emperors were likened to the Sun, and Nero, most notably, had been represented as Apollo, the Sun-God, riding his chariot. For Christians, Christ was the Sun of Justice and, as early as the second century, some Christian mosaics in Rome portray him as Apollo the charioteer. During the fourteenth century, in Western Europe, the chiefs of small principalities, Gaston de Foix, the Duc de Bourgogne, sometimes adopted the Sun as [an] emblem; emblem of power and glory. So did the king of France. Charles V, was the first to add the Sun to the monarchical emblem. For his marriage in 1385, Charles VI took up the image of a golden Sun as his sign. The Sun would no longer leave the arms, emblems and devices of the kings of France. Louis XI himself, the "roi bourgeois," diffused it by coining the Sun crown, which was still circulating by the time of Louis XIV. Charles IX, Henri III, [and] Henri IV were Sun-Kings. In the course of the sixteenth century, under the influence of Roman mythology, popularized by the humanists and artists of the Renaissance, the Sun was increasingly represented as a young prince, already crowned, seated on his chariot in the manner of Apollo. The symbol of the Sun was assigned by the people, by the Lyonnais in 1622, the Parisians in 1624, to Louis XIII, Sun-King and Apollo the bowman. . . . Louis XIV was born the Sun. (109–10; my translation)

Only with Louis XIV, however, was the idea of the king as sun integrated into a philosophical view of the world, a view that transcended the purely allegorical to become an element of "the real."

42. François Dumont, "French Kingship and Absolute Monarchy in the Seventeenth

Century," in *Louis XIV and Absolutism,* ed. Ragnhild Hatton (Columbus: Ohio State University Press, 1976), 55–84.

43. Ibid., 57–58.

44. For an overview of the history of France during that period, see Emmanuel Le Roy Ladurie, *The Royal French State, 1460–1610* (Oxford, Basil Blackwell, 1994).

45. Brittany, for instance, did not become part of France until 1532; Provence, not until 1481, when the king assumed power only under the title of "count of Provence"; the Dauphiné was annexed in 1560; the lands of the house of Foix-Navarre, which included the territories of Béarn, Navarre, Foix, Périgord, Bigorre, Nebouzan, and Soule, a vast territory indeed, stayed out of royal control for long after that. Independent administrations developed in Béarn, Provence, and Languedoc; Burgundy, Dauphiné, Provence, Languedoc, Guyenne, and Normandy secured to themselves the right to negotiate taxes with the crown and to raise them through their own institutional arrangements. As a way to gain the allegiance of Bordeaux, a city ruled by the English until 1451, its population was exempted from paying taxes altogether and allowed to maintain a significant degree of political autonomy. The same was true regarding La Rochelle, and cities like Bourges, Toulouse, and Marseille, whose tradition of independence was not repressed until much later. Many other towns and regions, usually dominated by a noble family or a small group of bourgeois, were given the privilege of setting up local *parlements* and allowed to administer justice according to their own rules and laws. See Parker, *Making of French Absolutism,* 13–27.

46. La Bruyère, *Characters,* 258–59.

47. See, for example, Levron, *Daily Life at Versailles,* 39.

48. Saint-Simon, quoted in Levron, *Daily Life at Versailles,* 39.

49. Ibid.

50. I do not want to give the impression that the new *honnêteté* was the only alternative to royal centrality. For one, the church continued to have significant effects on the definition of the desirable, in particular outside of the court. It dominated education, reached vast numbers of people through services, and, as much of the literature attests, often invested the discourse on propriety with a moralizing tone, if not with moral ideas. The critical point for this study, however, concerns the extent to which something new and different emerges from these alternatives, something that, because of the power of the people among which it forms, has the potential to transform society. Although ecclesiastical power was significant in France at the time, it could claim few transformative effects.

51. Chevalier de Méré, "De la vraïe honnêteté," in *Œuvres posthumes,* ed. Charles-H. Boudhors (Paris: Editions Fernand Roches, 1930). For a comprehensive study of Méré's *honnête homme,* see Dens, *L'honnête homme et la critique du goût.* Dens stresses the aesthetics of the *honnête homme* and of sociability in general, a property that I see as an expression of a more fundamental imprecision in the very formation that the new *honnêteté* helps constitute. See also his "L'honnête homme et l'esthétiqueé du paraitre," *Papers on French Seventeenth-Century Literature* 6 (1976–77): 69–82.

52. Ibid., 70; my translation.

53. Ibid., 69.

NOTES TO PAGES 142–148

54. Ibid.

55. Ibid.

56. See, for example, Méré, "De la vraïe honnêteté," and "Du commerce du monde," in *Œuvres posthumes,* 80, 90; 143, 144.

57. Méré, "De la vraïe honnêteté," 99.

58. Ibid.

59. Ibid., 79.

60. On noble culture in France during the seventeenth century, see Jonathan Dewald, *Aristocratic Experience and the Origins of Modern Culture: France, 1570–1715* (Berkeley: University of California Press, 1993).

61. Abbé Prévost, *Manon Lescaut* (New York: New American Library, 1961).

62. Here I am following Simmel's striking discussions on love, especially in "On Love (a fragment)," in *Georg Simmel: On Women, Sexuality, and Love,* ed. Guy Oakes (New Haven: Yale University Press, 1984), 153–92; and "Eros, Platonic and Modern," in *Georg Simmel: On Individuality and Social Forms,* ed. Donald N. Levine (Chicago: University of Chicago Press, 1971), 235–48. For a discussion of this aspect of Simmel's sociology, see Guy Oakes, "Eros and Modernity: Georg Simmel on Love," in *The Sociology of Emotions,* ed. David Franks and E. Doyle McCarthy (Greenwich, CT: JAI, 1989).

63. Méré, "Du commerce du monde," 141; emphasis in original. Méré has already warned, "It is then necessary to instruct oneself, as far as is possible, in life, and it is not what is usually called *morals* or *politics*" ("De la vraïe honnêteté," 72).

64. Even honor, once the prerogative of royal grace, becomes in Méré an expression of "love": to be an *honnête homme,* to earn the affection of one's peers, Méré tells us, is "the surest way to acquire honor." See "Suite de la vraïe honnêteté," in *Œuvres posthumes,* 90.

65. La Bruyère, *Characters,* 184.

66. Ibid., 219–20.

67. La Bruyère writes, for instance, "Courtiers speak well of a man for two reasons: firstly, that he may know they have commended him; and secondly, that he may say the same of them," and "It is as dangerous at court to make any advances as it is embarrassing not to make them" (ibid., 196). And, ironically prefiguring one of the central theorems of network theory, he says, "There is a highroad or a beaten road, as it is called, which leads to grand offices, and there is a cross or bye-way which is much the shortest" (ibid., 200). The theory I refer to is Marc Granovetter's "strength of weak ties" theory. See his *Getting a Job: A Study of Contacts and Careers* (Cambridge: Harvard University Press, 1974).

68. William Doyle, *The Old European Order, 1600–1800* (Oxford: Oxford University Press, 1978), 88.

69. Emile Durkheim, *The Division of Labor in Society,* with an introduction by Lewis A. Coser (New York: Free Press, 1984).

70. See my initial discussion of mechanical solidarity in the context of ecclesias and coalescence in the section of chapter 2 entitled "The Ontological Condition of Coalescence."

71. Indeed, within and outside the court, the aristocracy was divided into factions competing for power, both in terms of the mechanisms of royal centrality and in terms of

precedence and control of the new social formations. In the second case, conflict and competition among aristocrats can be seen as equivalent to conflict and competition among capitalists—which does not prevent them from being a class. On the divisions within the court, see Duindam, *Myths of Power,* 137–58. On the topic in general, see Roger Mettam, *Power and Faction in Louis XIV's France* (New York: Basil Blackwell, 1988).

72. See Simmel, "On Love (a fragment)," and "Eros, Platonic and Modern."

73. For a thorough description of this double effect, see Dewald, *Aristocratic Experience*—although Dewald's analytical apparatus, grounded on more conventional categories opposing "hierarchy" to "freedom," is very different from my own. Referring to a more moralistic literature developing in conjunction with Méré's in the aristocratic salons, and following the conventional interpretation of Faret, Gordon, in *Citizens without Sovereignty,* speaks of the coexistence between an "amoral courtly literature" and "a more moralistic salon literature" (122). My own distinction is very different and depends on the recognition of the different infrastructures of social relations and the different types of social formation that each discourse helped generate.

74. See Levron, *Daily Life at Versailles,* 29.

75. Guy Chaussinand-Nogaret, *The French Nobility in the Eighteenth Century: From Feudalism to Enlightenment* (Cambridge: Cambridge University Press, 1985), 9–10. The phrase "gilded ghetto" appears in the title of the introduction, appropriately called "The Gilded Ghetto of Royal Nobility."

76. La Bruyère, *Characters,* 185.

77. On this particular example, see René Pomeau, *L'age classique III: 1680–1720* (Paris: Arthaud, 1971), 116–17.

78. Père Bouhours, *Les entretiens d'Ariste et d'Eugène* (Paris: Editions Bossard, 1920). For a study of Bouhours, see George Doncieux's book, originally published in 1886, *Le Père Bouhours: Un Jésuite homme de lettre au dix-septième siècle* (Genève: Slatkin Reprints, 1970).

79. Bouhours, *Entretiens,* 195–96.

80. Bouhours, *Entretiens,* 197 ff.

Chapter Six

1. See Sidney Anglo, "The Courtier: The Renaissance and Changing Ideals," in *The Courts of Europe: Politics, Patronage, and Royalty, 1400–1800,* ed. A. G. Dickens (London: Thames and Hudson, 1977), 51 ff.

2. Sydney Anglo's comment on Ducci parallels Magendie's on Faret. To Anglo, Ducci's courtier was but "an unashamed climber," a flatterer and an opportunist, and he wonders at the seriousness with which these ideas were expressed. He also wonders at what he deems "a bizarre development in the history of the idea of the courtier," namely, the unquestioned acceptance of its "topsy-turvy morality" and its subsequent systematization into a complex body of behavioral rules. Clearly, however, the same comments that I made regarding Magendie apply to Anglo. Indeed, the English public seems odd only from the perspective of an outsider to the group. For Anglo's comments, see "The Courtier," 51–52.

3. Writing on the power of the Tudors, G. W. Bernard, in *The Power of the Early Tudor*

Nobility: A Study of the Fourth and Fifth Earls of Shrewsbury (Totowa, NJ: Barnes & Noble, 1985), reminds us of the manufactured character of the English monarchy:

> There has been a tendency to "reify" monarchy: in fact monarchical authority had to be created and constantly adjusted and maintained by Tudor monarchs. Henry IV of France, it has been suggested, "had consciously to create the stability of his regime after the wars. There was nothing natural or automatic about it. It was a deliberate, in some senses artificial creation, which could have easily been overturned, and which was constantly being tested, but which became stronger the longer it lasted." Much the same was true of early Tudor monarchy. That meant that circumstances were highly important. The monarchy was weakest on the death and accession of a king, or during the reign of a usurper or a minor. A young king such as Edward VI could not rule like an adult: popular rebellions, courtly intrigue, and noble coups mark his reign. Usurpers of doubtful legitimacy like Henry VII had to fight and win their battles before they become fully accepted within their realm and without. . . . Even kings who acceded without challenge might find it prudent to sacrifice the unpopular ministers of the former regime. (198)

4. See Lawrence Stone's magisterial *The Crisis of the Aristocracy, 1558–1641* (Oxford: Oxford University Press, 1965), chapter 8. For a description of life in Elizabeth's court, see Neville Williams, "The Tudors: Three Contrasts in Personality," in *The Courts of Europe: Politics, Patronage, and Royalty, 1400–1800,* ed. A. G. Dickens (London: Thames and Hudson, 1977). R. Malcolm Smuts, in *Court Culture and the Origins of a Royalist Tradition in Early Stuart England* (Philadelphia: University of Pennsylvania Press, 1987), gives an example of the workings of royal hegemony during Elizabeth's reign:

> Whenever Elizabeth passed through a town on progress, she was honored by an oration, and sometimes a civic pageant. When she settled for the night at the house of some unfortunate lord, complete with her massive train, she expected to be elaborately complimented and entertained. Borough corporations and country landowners thus found themselves pressed into the work of glorifying their royal mistress, and a few rose to the challenge with remarkable energy. When the Earl of Hertford heard she was moving toward one of his small country residences in 1591, he hired 280 workmen to erect a small village to house the court and construct the setting for a pageant. They dug a pond in the shape of a crescent moon of Diana, goddess of chastity. In it stood an island fortress and a ship, to symbolize England and her navy, and a huge snail made of trimmed hedges, to represent the queen's enemies. When Elizabeth arrived, water deities came out of this enchanted pool to pay homage in song and verse to the mistress of the seas. Then the ship and fortress attacked the snail with blazing cannon, blowing it up in a profusion of fireworks. The entertainment dragged on through three days of drizzle as both court and country folk watched. Finally Elizabeth departed, to the doleful laments of the water gods, whose mistress was deserting them, in the direction of the next host. (17–18)

Whether Hertford considered himself "unfortunate" is questionable, however. To him, most probably, the queen's visit was neither an inconvenience nor simply an opportunity to please his monarch; it was, quite literally, an honor. For an insightful analysis of the pageant of royalty, see Roy Strong's *Splendor at Court: Renaissance Spectacle and the Theater of Power* (Boston: Houghton Mifflin, 1973), especially chap. 2.

5. R. O. Bucholz, "'Nothing but Ceremony': Queen Anne and the Limitations of Royal Ritual," *Journal of British Studies* 30, no. 3 (July 1991): 288–323; and *The Augustan Court: Queen Anne and the Decline of Court Culture* (Stanford: Stanford University Press, 1993).

6. Lawrence Stone, "The Reformation," in *The Past and the Present* (Boston: Routledge & Kegan Paul, 1981), 102.

7. This thesis, first presented by J. E. Neale during the 1950s and still representing the dominant interpretation of the English parliament before the Puritan revolution, has been severely questioned since the late 1970s. Minute readings of parliamentary debates seem to indicate that for most of the first half of the seventeenth century the parliament, instead of being a force acting against the crown, was highly supportive of the monarchy and almost completely opposed to any kind of political reform. The extent to which parliamentary debates can or should be taken at face value remains an open question, however. The personal diaries of members of parliament show a more ambiguous situation, and may attest to significant undercurrents of antagonism to the crown that were kept alive by the very fact of the parliament's existence. For the original formulation of the thesis, see J. E. Neale, *Elizabeth I and Her Parliaments: 1559–1582* (London: Cape, 1953). The major criticism of Neale's thesis is Conrad Russell, *Parliaments and English Politics, 1621–29* (New York: Oxford University Press, 1979). For a response, see Christopher Hill, "Political Discourse in Early-Seventeenth-Century England," in Colin Jones, Malyn Newitt, and Stephen Roberts, eds., *Politics and People in Revolutionary England* (Oxford: Basil Blackwell, 1986), 41–64; and Christopher Hill, *A Nation of Change and Novelty: Radical Politics, Religion, and Literature in Seventeenth-Century England* (London: Routledge, 1990). Barry Coward's article in the Jones, Newitt, and Roberts volume, "Was There an English Revolution in the Middle of the Seventeenth Century?" presents a brief review of the topic in terms sympathetic to the revisionist interpretation of parliamentary politics.

8. See Coward, "Was There an English Revolution?," 18–20.

9. "So far as it conveyed to the ordinary man and woman the true meaning of Christianity," writes Stone, "the sixteenth century was far more effective than all the long centuries of the Middle Ages, and it is no wild paradox to speak of the sixteenth century as the era of the rise of Christian Europe—and of the decline of the bourgeoisie"; see Stone, "The Reformation," 103.

10. Martin Luther, *On Christian Liberty*, in *Introduction to Contemporary Civilization in the West: A Source Book*, vol. 1 (New York: Columbia University Press, 1954), 634.

11. As I discuss below, it is not necessary to subscribe to Weber's thesis linking Puritanism with capitalism in order to recognize the effects of Protestantism as a whole on individuation. Weber's general thesis can be significantly questioned on empirical grounds. For one thing, the Puritan movements of the post-Reformation period do not seem to have

been as sympathetic to capitalistic practices as Weber assumed. Although they did entail, as Weber claimed, a work ethic, they were deeply hostile to the idea of acquisitiveness, or to the *laissez-faire* mentality that characterizes a market economy. The suggestion that the Reformation fostered an individualized perception of self and other, as David Zaret showed, remains unaffected by this sort of criticism, however. See Max Weber, *The Protestant Ethic and the Spirit of Capitalism* (New York: Charles Scribner's Sons, 1958); David Zaret, *The Heavenly Contract: Ideology and Organization in Pre-Revolutionary Puritanism* (Chicago, University of Chicago Press, 1985), 199–208.

12. Henry Peacham, *The Compleat Gentleman; Fashioning Him Absolute in the Most Necessary and Commendable Qualities Concerning Minde or Bodie That May Be Required in a Noble Gentleman* (Amsterdam and New York: Theatrum Orbis Terrarum and Da Capo Press, 1968), 1.

13. William Shakespeare, *Henry IV, Part 1,* ed. David Bevington (New York: Oxford University Press, 1987). Unless otherwise indicated, I am mostly following Bevington's indications regarding textual comments and stage directions. I am also following the traditional form of citation, indicating in parentheses in the text first the number of the act, then the scene, then the numbers of the cited lines.

14. Northrop Frye, *On Shakespeare* (New Haven: Yale University Press, 1986), 74. Other authors have seen Falstaff, in addition to all of the above, as a homosexual, a serious criminal, a Machiavellian nationalist, an incarnation of pure lust, a corrupt military officer, a decadent nobleman, and much more, some of which he very overtly is, some of which seem far-fetched. For some reviews of these views, see David Bevington's introduction (28) to the sourcebook cited above and Harold Bloom, "Introduction," in *William Shakespeare: Histories and Poems,* ed. Harold Bloom (New York: Chelsea House Publishers, 1986), 3.

15. Later in the same dialog, Falstaff calls Hal "sweet swag," which he repeats a few lines later (1.2.22; 1.2.55), and "the most comparative, rascalliest, sweet young prince" (1.2.77–78).

16. See Frye, *On Shakespeare,* 77.

17. Bloom, "Introduction," 3; emphasis in original.

18. On this point, see Alvin B. Kernan's seminal study "'The Henriad': Shakespeare's Major History Plays," in *William Shakespeare: History and Poems,* ed. Bloom, 211–43.

19. Just before the battle of Shrewsbury, Hal bids Falstaff farewell, "Say thy prayers, and farewell." "I would 'twere bedtime, Hal, and all well" jokes Falstaff; to which the Prince replies, quite suggestively as we learn later, "Why, thou owest God a death." Left alone, Falstaff reflects on that last remark.

'Tis not due yet; I would be loath to pay him before his day. What need I be so forward with him that calls not on me? Well, 'tis no matter; honour pricks me on. Yea, but how if honour prick me off when I come on? How then? Can honour set to a leg? No. Or an arm? No. Or take away the grief of a wound? No. Honour hath no skill in surgery, then? No. What is honour? A word. What is in that word honour? What is that honour? Air. A trim reckoning. Who hath it? He that died o' Wednesday. Doth he feel it? No. Doth he hear it? No. 'Tis insensible, then? Yea, to the dead. But will it not live with the living? No. Why? Detraction will not suffer it. Therefore I'll none of it. Honour is a mere scutcheon. And so ends my catechism. (*1 Henry IV*, 5. 1.124–40)

20. Eric Auerbach, *Mimesis: The Representation of Reality in Western Literature* (Princeton: Princeton University Press, 1953), chap. 13.

21. See, for instance, Frye, *On Shakespeare*, 53–69; Kernan, "The Henriad," 211–19.

22. For instance, see his monologue during the second scene of act 1 regarding his misgivings about participating in a robbery planned by Falstaff; later, however, he takes part in the crime with very real delight (2.2.). Moreover, he actively participates in its preparation, even assuming at times a position of leadership.

23. The idea of life as a journey, often conceived in religious terms of pilgrimage, was common at the time. Bunyan's *Pilgrim's Progress* is the best known of the many books that embraced the idea. As I discuss below, it instructs most of the major civility manuals published in England during the seventeenth century. For a brief review of this literature, see Christopher Hill, *A Turbulent, Seditious, and Factious People: John Bunyan and His Church, 1628–1688* (Oxford: Clarendon Press, 1988), 201–6.

24. For a very similar argument, though much more elaborate, see Jonathan Hart, *Theater and World: The Problematics of Shakespeare's History* (Boston: Northeastern University Press, 1992), in particular 4–5 and chap. 4.

25. For an analysis of the multifaceted languages of politics at the time, see Conal Condren, *The Language of Politics in Seventeenth-Century England* (New York: St. Martin's Press, 1994).

26. See, for example, Mason, *Gentlefolk in the Making*, 23; Nicholas Orme, *From Childhood to Chivalry: The Education of the English Kings and Aristocracy, 1066–1530* (New York: Methuen, 1984), 224–31; Foster Watson, "Introduction," in Thomas Elyot, *The Boke Named the Gouernor* (London: J. M. Dent, 1907), xi. A comprehensive analysis of English courtesy literature during the sixteenth century is provided by Ruth Kelso in *The Doctrine of the English Gentleman in the Sixteenth Century* (Gloucester, MA: Peter Smith, 1964), originally published in 1929. The full text of the *Gouernour*, comprising three "books," is reproduced in Foster Watson's edition of the treatise. Unless otherwise stated, however, I quote from John M. Major's modernized version of book 1 of the *Gouernor* (New York: Teachers College Press, Columbia University, 1969). The quotation in the text is from page 29.

27. Elyot, *Gouernor*, 41.

28. Ibid., 42–43.

29. "Now to conclude my first assertion or argument: where all thing is common, there lacketh order; and where order lacketh, there all thing is odious and uncomely" (ibid., 47), writes Elyot to end the first chapter.

30. Ibid., 45–46.

31. Ibid., 48.

32. Ibid., 48–49.

33. Ibid., 50.

34. Thomas Hobbes, *Leviathan: Or the Matter, Forme, and Power of a Commonwealth Ecclesiasticall and Civil*, ed. Michael Oakeshott (New York: Collier Books, 1962), 125.

35. Ibid.

36. Ibid., 127.

37. I should also note that nowhere does Elyot use the term *civility;* the word had not yet entered the English language. The term is accurate, however, for the kind of behavior that Elyot advocates.

38. This is indicated by his differentiation between *populus* and *plebs,* the first having received the gift of understanding. Elyot explains:

> And therefore it appeareth that God giveth not to every man like gifts of grace, or of nature, but to some more, some less, as it liketh his divine majesty. Ne they be not in common (as fantastical fools would have all things), nor one man hath not all virtues and good qualities [so much for the divinity of the king]. Notwithstanding, for as much as understanding is the most excellent gift that man can receive in his creation, whereby he doth approach most nigh unto the similitude of God, which understanding is the principal part of the soul, it is therefore congruent, and according, that as one excelleth another in that influence, as thereby being next to the similitude of his maker, so should the estate of his person be advanced in degree, or place, where understanding may profit; which is also distributed into sundry uses, faculties, and offices necessary for the living and governance of mankind.

To which later he adds: "[I]t is of good congruence that they which be superior in condition or havior should have also pre-eminence in administration, if they be not inferior to other in virtue" (*Gouernour,* 45, 59–60).

39. The *honneste-Homme* did, at one point, contain an idea that resembles Elyot's: "[T]he true and lawful power of sovereigns is nothing but the tying and uniting of authority and justice for the preservation of the public good," wrote Faret (see chapter 6). Authority is distributed among many people, Faret suggested, and the king unites in his own the powers of the many. Moreover, the good of the public attains material expression in the king, so that monarch and nation become one, their fates tied, their interests blending into one another. But in Faret the tying and uniting was done from above, as a consequence of the will of the king, which is but a reflection of the will of God. In Faret's world the people renounce their power, or rather, are made to renounce their power; they do not vest it in another person. The aim of anyone therefore is to serve the one source of real value: the king. The idea of a public weal does lurk in Faret's conception of the social. In the background of all action, underlying the meaning of kingship itself, lies "the public good," something that has a value in and for itself. Kings come and go only for its sake, he suggested—for one moment stressing the preeminence of the community at large over that of the crowned head. Nevertheless, in the classical philosophy of the *honnête homme,* the king occupies center stage, the good of the public receiving an utterly secondary role. *L'honneste-Homme* is overwhelmed by the presence and importance of the king and thus the idea of a public weal melts away, ultimately becoming wholly insubstantial.

40. Both John M. Major in his introduction to the Teachers College edition of the *Gouernour*, 16–27, and John E. Mason in his *Gentlefolk in the Making*, 23–27, provide brief overviews of Elyot's educational program. For a study on education in general at the time, see Orme, *From Childhood to Chivalry*.

41. Almost all of the third book of the *Gouernor* is devoted to a discussion of *mediocritas* and to its application in the practical aspects of life.

42. Elyot, *Gouernour*, ed. Watson, 280, 284–85.

43. Ibid., 285–86.

44. Peacham, *Compleat Gentleman*, 1.

45. Ibid., 3.

46. Ibid., 2.

47. Ibid., 18.

48. Ibid., 2.

49. Take, for instance, the following passage. Peacham speaks of the nature of kingship:

> Since learning then joyned with the feare of God, is so faithfull a guide, that without it Princes undergoe but lamely (as *Chrysostome* faith) their greatest af-faires; they are blinde in direction, ignorant in knowledge, rude and barbarous in manners and living: the necessitie of it in Princes and Nobilitie, may easily be gathered, who howsoever they flatter themselves, with the favourable Sunshine of their great Estates and Fortunes, are indeede of no other account and reckoning with men of wisedome and understanding, then Glowormes that onely shine in the darke of Ignorance, and are admired of Ideots and the vulgar for the out-side . . . (ibid., 20)

It is significant that *The Compleat Gentleman* does not contain a separate section on kingship. All the discussions regarding kingship are integrated within larger discussions on the nobility.

50. This changing aspect of the British aristocracy has been emphasized most recently by David Cannadine in *Aspects of Aristocracy: Grandeur and Decline in Modern Britain* (New Haven: Yale University Press, 1994).

51. Peacham even complains that the Continental languages have no special word to address a noble person. Of the French, for instance, he writes, "In France, euery Peasant and common Lacquay, is saluted by name of *Monsieur,* or *Sire,* the King himselfe hauing no other Title." Of the Italian: "In *Venice* likewise, euery Mechanique is a *Magnifico,* though his *magnificenza* walketh the Market but with a *Chequin* [common clothing]" (*Compleat Gentleman,* 15).

52. See the entire first chapter, entitled "Youth," in Richard Brathwait, *The English Gentleman; Containing Sundry excellent Rules or exquisite Observations, tending to Direction of every Gentleman, of selecter ranke and quality; How to demeane or accomodate himselfe in the manage of publike or private affaires,* (Amsterdam and Norwood, NJ: Theatrum Orbis Terrarum and Walter J. Johnson, 1975).

53. Brathwait, *English Gentleman,* 374.

54. Owen Feltham, *Resolves, A Duple Century.* 3d ed. (Amsterdam and Norwood, NJ: Theatrum Orbis Terrarum and Walter J. Johnson 1975), 80, 185, 200, 344, 438.

55. Thomas Gainsford, *The Rich Cabinet: Containing Descriptions, Characters, Discourses, and Histories; Divine and Morall* (Amsterdam and New York: Theatrum Orbis Terrarum and Da Capo Press, 1972). The book dates from 1616. Under the caption "citizen" we read, for instance: "A Citizen is a professor of civilitie; and living in a glorious quiet, maketh the Common-wealth to flourish" (27); under the caption "honour": "Honour that is gracious, is gotten by vertue, and noble merit: it is never at full height, till vertue bring it to heaven" (63); or, "Honour in some cases is inferior to Gentilitie: for the ancestrie of bloud must needes have preheminence over a familie newly erected," and then he recounts, "Whereupon I remember a story of *Henry* the eight: who beeing entreated to make a clowne a gentleman, answered suddenly, hee could make him a noble man, or person of Honour, as in the estimation of the Common-wealth it passed currant: but a Gentleman must boast of his famous ancestors vertues, and his owne worthy merit" (63). On the other hand, he wrote, "Kings as they be gracious and worthy of their Scepters, are Gods Lieuetenants, and so they make Nobles vertuous, Officers just, Judges upright, Lawyers perfect, Preachers zealous, Merchants industrious, the Citizen honest, the Countrey-man laborious, the Scholler studious, the Souldier vigilant, all estates orderly dutifull, and the whole land peaceable and plentifull" (74). In view of the previous story regarding Henry VIII's power to bestow "vertue," this last statement is not very credible.

56. James Cleland, *The Institution of a Young Noble Man* (New York: Scholars' Facsimiles & Reprints, 1948).

57. The others are Peacham's and Brathwait's. See, for instance, Mason, *Gentlefolk in the Making,* 143.

58. See in particular the book's preface, which involves a definition of nobility, and the "Third Book," which discusses a nobleman's duties towards God, the king, and the country.

59. John Bunyan, *The Pilgrim's Progress* (London: Henry Frowde, Oxford University Press Warehouse, 1903). Studies on Bunyan and *The Pilgrim's Progress* include Beatrice Batson, *John Bunyan's Grace Abounding and The Pilgrim's Progress: An Overview of Literary Studies, 1960-1987* (New York: Garland, 1988); Julie Campbell, "Pilgrim's Progress/Regress/Stasis: Some Thoughts on the Treatment of the Quest in Bunyan's 'Pilgrim's Progress' and Beckett's 'Mercier and Camier,'" *Comparative Literature Studies* 30 (spring 1993): 137–52; Hill, *A Turbulent, Seditious, and Factious People;* Anne Laurence, W. R. Owens, and Stuart Sim, eds., *John Bunyan and His England* (London: The Hambledon Press, 1990); Vincent Newey, ed., *The Pilgrim's Progress: Critical and Historical Views* (Liverpool: Liverpool University Press, 1980); M. van Os and G. J. Schutte, eds., *Bunyan in England and Abroad: Papers Delivered at the John Bunyan Tercentenary Symposium, Vrije Universiteit, Amsterdam, 1988* (Amsterdam: VU University Press, 1990).

60. *The Pilgrim's Progress* brings to light an additional aspect of the development of multicenteredness, for we may see the book as expressing the individual's sense of "de-

centeredness" that results from a reality marked by multicenteredness, and of this individual's search for a new center, one no longer available within the realities of the social. The discourse of identity that it conveys thus becomes the mirror image of the discourses of multicenteredness within which it emerges. *The Pilgrim's Progress* is without question a primarily religious book, intended for the religious edification of its readers. But it is also the story of "an individual fighting alone to save his soul, which is his and only his," to use Christopher Hill's formulation in *A Turbulent, Seditious, and Factious People* (200). And it is also an allegory about that individual's "quest for some spiritual enlightenment in a disunified world," to quote Julie Campbell ("Pilgrim's Progress/Regress/Stasis," 137). Early in the narrative (*Pilgrim's Progress*, 37) the pilgrim loses the material token of his spiritual as well as his psychological identity, a scroll given to him at the House of the Interpreter (as a mark is simultaneously set in his forehead) sealing the change of his name from Graceless to Christian. The "progress" of the book's title refers to the psychological and spiritual journey through which the pilgrim recaptures his identity. It refers to the inner struggles by which he attains something that he can hold and make his own, something that defines his sense of being, something in terms of which he can orient his actions and make sense of reality. Through the struggles by which he becomes established in the truths inherent in his faith, he develops a center—an inner center entirely his own.

The Pilgrim's Progress can in fact be seen as a double mirror of the realities of multicenteredness. It first reflects the new realities from the perspective of the individual. Faced with a multiplicity of centers, the individual has no singular point of orientation, no singular axis in terms of which to determine a position in relation to others. In a way, the person becomes "decentered." But the book also provides a reversed image of this experience of "decenteredness." For the absence of a center prompts a discourse of recenteredness; since a center can no longer be found outside the individual, it is now located inside the individual. The discourses of identity reflect a reality in which identity has become problematic—something that is fully manifested a few years later in the works of John Locke.

61. Peacham, *Compleat Gentleman*, 12.

62. Ibid., 189.

63. Feltham, *Resolves, A Duple Century*, 152.

64. As Peacham advises, "In your discourse be free and affable, giving entertainment in a sweete and liberall manner, and with a cheerefull courtesie, seasoning your talke at the table among grave and serious discourses, with conceipts of wit and pleasant invention, as ingenious Epigrammes, Emblemes, Anagrammes, merry tales, wittie questions and answers, Mistakings, as a melancholy Gentleman sitting one day at a table, where I was, started up upon the suddaine, and meaning to say, *I must goe buy a dagger*, by transposition of the letters, said: Sir, *I must goe dye a begger*" (*Compleat Gentleman*, 196).

65. This is particularly stressed in Cleland, *Institution*, 90–95.

66. Incidentally, and perhaps not surprisingly, the only author to discuss behavior at court at any length is Cleland. The six pages or so that he devotes to the topic, however, offer no advice whatsoever on how to gain favor. The court is a place where the highest

majesty is found, and therefore where one can learn about majesty, the mark of nobility. It is a place of example, not of competition. And although to "be in favour" at court is not a bad thing, it should not become a goal in itself, Cleland cautions (*Institution,* 172 ff).

67. For this, however, Peacham proposes a short-cut: marry well, he tells the still unmarried youngster (*Compleat Gentleman,* 189).

68. Ibid.

69. Ibid., and see especially Brathwait's chapter on "Acquaintance," in *The English Gentleman,* 233 ff.

70. Luther, *On Christian Liberty,* 642.

71. Ibid.

72. Ibid., 645.

73. The anti-Puritan bent of much of the literature on the gentleman is well illustrated in the following passage from Feltham:

> Absolutely to define him [the Puritan], is a worke, I thinke, of *Difficulty;* some I know that rejoyce in the *name;* but sure they be such, as least *understand* it. As hee is more generally in these times taken, I suppose we may call him *a Church-Rebell,* or one that would exclude *order,* that his *braine* might rule. To *decline offences;* to be carefull and conscionable in our severall *actions,* is a *Purity,* that every man ought to labour for, which we may well doe, without a sullen *Segregation* from all *Society.* (*Resolves,* 11]

And he will ask, for instance, "If *Wine* were given to cheere the *heart,* why should I feare to use it for that end?" To which he replies, "Surely, the *merry soule* is freer from intended *mischiefe,* than the *thoughtfull man. . . .* God delights in nothing more, then in a *cheerefull heart,* carefull to performe him service" (ibid.). Drunkenness is to be avoided, for as Peacham explains, from drunkenness "proceede quarrelling, reviling, and many times execrable murders" (*Compleat Gentleman,* 194). He who drinks in excess acts against the good of the common weal; taken in moderation, however, "it preserveth health, comformeth and disperseth the naturall heate over all the whole body, allayes cholericke humours, expelling the same with the sweate, &c. tempereth Melancholly. And as one saith, hath in itselfe . . . a drawing vertue to procure friendship" (ibid., 195).

74. See Weber, *The Protestant Ethic and the Spirit of Capitalism.*

75. For a thorough discussion of this point, see Wolfgang Schluchter, *The Rise of Western Rationalism: Max Weber's Developmental History* (Berkeley: University of California Press, 1981), in particular 141–48.

76. For an excellent discussion of the *Protestant Ethic* and the many controversies surrounding it, see Gordon Marshall, *In Search of the Spirit of Capitalism: An Essay on Max Weber's Protestant Ethic Thesis* (New York: Columbia University Press, 1982). A shorter review of the literature appears in Benjamin Nelson, "Weber's Protestant Ethic: Its Origins, Wanderings, and Foreseeable Future," in *Beyond the Classics? Essays in the Scientific Study of Religion,* ed. C. Y. Glock and P. E. Hammond (New York: Harper and Row, 1973), 71–130.

77. See, for example, Charles H. George and Katherine George, *The Protestant Mind of the English Reformation, 1570–1640* (Princeton: Princeton University Press, 1961), 3–19; Michael Waltzer, *The Revolution of the Saints: A Study in the Origins of Radical Politics* (London: Weidenfeld and Nicolson, 1961).

78. For example, H. M. Robertson, *Aspects of the Rise of Economic Individualism: A Criticism of Max Weber and His School* (Cambridge: Cambridge University Press, 1933); Robin Briggs, "The Catholic Puritans: Jansenists and Rigorists in France," in *Puritans and Revolutionaries: Essays in Seventeenth-Century History Presented to Christopher Hill,* ed. Donald Pennington and Keith Thomas (Oxford: Clarendon Press, 1978), 333–54.

79. This interpretation of elective affinity as correlation comes from Parsons's translation of the *Protestant Ethic,* 91.

80. The affinities between the complex of practices at the core of etiquette and those formative of a market economy are actually best explained using Simmel's theories of modernization and economic interactions. Simmel stresses the interactive dimensions of economic configurations and explains the emergence of capitalism as a transformation in the configuration of economic interactions. Since in his view a society is no more than the sum of interactions that compose it, the economic, like any other aspect of society, should be understood in terms of the interactions that incorporate its activities. Now, to Simmel, the process of individuation that marks the coming of modernity, and that I have suggested becomes formative of the infrastructures of social relations developing in Europe at the time, changes the foundational configurations of economic interaction as radically as anything else—and he views this change as a condition for the emergence of capitalism. Individuation promotes an objectivistic perception of self and other. As the boundaries separating people grow, self and other become entities external to one another and thus become objects for one another, as for themselves. A configuration characterized by objectivity sets in. Action becomes increasingly objectified, and a tendency to behave objectively, that is, in terms akin to Weber's instrumental rationality, develops. This objectification and rationalization of action, for Simmel, make possible a form of exchange compatible with the requirements of a market economy, and therefore provide a ground for the emergence of capitalism. For Simmel's definition of economic activity in terms of interaction and exchange, see Georg Simmel, *The Philosophy of Money,* trans. Tom Bottomore and David Frisby (London: Routledge & Kegan Paul, 1978), 83–84. For his thesis on capitalism and objectification, see *The Philosophy of Money,* and his "Metropolis and Mental Life," in *Georg Simmel: On Individuality and Social Forms,* ed. Donald Levine (Chicago, University of Chicago Press, 1971), 324–39.

81. *Webster's Unabridged Dictionary,* 1979, s.v. "analogy."

82. I suggest this in my brief discussion of Simmel in note 80 above.

83. For a detailed account of the English case, see David Zaret's *The Heavenly Contract.*

84. See, for instance, V. G. Kiernan's synoptic *State and Society in Europe: 1550–1650* (New York: St. Martin's Press, 1980).

85. *Introduction to Contemporary Civilization in the West,* 677.

86. For a detailed analysis of this multilayered process, see Zaret, *The Heavenly Con* especially chaps. 3–6.

87. Some relevant passages in this anti-Catholic vein are reproduced in the volume *The Protestant Reformation,* ed. Hans J. Hillerbrand (New York: Harper Torchbooks, 1968), 240–47.

Chapter Seven

1. See chapter 1.

2. I am using the text of "Some Thoughts Concerning Education," published in *John Locke on Education,* edited, with an introduction and notes by Peter Gay (New York: Teachers College, Columbia University, 1964), 99, sec. 134. For a short study of Locke's educational philosophy, see M. V. C. Jeffreys, *John Locke: Prophet of Common Sense* (London: Methuen, 1967); for a more recent and comprehensive analysis, see Nathan Tarcov, *Locke's Education for Liberty* (Chicago: University of Chicago Press, 1984). See also James L. Axtell's introduction in *The Educational Writings of John Locke: A Critical Edition with Introduction and Notes* (Cambridge: Cambridge University Press, 1968); and Gay's introduction to *John Locke on Education.* For a discussion of Locke's civility in the context of his general moral thought, see John Marshall, *John Locke: Resistance, Religion, and Responsibility* (Cambridge: Cambridge University Press, 1994). Marshall's study, however, is not based on the "Thoughts" but on Locke's philosophical writings. The conception of civility that ensues is very different from, yet not incompatible with, the one that I introduce in this study. Admittedly, neither the "Thoughts" nor Locke's thoughts on civility, manners, and education in general are considered among his most important contributions, and little of the voluminous literature on Locke deals with either the book or the subjects that I discuss here. Typical of this situation is *The Cambridge Companion to Locke,* edited by Vere Chappell (Cambridge: Cambridge University Press, 1994). The recently published collection includes no chapter on education, no significant discussion of civility, and only two citations of the "Thoughts."

3. Locke, "Thoughts," 99, sec. 136.

4. Ibid., 102, sec. 140.

5. Ibid., 109, sec. 147.

6. Ibid., 99, sec. 134.

7. Ibid., 103–4, sec. 143; emphasis added.

8. Ibid, 104.

9. See Tarcov, *Locke's Education for Liberty,* 188 ff.

10. Jeffreys, *John Locke,* 78–79.

11. Locke, "Thoughts," 101, sec. 139.

12. Ibid., 101–2, sec. 139.

13. Locke does not establish a hierarchy among the lower virtues; given the centrality of civility in the definition of breeding, however, it may be assigned a certain priority over the other elements of a "good nature."

14. On this point, see Tarcov, *Locke's Education for Liberty,* 137–41. I base much of the discussion below on Tarcov's analysis.

15. Ibid., 139. This, incidentally, is the point stressed by John Marshall in his analysis of Locke's civility.

16. Nathan Tarcov explains how in Locke the nurturing of love and esteem replaces the more openly coercive mechanisms of power. In the spheres of civility, Tarcov writes, a "desire for winning esteem from others replaces the desire for mastery over them—for making them submit their wills to one's own. By teaching and even molding children by getting them to do freely what one wants, one teaches them to act in the same way: to get others to be useful to them freely or from a concern for their esteem and not by mastery" (ibid., 137).

17. Ibid., 191.

18. Michel Foucault, *The Order of Things: An Archaeology of the Human Sciences* (New York: Vintage, 1970); *The Archaeology of Knowledge* (New York: Pantheon, 1972).

19. Foucault, *Order of Things,* xvi–xvii.

20. Truth, rightness, truthfulness, and comprehensibility are the four validity claims, each associated with a different domain of reality, specified by Habermas. See his "What Is Universal Pragmatics," in *Jürgen Habermas: Communication and the Evolution of Society* (Boston: Beacon Press, 1979), 1–68.

21. Gay, "Introduction," 5.

22. This, as I discuss below, is the type of honor that Steven Shapin analyzes in his study of civility and science in seventeenth-century England. Shapin's study beautifully shows how questions about trustworthiness are historically particular. My own thesis about the historicity of pragmatics in general fits Shapin's thesis nicely. See Steven Shapin, *A Social History of Truth: Civility and Science in Seventeenth-Century England* (Chicago, University of Chicago Press, 1994).

23. Samuel Pepys, *The Diary of Samuel Pepys, a New and Complete Transcription,* ed. Robert Latham and William Matthews (Berkeley: University of California Press, 1983). Below, I quote from *The Shorter Pepys,* selected and edited by Robert Latham (Berkeley: University of California Press, 1985).

24. Pepys, *Shorter Pepys,* 470–71.

25. See Robert Latham, "Introduction" to *Shorter Pepys,* xxiv. The most comprehensive study on Pepys and his diary is the *Companion* (vol. 10) of the full edition of the text. The volume includes essays by various authors on the persons, places, and subjects that Pepys met, visited, or discussed in the years of his writing. See also Richard Ollard, *Pepys: A Biography* (London: Hodder and Stoughton, 1974); and Ivan E. Taylor, *Samuel Pepys: Updated Edition* (Boston: Twayne Publishers, 1989).

26. Pepys, *Shorter Pepys,* 470–71.

27. So, for instance, on 24 January 1667, after an evening of entertainment:

After supper to dancing again and singing, and so continued till almost 3 in the morning and then with extraordinary pleasure broke up; only, towards morning Knipp [an actress in the King's Company] fell a little ill, and so my wife home with her to put her to bed, and we continued dancing—and singing; and among other things, our Mercer unexpectedly did happen to sing an Italian song I knew not, of which they two sung the other two parts too, that did almost ravish me and made me in love with her more than ever with her singing. As late as it was, yet Rolt and Harris would go home tonight, and walked it, though I had a bed for them; and it proved dark, and a misly night—and very windy. The company being all gone to their homes, I up with Mrs. Pierce to Knipp, who was in bed; and we waked her and there I handled her breasts and did baiser la and sing a song, lying by her on the bed; and then left my wife to see Mrs. Pierce in bed with her in our best chamber, and so to bed myself—my mind mightily satisfied with all this evening's work, and thinking it to be one of the merriest enjoyments I must look for in the world, and did content myself therefore at the thoughts of it, and so to bed. (ibid., 718–19)

28. Ibid., 471.

29. Latham, "Introduction," xxxiii–iv.

30. Pepys, *Shorter Pepys*, 471.

31. In all fairness, it should be mentioned that Pepys did not seem to have visited the hot-house more often than his wife, or cared much about his own cleanliness. On Pepys's washing and bathing practices, see the *Companion*, 103–4.

32. And Ivan E. Taylor reminds us that Pepys was rather mild and cautious, at least as far as his relations with women were concerned. See Taylor, *Samuel Pepys*, 59–64.

33. See, for example, Pepys, *Shorter Pepys*, 579; on Pepys and the Great Plague of 1665, see Christopher Morris's article in the *Companion*, 328–37.

34. Pepys, *Shorter Pepys*, 659–72.

35. Although, if we must believe him, it was somewhat more than that: "Thus I ended this month," he wrote after telling of the wedding, "with the greatest joy that ever I did any in my life, because I have spent the greatest part of it with abundance of joy and honour, and pleasant Journys and brave entertainments, and without cost of money" (ibid., 511).

36. Ibid., 510–11.

37. The reasons why the English started to keep an increasing number of diaries during the seventeenth century are not well understood, yet the practice seems to have become fairly common. Latham mentions the rise of literacy, the growing interest in travel, the habit of keeping household accounts, and, in particular, the impulse to self-examination provoked by Protestantism as possible causes; see his "Introduction," xxxii. See also Robert A. Fothergill, *Private Chronicles: A Study of English Diaries* (London: Oxford University Press, 1974); Margaret Willy, *English Diarists: Evelyn and Pepys* (London: Longmans, Green, 1963); and, in particular, Elisabeth Bourcier, *Les journaux privés en Angleterre de 1600 à 1660* (Paris: Publications de la Sorbonne, 1976). For a comprehensive study of Englishwomen's diaries ranging from the seventeenth to the twentieth centuries, see Harriet Blodgett, *Centu-*

ries of Female Days: Englishwomen's Private Diaries (New Brunswick, NJ: Rutgers University Press, 1988).

38. The text of Anne Clifford's diary from her last year appears as an appendix "Pages from Lady Anne Clifford's Final Diary, 1676," in Blodgett, *Centuries of Female Days,* 249–57; and in George C. Williamson, *Lady Anne Clifford: Her Life, Letters, and Work* (Wakefield, England: S. R. Publishers, 1967), 270–80. The quotation is from Blodgett, pp. 252–53. The text of Clifford's better-known early journal, written from 1616 to 1619, was published as *The Diary of Lady Anne Clifford,* ed. Vita Sackville-West (London: William Heinemann, 1924). Portions of the earlier diary have been published in Elspeth Graham, Hilary Hinds, Elaine Hobby, and Helen Wilcox, eds., *Her Own Life: Autobiographical Writings by Seventeenth-Century Englishwomen* (London: Routledge, 1989). Williamson's book remains the best study exclusively devoted to Clifford. Bourcier's *Les journaux privés en Angleterre,* pp. 397–411, contains an excellent summary of Clifford's diaries.

39. Substantial parts of Evelyn's diary were first published in two volumes in 1818 under the title *Memoirs, Illustrative of the Life and Writings of John Evelyn, Esq., F.R.S., Comprising His Diary, from the Year 1641 to 1505–6, and a Selection of His Familiar Letters,* ed. W. Bray, (London: J. M. Dent; New York: E. P. Dutton, 1907). The complete, definitive edition of the diary was published in six volumes in 1955 as *Kalendarium. My Journal etc., 1620–1649: The Diaries of John Evelyn,* ed. E. S. de Beer (Oxford: Clarendon Press, 1955). For practical matters in the passages below I quote from the modernized language of the Bray edition. For comprehensive studies of Evelyn and his diary, see John Bowle, *John Evelyn and His World: A Biography* (London: Routledge & Kegan Paul, 1981); Florence Higham, *John Evelyn Esquire: An Anglican Layman of the Seventeenth Century* (London: SCM Press, 1968); W. G. Hiscock, *John Evelyn and His Family Circle* (London: Routledge & Kegan Paul, 1955); Beatrice Saunders, *John Evelyn and His Times* (Oxford: Pergamon Press, 1970); and Jeanne K. Welcher, *John Evelyn* (New York: Twayne, 1972). All these studies tend to minimize Evelyn's conscious address to an audience and present a more literal interpretation of the diary, and a more sympathetic view of its author, than I do.

40. For example, see Evelyn, *Memoirs:* "2d September, 1666. This fatal night, about ten, began the deplorable fire, near Fish street, in London" (2: 11). This is the entire entry for that day, obviously written long after the fact.

41. Ibid., 1: 372.

42. Ibid.

43. Ibid., 2: 40. The entry is dated 29 January 1669; the previous entry is from 3 January; the following is from 13 February.

44. Ibid., 2: 24–25.

45. Ralph Josselin, *The Diary of Ralph Josselin, 1616–1683,* ed. Alan MacFarlane, Records of Social and Economic History, n.s., 3 (London: Oxford University Press, 1976). The most comprehensive study on Josselin is Alan MacFarlane's *The Family Life of Ralph Josselin, a Seventeenth-Century Clergyman* (New York: W. W. Norton, 1970). See also Bourcier, *Les journaux privés en Angleterre,* 411–29.

46. Quoted in Gay, "Introduction," 13.

47. *The Shorter Pepys,* 471.

48. Ibid., 472.

49. Ibid., 478.

50. For information on the different characters, see the *Companion* volume to the complete edition of the diary.

51. The same pattern can be seen in Josselin. Although totally devoted to his congregation, Josselin cannot avoid marking subtle distinctions among his parishioners. His equals, like the various schoolmasters who worked for some time in Josselin's town, are always addressed as "Mr. Ludgater" or "Mr. Cosins." People of lower status—the yeomen, shopkeepers, bricklayers, millers, tailors, and so on—are virtually without exception called by their last names. The "notables"—the people who come into sight the most in the diary—if seldom more than Mr. or Mrs. are regularly treated with more dignity and regard than his peers. Josselin records their illnesses, financial fortunes, trips, family problems, and so on. He deplores their woes, prays for them, and now and then punctuates his writing with an expression of affection or deference. In the rare moments when he comes close to someone of the aristocracy, his admiration and reverence attain their highest expression: "A choice day of civil concourse mixt with religious at the L. Honywoods whither came the Countesse Dowager of Warwicke. and her sister the L. Renula: goodness and greatness sweetly mett in them, I writt to the Countesse who invited mee to Leez" (Josselin, *Diary,* 577; the entry is dated 2 July 1674).

52. Anne Clifford's late diary exhibits the same pattern but from the perspective of the center. Nearing her death, she sees many visitors, whom she dutifully receives every day in her chambers. Some come out of genuine feeling, some with the intention of gaining some material profit. Some are family members, some are fellow aristocrats, some are people for whom she very clearly serves as a center of distinction. To almost everyone she gives a present, money or jewelry. And here, indeed, we see the mirror image of what we have just seen in Pepys: the value of the gift varies according not only to family relationship, but to the distinction of the visitor.

53. Evelyn, *Memoirs,* 2: 59.

54. For example, on 18 April 1667, he goes "to make court to the Duke and Duchess of Newcastle, at their house in Clerkenwell, being newly come out of the north." He is received "with great kindness," and "was much pleased with the extraordinary fanciful habit, garg [*sic*], and discourse of the Duchess" (ibid., 24).

55. Ibid., 8 (3 August 1665); 13 (8 February 1666), for example.

56. For detailed analyses of life at court during the late seventeenth and early eighteenth centuries in England, see John M. Beattie, *The English Court in the Reign of George I* (Cambridge: Cambridge University Press, 1967); and especially R. O. Bucholz, "'Nothing but Ceremony': Queen Anne and the Limitations of Royal Ritual," *Journal of British Studies* 30 (July 1991): 288–323; and *The Augustan Court: Queen Anne and the Decline of Court Culture* (Stanford: Stanford University Press, 1993). Bucholz sustains the thesis of a strong yet largely inconsequential presence of what I have called the pragmatics of grace during the early eighteenth century.

57. Evelyn, *Memoirs*, 2: 181.

58. Ibid.

59. Pepys, *Shorter Pepys*, 483.

60. For a detailed analysis of Catholicism in relation to English politics, see John Miller, *Popery and Politics in England, 1660–1688* (Cambridge: Cambridge University Press, 1973).

61. See Barry Coward, "Was There an English Revolution?" in *Politics and People in Revolutionary England*, ed. Colin Jones, Malyn Newitt, and Stephen Roberts (Oxford: Basil Blackwell, 1986), 18–20.

62. For detailed accounts of James II's reign, see Maurice Ashley, *James II* (Minneapolis: University of Minnesota Press, 1977); John Miller, *James II: A Study in Kingship* (London: Methuen, 1989); and Michael A. Mullett, *James II and English Politics—1678–1688* (London: Routledge, 1994).

63. Evelyn carefully recorded the progressive turn towards Catholicism as well as his growing bewilderment at the king's actions. On 2 October 1685, shortly after James II succeeded his brother at the throne, Evelyn wrote approvingly of the king's openness about his faith, accepting without question the king's right to do whatever he pleased (*Memoirs*, 240). Then, slowly, he began reporting the increasing number of positions assigned to "Popists" and of the changed practices of behavior at court (for the first, see, for example, 241, 243, 250; for the second, 246, 265). Overwhelmed by the transformations, on 5 May 1686, when the king's move was still only at its beginning, he exclaimed, "All engines being now at work to bring in Popery, which God in mercy prevent!" (256). He was equally clear on the growth of absolutism, sharing in the astonishment and objection of his peers. On 27 June 1686, for instance, deeply offended, he expressed his outrage at the new Lord Chief-Justice's declaration of intention, which laid out the basis for an absolutism on the French model (258). He would finally, and quite painfully, be brought to support the interests of his class against the king.

64. So, for instance, at the same time that we see Evelyn take his distance from the monarch, we see him writing as eloquently as ever of the ceremonials at court (see, for example, ibid., 245, 256). Or at the same time that we see him unable to comply with his duties to the crown, we see him—as if the contrary were inconceivable—asking the king permission to marry his daughter (249, 252; 248–49). Or as James was fleeing England and William and Mary were being crowned, we see Evelyn simultaneously supporting the events yet wishing for a return to what he believed to be a bygone world (283 ff).

65. On this point, see Bowle, *John Evelyn and His World*. On the attitudes of the aristocracy in general, see again, Bucholz, "'Nothing but Ceremony'" and *Augustan Court*.

66. We see this also in Pepys. The sense of being lost that assails him during his meeting with the king, the subtle embarrassment that marks his behavior, his inability to experience anything significant, point, in effect, to this blurring of the forms of being that were generated by royal centrality. Pepys did not experience the awe or the almost ecstatic joy that the men and women of his condition used to experience in the presence of the monarch. To him the encounter seems to have been little more than an abstraction, something that he knew should have been of the utmost significance yet failed to elicit any real feelings.

The actual contact with the king, therefore, startled more than gratified him, putting Pepys in a situation he did not know how to interpret.

67. The two most comprehensive studies on Chesterfield date from the 1930s. Of the two, Willard Connely, *The True Chesterfield: Manners—Women—Education* (London: Cassell and Company, 1939), is the most detailed, but it is often inane. Samuel Shellabarger's *Lord Chesterfield* (London: Macmillan, 1935), is less exhaustive but preferable. David Roberts's introduction to the World's Classics collection of letters provides an excellent account of Chesterfield and his work, a short historiography of early editions, and an updated, selected bibliography. See *Lord Chesterfield: Letters,* edited with an introduction by David Roberts (Oxford: Oxford University Press, 1992).

68. Lord Chesterfield, *Letters Written by the Late Honourable Philip Dormer Stanhope, Earl of Chesterfield, to His Son, Philip Stanhope, Esq; Late Envoy Extraordinary at the Court of Dresden: Together with Several Other Pieces on Various Subjects* (London: J. Dodsley, 1774). Several collections of letters have appeared over the years, including David Robert's volume cited above, itself a new edition of a selection by Phyllis M. Jones, originally published in 1929. I use a somewhat different selection published in slightly modernized English under the title *Lord Chesterfield: Letters Written to His Natural Son on Manners and Morals* (Mount Vernon, NY: Peter Pauper Press, n.d.).

69. Here I use the word *society* in the sense of a social structure—of a system of hierarchies, of power relations, of openings and closures, and so on—as well as the sense of what used to be called "polite society," the *beau monde,* "high life."

70. Samuel Johnson, Quoted in John E. Mason, *Gentlefolk in the Making* (New York: Octagon Books, 1971), 106.

71. Ibid.

72. Ibid.

73. On Chesterfield's connection with French culture, see Rex A. Barrell, *Chesterfield et la France* (Paris: Nouvelles Editions Latines, 1968). Chesterfield actually wrote many of the letters in French, especially the ones that were more literally didactic in character, as when he was teaching his son about history or literature.

74. Chesterfield, *Lord Chesterfield,* 8.

75. Ibid., 76; emphasis in original.

76. Ibid., 52–53.

77. Ibid., 12, 16, 20, 28.

78. Ibid., 49.

79. Ibid., 44.

80. Ibid., 28.

81. E.g., ibid., 106.

82. A position, incidentally, shared by Locke; on Locke's defense of hypocrisy, see Tarcov, *Locke's Education for Liberty,* 188 ff.

83. Chesterfield, *Lord Chesterfield,* 45–46. See also, for example, Roberts, ed., *Lord Chesterfield: Letters,* 170.

84. Peter Gay reminds us of the elitist nature of Locke's treatise on education. "The

very real affinity of Locke's radical notions with our age of democratic education should not blind us to their equally real distance from it," Gay warns. "Locke was, after all, addressing his little book on education to a gentleman. . . . It never occurred to him that every child should be educated or that all those to be educated should be educated alike" (Gay, "Introduction," 12). Indeed, in the "Thoughts" the class of the poor is a nonentity, and Locke's ideas on the subject are far from being in tune with his ideas concerning the rich.

85. See Max Weber, *Economy and Society,* ed. Guenther Roth and Claus Wittich (Berkeley: University of California Press, 1978); Norbert Elias, *The Civilizing Process* (Oxford: Basil Blackwell, 1994); Pierre Bourdieu, *Distinction: A Social Critique of the Judgment of Taste* (Cambridge: Harvard University Press, 1984); Frank Parkin, *Marxism and Class Theory: A Bourgeois Critique* (New York: Columbia University Press, 1979). For a recent discussion of this literature, see Jeff Manza, "Classes, Status Groups, and Social Closure: A Critique of Neo-Weberian Social Theory," *Current Perspectives in Social Theory* 12 (1992): 275–302.

86. Chesterfield, *Lord Chesterfield,* 62; emphasis in original; see also 34.

87. This, interestingly enough, seems to have been the pattern in the United States, too. Indeed, the puritanical bent of the behavioral literature in America before Chesterfield was as strong as in England. As in England, eminently Puritan books continued to achieve considerable success in America until the beginning of the nineteenth century. Many of the most widely read books in the United States were actually the same, and the few native ones, Elaezar Moody's *The School of Good Manners* (1715) or Benjamin Colman's *A Sermon for the Reformation of Manners* (1716), were no exception to the rule. Yet as in England, most of this literature disappeared during the early nineteenth century—as etiquette became dominant and, in the United States, highly Americanized. For the history of manners in the United States, see Arthur M. Schlesinger, *Learning How to Behave: A Historical Study of American Etiquette Books* (New York: Macmillan, 1947); Gerald Carson, *The Polite Americans: A Wide-Angle View of Our More or Less Good Manners over Three Hundred Years* (New York: William Morrow, 1966). For an account of the British pattern and the overwhelming influence of Chesterfield during the nineteenth century, see Mason, *Gentlefolk in the Making,* and Nicolson, *Good Behavior.*

88. This argument would actually fit theories as different as, for instance, Georg Simmel's, Neil Smelser's and Jürgen Habermas's. Indeed, the idea that the development of "modernity," and in particular the forms of being that we associate with it, is a consequence of the division of labor and its concomitant multiplication of social spheres is, of course, one of the paradigmatic ideas of sociology today.

89. Max Weber, "Politics as a Vocation," in *From Max Weber: Essays in Sociology,* ed. H. H. Gerth and C. Wright Mills (New York: Oxford University Press, 1946), 77–128.

90. Honor has been always identified as a mark of the gentleman, and practically all discussions of the gentleman include honor as one of his major traits. However, the distinction between honor that follows from an affirmation of the integrity of the group and honor that follows from the circulation of grace is seldom recognized. For the most part, the two types are confused and are seen as a function of one and the same civility. For a relatively

recent example, see David Castronovo, *The English Gentleman: Images and Ideals in Literature and Society* (New York: Ungar, 1987). An exception is Shapin's book, which I discuss below.

91. Shapin, *Social History of Truth.*

92. See my earlier discussion of mechanical solidarity and coalescence in chapter 2, section entitled "The Ontological Condition of Coalescence."

93. See chapter 6, section entitled "Protestantism and the Doctrine of the English Gentleman."

94. I am defining mechanistic models of order as a subset of systemic models in general.

95. Shapin, *Social History of Truth;* on this, see also Steven Shapin, "A Scholar and a Gentleman: The Problematic Identity of the Scientific Practitioner in Early Modern England," *History of Science* 29 (1991): 279–327.

96. John Cannon, *Aristocratic Century: The Peerage of Eighteenth-Century England* (Cambridge: Cambridge University Press, 1984), viii.

97. Ibid., ix.

98. I should note that, if not truly capitalistic, the aristocracy was not medieval, either. Describing the English aristocracy much before the time that we are discussing at this point, Lawrence Stone writes, for instance, in *The Crisis of the Aristocracy,*

> There was nothing particularly feudal about the peers in 1641: if they fought for the State, they were paid for their services; their seats in the House of Lords bore no relation to feudal tenure; their client gentry were bound to them by personal not feudal ties; the feudal aspect of their relationships with their tenants was confined to the intermittent enforcement of obsolete taxes like fines for wardship; their estate management was as modern as the times and as their paternalistic notions of fair treatment of tenants would allow; their zest for new industrial and commercial ventures was keener than that of the merchants; the challenge to their authority came not from capitalists or bourgeoisie, but from solid landowners one notch farther down the social and economic ladder, the squires and greater gentry. (11)

Chapter Eight

1. For a short yet incisive discussion, see his remarks on reflexivity in Pierre Bourdieu and Loïc J. D. Wacquant, *An Invitation to Reflexive Sociology* (Chicago, University of Chicago Press, 1992), 62–74.

2. Eiko Ikegami, *The Taming of the Samurai: Honorific Individualism and the Making of Modern Japan* (Cambridge: Harvard University Press, 1995).

3. This is how Gramsci conceives of cultural hegemony. To him, cultural hegemony is a result of power mechanisms that fashion the preconscious of the dominated, both in terms of the categories they use to think as well as the practices they engage in every day, and thus set the conditions for false consciousness. The language of permeation, fully compatible with Gramsci, allows for conceiving of hegemony as a variable rather than as a total and totalizing power, and therefore for the use of a language of fashioning, as opposed to a

language of determinations. See, in particular, the essays cited in chapter 1, "State and Civil Society," and "Americanism and Fordism" in Antonio Gramsci, *Selections from the Prison Notebooks,* ed. and trans. Quintin Hoare and Geoffrey Nowell Smith (New York: International Publishers, 1971).

4. For brilliant discussions of "creativity" in its multiple articulations, see the essays in Hans Joas, *Pragmatism and Social Theory* (Chicago: University of Chicago Press, 1993).

Adam, Antoine. 1968. *L'age classique. I, 1624–1660.* Paris: B. Arthaud.

Alighieri, Dante. 1954. *The Inferno.* Translated by John Ciardi. New York: Mentor.

Anglo, Sydney. 1990. "How to Kill a Man at Your Ease: Fencing Books and the Duelling Ethic." In *Chivalry in the Renaissance,* edited by Sydney Anglo, 1–12. Woodbridge, Suffolk: Boydell.

———. 1983. *The Courtier's Art: Systematic Immorality in the Renaissance.* An Inaugural Lecture delivered at the University College of Swansea. 1983.

———. 1977. "The Courtier: The Renaissance and Changing Ideals." In *The Courts of Europe: Politics, Patronage, and Royalty, 1400–1800,* edited by A. G. Dickens. London: Thames and Hudson.

Arac, Jonathan, ed. 1988. *After Foucault: Humanistic Knowledge, Postmodern Challenges.* New Brunswick: Rutgers University Press.

Arden, Heather M. 1987. *The Romance of the Rose.* Boston: Twayne Publishers.

Arditi, Jorge. 1994. "Geertz, Kuhn, and the Idea of a Cultural Paradigm," *British Journal of Sociology* 45 (December): 597–617.

———. 1987. "Role as a Cultural Concept," *Theory and Society* 16: 565–591.

Aresty, Esther. 1970. *The Best Behavior: The Course of Good Manners—From Antiquity to the Present—as Seen Through Courtesy and Etiquette Books.* New York: Simon and Schuster.

Ariès, Philippe. 1977. *L'homme devant la mort.* Paris: Seuil.

Ariès, Philippe, and Georges Duby, eds. 1987–91. *A History of Private Life.* 4 vols. Cambridge: Harvard University Press.

Armstrong, Timothy J., ed. 1992. *Michel Foucault, Philosopher.* New York: Routledge.

Asch, Ronald G., and Adolf M. Birke, eds. 1991. *Princes, Patronage, and the Nobility: The Court at the Beginning of the Modern Age, c. 1450–1650.* New York: Oxford University Press.

Ashley, Maurice. 1977. *James II.* Minneapolis: University of Minnesota Press.

Aubailly, Jean-Claude, ed. 1987. *Fabliaux et contes moraux du Moyen Age.* Paris: Poche.

Auerbach, Erich. 1973. "Figura." In *Scenes from the Drama of European Literature.* Gloucester, MA: Peter Smith.

———. 1953. *Mimesis: The Representation of Reality in Western Literature.* Princeton: Princeton University Press.

Axtell, James L. 1968. *The Educational Writings of John Locke: A Critical Edition with Introduction and Notes.* Cambridge: Cambridge University Press.

Balmas, Enea. 1974. *La Renaissance; II, 1548–1570.* Paris: B. Arthaud.

Banton, Michael. 1965. *Roles: An Introduction to the Study of Social Relations.* New York: Basic Books.

Barbazan, Etienne. 1976. *Fabliaux et contes des poètes francois des 11e, 12e, 13e, 14e, et 15e siècles.* Genève: Slatkin Reprints.

Barber, Malcolm. 1992. *The Two Cities: Medieval Europe, 1050–1320*. New York: Routledge.

Barber, Richard W., and Juliet R. V. Barker. 1989. *Tournaments: Jousts, Chivalry, and Pageants in the Middle Ages*. Woodbridge, Suffolk: Boydell.

Barker, Juliet R. V. 1986. *The Tournament in England, 1100–1400*. Woodbridge, Suffolk: Boydell.

Barrell, Rex A. 1968. *Chesterfield et la France*. Paris: Nouvelles Editions Latines.

Barstow, Anne Llewellyn. 1994. *Witchcraze: A New History of the European Witch Hunts*. San Francisco: Pandora.

Barthélemy, Dominique, and Philippe Contamine. 1988. "The Use of Private Space." In *Revelations of the Medieval World*, ed. Georges Duby, 395–505. Cambridge: Harvard University Press.

Batson, Beatrice. 1988. *John Bunyan's Grace Abounding and The Pilgrim's Progress: An Overview of Literary Studies, 1960–1987*. New York: Garland.

Baumgartner, Emmanuèle, trans. 1979. *La quête du Saint Graal*. Paris: Honoré Champion.

Baumgartner, Emmanuèle. 1981. *L'Arbre et le Pain: Essai sur "La Queste del saint graal."* Paris: SEDES.

Beattie, John M. 1967. *The English Court in the Reign of George I*. Cambridge: Cambridge University Press.

Bec, Christian. 1974. "La Politique de Giovanni della Casa." *Pensiero Pol* 7, no. 3: 362–78.

Beckwith, Sarah. 1993. *Christ's Body: Identity, Culture, and Society in Late Medieval Writings*. New York: Routledge.

Bellah, Robert, N., Richard Madsen, William M. Sullivan, Ann Swidler, and Steven Tipton. 1991. *The Good Society*. New York: Knopf.

Bellenger, Yvonne, ed. 1986. *Le temps et la durée dans la littérature au Moyen Age et à la Renaissance*. Paris: Nizet.

Bénichou, Paul. 1948. *Morales du grand siècle*. Paris: Gallimard.

Bernard, G. W. 1985. *The Power of the Early Tudor Nobility: A Study of the Fourth and Fifth Earls of Shrewsbury*. New Jersey: Barnes & Noble Books.

Bertelli, Sergio, and Giulia Calvi. 1985. "Rituale, Cerimoniale, Etichetta nelle Corti Italiane." In *Rituale, Cerimoniale, Etichetta*, ed. Sergio Bertelli and Giuliano Crifo, 11–27. Milano: Bompiani.

Biddle, Bruce J., and Edwin J. Thomas. 1966. *Role Theory: Concepts and Research*. New York: John Wiley.

Bierlaire, Franz. 1978. "Erasmus at School: The *De civilitate morum puerilium libellus*." In *Essays on the Works of Erasmus*, edited by Richard L. DeMolen, 239–51. New Haven: Yale University Press.

Billacois, François. 1990. *The Duel: Its Rise and Fall in Early Modern France*. New Haven: Yale University Press.

Black, C., M. Greengrass, D. Howarth, J. Lawrance, R. Mackenney, M. Rady, and E. Wech. 1993. *Atlas of the Renaissance*. London: Cassell.

Bloch, Marc. 1961. *Feudal Society*. Chicago: University of Chicago Press.

Bloch, Oscar, and Walter von Wartburg. 1968. *Dictionnaire étymologique de la langue française*. Paris: Presses Universitaires de France.

Bloch, R. Howard. 1986. *The Scandal of the Fabliaux*. Chicago: University of Chicago Press.

Blodgett, Harriet. 1988. *Centuries of Female Days: Englishwomen's Private Diaries.* New Brunswick, NJ: Rutgers University Press.

Bloom, Harold, ed. 1986. "Introduction." In *William Shakespeare: Histories and Poems,* edited by Harold Bloom. New York: Chelsea House Publishers.

Bluche, François. 1990. *Louis XIV.* New York: Franklin Watts.

Boggs Jr., Carl. 1971. "Gramsci's 'Prison Notebooks,' Part 1." *Socialist Revolution,* 10 (winter 1971): 79–118.

Borges, Jorge Luis. 1964. *Labyrinths: Selected Stories and Other Writings.* Edited by Donald A. Yates and James E. Irby. New York: New Directions.

Bornstein, Diane. 1975. *Mirrors of Courtesy.* Hamden, Connecticut: Archon.

Borst, Arno. 1992. "Three Studies of Death in the Middle Ages." In *Medieval Worlds: Barbarians, Heretics, and Artists in the Middle Ages,* 215–43. Chicago: University of Chicago Press.

Bouhours, Père. 1920. *Les entretiens d'Ariste et d'Eugène.* Paris: Editions Bossard.

Bourcier, Elisabeth. 1976. *Les journaux privés en Angleterre de 1600 à 1660.* Paris: Publications de la Sorbonne.

Bourdieu, Pierre. 1994. "Rethinking the State: Genesis and Structure of the Bureaucratic Field," *Sociological Theory,* vol. 12, March: 1–18.

———. 1990. *The Logic of Practice.* Stanford: Stanford University Press.

———. 1984. *Distinction: A Social Critique of the Judgment of Taste.* Cambridge: Harvard University Press.

———. 1977. *Outline of a Theory of Practice.* New York: Cambridge University Press.

Bourdieu, Pierre, and Loïc J. D. Wacquant. 1992. *An Invitation to Reflexive Sociology.* Chicago: University of Chicago Press.

Boureau, Alain. 1988. *Le Simple Corps de Roi: L'Impossible Sacralité des Souverains Français, XV–XVIII Siècle.* Paris: Les Editions de Paris.

Bowle, John. 1981. *John Evelyn and his World: A Biography.* London: Routledge & Kegan Paul.

Bradbury, Malcolm, Bryan Heading, and Martin Hollis. 1972. "The Man and the Mask: A Discussion of Role Theory." In *Role,* edited by J. A. Jackson, 41–64. Cambridge: Cambridge University Press.

Bradley, A. C. 1968. "Shakespeare's tragic period—*Hamlet.*" In *Twentieth-Century Interpretations of Hamlet,* edited by David Bevington, 13–21. Englewood Cliffs, NJ: Prentice-Hall.

Brathwait, Richard. 1975. *The English Gentleman; Containing Sundry excellent Rules or exquisite Observations, tending to Direction of every Gentleman, of selecter ranke and quality; How to demeane or accomodate himselfe in the manage of publike or private affaires.* Amsterdam: Theatrum Orbis Terrarum; Norwood, NJ: Walter J. Johnson.

Bray, Bernard. 1990. "Praise: A Requirement of Courtesy and Epistolary Practice in the Seventeenth Century." *Dix-septième Siècle* 42, no. 2 (1990): 135–53.

Bremmer, Jan, and Herman Roodenburg, eds. 1991. *A Cultural History of Gesture.* Ithaca, NY: Cornell University Press.

Briggs, Robin. 1978. "The Catholic Puritans: Jansenists and Rigorists in France." In *Puritans and Revolutionaries: Essays in Seventeenth-Century History Presented to Christopher Hill,* edited by Donald Pennington and Keith Thomas, 333–54. Oxford: Clarendon Press.

Broughton, Bradford B. 1986. *Dictionary of Medieval Knighthood and Chivalry: Concepts and Terms.* New York: Greenwood.

Brubaker, Rogers. 1991. "Comments on Pizzorno." In *Social Theory for a Changing Society,* edited by Pierre Bourdieu and James S. Coleman, 234–38. Boulder, CO: Westview.

Bruckner, Matilda Tomaryn. 1993. *Shaping Romance: Interpretation, Truth, and Closure in Twelfth-Century French Fictions.* Philadelphia: University of Pennsylvania Press.

Bryant, Lawrence M. 1986. *The King and the City in the Parisian Royal Entry Ceremony: Politics, Ritual, and Art in the Renaissance.* Genève: Droz.

Bryant, Nigel, ed. and trans. 1978. *The High Book of the Grail: A Translation of the Thirteenth-Century Romance of Perlesvaus.* Ipswich: D. S. Brewer.

Bucholz, R. O. 1993. *The Augustan Court: Queen Anne and the Decline of Court Culture.* Stanford: Stanford University Press.

———. 1991. "'Nothing but Ceremony': Queen Anne and the Limitations of Royal Ritual," *Journal of British Studies* 30, no. 3 (July): 288–323.

Bunyan, John. 1903. *The Pilgrim's Progress.* London: Henry Frowde, Oxford University Press Warehouse.

Burke, Peter. 1992. *The Fabrication of Louis XIV.* New Haven: Yale University Press.

———. 1991. "The Language of Gesture in Early Modern Italy." In *A Cultural History of Gesture,* edited by Jan Bremmer and Herman Roodenburg, 71–83. Ithaca, New York: Cornell University Press.

Burns, E. Jane. 1985. *Arthurian Fictions: Rereading the Vulgate Cycle.* Columbus: Ohio State University Press.

Burns, Elizabeth. 1972. *Theatricality: A Study of Convention in the Theatre and in Social Life.* London: Longman.

Burns, Tom R. 1994. "Two Conceptions of Human Agency: Rational Choice Theory and the Social Theory of Action." In *Agency and Structure: Reorienting Social Theory,* edited by Piotr Sztompka, 197–250. Yverdon, Switzerland: Gordon and Breach.

Calderón de la Barca. 1978. *La vida es sueño.* With an introduction by Alberto Porqueras-Mayo. Madrid: Espasa-Calpe.

Campbell, Julie. 1993. "Pilgrim's Progress/Regress/Stasis: Some Thoughts on the Treatment of the Quest in Bunyan's 'Pilgrim's Progress' and Beckett's 'Mercier and Camier.'" *Comparative Literature Studies* 30 (spring): 137–53.

Cannadine, David. 1994. *Aspects of Aristocracy: Grandeur and Decline in Modern Britain.* New Haven: Yale University Press.

Cannon, John. 1984. *Aristocratic Century: The Peerage of Eighteenth-Century England.* Cambridge: Cambridge University Press.

Capellanus, Andreas. 1982. *On Love.* Translated by P. G. Walsh. London: Gerald Duckworth.

———. 1941. *The Art of Courtly Love.* Translated by John Jay Parry. New York: Columbia University Press.

Carman, J. Neale. 1946. "The symbolism of *Perlesvaus,*" *P.M.L.A.* 61 (March): 42–83.

Carr, Raymond. 1976. *English Fox Hunting: A History.* London: Weidenfeld and Nicolson.

Carson, Gerald. 1966. *The Polite Americans: A Wide-Angle View of Our More or Less Good Manners over Three Hundred Years.* New York: William Morrow.

Cassirer, Ernst. 1963. *The Individual and the Cosmos in Renaissance Philosophy.* New York: Barnes and Noble.

Castiglione, Baldesar. 1959. *The Book of the Courtier.* Translated by Charles S. Singleton. Garden City, NY: Anchor Books.

Castronovo, David. 1987. *The English Gentleman: Images and Ideals in Literature and Society.* New York: Ungar.

Cervantes, Miguel de. 1986. *Don Quixote de la Mancha.* Translated by Tobias Smollett. New York: Farrar, Straus, and Giroux.

Ceva, Bianca. 1965. *Brunetto Latini: L'Uomo e l'Opera.* Milano: R. Ricciardi.

Chapelot, Jean, and Robert Fossier. 1985. *The Village and House in the Middle Ages.* Berkeley: University of California Press.

Chappell, Vere, ed. 1994. *The Cambridge Companion to Locke.* Cambridge: Cambridge University Press.

Chartier, Roger. 1994. *The Order of Books: Readers, Authors, and Libraries in Europe between the Fourteenth and the Eighteenth Centuries.* Stanford: Stanford University Press.

Chaussinand-Nogaret, Guy. 1985. *The French Nobility in the Eighteenth Century: From Feudalism to Enlightenment.* Cambridge: Cambridge University Press.

Chesterfield, Lord. 1992. *Lord Chesterfield: Letters.* Edited with an introduction by David Roberts. Oxford: Oxford University Press.

———. 1774. *Letters Written by the Late Honourable Philip Dormer Stanhope, Earl of Chesterfield, to his Son, Philip Stanhope, Esq; Late envoy Extraordinary at the Court of Dresden: Together with Several Other Pieces on Various Subjects.* London: J. Dodsley, 1774.

———. n.d. *Lord Chesterfield: Letters Written to his Natural Son on Manners and Morals.* Mount Vernon, NY: Peter Pauper Press.

Cholakian, Patricia Francis. 1993. "Heroic Infidelity: Novella 15." In *Heroic Virtue, Comic Infidelity: Reassessing Marguerite de Navarre's Heptaméron,* edited by Dora E. Polachek, 62–76. Amherst, MA: Hestia Press.

Ciccuto, Marcello. 1985. "Introduzione." In *Brunetto Latini, Il Tesoretto,* edited by Marcello Ciccuto, 5–54. Milano: Biblioteca Universale Rizzoli.

Cleland, James. 1948. *The Institution of a Young Noble Man.* New York: Scholars' Facsimiles & Reprints.

Clifford, Lady Anne. 1988. "Pages from Lady Anne Clifford's Final Diary, 1676." In Harriet Blodgett, *Centuries of Female Days: Englishwomen's Private Diaries.* New Brunswick, New Jersey: Rutgers University Press.

———. 1924. *The Diary of Lady Anne Clifford.* Edited by Vita Sackville-West. London: William Heinemann.

Clough, Cecil H. 1978. "Francis I and the Courtiers of Castiglione's *Courtier.*" *European Studies Review* 8, no. 1: 23–70.

Condren, Conal. 1994. *The Language of Politics in Seventeenth-Century England.* New York: St. Martin's Press.

Connely, Willard. 1939. *The True Chesterfield: Manners—Women—Education.* London: Cassell and Company.

Cook, Deborah. 1993. *The Subject Finds a Voice: Foucault's Turn Toward Subjectivity.* New York: P. Lang.

Corneille, Pierre. 1959. "The Cid." In *Six Plays by Corneille and Racine,* edited and with an introduction by Paul Landis. New York: The Modern Library.

———. 1978. *Le Cid: The Text of the Original Edition (1637).* Ed. Peter H. Nurse, with introduction, notes, and variants. Baton Rouge: Louisiana State University Press.

Correll, Barbara. 1990. "Malleable Material, Models of Power: Women in Erasmus's 'Marriage Group' and 'Civility in Boys.'" *English Literary History* 57, no. 2: 241–62.

Coser, Lewis A. 1977. *Masters of Sociological Thought*. New York: Harcourt Brace Jovanovich.

Coser, Rose Laub. 1991. *In Defense of Modernity: Role Complexity and Individual Autonomy.* Stanford: Stanford University Press.

Coward, Barry. 1986. "Was There an English Revolution?" In *Politics and People in Revolutionary England*, edited by Colin Jones, Malyn Newitt, and Stephen Roberts. Oxford: Basil Blackwell.

Cox Balmaceda, Virginia. 1992. *The Renaissance Dialog: Literary Dialog in Its Social and Political Contexts, Castiglione to Galileo.* New York: Cambridge University Press.

Cuénin, Micheline. 1990. "Evolution and Revolutions in the Pursuit of Happiness in France from 1688 to 1750." In *Culture and Revolution,* ed. Paul Dukes and John Dunkley. London: Pinter Publishers.

Curran, Patricia. 1989. *Grace Before Meals: Food Ritual and Body Discipline in Convent Culture.* Urbana: University of Illinois Press.

Curtius, E. 1953. *European Literature and the Latin Middle Ages.* London: Routledge.

Deleuze, Gilles. 1988. *Foucault.* Minneapolis: University of Minnesota Press.

Della Casa, Giovanni. 1986. *Galateo.* Translated, with an introduction and notes, by Konrad Eisenbichler and Kenneth R. Bartlett. Toronto: Centre for Reformation and Renaissance Studies.

———. 1985. *Galateo.* Edited and with an introduction by Giuseppe Prezzolini. Milano: Rizzoli.

Delort, Robert. 1983. *Life in the Middle Ages.* New York: Crown.

DeMolen, Richard L. 1978. "Introduction, *Opera Omnia Desiderii Erasmi.*" In *Essays on the Works of Erasmus,* edited by Richard L. DeMolen. New Haven: Yale University Press.

Dens, Jean-Pierre. 1981. *L'honnête homme et la critique du goût: Esthétique et société au XVIIè siècle.* Lexington, KY: French Forum Publishers.

———. 1976–77. "L'honnête homme et l'esthétique du paraitre." *Papers on French Seventeenth Century Literature,* 6: 69–82.

Dewald, Jonathan. 1993. *Aristocratic Experience and the Origins of Modern Culture: France, 1570–1715.* Berkeley: University of California Press.

Dickens, A. G., ed. 1977. *The Courts of Europe.* London: Thames and Hudson.

Doncieux, Georges. 1970. *Le Père Bouhours: Un Jésuite homme de lettre au dix-septième siècle.* Genève: Slatkin Reprints.

Doubrovsky, Serge. 1963. *Corneille et la dialectique du héros.* Paris: Gallimard.

Doyle, William. 1978. *The Old European Order, 1600–1800.* Oxford: Oxford University Press.

Dreyfus, Hubert L., and Paul Rabinow. 1983. *Michel Foucault: Beyond Structuralism and Hermeneutics.* Chicago: University of Chicago Press.

Duby, Georges. 1987. *Le Moyen Age: De Hugues Capet à Jeanne d'Arc.* Paris: Hachette.

———. 1984. *Guillaume le Maréchal, ou le meilleur chevalier du monde.* Paris: Fayard.

———. 1980. *The Three Orders: Feudal Society Imagined.* Chicago: University of Chicago Press.

———. 1977. *The Chivalrous Society.* Berkeley: University of California Press.

Duby, Georges, ed. 1988. *Revelations of the Medieval World.* Vol. 2 of *A History of Private Life,* edited by Philippe Ariès and Georges Duby. Cambridge: Harvard University Press.

Duby, Georges, Dominique Barthélemy, and Charles de la Roncière. 1988. "Portraits." In *Revelations of the Medieval World,* edited by Georges Duby, 33–309. Cambridge: Harvard University Press.

Duby, Georges, and Philippe Braunstein. 1988. "The Emergence of the Individual." In *Revelations of the Medieval World,* edited by Georges Duby, 507–630. Cambridge: Harvard University Press.

Duindam, Jeroen. 1994. *Myths of Power: Norbert Elias and the Early Modern European Court.* Amsterdam: Amsterdam University Press.

Dumont, François. 1976. "French Kingship and Absolute Monarchy in the Seventeenth Century." In *Louis XIV and Absolutism,* edited by Ragnhild Hatton, 55–84. Columbus: Ohio State University Press.

Dupin, Henri. 1973. *La Courtoisie au Moyen Age.* Genève: Slatkin Reprints.

Durkheim, Emile. 1984. *The Division of Labor in Society.* Introduction by Lewis A. Coser. New York: Free Press.

———. 1982. *The Rules of Sociological Methods.* Edited and with an introduction by Steven Lukes. New York: The Free Press.

———. 1965. *The Elementary Forms of the Religious Life.* New York: Free Press.

Dyer, Christopher. 1994. *Everyday Life in Medieval England.* London: Hambledon Press.

Elias, Norbert. 1994. *The Civilizing Process: The History of Manners, and State Formation and Civilization.* Oxford: Basil Blackwell.

———. 1987. *Involvement and Detachment.* New York: Basil Blackwell.

———. 1983. *The Court Society.* New York: Pantheon.

Elyot, Thomas. 1907. *The Boke Named the Gouernor.* Edited by Foster Watson. London: J. M. Dent.

———. 1969. *The Book Named the Governor.* Edited by John M. Major. New York: Teachers College Press, Columbia University.

Ennen, Edith. 1989. *The Medieval Woman.* Oxford: Basil Blackwell.

Erasmus, Desiderius. 1985. "De Civitate morum puerilium." Translated by Brian McGregor. In *The Collected Works of Erasmus,* vol. 25, edited by J. K. Sowards, 273–89. Toronto: University of Toronto Press.

———. 1977. *La civilité puérile.* Translated and with an introduction by Alcide Bonneau. Paris: Editions Ramsay.

Eribon, Didier. 1991. *Michel Foucault.* Cambridge: Harvard University Press.

Evelyn, John. 1955. *Kalendarium. My Journal etc., 1620–1649: The Diaries of John Evelyn.* Edited by E. S. de Beer. Oxford: Clarendon Press.

———. 1907. *Memoirs, Illustrative of the Life and Writings of John Evelyn, Esq., F.R.S., Comprising His Diary, from the Year 1641 to 1705–6, and a Selection of His Familiar Letters.* Edited by William Bray. London: J. M. Dent; New York: E. P. Dutton.

Faret, Nicolas. 1630. *L'honneste-Homme ou, L'Art de Plaire à la Court.* Paris: Chez Toussaincts du Bray.

Febvre, Lucien. 1977. *Life in Renaissance France.* Cambridge: Harvard University Press.

Feher, Michel, ed. 1990. *Fragments for a History of the Human Body.* 3 vols. New York: Zone.

Feltham, Owen. 1975. *Resolves, A Duple Century.* Amsterdam: Theatrum Orbis Terrarum; Norwood, NJ: Walter J. Johnson.

Field, P. J. C. 1993. *The Life and Times of Sir Thomas Malory.* Cambridge: D. S. Brewer.

Fiero, Gloria K., Wendy Pfeffer, and Mathe Allain, eds. 1989. *Three Medieval Views of Women.* New Haven: Yale University Press.

Finucci, Valeria. 1992. *The Lady Vanishes: Subjectivity and Representation in Castiglione and Ariosto.* Stanford: Stanford University Press.

Flint, Valerie I. J. 1991. *The Rise of Magic in Early Medieval Europe.* Princeton: Princeton University Press.

Foss, Michael. 1975. *Chivalry.* London: Michael Joseph.

Fothergill, Robert A. 1974. *Private Chronicles: A Study of English Diaries.* London: Oxford University Press.

Foucault, Michel. 1984. "Nietzsche, Genealogy, History." In *The Foucault Reader,* edited by Paul Rabinow, 76–100. New York: Pantheon.

———. 1980. *Power/Knowledge: Selected Interviews and Other Writings, 1972–1977.* Edited by Colin Gordon. New York: Pantheon.

———. 1978. *A History of Sexuality.* Vol. 1. *An Introduction.* New York: Vintage.

———. 1977. *Discipline and Punish: The Birth of the Prison.* New York: Vintage.

———. 1975. *The Birth of the Clinic: An Archeology of Medical Perception.* New York: Random House.

———. 1972. *The Archaeology of Knowledge.* New York: Pantheon.

———. 1970. *The Order of Things: An Archaeology of the Human Sciences.* New York: Vintage.

———. 1965. *Madness and Civilization: A History of Insanity in the Age of Reason.* New York: Vintage.

Franklin, Julian H. 1973. *Jean Bodin and the Rise of Absolutist Theory.* Cambridge: Cambridge University Press.

Freccero, Carla. 1993. "Unwriting Lucrecia: 'Heroic Virtue' in the *Heptaméron.*" In *Heroic Virtue, Comic Infidelity: Reassessing Marguerite de Navarre's Heptaméron,* edited by Dora E. Polachek, 77–89. Amherst, MA: Hestia Press.

Frye, Northrop. 1986. *On Shakespeare.* New Haven: Yale University Press.

Frye, Susan. 1993. *Elizabeth I: The Competition for Representation.* New York: Oxford University Press.

Gagliardi, Antonio. 1989. *La misura e la grazia: Sul Libro del Cortegiano.* Torino: Tirrenia Stampatori.

Gainsford, Thomas. 1972. *The Rich Cabinet: Containing Descriptions, Characters, Discourses, and Histories; Divine and Morall.* Amsterdam: Theatrum Orbis Terrarum; New York: Da Capo Press.

Gay, Peter. 1964. "Introduction." In *John Locke on Education,* edited by Peter Gay. New York: Teachers College, Columbia University.

Geertz, Clifford. 1983. *Local Knowledge: Further Essays in Interpretive Anthropology.* New York: Basic Books.

Genicot, Leopold. 1968. *Le XIIIe siècle Européen.* Paris: Presses Universitaires de France.

———. 1967. *Contours of the Middle Ages.* London: Routledge & Kegan Paul.

George, Charles H., and Katherine George. 1961. *The Protestant Mind of the English Reformation, 1570–1640.* Princeton: Princeton University Press.

Gies, Joseph, and Frances Gies. 1969. *Life in a Medieval City.* New York: Thomas Crowell.

Giraud, Yves, and Marc-René Jung. 1972. *La Renaissance, I: 1480–1548.* Paris: Arthaud.

Goetz, Hans-Werner. 1993. *Life in the Middle Ages: From the Seventh to the Thirteenth Century.* Notre Dame: University of Notre Dame Press.

Goffman, Erving. 1974. *Frame Analysis: An Essay on the Organization of Experience.* Cambridge: Harvard University Press.

Gordon, Daniel. 1994. *Citizens without Sovereignty: Equality and Sociability in French Thought, 1670–1789.* Princeton: Princeton University Press.

Gouron, André, and Albert Rigaudière, eds. 1988. *Renaissance du pouvoir législatif et genèse de l'état.* Montpellier: Société d'Histoire du Droit.

Goyard-Fabre, Simone. 1989. *Jean Bodin et le droit de la république.* Paris: Presses Universitaires de France.

Graham, Elspeth, Hilary Hinds, Elaine Hobby, and Helen Wilcox, eds. 1989. *Her Own Life: Autobiographical Writings by Seventeenth-Century Englishwomen.* London: Routledge.

Gramsci, Antonio. 1971. *Selections from the Prison Notebooks.* Edited and translated by Quintin Hoare and Geoffrey Nowell Smith. New York: International Publishers.

Granovetter, Marc. 1974. *Getting a Job: A Study of Contacts and Careers.* Cambridge: Harvard University Press.

Gravdal, Kathryn. 1989. *Vilain and Courtois: Transgressive Parody in French Literature of the Twelfth and Thirteenth Centuries.* Lincoln: University of Nebraska Press.

The Great Tournament Roll of Westminster: A Collotype Reproduction of the Manuscript. 1968. With an introduction by Sydney Anglo. Oxford: Clarendon Press.

Green, Dennis H. 1979. *Irony in the Medieval Romance.* Cambridge: Cambridge University Press.

Greenblatt, Stephen Jay. 1980. *Renaissance Self-Fashionings: From More to Shakespeare.* Chicago: University of Chicago Press.

Greene, Thomas M. 1983. "*Il Cortegiano* and the Choice of a Game." In *Castiglione: The Ideal and the Real in Renaissance Culture,* edited by Robert W. Hanning and David Rosand, 1–15. New Haven: Yale University Press.

Guenée, Bernard, and Françoise Lehoux. 1968. *Les entrées royales françaises de 1328 à 1515.* Paris: Centre National de la Recherche Scientifique.

Guetz, Mary Paul. 1935. *The Concept of Nobility in German Didactic Literature of the Thirteenth Century.* New York: Ams Press.

Habermas, Jürgen. 1979. "What Is Universal Pragmatics?" In *Jürgen Habermas: Communication and the Evolution of Society,* translated by Thomas McCarthy, 1–68. Boston: Beacon Press.

Hale, J. R. 1983. "Castiglione's Military Career." In *Castiglione: The Ideal and the Real in Renaissance Culture,* edited by Robert W. Hanning and David Rosand, 143–64. New Haven: Yale University Press.

Hanning, Robert W., and David Rosand eds. 1983. *Castiglione: The Ideal and the Real in Renaissance Culture.* New Haven: Yale University Press.

Hart, Jonathan. 1992. *Theater and World: The Problematics of Shakespeare's History.* Boston: Northeastern University Press.

Hatton, Ragnhild. 1977. "Louis XIV: At the Court of the Sun King." In *The Courts of Europe: Politics, Patronage, and Royalty—1400–1800,* edited by A. G. Dickens. London: Thames and Hudson.

Hay, Denys. 1979. "Historians and the Renaissance during the Last Twenty-Five Years."

In *The Renaissance: Essays in Interpretation,* edited by André Chastel et al., 1–32. New York: Methuen.

Henshall, Nicholas. 1992. *The Myth of Absolutism: Change and Continuity in Early Modern European Monarchy.* New York: Longman.

Hewitt, John P. 1989. *Dilemmas of the American Self.* Philadelphia: Temple University Press.

Higham, Florence. 1968. *John Evelyn Esquire: An Anglican Layman of the Seventeenth Century.* London: SCM Press.

Hill, Christopher. 1990. *A Nation of Change and Novelty: Radical Politics, Religion, and Literature in Seventeenth-Century England.* London: Routledge.

———. 1988. *A Turbulent, Seditious, and Factious People: John Bunyan and His Church, 1628–1688.* Oxford: Clarendon Press.

———. 1986. "Political Discourse in Early-Seventeenth-Century England." In *Politics and People in Revolutionary England,* edited by Colin Jones, Malyn Newitt, and Stephen Roberts, 41–64. Oxford: Basil Blackwell.

Hillerbrand, Hans J., ed. 1968. *The Protestant Reformation.* New York: Harper Torchbooks.

Hiscock, W. G. 1955. *John Evelyn and His Family Circle.* London: Routledge & Kegan Paul.

Hobbes, Thomas. 1962. *Leviathan: Or the Matter, Forme, and Power of a Commonwealth Ecclesiasticall and Civil.* Edited by Michael Oakeshott. New York: Collier Books.

Houdard, Sophie. 1992. *Les sciences du diables: Quatres discours sur la sorcellerie.* Paris: Cerf.

Holloway, Julia Bolton. 1993. *Twice-Told Tales: Brunetto Latino and Dante Alighieri.* New York: P. Lang.

———. 1986. *Brunetto Latini: An Analytic Bibliography.* London: Grant & Cutler.

Holmes, Urban T. 1980. *Medieval Man.* Chapel Hill: University of North Carolina Press.

Huguet, Edmond. 1925. *Dictionnaire de la langue française du seizième siècle.* 7 vols. Paris: Librairie Ancienne Edouard Champion.

Huizinga, Johan. 1984. *Erasmus and the Age of Reformation.* Princeton: Princeton University Press.

———. 1954. *The Waning of the Middle Ages.* Garden City: Doubleday Anchor Books.

Huovinen, Lauri. 1975. "Renaissance Ideals of Personality," (in Finnish) *Historiallinen Arkisto* 70: 46–60;

Ihle, Sandra Ness. 1983. *Malory's Grail Quest: Invention and Adaptation in Medieval Prose Romance.* Madison: University of Wisconsin Press.

Ikegami, Eiko. 1995. *The Taming of the Samurai: Honorific Individualism and the Making of Modern Japan.* Cambridge: Harvard University Press.

Introduction to Contemporary Civilization in the West: A Source Book. Vol 1. 1954. New York: Columbia University Press.

Jackson, William H. 1990. "Tournaments and the German Chivalric *Renovatio*: Tournament Discipline and the Myth of Origins." In *Chivalry in the Renaissance,* edited by Sydney Anglo, 77–91. Woodbridge, Suffolk: Boydell.

Jaeger, C. Stephen. 1985. *The Origins of Courtliness: Civilizing Trends and the Formation of Courtly Ideals, 923–1210.* Philadelphia: University of Pennsylvania Press.

Jauss, Hans Robert. 1979. "The Alterity and Modernity of Medieval Literature." *New Literary History* 10: 181–230.

Javitch, Daniel. 1983. "*Il Cortegiano* and the Constraints of Despotism." In *Castiglione: The Ideal and the Real in Renaissance Culture,* edited by Robert W. Hanning and David Rosand, 17–28. New Haven: Yale University Press.

Jeffreys, M. V. C. 1967. *John Locke: Prophet of Common Sense.* London: Methuen.

Joas, Hans. 1993. *Pragmatism and Social Theory.* Chicago: University of Chicago Press.

Josselin, Ralph. 1976. *The Diary of Ralph Josselin, 1616–1683.* Edited by Alan MacFarlane. Records of Social and Economic History, n.s., 3. London: The Oxford University Press.

Kantarowicz, Ernst H. 1957. *The King's Two Bodies: A Study in Mediaeval Political Theology.* Princeton: Princeton University Press.

Keen, Maurice. 1984. *Chivalry.* New Haven: Yale University Press.

Keiser, Elizabeth. 1980. "The Festive Decorum of *Cleanness.*" In *Chivalric Literature; Essays on the Relations between Literature and Life in the Later Middle Ages,* edited by Larry D. Benson and John Leyerle. Kalamazoo: Western Michigan University Press.

Kelly, Douglas. 1993. *Medieval French Romance.* New York: Twayne Publishers.

Kelso, Ruth. 1964. *The Doctrine of the English Gentleman in the Sixteenth Century.* Gloucester, MA: Peter Smith.

Kernan, Alvin B. 1986. "'The Henriad': Shakespeare's Major History Plays." In *William Shakespeare: Histories and Poems,* edited by Harold Bloom, 211–43. New York: Chelsea House Publishers.

Kettering, Sharon. 1993. "Brokerage at the Court of Louis XIV." *Historical Journal* 36, no. 1: 69–87.

———. 1992. "Patronage in Early-Modern France." *French Historical Studies* 17, no. 4: 839–62.

———. 1986. *Patrons, Brokers, and Clients in Seventeenth-Century France.* New York: Oxford University Press.

Kieckhefer, Richard. 1994. "The Specific Rationality of Medieval Magic," *American Historical Review* 99 (June): 813–36.

———. 1989. *Magic in the Middle Ages.* New York: Cambridge University Press.

Kiernan, V. G. 1988. *The Duel in European History: Honour and the Reign of Aristocracy.* New York: Oxford University Press.

———. 1980. *State and Society in Europe: 1550–1650.* New York: St. Martin's Press.

King, Preston T. 1974. *The Ideology of Orders: A Comparative Analysis of Jean Bodin and Thomas Hobbes.* New York: Barnes & Noble.

Kinney, Arthur F. 1989. *Continental Humanist Poetics: Studies in Erasmus, Castiglione, Marguerite de Navarre, Rabelais, and Cervantes.* Amherst: University of Massachusetts Press.

Kirshner, Julius, and Suzanne F. Wemple, eds. 1985. *Women in the Medieval World: Essays in Honor of John H. Mundy.* New York: Basil Blackwell.

Klapisch-Zuber, Christiane, ed. 1992. *A History of Women in the West.* Vol. 2. *Silences of the Middle Ages.* Cambridge: Harvard University Press.

Kristeller, Paul Oskar. 1943. *The Philosophy of Marsilio Ficino.* New York: Columbia University Press.

Kuhn, Thomas. 1970. *The Structure of Scientific Revolutions.* Chicago: University of Chicago Press.

Labarge, Margaret Wade. 1982. *Medieval Travelers: The Rich and Restless.* London: Hamish Hamilton.

La Bruyère, Jean de. 1929. *The Characters of Jean de la Bruyère.* Translated by Henri van Laun. New York: Brentano's.

Lacroix, Paul. 1963. *France in the Middle Ages: Customs, Classes, and Conditions.* New York: Ungar.

La Fontaine Verway, Herman de. 1971. "The First 'Book of Etiquette' for Children," *Quaerendo* 1: 19–30.

Lakatos, Imre. 1970. "Falsification and the Methodology of Scientific Research Programmes." In *Criticism and the Growth of Knowledge,* edited by Imre Lakatos and Alan Musgrave. Cambridge: Cambridge University Press.

Lamont, Michele. 1992. *Money, Morals, and Manners: The Culture of the French and American Upper-Middle Class.* Chicago: University of Chicago Press.

Lanham, Richard. 1976. *The Motives of Eloquence.* New Haven: Yale University Press.

Latham, Robert. 1985. "Introduction." In Samuel Pepys, *The Shorter Pepys.* Berkeley: University of California Press.

Latini, Brunetto. 1981. *Il Tesoretto.* Edited and translated by Julia Bolton Holloway. New York: Garland.

Laurence, Anne, W. R. Owens, and Stuart Sim, eds. 1990. *John Bunyan and His England.* London: The Hambledon Press.

Layder, Derek. 1994. *Understanding Social Theory.* Thousand Oaks, CA: Sage.

Lecoy, Felix, ed. 1955. *Le Chevalier au barisel: Conte pieux du XIIIe siècle.* Paris: Champion.

Ledrut, Raymond. 1990. "L'Homme et l'Espace." In *Histoire des moeurs,* edited by Jean Poirier, 1: 59–114. Paris: Gallimard.

Le Goff, Jacques. 1967. *La civilisation de l'occident médiéval.* Paris: Arthaud.

Le Roy Ladurie, Emmanuel. 1994. *The Royal French State, 1460–1610.* Oxford: Blackwell.

———. 1985. "Auprès du roi, la cour," *Annales ESC,* vol. 40, no. 1.

———. 1979. *Montaillou: The Promised Land of Error.* New York: Vintage.

———. 1978. "Système de la cour." In *Le territoire de l'historien,* vol. 2, 275–99. Paris: Gallimard.

Levack, Brian P., ed. 1992. *Witchcraft in the Ancient World and the Middle Ages.* New York: Garland.

Levin, William C. 1984. *Sociological Ideas: Concepts and Applications.* Belmont, CA: Wadsworth.

Levron, Jacques. 1977. *Daily Life at Versailles in the Seventeenth and Eighteenth Centuries.* New York: Macmillan.

Locke, John. 1964. "Some Thoughts Concerning Education." In *John Locke on Education,* edited by Peter Gay. New York: Teachers College, Columbia University.

Lorcin, Marie-Thérèse. 1979. *Façons de sentir et de penser: Les fabliaux français.* Paris: Honoré Champion.

Lorris, Guillaume de. 1962. *Romance of the Rose.* Translated by Harry W. Robbins. New York: E. P. Dutton.

Lossky, Andrew. 1994. *Louis XIV and the French Monarchy.* New Brunswick: Rutgers University Press.

Lucas, Angela M. 1983. *Women in the Middle Ages: Religion, Marriage, and Letters.* New York: St. Martin's.

Luther, Martin. 1954. "On Christian Liberty." In *Introduction to Contemporary Civilization in the West; A Source Book.* Vol. 1. New York: Columbia University Press.

MacFarlane, Alan. 1970. *The Family Life of Ralph Josselin, a Seventeenth-Century Clergyman.* New York: W. W. Norton.

Magendie, Maurice. 1925. "Introduction." In Nicolas Faret, *L'Honnête Homme ou, L'Art de Plaire à la Court.* Paris: Presses Universitaires de France.

————. 1970. *La politesse mondaine, et les théories de l'honnêteté, en France au XVIIè siècle, de 1600 à 1660.* Genève: Slatkin Reprints.

Malory, Sir Thomas. 1906. *Le Morte d'Arthur.* London: J. M. Dent.

Mansfield, Bruce. 1992. *Man on His Own: Interpretations of Erasmus, c. 1750–1920.* Toronto: University of Toronto Press.

————. 1979. *Phoenix of His Age: Interpretations of Erasmus, c. 1550–1750.* Toronto: University of Toronto Press.

Manza, Jeff. 1992. "Classes, Status Groups, and Social Closure: A Critique of Neo-Weberian Social Theory." *Current Perspectives in Social Theory* 12: 275–302.

Margolies, David. 1992. *Monsters of the Deep: Social Dissolution in Shakespeare's Tragedies.* Manchester: Manchester University Press.

Marshall, Gordon. 1982. *In Search of the Spirit of Capitalism: An Essay on Max Weber's Protestant Ethic Thesis.* New York: Columbia University Press.

Marshall, John. 1994. *John Locke: Resistance, Religion, and Responsibility.* Cambridge: Cambridge University Press.

Marx, Karl. 1978. "Contribution to the Critique of Hegel's *Philosophy of Right:* Introduction." In *The Marx-Engels Reader,* edited by Robert C. Tucker, 53–65. New York: Norton.

Mason, John E. 1971. *Gentlefolk in the Making.* New York: Octagon Books.

Matarasso, P. M. 1969. *The Quest of the Holy Grail.* London: Penguin.

Mauss, Marcel. 1973. "The Techniques of the Body." *Economy and Society* 2 (February): 70–88.

May, Todd. 1993. *Between Genealogy and Epistemology: Psychology, Politics, and Knowledge in the Thought of Michel Foucault.* University Park, PA: Pennsylvania State University Press.

McNay, Lois. 1993. *Foucault and Feminism: Power, Gender, and the Self.* Boston: Northeastern University Press.

Mennell, Stephen. 1989. *Norbert Elias: Civilization and the Human Self-Image.* New York: Basil Blackwell.

Méré, Chevalier de. 1930. *Œuvres Posthumes.* Edited by Charles-H. Boudhors. Paris: Editions Fernand Roches.

Mettam, Roger. 1988. *Power and Faction in Louis XIV's France.* New York: Basil Blackwell.

Michaud, Claude. 1973. *L'Europe de Louis XIV.* Paris: Bordas.

Miller, James. 1993. *The Passion of Michel Foucault.* New York: Simon and Schuster.

Miller, John. 1989. *James II: A Study in Kingship.* London: Methuen.

————. 1973. *Popery and Politics in England, 1660–1688.* Cambridge: Cambridge University Press.

Molière. 1909. "Le Tartuffe." Translated by Katharine Prescott Wormeley. In *The Plays of Molière.* Boston: Little, Brown.

Montaigne, Michel de. 1985. "De l'inequalité qui est entre nous." In *Les Essais.* Paris: Presses Universitaires de France.

Moore, Thomas. 1982. *The Planets Within: Marsilio Ficino's Astrological Psychology.* Lewisburg: Bucknell University Press.

Morris, Christopher. 1983. "The Plague." In *The Diary of Samuel Pepys, a New and Complete Transcription,* vol. 10, *Companion,* edited by Robert Latham and William Matthews, 328–37. Berkeley: University of California Press.

Mousnier, Roland. 1965. "Le Roi-Soleil." In Georges Mongrédien et al., *La France au Temps de Louis XIV.* Paris: Hachette, 1965.

Muir, Edward. 1993. *Mad Blood Stirring: Vendetta and Factions in Friuli during the Renaissance.* Baltimore: Johns Hopkins University Press.

Mullett, Michael A. 1994. *James II and English Politics—1678–1688.* London: Routledge.

Murray, Alexander. 1978. *Reason and Society in the Middle Ages.* Oxford: Clarendon Press.

Neale, J. E. 1953. *Elizabeth I and Her Parliaments: 1559–1581.* London: Cape.

Nelson, Benjamin. 1973. "Weber's Protestant Ethic: Its Origins, Wanderings, and Foreseeable Future." In *Beyond the Classics? Essays in the Scientific Study of Religion,* edited by C. Y. Glock and P. E. Hammond, 71–130. New York: Harper and Row.

Newey, Vincent, ed. 1980. *The Pilgrim's Progress: Critical and Historical Views.* Liverpool: Liverpool University Press.

Nicholas, David. 1988. *The Van Arteveldes of Ghent: The Varieties of Vendetta and the Hero in History.* Ithaca, NY: Cornell University Press.

Nickel, Helmut. 1988. "The Tournament: An Historical Sketch." In *The Study of Chivalry: Resources and Approaches,* edited by Howell Chickering and Thomas H. Seiler, 213–62. Kalamazoo, MI: Medieval Institute Publications, Western Michigan University.

Nicolson, Harold. 1960. *Good Behavior.* Boston: Beacon.

Nietzsche, Friedrich. 1982. *Daybreak: Thoughts on the Prejudices of Morality.* Translated by R. J. Hollingdale. New York: Cambridge University Press.

———. 1967. *On the Genealogy of Morals.* Translated by Walter Kaufman and R. J. Hollingdale. New York: Vintage.

Oakes, Guy. 1989. "Eros and Modernity: Georg Simmel on Love." In *The Sociology of Emotions,* edited by David Franks and E. Doyle McCarthy. Greenwich, CT: JAI.

Ollard, Richard. 1974. *Pepys: A Biography.* London: Hodder and Stoughton.

Orme, Nicholas. 1984. *From Childhood to Chivalry: The Education of the English Kings and Aristocracy, 1066–1530.* New York: Methuen.

Os, M. van, and G. J. Schutte, eds. 1990. *Bunyan in England and Abroad: Papers Delivered at the John Bunyan Tercentenary Symposium, Vrije Universiteit Amsterdam, 1988.* Amsterdam: VU University Press.

Ossola, Carlo, ed. 1980. *La corte e il "Cortegiano."* Vol. 1. *La scena del testo.* Roma: Bulzoni Editore.

Palladio degli Olivi, Giovanni Francesco. 1966. *Historie della Provincia del Friuli.* Bologna: Forni.

Pardailhé-Galabrun, Annik. 1991. *The Birth of Intimacy: Privacy and Domestic Life in Early Modern Paris.* Philadelphia: University of Philadelphia Press.

Parker, David. 1983. *The Making of French Absolutism.* New York: St. Martin's Press.

Parkin, Frank. 1979. *Marxism and Class Theory: A Bourgeois Critique.* New York: Columbia University Press.

Payen, Jean-Charles. 1984. *Littérature française.* Vol. 1. *Le Moyen Age.* Paris: Arthaud.

Peacham, Henry. 1968. *The Compleat Gentleman; Fashioning Him Absolute in the Most Necessary and Commendable Qualities Concerning Minde or Bodie That May Be Required in a Noble Gentleman.* Amsterdam: Theatrum Orbis Terrarum; New York: Da Capo Press.

Perier, A., ed. 1948. *Fabliaux et contes choisis du Moyen Age.* Paris: Hatier.

Pepys, Samuel. 1985. *The Shorter Pepys.* Selected and edited by Robert Latham. Berkeley: University of California Press.

————. 1983. *The Diary of Samuel Pepys, a New and Complete Transcription.* Edited by Robert Latham and William Matthews. Berkeley: University of California Press.

Perrin, M., ed. 1990. *Dire le Moyen Age: Hier et aujourd'hui.* Paris: Presses Universitaires de France.

Persels, Jeffery C. 1993. "'Qui sommes tous cassez du harnoys' or, the *Heptaméron* and Uses of the Male Body." In *Heroic Virtue, Comic Infidelity: Reassessing Margurite de Navarre's Heptaméron,* edited by Dora E. Polachek, 90–102. Amherst, MA: Hestia Press.

Poirier, Jean, ed. 1990–91. *Histoire des Moeurs.* Paris: Gallimard.

Poirion, Daniel. 1974. *Le roman de la rose.* Paris: Hatier.

Polachek, Dora E., ed. 1993. *Heroic Virtue, Comic Infidelity: Reassessing Margurite de Navarre's Heptaméron.* Amherst, MA: Hestia Press.

Polhemus, Ted, ed. 1978. *The Body Reader: Social Aspects of the Human Body.* Harmondsworth: Penguin.

Pomeau, René. 1971. *L'age classique III: 1680–1720.* Paris: Arthaud.

Prévost, Abbé. 1961. *Manon Lescaut.* New York: New American Library.

Prigent, Michel. 1986. *Le héros et l'état dans la tragédie de Pierre Corneille.* Paris: Presses Universitaires de France.

Rebhorn, Wayne A. 1978. *Courtly Performances: Masking and Festivity in Castiglione's "Book of the Courtier."* Detroit: Wayne State University Press.

Reiss, Edmund. 1977. "Fin'Amors: Its History and Meaning in Medieval Literature." *Medieval and Renaissance Studies* 8.

Revel, Jacques. 1989. "The Uses of Civility." In *A History of Private Life: Passions of the Renaissance,* edited by Roger Chartier, 167–205. Cambridge: Harvard University Press.

Ribard, Jacques. 1989. *Du philtre au Graal: Pour une Interpretation théologique du "Roman de Tristan" et du "Conte du Graal."* Paris: Champion.

Rickert, Edith, ed. 1966. *The Babees' Book: Medieval Manners for the Young.* New York: Cooper Square.

Rieupeyroux, Francis. 1984. *La chasse en France de la fin du Moyen-Age à la révolution.* Poitiers: CNDP.

Robert, Paul. 1960. *Dictionnaire alphabétique et analogique de la langue française.* Paris: Société du Nouveau Littré.

Roberts, David. 1992. "Introduction." In *Lord Chesterfield: Letters,* edited with an introduction by David Roberts, ix–xxix. Oxford: Oxford University Press.

Robertson Jr., D. W. 1962. *A Preface to Chaucer: Studies in Medieval Perspectives.* Princeton: Princeton University Press.

Robertson, H. M. 1933. *Aspects of the Rise of Economic Individualism: A Criticism of Max Weber and His School.* Cambridge: Cambridge University Press.

Rooryck, Guy. 1992. *Les "Mémoires" du Duc de Saint-Simon: De la parole du témoin au discours du mémorialiste.* Genève: Droz.

Rose, Mary Beth, ed. 1986. *Women in the Middle Ages and the Renaissance: Literary and Historical Perspectives.* Syracuse: Syracuse University Press.

Rouche, Michel, and Jean Heuclin, eds. 1990. *La femme au Moyen Age.* Paris: J. Touzot.

Russell, Conrad. 1979. *Parliaments and English Politics, 1621–29.* New York: Oxford University Press.

Saccaro Battisti, Giuseppa. 1980. "La donna, le donne nel Cortegiano." In *La corte e il*

"Cortegiano." Vol. 1. *La scena del testo,* edited by Carlo Ossola, 219–49. Roma: Bulzoni Editore.

Saccone, Eduardo. 1983. *"Grazia, Sprezzatura, Afettazzione* in the *Courtier."* In *Castiglione: The Ideal and the Real in* Renaissance Culture, edited by Robert W. Hanning and David Rosand, 45–67. New Haven: Yale University Press.

Saint-Simon, Louis de Rouvroy, Duc de. 1983. *Mémoires,* Paris, Gallimard.

———. 1913. *The Memoirs of the Duke of Saint-Simon on the Reign of Louis XIV and the Regency.* Translated by Bayles St. John. London: George Allen & Company.

Saunders, Beatrice. 1970. *John Evelyn and His Times.* Oxford: Pergamon Press.

Sawicki, Jana. 1991. *Disciplining Foucault: Feminism, Power, and the Body.* New York: Routledge.

Scaglione, Aldo. 1991. *Knights at Court: Courtliness, Chivalry, and Courtesy from Ottonian Germany to the Italian Renaissance.* Berkeley: University of California Press.

Schlesinger, Arthur M. 1947. *Learning How to Behave: A Historical Study of American Etiquette Books.* New York: Macmillan.

Schluchter, Wolfgang. 1981. *The Rise of Western Rationalism: Max Weber's Developmental History.* Berkeley: University of California Press.

Schmitt, Charles B., and Quentin Skinner, eds. 1988. *The Cambridge History of Renaissance Philosophy.* Cambridge: Cambridge University Press.

Schmitt, Jean-Claude. 1990. *La raison des gestes dans l'occident médiéval.* Paris: Gallimard.

Schneider, Robert A. 1984. "Swordplay and Statemaking: Aspects of the Campaign Against the Duel in Early Modern France." In *Statemaking and Social Movements: Essays in History and Theory,* edited by Charles Bright and Susan Harding, 265–96. Ann Arbor: University of Michigan Press.

Sewell Jr., William H. 1992. "A Theory of Structure: Duality, Agency, and Transformation." *American Journal of Sociology* 98: 1–29.

Shahar, Shulamit. 1990. *The Fourth State: A History of Women in the Middle Ages.* New York: Routledge.

Shakespeare, William. 1987. *Henry IV, Parts I and II.* Edited by David Bevington. New York: Oxford University Press.

Shapin, Steven. 1994. *A Social History of Truth: Civility and Science in Seventeenth-Century England.* Chicago: University of Chicago Press.

———. 1991. "A Scholar and a Gentleman: The Problematic Identity of the Scientific Practitioner in Early Modern England." *History of Science* 29: 279–327.

Shellabarger, Samuel. 1935. *Lord Chesterfield.* London: Macmillan.

Simmel, Georg. 1984. "On Love (a fragment)." In *Georg Simmel: On Women, Sexuality, and Love,* edited by Guy Oakes, 153–92. New Haven: Yale University Press.

———. 1978. *The Philosophy of Money.* Translated by Tom Bottomore and David Frisby. London: Routledge.

———. 1971a. *On Individuality and Social Forms: Selected Writings.* Edited by Donald N. Levine. Chicago: University of Chicago Press.

———. 1971b. "Eros, Platonic and Modern." In *Georg Simmel: On Individuality and Social Forms,* edited by Donald N. Levine, 235–48. Chicago: University of Chicago Press.

———. 1971c. "The Metropolis and Mental Life." In *Georg Simmel: On Individuality and Social Forms,* edited by Donald N. Levine, 324–39. Chicago: University of Chicago Press.

Smith, Molly. 1991. *The Darker World Within: Evil in the Tragedies of Shakespeare and His Successors.* Newark: University of Delaware Press.

Smuts, R. Malcolm. 1987. *Court Culture and the Origins of a Royalist Tradition in Early Stuart England.* Philadelphia: University of Pennsylvania Press.

Sommer, O. 1910. *The Vulgate Version of Arthurian Romance.* Washington, DC: Carnegie Institution.

Stanton, Domna C. 1980. *The Aristocrat as Art.* New York: Columbia University Press.

Staves, Susan. 1989. "The Secrets of Genteel Identity in the Man of Mode: Comedy of Manners vs. the Courtesy Book." *Studies in Eighteenth-Century Culture* 19 (1989): 117–28.

Stone, Lawrence. 1981. *The Past and the Present.* Boston: Routledge & Kegan Paul.

———. 1965. *The Crisis of the Aristocracy, 1558–1641.* Oxford: Oxford University Press.

Strong, Roy. 1984. *Art and Power: Renaissance Festivals, 1450–1650.* Berkeley: University of California Press.

———. 1973. *Splendour at Court: Renaissance Spectacle and the Theater of Power.* Boston: Houghton Mifflin.

Strutt, Joseph. 1968. *The Sports and Pastimes of the People of England.* Detroit: Gale.

Stuard, Susan Mosher, ed. 1987. *Women in Medieval History and Historiography.* Philadelphia: University of Pennsylvania Press.

Sztompka, Piotr, ed. 1994. *Agency and Structure: Reorienting Social Theory.* Amsterdam: Gordon and Breach.

Tarcov, Nathan. 1984. *Locke's Education for Liberty.* Chicago: University of Chicago Press.

Taylor, Ivan E. 1989. *Samuel Pepys: Updated Edition.* Boston: Twayne Publishers.

Thiebaux, Marcelle. 1962. "The Medieval Chase" *Speculum* 37: 260–74.

Tilly, Charles. 1990. *Coercion, Capital, and European States, A.D. 990–1990.* Oxford: Basil Blackwell.

Tonnies, Ferdinand. 1957. *Community and Society.* New York: Harper.

Trafton, Dain A. 1983. "Politics and the Praise of Women: Political Doctrine in the *Courtier*'s Third book." In *Castiglione: The Ideal and the Real in Renaissance Culture,* edited by Robert W. Hanning and David Rosand, 29–44. New Haven: Yale University Press.

Treasure, Geoffrey. 1985. *The Making of Modern Europe, 1648–1780.* London and New York: Methuen.

Tribby, Jay. 1992. "Body/Building: Living the Museum Life in Early Modern Europe," *Rhetorica* 10, no. 2: 139–63.

Trinkaus, Charles. 1990. "Renaissance Ideas and the Idea of the Renaissance." *Journal of the History of Ideas* 51: 667–84.

———. 1982. "Themes of a Renaissance Anthropology." In *The Renaissance: Essays in Interpretation,* edited by André Chastel et al., 83–125. New York: Methuen.

Turner, Bryan S. 1987. *Medical Power and Social Knowledge.* London: Sage.

Turner, Jonathan H. 1991. *The Structure of Sociological Theory.* Belmont, CA: Wadsworth.

Uitz, Erika. 1990. *Women in the Medieval Town.* London: Barrie and Jenkins.

Ullman, Walter. 1982. "The Medieval Origins of the Renaissance." In *The Renaissance: Essays in Interpretation,* edited by André Chastel et al., 33–82. New York: Methuen.

Vale, Juliet. 1982. *Edward III and Chivalry: Chivalric Society and Its Context, 1270–1350*. Woodbridge, Suffolk: Boydell Press.

Van Laan, Thomas F. 1978. *Role-Playing in Shakespeare*. Toronto: University of Toronto Press.

Vance, Eugene. 1986. *Marvelous Signals: Poetics and Sign Theory in the Middle Ages*. Lincoln: University of Nebraska Press.

Vienne, Philibert de. 1990. *Le philosophe de court*. Edited and with an introduction by P. M. Smith. Genève: Droz.

Vigh, Eva. 1987. "Court and Courtiers in Sixteenth-Century Italy" (in Hungarian). *Vilagtortenet* 1: 3–15.

Waltzer, Michael. 1966. *The Revolution of the Saints: A Study in the Origins of Radical Politics*. London: Weidenfeld and Nicolson.

Watson, Foster. 1907. "Introduction." In Thomas Elyot, *The Boke Named the Gouernor*. London: J. M. Dent.

Weber, Max. 1978. *Economy and Society*. Edited by Guenther Roth and Claus Wittich. Berkeley: University of California Press.

———. 1958. *The Protestant Ethic and the Spirit of Capitalism*. New York: Charles Scribner's Sons.

———. 1946. "Politics as a Vocation." In *From Max Weber: Essays in Sociology,* edited by H. H. Gerth and C. Wright Mills, 77–128. New York: Oxford University Press.

Welcher, Jeanne K. 1972. *John Evelyn*. New York: Twayne.

Wildeblood, Joan, and Peter Brinson. 1965. *The Polite World: A Guide to English Manners and Deportment from the Thirteenth to the Nineteenth Century*. London: Oxford University Press.

Williams, Neville. 1977. "The Tudors: Three Contrasts in Personality." In *The Courts of Europe: Politics, Patronage, and Royalty, 1400–1800,* edited by A. G. Dickens. London: Thames and Hudson.

Williamson, George C. 1967. *Lady Anne Clifford: Her Life, Letters, and Work*. Wakefield, England: S. R. Publishers.

Willy, Margaret. 1963. *English Diarists: Evelyn and Pepys*. London: Longmans, Green.

Wilson, Anne. 1988. *The Magical Quest: The Use of Magic in Arthurian Romance*. Manchester: Manchester University Press.

Woodhouse, J. R. 1978. *Baldesar Castiglione. A Reassessment of The Courtier*. Edinburgh: Edinburgh University Press.

Worthen, William B. 1984. *The Idea of the Actor: Drama and the Ethics of Performance*. Princeton: Princeton University Press.

Zanier, Giancarlo. 1977. *La medicina astrologica e la sua teoria: Marsilio Ficino e i suoi critici contemporanei*. Roma: Edizioni dell'Ateneo.

Zaret, David. 1985. *The Heavenly Contract: Ideology and Organization in Pre-Revolutionary Puritanism*. Chicago: University of Chicago Press.

Zerclaere, Thomasin Von. 1981. "Der Waelsche Gast." In *Queene Elizabethes Achademy,* edited by Frederick J. Furnivall. Early English Text Society, extra series, no. 8; reprinted, New York: Kraus Reprint.

———. 1965. *Der Waelsche Gast*. Edited by H. Ruckert. Berlin: de Gruyter.

Boureau, Alain, 248n. 54
Bowle, John, 280n. 39, 282n. 65
Bradbury, Malcolm, 90, 251n. 2, 251n. 3, 251n. 12
Bradley, A. C., 90
Brathwait, Richard, 172, 177, 272n. 52, 275n. 69
Bray, Bernard, 135, 256n. 79
Briggs, Robin, 276n. 78
Bruckner, Matilda Tomaryn, 27, 237n. 20, 242n. 90
Brunetto Latini, 55–61, 64, 67, 185–186; compared to Thomasin, 68–69, 72–73. See also *Tesoretto, Il*
Bryant, Nigel, 235n. 2, 241n. 68
Bucholz, R. O., 156, 281n. 56, 282n. 65
Bunyan, John, 158, 173, 214, 270n. 23, 273–274n. 60
Burke, Peter, 255n. 50, 263n. 40
Burns, E. Jane, 242n. 90, 244n. 113
Burns, Elizabeth, 251n. 6
Burns, Tom R., 244n. 112

Calderón de la Barca, 87, 97, 251n. 7
Calvi, Giulia, 250n. 74
Cambridge History of Renaissance Philosophy, The, 100
Campbell, Julie, 274n. 60
Cannadine, David, 272n. 50
Cannon, John, 219–220
Capellanus, Andreas, 47–48, 57, 243n. 101, 244n. 107. See also *On Love*
Carman, J. Neale, 237n. 19
Carr, Raymond, 250n. 73
Carson, Gerald, 284n. 87
Cassirer, Ernst, 34–36, 37
Castiglione, Baldesar, 4, 14; and Faret, 125–129; on grace, 54–55, 101–113; on manners, 15; military element, 76; in relation to Machiavelli, 110–111. See also *Book of the Courtier, The*
Castoriadis, Cornelius, 227
Castronovo, David, 285n. 90
centeredness, 8–9, 14; in *The Book of the Courtier,* 110–113; in *ecclesias,* 33–39; in *L'honneste-Homme,* 124–129; manifestations in England, 156–158; permeation in *res civile,* 118–119; role in fashioning everyday life, 36–39; as vehicle of power, 38–39

Cervantes, Miguel de, 87, 89, 96, 146
Chappell, Vere, 277n. 2
Charles I, 157, 205–206
Chartier, Roger, 254n. 39
Chesterfield, Lord, 1, 14, 147–148, 183, 208–220; and the little ethics, 209–210; and the idea of a social absolute, 211–220. See also *Letters of Lord Chesterfield*
chevalier au barisel, Le, 22–25; Christian dimension 26
Cholakian, Patricia Francis, 253n. 33
Chomsky, Noam, 11
Cid, Le, 91–97, 261n. 21; compared to *Henriad,* 159, 163–164; as affirmative of *res civile,* 94–96; and courtesy, 95. See also Corneille, Pierre
civility: advent of, 4; behavioral expressions, in England, 173–175; in Castiglione, 101–113; development in England, 158, 163–175; Elias on, 3–4; in Erasmus, 113–121; in della Casa, 113–121; in Locke, 184–190; multiple historicities of, 183–184
Cleland, James, 172–173, 274n. 65, 274n. 66
Clifford, Lady Anne, 196–197, 207–208, 281n. 52
Clough, Cecil H., 254n. 44
coalescence, social, 39–45, 84–85; definition of, 40; as opposite to attachment, 40, 43–44, 148–149; as opposite of individuation, 40; and material conditions, 42–43
Colin, Jacques, 102
Colman, Benjamin, 284n. 87
Compleat Gentleman, The, 272n. 49, 272n. 51, 274n. 64, 275n. 67, 275n. 73; aristocratic definition of value in, 170–172, 215; compared to *L'honneste-Homme,* 158, 170–175; on multicenteredness, 170–171. See also Peacham, Henry
Condren, Conal, 270n. 25
Connelly, Willard, 283n. 67
Contamine, Philippe, 241n. 72
contes pieux, 25–26, 91, 236n. 14
Cooper, Florence Kendrick, 94
Corneille, Pierre, 91–97. See also *Cid, Le*
Correll, Barbara, 259n. 103

everyday life in seventeenth-century England, 193–201; as combination of roughness and urbanity, 195–197; fragility of the taken-for-granted, 199–201

fabliaux, 41, 45, 236n. 14, 241n. 69, 242n. 90
Faret, Nicolas, 4, 14, 125–136; and Castiglione, 125–129; on dueling, 130–132. See also *honneste-Homme, L', ou l'Art de plaire à la Court*
Febvre, Lucien, 80
Feltham, Owen, 172, 174–175, 275n. 73
feudal polity, 61, 62–63
Ficino, Marsilio, 98
figural interpretation, 29–30
Finucci, Valeria, 256n. 64
Flint, Valerie I. J., 238n. 40, 239n. 45, 239n. 48, 239n. 49
Foss, Michael, 249n. 66
Fothergill, Robert A., 279n. 37
Foucault, Michel, 29, 190; on discontinuities, 7–8, 12, 232n. 25; on foundational incommensurability, 191; and heterogeneity, 10, 29–30; and method, 16–17; on Nietzsche, 229n. 9, 233n. 27; and normalization, 52; on practice as deployment, 11; power in, 12–13; on self-control, 60; image of *ship of fools,* 233n. 28; on similarity and difference, 7; on systems of ordering, 6–7, 29–30, 230n. 13, 231n. 16, 232n. 20
Fougères, Stephen de, 52–53, 57
Franklin, Julian H., 260n. 14
Freccero, Carla, 253n. 33, 253n. 34
Frye, Northrop, 160, 269n. 16, 270n. 21
Frye, Susan, 248n. 62

Gainsford, Thomas, 172, 273n. 55
Galateo, 113, 116–121, 259n. 106; on grace, 259n. 104; masculinity in, 117–118. *See also* della Casa, Giovanni
Gay, Peter, 192, 277n. 2, 280n. 46, 283n. 84
Geertz, Clifford, 232n. 22, 232n. 23, 241n. 67
Genicot, Leopold, 246n. 27
gentleman, doctrine of, 170–175; ambiguous discourse of power, 158–164; hostility to Puritanism, 177; and Protestantism, 176–181
Gentleman's Magazine, 209

George, H. Charles, 276n. 77
George, Katherine, 276n. 77
Giraud, Yves, 254n. 44
Goffman, Erving, 60, 90, 232n. 22, 233n. 29, 253n. 31
Gordon, Daniel, 260n. 6, 261n. 25, 262n. 31, 266n. 73
Gouvernour, The, 165–170, 181; and ambiguities of power, 166–167; compared to *L'honneste-Homme,* 166–169, 271n. 39; liminal character, 168; on monarchical authority, 166–169; multicenteredness in, 168–169. *See also* Elyot, Thomas
Goyard-Fabre, Simone, 260n. 14
grace: acquisition of, 102–103; as aesthetic concept 102–107; Castiglione on, 54–55, 101–113; circular logic, 104–107, 111; as expression of collective self, 73, 104–107; as moral concept, 73, 107–108; permeation outside the courts, 113–121, 150–151; as political concept 110–113; presence in England, 155–156, 158; and technologies of the body, 103–107
grace, pragmatics of, 9, 14, 55; manifestations in practice, 122–125; permeation outside the courts, 113–121; presence in England, 155–156, 158, 191; as expression of collective self, 73, 104–107; in relation to pragmatics of systemic relationality, 191–192, 201–208; subjectivity in, 133
Gramsci, Antonio, 227, 233n. 28, 285n. 3
Granovetter, Marc, 265n. 67
Gravdal, Kathryn, 236n. 7, 237n. 20, 239n. 52, 242n. 90
Green, Dennis H., 242n. 90
Greenblatt, Stephen, 106, 255n. 61
Greene, Thomas M., 108, 109, 256n. 68, 257n. 85
Guetz, Mary Paul, 247n. 41
Guillaume de Lorris, 48–52, 56, 57, 67

Habermas, Jürgen, 232n. 18, 278n. 20, 284n. 88
Hale, J. R., 255n. 63
Hamlet, 5, 88–90, 95, 159–161
Hart, Jonathan, 270n. 24
Hatton, Ragnhild, 263n. 40
Hay, Denys, 250n. 1

Kelly, Douglas, 45, 243n. 91
Kelso, Ruth, 270n. 26
Kernan, Alvin B., 269n. 18, 270n. 21
Kettering, Sharon, 256n. 79, 262n. 35
Kieckhefer, Richard, 31–33, 239n. 47
Kiernan, V. G., 131, 276n. 84
King, Preston, 261n. 15
Kinney, Arthur, 104–105, 254n. 44, 255n. 52
Knights at Court, 66–67, 76
Kristeller, Oskar, 253n. 36
Kuhn, Thomas, 7, 232n. 22

Labarge, Margaret Wade, 250n. 76
La Bruyère, Jean de, 135, 140, 145–147, 151, 265n. 67
Lakatos, Imre, 82
Lamont, Michele, 234n. 32
Latham, Robert, 195, 278n. 25, 279n. 37
Latini, Brunetto. *See* Brunetto Latini
Layder, Derek, 234n. 29
Ledrut, Raymond, 238n. 30
Le Goff, Jacques, 241n. 65, 241n. 66, 241n. 75
Leonardo da Vinci, 98
Le Roy Ladurie, Emmanuel, 124, 237n. 27, 264n. 44
Letters of Lord Chesterfield, 183, 208–220; and affirmation of aristocracy, 211–220; reactions to, 208–209; definition of a social absolute, 211–220; dissociation of manners from ethics, 209–210. *See also* Chesterfield, Lord
Lettres Portugaises, 143
Leviathan, 128, 167–168, 260n. 15
Lévi-Strauss, Claude, 11
Levron, Jacques, 140, 262n. 29, 263n. 40, 266n. 74
Locke, John, 274n. 60, 283n. 82, 283n. 84; and Chesterfield, 209; on civility, 183, 184–190; and Newton's model of order, 192, 218–219; ambiguous attitude to violence, 199
Lorris, Guillaume de. *See* Guillaume de Lorris
Louis XIII, 137
Louis XIV, 122–125, 136–137, 140–141
Luther, Martin, 83, 98, 157–158, 176–181

MacFarlane, Alan, 280n. 45
Machiavelli, 61, 120; in relation to Castiglione, 110–111

Madness and Civilization, 232n. 25, 233n. 28, 238n. 37
Magendie, Maurice, 125, 132, 260n. 6, 260n. 7, 266n. 2
magic, during Middle Ages, 30–33
Major, John M., 270n. 26, 272n. 40
Malory, Sir Thomas, 20–22
manners: dissociation from ethics, 186–190, 209–211; and ethics, 4–6, 73; as self-referential, 72–73, 211; as translation of ethics, 46–53
Manon Lescaut, 144
Mansfield, Bruce, 258n. 92
Manza, Jeff, 284n. 85
Margolis, David, 252n. 17
Marguerite de Navarre, 97
Marshall, Gordon, 275n. 76
Marshall, John, 277n. 2, 278n. 15
Marx, Karl, 35–36, 148
Mason, John E., 270n. 26, 272n. 40, 284n. 87
Mauss, Marcel, 249n. 67
McGregor, Brian, 257n. 87
medieval church. *See* ecclesias
Mennell, Stephen, 229n. 4
Méré, Chevalier de (Antoine Gambaud), 142–148, 152, 265n. 63, 265n. 64; compared to Locke, 188–189; departure from pragmatics of grace, 144–145; new *honnêteté* as cementing property, 148–149
Mettam, Roger, 266n. 71
Michaud, Claude, 260n. 11
Miller, John, 282n. 60, 282n. 62
Montaigne, 87
Moody, Eleazar, 284n. 87
Moore, Thomas, 253n. 36
More, Thomas, 98
Morris, Christopher, 279n. 33
Mousnier, Roland, 263n. 41
Muir, Edward, 246n. 25, 247n. 42
Mullett, Michael A., 282n. 62
multicenteredness, 9; conditions for the consolidation of, 190–193, 197; as construct of aristocracy, 14, 211–220; discursive manifestations, 170–173; as dispersion of centers, 146–147; as foundation of power, 149; in *The Gouernour*, 168–169; in the *Letters of Lord Chesterfield*, 217–220; and Protestantism, 157
Murray, Alexander, 240n. 63